W9-CUJ-156

A. J. P. TAYLOR

A. J. P. Taylor

The Traitor within the Gates

Robert Cole
Utah State University
Logan, Utah

St. Martin's Press   New York

First published in the United States of America in 1993

Printed in Great Britain

ISBN 0–312–10066–3

Library of Congress Cataloging-in-Publication Data
Cole, Robert, 1939–
A. J. P. Taylor : the traitor within the gates / Robert Cole.
p. cm.
Includes bibliographical references and index.
ISBN 0–312–10066–3
1. Taylor, A. J. P. (Alan John Percivale), 1906–90. 2. Great
Britain—Historiography. 3. Europe—Historiography. I. Title.
DA3.T36C65   1993
907'.202—dc20   93–13506
                                                      CIP

To Ilona Jappinen, with love

Contents

List of Abbreviations		viii
Preface		ix
Introduction		1
1	Historian of Foreign Policy: *The Italian Problem in European Diplomacy, 1847–1849* (1934)	9
2	Slav Troubles: *The Habsburg Monarchy, 1815–1918* (1941)	38
3	Europe and the Germans: *The Course of German History* (1946); *Bismarck: The Man and the Statesman* (1955)	75
4	The Precarious Balance: *The Struggle for Mastery in Europe, 1848–1918* (1954)	111
5	'Speak for England': *The Troublemakers: Dissent Over Foreign Policy, 1792–1939* (1957)	143
6	Storm Over War Origins: *The Origins of the Second World War* (1961)	170
7	'Land of Hope and Glory': *English History, 1914–1945* (1965)	204
8	'What Was It All About, Alan?': *Beaverbrook* (1972)	230
	Notes	241
	Select Bibliography	265
	Index	275

List of Abbreviations

AAAPSS	Annals of the American Academy of Political and Social Sciences
AHR	American Historical Review
BBMN	Bulletin of Bibliography and Magazine Notes
CHR	Canadian Historical Review
CSM	Christian Science Monitor
CST	Chicago Sunday Times
EHR	English Historical Review
GO	Government and Opposition
HR	Historical Review
HT	History Today
JMH	Journal of Modern History
LJ	Library Journal
MG	Manchester Guardian
MGW	Manchester Guardian Weekly
NR	New Republic
NS	New Statesman
NSN	New Statesman and Nation
NYHTWR	New York Herald Tribune Weekly Review
NYRB	New York Review of Books
NYT	New York Times
NYTBR	New York Times Book Review
PP	Past and Present
PQ	Political Quarterly
PSQ	Political Science Quarterly
RH	Revue Historique
RN	Reynolds News
RP	Review of Politics
SE	Sunday Express
SFC	San Francisco Chronicle
SRL	Saturday Review of Literature
TLS	The Times Literary Supplement
TT	Time and Tide
WLB	Wiener Library Bulletin
WP	World Politics

Preface

A. J. P. Taylor died on 7 September 1990. The obituary notice in *The Times* speculated that in his prime, he was 'probably the most controversial' as well as best known historian in the English-speaking world, who had 'attracted – and usually bewitched – a wider following than Macaulay ever dreamt of'. The *Washington Post* recalled Taylor's controversiality and placed him among the most influential twentieth-century scholars. *The Times* also described him as 'something of a card, a quick-witted debater playing the role of a latter-day Cobbett', to which the *Guardian* added that he was 'always with the iconoclastic minority, whether speaking out against appeasement in the 1930s, attacking the Cold War in the 1940s, or helping to launch the Campaign for Nuclear Disarmament in 1958'.[1]

As these observations suggest, Taylor wrote and lectured on history and at the same time played a role as a dissenter. The historian wrote on Europe, Germany, the Habsburg monarchy, and England; the dissenter wrote on nearly everything pertaining to contemporary political and diplomatic affairs. He was noted for his prolificacy and controversiality, and was criticised as frequently as he was praised for what he had to say. Sometimes he was refuted and occasionally even denounced. What he was not, was ignored. Historians, the likes of Denis Judd, Keith Robbins, Martin Gilbert, and Betty Kemp, learnt their skills at his feet. Robbins recalled that as a teacher Taylor's 'technique was superb', and called his writings 'among the most distinguished of his generation of English historians'. Denis Judd credited Taylor with making him 'a more radical historian – that is, readier to challenge "established theories"'.[2]

Meanwhile, millions of others got to know Taylor from radio, television, and the popular press as well as from his historical writing. Their perception of history, or at least their thinking about aspects of the past, must have been influenced to a considerable extent, if not actually shaped, by exposure to his interpretations, manner, and style. Taylor was, perhaps, the first English historian who appealed to a mass audience both as

ix

historian and political commentator. It can be instructive to submit both the historical and polemical writings of such a figure to scrutiny, and that is the purpose of this book.

A caveat, however: anyone expecting a 'life' of A. J. P. Taylor in these pages will be disappointed. I have no interest in discussing his relationships with his wives (he had three) or children (he had six), what he ate for lunch, how much money he earned, where and how often he went on holiday (unless he claimed to have learnt something of value to his work from the experience), or why he was addicted to bow ties. This is biography to the extent that it is intellectual biography, a study of the growth and evolution of his ideas as they appeared in his historical and political writing. Taylor's 'life' appears only in a brief sketch of his origins, early life in the North of England, and education, as well as reference to those events and personalities which appear to have influenced his writings later, and the way he perceived their purpose. I am happy to leave the rest to others.

Having said that, a word about sources is also in order. This study is drawn mainly from Taylor's major works of diplomatic and political history, from his writings in the popular press, supplemented from correspondence and interviews, and Taylor's autobiographical commentaries. His bibliography runs to more than 1000 entries, only a portion of which are useful for this study, namely those books which were distinguished both for their scholarship and originality, and from which it is possible to gain insight into both the quality and nature of his historical mind.[3] These volumes include: *The Italian Problem in European Diplomacy, 1847–1849* (1934); *Germany's First Bid for Colonies, 1884–1885* (1938); *The Habsburg Monarchy, 1815–1918* (1941, and a revised edition published in 1948); *The Course of German History* (1946); *The Struggle for Mastery in Europe, 1848–1918* (1954); *Bismarck: The Man and the Statesman* (1955); *The Troublemakers: Dissent Over Foreign Policy, 1792–1939* (1957, the published edition of Taylor's Ford Lectures given at Oxford University the year before); *The Origins of the Second World War* (1961); *English History, 1914–1945* (1965); and *Beaverbrook* (1972). The last of these is a largely hagiographic work which figures only in terms of Taylor's relationship with its subject. Beaverbrook was his great friend and was influential in affirming, if not actually shaping, Taylor's views on English history, politics, and life as he expressed them in the 1950s and 1960s.

The short pieces, many of which were later collected and published as books of historical and critical essays, are where Taylor most obviously expressed the individualism, populism, egalitarianism, and iconoclasm which provided the bond between his historiography and political commentary. The pieces used are drawn from such journals and newspapers as the *Manchester Guardian*, the *New Statesman*, *The Times Literary Supplement*, and the *Sunday Express*, among others.

This book actually began a long time ago, but was put away for a number of years before being taken out, dusted off, and finally completed. I owe a special debt of gratitude to Denis Judd for never letting me forget that the book needed writing, to my wife, Ilona Jappinen, who sustained me with sound advice and encouragement whenever I was stuck, and to Eva Haraszti-Taylor for granting permission to quote from her late husband's work and for being enthusiastic about my efforts. I am also grateful to audiences at Western Conference on British Studies meetings for listening on more than one occasion, with patience, curiosity, and a healthy scepticism, to my efforts at explaining aspects of A. J. P. Taylor's contribution to historiography.

Perhaps most of all I owe the man himself, for having provided, over the years, some of the most stimulating and infuriating reading I have ever encountered.

Introduction

A. J. P. Taylor was a British diplomatic historian who also wrote commentaries on politics and international affairs – which is like observing that Vanessa Redgrave is a British actress who sometimes does film. There is rather more to it. Like Ms Redgrave, Taylor brought to his work an outlook shaped by his personal response to the times in which he lived, using a style that lay somewhere between scholarly objectivity, journalism and theatre, and which, he maintained, was uniquely his own. Television and journalism, he once argued, are done in a rush and may appear inaccurate or imprecise, as compared to a scholarly text. But 'you cannot chop a human being into different creatures as a scholar and a play-boy. He is all of a piece.'[1]

This 'piece' was politically 'engaged' throughout, which Taylor thought was perfectly natural, and often marvelled that a historian could be otherwise. 'Every historian tries to be a detached and impartial scholar', he once wrote. 'Yet, as a human being living in a community, he responds even if unconsciously to the needs of his time.'[2] These 'needs' had to do with both historical interpretation and participation in political life, and the result, for Taylor, was that while his format embraced accepted conventions, his ideas challenged accepted views. 'This is', he supposed, 'why my books annoy some people – I am a traitor within the gates.'[3]

The popular historian-writer and the academic scholar were equally part of Taylor. He wrote serious books and published in academic journals, and wrote for the popular press and performed on radio and television, once with former US President Richard M. Nixon. He enjoyed his reputation as an *enfant terrible* pressing alternatives to orthodoxy upon his colleagues. He regarded this perspective as the viewpoint equally of a radical committed to being out of step with the larger community, and a scientific historian aware that new evidence, or new points of view about old evidence, inevitably led to changed perceptions of reality. His description of dissenters fostering opposition to authority as that 'stage army of the good, with its slightly

1

ridiculous reappearances, which alone keeps our liberties alive', was more than a little autobiographical.[4]

Taylor's principal subject, at least up to 1961, was the history of European foreign policy, with occasional forays into aspects of national history. The scope of diplomatic history appealed to him. 'Diplomacy', he wrote, 'deals with the greatest of themes – with the relations of states, with peace and war, with the existence and destruction of communities and civilizations'.[5] His writing covered the nineteenth and twentieth centuries, and addressed such fundamental questions as whether a united Germany is viable within Europe? Can ethnically diverse peoples be successfully amalgamated within national states? Is there a viable alternative to the balance of power in international politics? Can there be a genuine peace between nations or is peace merely the breathing space between wars? He also wondered if Britain could ever be comfortable as part of Europe, and whether ordinary people, English or others, ever could have justice from men or nations in positions of power? Taylor made it perfectly clear that these were questions with no permanent answers. On the other hand, the manner in which he dealt with them revealed that, as both a historian and commentator on contemporary affairs, he regretted that this was so. His treatment of these questions also indicated that he was a thorough populist in politics, an advocate of Little England in foreign affairs, and above all else, an Englishman.

Who was this *enfant terrible*, then, who asked hard questions and sometimes provided even harder answers, and who always appeared to be part of the 'stage army of the good?' Taylor came from Lancashire, where there was a tradition of Northern non-conformist radicalism. His family included Quakers, Baptists, Methodists, and Congregationalists committed to moral progress, popular control, and independence from religious, political, or social Establishment.[6] They ran a prosperous cotton business – which in no way contradicted their radical principles, which were, after all, singularly individualistic. Taylor grew up surrounded by all the amenities of plutocratic life including cars, telephones, and continental holidays.[7]

Alan John Percivale Taylor was born on March 25, 1906 in Birkdale, near Manchester, the only surviving child of Percy and Constance Taylor. Before the Great War, Taylor's parents were radical-liberal in politics, supported the pro-Boer Henry

Campbell-Bannerman in 1906, and were part of the 'Birkdale Common' which opposed the oligarchical rule of the old guard 'Birkdale Park' in local politics.[8] The Taylors became socialists under the impact of the war, and especially the Conscription Act of 1916, which compelled men to go to war against their will.[9] At that point, Constance Taylor gravitated towards the Communist Party, although she never joined. She became involved with various Communists, however, and fell under the scrutiny of Scotland Yard's Special Branch for the company she kept. Percy Taylor did not follow her. He thought that socialism meant leaving the workers to run their own affairs, and that the Moscow-orientation of his wife's new friends missed the point. Percy became a trade unionist more or less in defiance of Constance, and in 1926, he served on the Preston General Strike Committee.

An incident in 1917 characterised Percy's jaded view of Britain's would-be Communist revolutionaries, and also revealed an inclination towards perversity which his son clearly inherited. J. T. Walton Newbold, an anti-war journalist who 'thought he would be the English Lenin', was a guest in the Taylor home.[10] Constance was impressed, as was young Alan, who, only eleven years at the time, was allowed to stay up late to meet 'the great man'. Percy, on the other hand, saw through the self-styled Bolshevik's pretentiousness. At a certain point Newbold assured his hosts that 'I am in touch with Moscow', and Percy, slightly deaf certainly, but always more so when he wished to be, raised an eyebrow and repeated 'Glasgow?'[11] It was a story Taylor loved to tell in later years.

In 1919, Taylor entered Bootham, the famous Quaker school in York. When Lord Beaverbrook learned of this years later, he found the idea amusing. 'I used to wonder what influence the school had on him, but after the publication of a Quaker tract on sex, I began to wonder what influence Taylor had on the school.'[12] In fact, the school's philosophy affirmed Taylor's parents' views on encouraging brotherhood and tolerance while repudiating war, materialism, and power. Of course, Bootham values were predicated upon a religious foundation.[13] Typically, Taylor claimed it was at Bootham that he ceased to believe in God. All the same, he often suggested in later years that he was a Quaker in outlook, if not in religion.

At Bootham, Taylor at least leaned in the direction of becoming a historian by concentrating his studies on church archeology, a subject that held his interest throughout his life. He learned to approach every building with a blank mind, and to accept nothing second-hand, perspectives which later informed his approach to history, if not also to politics. His archeological work was described by the masters as 'very thorough, and is illustrated by excellent plans showing much detail on a large scale'. This was also characteristic of his historical writing. Taylor earned several prizes at Bootham for his archeological scholarship, and was selected in his final year to give the John Bright oration.[14]

In 1924, Taylor left Bootham for Oxford to read History. There was more to Oxford than books, however. The university's aristocratic and conservative mentality soon turned him into a Communist (in name, though the depth of conviction is questionable). He joined the Party in his second year, and also joined the Labour Club (the only member from Oriel College) where he regularly delivered Communist speeches. He was disappointed in 1926 when the General Strike did not initiate a Communist-led working-class revolution, but he played his part for Labour by going to the North and driving a car for his father's Strike Committee in Preston.

The Communist Party could no more capture Taylor than it could his father, and for similar reasons. Both concluded that the British Communist Party betrayed the workers in 1926, to which Taylor added that the Soviet Communist Party betrayed Leon Trotsky by expelling him in 1929:

> I ceased to have any sympathy with Communism, (a) when the Communist Party failed to play any part in the General Strike (b) when it expelled Trotsky – not that I agreed with him, but I didn't like a party that threw out its greatest man.

When the dust of his disillusionment had settled, he became, in his own words, 'an out-of-hand radical'.[15]

Taylor claimed that Oxford made little contribution to his becoming a historian, and in one sense this is true. His fellow undergraduates seemed interested mainly in beer, football, and persecuting intellectuals, while the history dons were uninterested in modern history, or at least what he considered modern history: the nineteenth century.[16] For instance, G. N. Clark, who, incidentally, had also been at Bootham School, was considered 'modern' because he dealt with the seventeenth century. As for Taylor's eventual subject: 'In my time at Oxford no-one . . . knew anything about the history of foreign policy.'[17]

Despite his avowed disappointment in Oxford, Taylor left in 1927 with a First, which if nothing else, he thought, demonstrated that he was clever at history. His future remained unclear, however, and for a time he considered a career in law. He spent six months as a solicitor's articled clerk in London, was miserable, and finally went home, to throw himself on his father's mercy. Percy gave him an allowance, and back he went to Oxford with the vague idea of reading on nineteenth-century radicals. G. N. Clark thought this was frivolous, and made pointed references to the advantages of getting a job and keeping it.

All the same, Clark arranged for Taylor to go to Vienna, where he could read diplomatic history with Alfred Francis Prîbrâm while he learned German. Prîbrâm's reputation was in the history of seventeenth-century diplomacy, but he had long since turned his attention to the origins of the First World War. He had published *Das Zeitalter des Imperialismus, 1884–1914*, and when Taylor arrived, he was preparing to give the Ford Lectures at Oxford in 1929.

Taylor began to develop as an historian in Vienna. Prîbrâm's lectures on nineteenth-century politics 'were a model of how to combine scholarship and excitement', and the archives were full of political and diplomatic records from the Habsburg monarchy which had not yet been fully explored. Also Prîbrâm, a half-Jewish Czech, constitutionalist, and later anti-Nazi, set Taylor's feet on the path of understanding the human aspect of European history by urging him not only to read in the archives, but to travel and 'see the Balkan people'.[18]

In 1930, on Prîbrâm's recommendation, Taylor was hired at Manchester University as a lecturer. He soon married and fell into a pleasant life of dinner parties, concerts (Taylor's wife reputedly participated in Hallé Orchestra activities), fell walking, and sojourns to the continent. The Taylors' companions included Kitty and Malcolm Muggeridge, retired philosophy professor Samuel Alexander, and Taylor's own professor, L. B. (later Sir Lewis) Namier. Meanwhile, Taylor learnt the art of lecturing, penned his first scholarly book, and became a journalist, regularly writing 600–1200 word review-commentaries for the

Manchester Guardian. The style in these pieces was critical, personal, and inflammatory, exploiting the relationship between past and present to a degree that infuriated many of his scholarly colleagues. It was a gay and exciting life as Taylor recalled it, enhanced by increasing involvement in radical politics. Later, as an Oxford don, he looked back and remarked that much as he enjoyed Oxford, 'by no means am I as happy as I was in noisy, industrial Manchester'.[19]

Taylor remained at Manchester University for eight years. He associated closely with Lewis Namier, the great historian of eighteenth-century parliament, and they became close friends. Namier joined Manchester in 1931 as Professor of Modern History, his reputation established with *The Structure of Politics at the Accession of George III* (1929) and *England in the Age of the American Revolution* (1930). Namier mixed psychological and sociological analysis of great masses of detail, in which people and personalities simply became part of large, abstract patterns. It was a novel and compelling methodology for explaining eighteenth-century politics, which some later enthusiasts thought had validity for explaining political history as shaped by the Cold War. Consequently, a strong Namier School emerged in the 1950s.

It did not include Taylor. To Ved Mehta he remarked (with characteristic cheek):

> It was thought that I was Namier's pupil. Strictly speaking, he was my pupil. . . . During my eight-year spell at Manchester University, I instructed him in marking examination papers, in the hours of his lectures, and even in the subject matter of his classes.[20]

It was more to the point that, compared with Namier, Taylor preferred straight historical narrative, described personalities in humanistic terms, and credited his human subjects with capacity for independent thought and action. Namier 'took the mind out of history', he claimed, whereas 'thinking myself, I assume others think as well'.[21]

Even so, Taylor appreciated Namier as friend and colleague. Namier convinced him that he had great qualities as a young historian, helped him place his first scholarly manuscripts, recommended his appointment to a fellowship at Magdalen College, Oxford, and gave him books to review for the *Man-*

chester Guardian. 'Professor L. B. Namier has given me advice and criticism with unfailing patience and wisdom', Taylor wrote in *The Italian Problem in European Diplomacy,* and he dedicated *The Habsburg Monarchy* 'to L. B. Namier: this token of gratitude, affection, and esteem'. Namier was a 'character', also, and Taylor believed that characters were living proof that life, academic or otherwise, need not be taken too seriously. They remained close until 1957, when a falling out over the appointment of the Regius Professor of Modern History at Oxford ended their friendship.[22]

At Manchester, Taylor began reading in the period of diplomatic history that would make his early scholarly reputation. It came about more or less by accident, which, he was always quick to point out, was true of nearly everything that ever happened to him. Namier arranged for Taylor to teach a special subject, a responsibility not usually given to assistant lecturers. The subject was Europe, 1871–1914. Taylor prepared for it by reading the multi-volume collection of documents for the period called *Die Große politik der europäischen Kabinette.* Soon he was a leading British expert on Bismarckian and Wilhelminian diplomacy. His research for *Germany's First Bid for Colonies* (1938), *The Habsburg Monarchy* (1941), *The Struggle for Mastery in Europe* (1954), and *Bismarck: The Man and the Statesman* (1955) began with this reading.[23]

Taylor also expanded his politics to international affairs during his Manchester years. In February 1934, the Austrian Government crushed a socialist workers' demonstration in Vienna. Taylor was among the speakers at a giant protest rally in Manchester. The *Manchester Guardian* reported that he condemned the Austrian Fascists for attacking the workers, but also the British Government for standing idly by while it happened, and contributing to it by having agreed to the arming of Austrian troops. It was the duty of British workers to learn from the Austrian example, he said, because 'capitalism knew no mercy to women and children when it had to defend its hold over the workers'. In June, he spoke at another rally protesting the rearmament plans of the National Government, and against the Incitement to Disaffection Bill which was aimed at 'all of us who are in favour of anti-war propaganda'.[24]

The following year, Taylor was a member of the Manchester Peace Council, where he protested against the Hoare–Laval plan that would have Britain and France acquiesce in Italy's conquest of Abyssinia. He spoke out against war, one or two nights a week in town halls, labour halls, and churches, until, on the eve of the Munich Crisis, he concluded that Adolf Hitler was out of control, and became an anti-appeaser.[25]

In 1938 Taylor left Manchester for Oxford University, elected to a Magdalen College Fellowship at the urging of Llewelyan Woodward, who was impressed with what he had seen of Taylor's scholarship. By then he was set. Over the next three decades he wrote voluminously and expanded his skills in the three careers he claimed to have had, historian, journalist, and television star. In each area, his efforts were bent toward furthering the individualistic, irreverent, iconoclastic, and seditious in historiography and politics. He also created, whether he meant to or not, what John W. Boyer described as a 'harmony between history as interpretive category and history as subjective cultural experience'.[26] This harmony became the focus for Taylor's historical and political thinking throughout his long and tempestuous career.

1

Historian of Foreign Policy

The Italian Problem in European Diplomacy, 1847–1849 (1934)

The foundations for Taylor's writing of diplomatic history were established in his first scholarly book, *The Italian Problem in European Diplomacy*, in 1934. The theme was the impact of diplomacy upon the European balance of power, and the style was 'technically old fashioned, straight political narrative', objective, detached, detailed, and without 'behavioural sauce'.[1] The study was sharp, ironic, and humorous as it concentrated on the thoughts and interactions of diplomats, statesmen and others – the human side of diplomacy. Taylor told a good story emphasising the drama of events, and he asserted that the accidental shared space with the deterministic, in explaining history. *The Italian Problem in European Diplomacy* was a viable beginning for what would come to be regarded widely as 'vintage Taylor'.

The novice historian had always loved history, a perspective that was, in his words, 'natural, just like loving music or the Lake District mountains', and in Vienna in 1928–30 with Alfred Francis Prîbrâm, Taylor turned that love into a profession.[2] Whether Prîbrâm formed Taylor's perspectives as a diplomatic historian, is open to question, if for no other reason than that Taylor denied that it did, while using curiously contradictory language. It is certain that Prîbrâm put him on to materials in the *Staatsarchiv*, out of which *The Italian Problem in European Diplomacy* grew, but it is not at all certain that the professor gave him specific direction once he began to work. On the one hand, Taylor claimed that Prîbrâm's Vienna University lectures provided the model when he became a lecturer at Manchester, and that when Prîbrâm was preparing to give the Ford Lectures at

Oxford University in 1929, he had assisted in putting the script into reasonable English.[3] Both experiences would have exposed Taylor to the interpretive ideas and assumptions upon which the professor based his diplomatic history. If it can be assumed that Taylor discussed with Příbrâm the direction that a study based on the archival collections would take, it is more than likely that the latter approved. Later, Taylor affirmed that he knew Příbrâm's thinking on diplomatic history and research methods. In 1934 he wrote: 'From Professor Pribram I first learnt what diplomatic history could be and he taught me the elements of scientific research.' Again, in 1966, he noted that '[Příbrâm] also taught me the rudiments of technique in studying diplomatic documents.'[4]

On the other hand, in 1931 Příbrâm published his Ford Lectures without including Taylor when recognising the translating help of 'some of my younger friends'.[5] Further, on several occasions, beginning in 1977, Taylor contradicted his earlier version of events in Vienna by claiming that he had 'gradually trained myself', receiving no direction or insights from Příbrâm at all. Again, in 1983, Taylor's memoirs made no reference to helping polish the English version of the Ford Lectures, but he did emphatically deny that Příbrâm's methods or outlook had taught him anything at all about researching or writing diplomatic history. Indeed, he claimed that, as a historical writer, his model was Heinrich Friedjung's The Struggle for Supremacy in Germany. As for Příbrâm, 'I did not even know he had a method or outlook.'[6]

There is no obvious explanation for Taylor's claims and counterclaims, except the rather vague one that the two versions of his scholarly relationship with Příbrâm simply qualify as 'vintage Taylor'. He never denied owing his appointment at Manchester University, which made him a professional historian, to Příbrâm, and he never referred to the Viennese professor in anything but the warmest terms. Taylor was always the contrary-minded maverick, a condition he nurtured carefully over a half-century. To both acknowledge and deny a methodological or intellectual debt to Příbrâm was quite consistent with the perverse way he perceived himself in relation to his profession. In the end, Taylor was reluctant to believe that he owed the learning of any part of his skills to anyone but himself.

However, Taylor's view in this regard is not entirely consistent with what can be gained from a comparison of perspective and methodology between *The Italian Problem in European Diplomacy* and Prîbrâm's *England and the International Policy of the European Great Powers, 1871–1914*, the 1931 published edition of his Ford Lectures. This comparison suggests a much closer link between them than Taylor admitted. It is not proof that Prîbrâm was his mentor exactly, but it provides clear indication that Taylor had at least read Prîbrâm and agreed with the fundamentals of his approach to diplomatic history.

The historian's primary responsibility, Prîbrâm began, is to respect the scientific nature of historical scholarship. The historian 'must always be tempted to incorporate into his work those ideals which appeal most to himself or to his hearers or readers'. However: 'Science . . . is a stern mistress who will not condone the opinions of the day. He who, through weakness or for ulterior reasons, yields to this temptation, breaks faith with her.'[7] In keeping faith with this 'stern mistress', the historian must avoid subjective judgement which seeks to praise or blame. Prîbrâm was particularly critical in this regard of those diplomatic historians writing in the 1920s who sought, for reasons more political than historical, malevolent and sinister motives behind the actions of European statesmen in the years before the First World War. In his words:

I have refrained from dealing with the causes of the World War and from discussing the question of what degree of so-called guilt – I should prefer to say responsibility – rests on individual people, not to say individual men, for having precipitated it.

The issues in the relations between the great powers were too complicated to allow historians to decide guilt or innocence. Wars do not result from the immoral machinations of statesmen, Prîbrâm argued, but from conflict over national principles or interests, and the European war of 1914–18 was no exception. National principles were the fundamental reality behind statecraft, and could not be overcome or changed by 'the wishes, personal feelings, and conscious actions of the leading men at the courts, in the chancelleries, and in the armies of the

European Great Powers'. Accordingly, Príbrâm narrated the story of the events which occurred in the relations between the leading European statesmen before 1914, purporting at the end to have 'let the men who exercised an influence upon the course of those events speak for themselves, and then to leave it to my hearers and readers to pronounce judgement upon the aims and conduct of the British statesmen'.[8]

Príbrâm's purpose, as he saw it, was not to praise or blame, but to explain the foundations upon which the motives and actions of participating statesmen rested. These were permanent, or nearly permanent, national principles and interests. His lectures were meant 'to indicate the policy pursued by leading British statesmen in decisive international questions of their time', through which he would 'reveal the principles which induced them to act as they did'. Of Lord Grey, for example, he wrote: 'Certain fundamental and enduring factors and influences that served to formulate and condition his policy must be ever present to his mind.'[9] Príbrâm connected British national interests with maintaining the continental balance of power (he called it a 'system of counterpoises'), freedom of the seas, and the security of Belgium, which Britain had guaranteed since that nation was born in 1832.[10]

On the whole, Príbrâm's philosophy of history as indicated in this volume of lectures, was deterministic. Statesmen served permanent interests, and these interests, stretching over generations, prevailed in policy-making and gave a general direction to the course of international relations which the momentary aberrations of historical actors might influence, but could not change.

Taylor's perspective in *The Italian Problem in European Diplomacy* differed from Príbrâm's only occasionally. Even the language was similar as he explained his views on the historian's responsibility and the large patterns of the diplomatic historical process. Like Príbrâm, Taylor avoided subjective judgement, arguing that the historian's work was to explain the 'contradictions and misunderstandings' between diplomats and states, not to 'provide the appeal court, which had been lacking in real life'.[11] He explained policy-making in terms of statesmen responding to events according to the common elements of their political experience, from which derived their understanding of national principle and interest. Like Príbrâm, he discounted 'secret forces' – the 'malignant influence of a Holstein or a Crowe' – as factors in determining foreign policy. There were no secret forces at work, only a set of virtually axiomatic assumptions to be found among the statesmen. These assumptions were the determining national principles central to the policy formation of every European power – the balance of power for Britain, the legitimacy principle for Austria, and the desire to be dominant in western Europe for France – and they admitted no absolute standard for moral judgement beyond the existence of the principles themselves; as for example England and the balance of power, in which England did not demand a particular balance, just so long as there was one. It came down to this, Taylor concluded that European history was not European struggles predicated upon conflicts between right and wrong, but between two rights. Unfortunately, in this situation the only appeal court was 'the arbitrament of war', which had little to do with right and wrong.[12]

These methodological and interpretive views reflected Prîbrâm's; not so Taylor's denial of the role played in diplomacy by public opinion. Historians writing in the new democratic age following the First World War were inclined to elevate the role of public opinion in the conduct of foreign affairs. Prîbrâm was no exception. *England and the Great Powers* argued that popular opinion in Germany and Britain determined certain German policy decisions following the Moroccan crisis of 1905. By gaining its Moroccan objectives, he explained, Germany created an anti-German public outcry in Britain, which, in turn, created an anti-British protest in Germany. As a result, Germany was forced to rethink its western European policies and seek a rapprochement with Russia in the east.[13]

This reasoning was flawed, Taylor thought, because it misunderstood both the nature of public opinion and the willingness of nineteenth-century statesmen to be led by it. Connecting public opinion and diplomacy was far less justified than its increasing popularity would suggest. The reality of public opinion, he argued, was the ease with which it was manipulated, a judgement most likely encouraged, if not shaped by the political propaganda disseminated across Europe in the early 1930s when this book was being written. Taylor's next comments support such an interpretation. Public opinion was not really public at all, he wrote, but rather the views of members of parliament, the 'less well instructed members of the

Cabinet', and newspaper editorial writers, all of whom were part of a small, 'politically conscious class . . . themselves on the fringe of diplomacy', who sought to determine not only the direction of policy but the direction of public response to it.

Taylor's scepticism went deeper. He argued also that no competent statesman would allow even this small and elite class of opinion holders to detract him from the real object of policy, the carrying forward of national interest. He compared nineteenth-century statesmen in this regard to earlier statesmen serving absolute monarchs: both used the 'phrases that would satisfy', but in neither case was policy essentially expressed in the phrases used. Historic continuity, not the momentary inspiration of an editorial writer in *The Times* or the *Guardian*, was the governing factor in diplomacy.[14]

Taylor set forth his views on history and diplomacy, other than by example, in *The Italian Problem in European Diplomacy* more so than in any subsequent book. In most particulars he shared Pribrâm's perspectives on the principles of scientific scholarship, and on foreign policy being determined by the interaction of the national principles of the several states, rather than by the whimsy which often determined personal likes and dislikes, or by 'the accidental delaying of a dispatch'. He accepted that such issues must be taken into account, but he denied that they determined the course of relations between states.[15]

In *The Italian Problem in European Diplomacy*, these perspectives applied to the diplomatic and political events of 1847–49 concerning dissatisfaction in Lombardy and Venetia, Italian provinces under Austrian rule since the late eighteenth-century. Taylor told the story of the European great powers interacting over northern Italy. His purpose was to explain how Prince Metternich's Concert of Europe, a system which imposed the doctrine of legitimacy upon the traditional European balance of power, broke down as a consequence of great power conflict in that context. His thesis was that the Concert aimed at solving the Italian unrest without encouraging either resurgent French expansionism or a general European war, and succeeded in the short run but failed in the long. A major war was avoided, which was the immediate goal. But in the process the Concert was seriously altered in form and outlook, as national egoism and the rule of force superseded the internationalist assumptions upon which the Concert rested.[16]

Taylor's interpretations of the diplomatic events of 1847–9 were strikingly original, the result both of his freshness and of the fact that by 1934 little had been written on his subject. In his words, 'the domestic events of 1848 were, in every continental country, so complicated and so important that historians have tended to forget that foreign affairs were still proceeding'.[17] Taylor did follow Přibrâm, in part, in understanding the motives behind foreign policy, but he offered his own interpretation of the way statesmen acted upon them. This element of *The Italian Problem in European Diplomacy* was a further indication that the book was characteristic, in general terms, of what was to come from him.

The emergence of *realpolitik* as a political doctrine in Europe was a principal theme of the book. National egoism and the rule of force dominated European politics from 1850 until the outbreak of the First World War. *Realpolitik* rested on the basic assumption that, as an anonymous nineteenth-century poet phrased it,

> We cling to the simple plan
> That they shall take
> Who have the power,
> And they shall keep, who can.

Tradition assigned *realpolitik* to the Germans, but Taylor challenged this thesis, as he would often challenge consensus in the years to come. Instead he argued that the French were the true practitioners of *realpolitik*. While the Germans had only Bismarck behaving as a *realpolitiker*, every French statesman behaved so. 'The statesmen of all other nations appear sometimes to be influenced by sentimental, idealistic, unselfish motives', he observed, but 'the French never.'[18]

Taylor described *realpolitik* as emerging more or less inevitably at mid-century in consequence of the system created at the Congress of Vienna in 1815 by Metternich, then Austrian foreign minister, and Lord Castlereagh, British foreign secretary. This system was referred to as the Concert of Europe, by which European peace and stability was to be maintained according to the standards of the *ancien régime*. The Concert was justified morally on the basis of the legitimacy principle, and as such, it embraced royal absolutism, unchanging commitments, and opposition to progress and change; in all, a quite unworkable long-term proposition in a Europe that, while momentarily surfeited with revolution, was also forever changed by it – unless, of course, the Concert was only a new way to describe continuing to do things the way they had always been done. This was Taylor's point. Basically, the Concert was an artifice, though few outside England thought so at the time.

Historians usually overplayed the Concert, Taylor argued, by purporting it to be a 'system'. It was nothing of the sort. They had borrowed the concept of 'system' from political scientists, who created systems by using history to demonstrate their contemporary theses. Consequently, they produced 'arrant nonsense' and historians obviously were wrong to pay attention to them.[19] Having made that methodological point, Taylor went on to propose that the Concert simply was a word imposed upon the balance of power. In reality, the balance of power had been and remained the substance of European diplomatic relations. The real issue, he contended, was this: on what basis did the balance of power rest before and after 1848, and to what extent was the difference, if any, a fundamental alteration in the assumptions upon which the foreign policies of the various powers rested? When he had answered this question, he was clear in his own mind that no substantive alteration in European diplomacy had been made at all. The national principles that were central to the formation of policy had been affirmed.

Taylor admitted that after the Vienna Congress in 1815, diplomacy had a definite European (international, as opposed to national) basis. Problems concerning territorial equilibrium, and political and social stability, were met through collective mediation – or direct joint intervention, in the case of revolution – as opposed to unilateral action. The state powers had interests in common, specifically a desire to see Europe at peace and secure from internal upheavals that threatened monarchy, aristocracy, established religion, or, as in the case of Austria, the survival of a multi-national empire, and, with reference to Britain, lucrative European markets into which to feed the outflow of its burgeoning industrial production. These interests prevailed – at least they were officially espoused by most European governments – until 1847.

Then, Italian liberals and nationalists rebelled in Lombardy against the crumbling Austrian administration – Taylor called this disintegration an extension of the general breakdown of the Imperial system of government – and the first major rifts appeared in the Concert. In 1847, Metternich, now Austrian chancellor, set out to organise Europe against this threat to the Empire from within Italy. The powers, acting in Concert, were to put down the revolution; it was not to be the work of Austria alone.[20] No other response was possible for Metternich. In his view, the unrest in Lombardy was no different than that which had occurred elsewhere in Europe over the prior three decades. Legitimacy, the only firm basis for the monarchy he served, was threatened as it had been in 1789, and with it, the stability of Europe and the prestige of imperial Austria. And that, Taylor urged, was the weakness of Metternich's position, the key to the collapse of his policy and of the collective diplomacy he had advocated since 1815.

In theory, legitimacy was a post-1815 doctrine of restoring the *ancien régime* and maintaining it by the powers acting together. Taylor was dubious. Perhaps legitimacy underlay the Congress of Vienna, but if it did, it was honoured more in its breach than in the observance. After all: 'How could the heirs of the mediatisation of the German princes talk of legitimacy?' In Taylor's interpretation, legitimacy was an excuse to restore the Bourbon to France, which, it was generally thought, would keep the French from again threatening Europe.[21] He acknowledged that Metternich took legitimacy as his principle and sought to impose it upon the powers before 1847. But in practice, Taylor wrote, legitimacy was a doctrine of convenience, to be discarded when it was no longer useful. This had to be understood in order to understand the Italian problem of 1847–9.

Taylor affirmed that the power relationship which actually determined European diplomacy after 1815 was the balance of power as it had been maintained at least since the Peace of Utrecht in 1713. Balance of power was meant to deter war as well as to protect the interests of the various states, and was marginally successful, even though limited warfare was a more or less regular feature of periodic adjustments within the balance. The eighteenth-century states demonstrated the system fairly well. States had changed sides and fought limited wars as they altered their relationships in connection with the rising importance of Prussia and Russia as great powers, and the relative decline of France and the Habsburg Empire.

But if balance of power was the actual system of 1815, actuality was obscured by rhetoric. Metternich's rhetoric and that of those Europeans who followed his lead asserted legitimacy as the principle which sustained eighteenth-century standards in politics, religion, society, and diplomacy; that is, absolutist government, state-supported religion, aristocratic privilege, and the domination of Europe by a set and permanent number of great powers, respectful of each other's territorial rights as defined by dynastic traditions, and prepared to act accordingly. Legitimacy was said to be rational and static, making it unnecessary to consider the alternative view, then taking root in Europe, which said 'change or die'.

However, the balance of power, by its nature, was a flexible system within which European states expanded and contracted in power and importance, and in so doing, necessitated adjustments within the system itself. Metternich's moment had come with the aberration of Bonapartism. Napoleon secured French domination of Europe together with revolutionary, liberal, and nationalist baggage, all an anathema to the Austrian statesman. When Napoleon had been defeated, Metternich linked Bonapartism absolutely with these doctrines, and France with Bonapartism. To save the French from themselves and Europe from the French, required restoration of the legitimate Bourbon dynasty. In this way, Metternich tacked legitimacy onto the 1815 settlement. Other statesmen acquiesced in Metternich's arrangements, notably Lord Castlereagh, because on the face of it, they could see no other way to preserve Europe from Bonapartism. There must be a Bourbon on the French throne, they agreed, and that could be justified only by declaring political reform to be illegitimate. In Taylor's view however, the change was superficial. The reality was that diplomacy continued to rely on the balance of power.

The legitimist framework made sense in 1815, given the mentality of the times, Taylor acknowledged, but the difficulty came when Metternich sought to invoke legitimacy through the Concert at a later time when the mentality had changed. In 1815, France had to be preserved as a great power to balance Russia, but in such a way as to prevent France also becoming a threat to western Europe. The Bourbon restoration fitted the bill, as it set in place a monarchy grateful to be alive and eager to repudiate those revolutionary enthusiasms which under Bonaparte had changed France from simply one of the powers into *the* power in Europe.[22] This alone was the function of legitimacy in 1815, Taylor argued. Metternich's call for a legitimist response to unrest in Lombardy in 1847 was merely an attempt to persuade European statesmen to maintain the 'system' he had created in 1815 as a fixed moral order with Austria at its center, a system he still regarded as the key to European security and equilibrium.

It was inevitable, Taylor continued, that Metternich would perceive both the problem and its solution in this manner. The servant of the Habsburgs, he understood implicitly that if revolutionary nationalism took root in Austria as it had in France, the Empire would be destroyed. He must deter war because any general European war would lead to the triumph of liberalism and nationalism, to both of which the Habsburg Empire was exceptionally vulnerable. Metternich had to preserve stability in eastern Europe, which indicated that the Empire was playing its historic role of preserving equilibrium among the particularist Slavs, without which European security was always in jeopardy. 'If the Habsburg Empire had not existed', Metternich is supposed to have remarked (no doubt he was not the first to say so), 'it would have been necessary to invent it.' He also had to preserve the internal stability of the Empire, because he knew it was militarily weak, incapable of change, and existed on the strength of dynastic and personal loyalty to the emperor, and on no other basis. For the rest of Europe to understand this, however, was to indicate that Austria had ceased to be necessary to Europe. Therefore, Europe had to intervene in Lombardy in order to ensure that Austrian weaknesses would remain unrevealed.

Then came the crisis of 1847. Metternich called upon the powers to act in concert with Austria to prevent an Italian revolution, an intervention to be orchestrated on the premise that Europe remained legitimist in diplomacy, if not always in politics. The reality, Taylor concluded, was something else. To the extent that it was legitimist, the Concert system denied progress and change, and by 1847, opposition to change was no longer realistic in national or international European politics. Many leading statesmen in 1847 understood this. Some, such as Lord Palmerston, the English foreign secretary and a Whig, even approved of it. Social and political reform of one kind or another was the rule rather than the exception among advancing industrial states, and Italy and Germany, both still geographic expressions waiting to be recognised as nations, identified reform with national self-determination. Even in diplomacy, the tendency since 1830 had been to treat eighteenth-century rationalism as form and nineteenth-century empiricism as actuality.

The middle third of the nineteenth century saw nationalism translate international co-operation into hard-eyed, clench-fisted expansionism, sometimes with pseudo-idealistic overtones, as in the claims of Napoleon III's Second Empire, but always with an eye toward self-aggrandisement. In Germany, in the 1860s, such nationalist zealots as the historian Heinrich von Treitschke, popularised the phrase 'national egoism'. But the concept already existed in principle by 1848, and emerged within a year or two as a fundamental element in diplomacy. Metternich's greatest fear was that national egoism, nationalism, or self-determination, by whatever name the striving for independence from foreign rule went, might become a determining factor in the internal politics of the Austrian Empire.[23] Consequently, as Taylor described it, this most rational of European statesmen behaved, in the long run, most irrationally.

The Italian Problem in European Diplomacy divided into four chronological periods, extending from mid-1847 through to mid-1849. Each period witnessed events and developments which characterised the eclipse of the Concert system and the elevation of *realpolitik*. During the first period, Metternich campaigned to Europeanise resolution of the Italian problem. During the second, he failed, due to misunderstanding both Britain's changed attitude toward the 1815 settlement and France's position regarding the future of Italy. The revolution of 1848 and war in northern Italy dominated the third period, when all of Metternich's hopes, plans, and policies were confounded. He fell from power after the initial uprising in Vienna in March, and the military clique of Field Marshals Radetzky and Windischgraetz behind the diplomatic leadership (or did they lead him?) of Prince Schwarzenberg, emerged to dominate Austrian policy-making.

The fourth period began with French threats to intervene on the side of the Italian rebels, and ended with Palmerston's successful mediation of the conflict in cautious co-operation with, first, the French Second Republic, and, second, the Bonapartist Second Empire. In this way, England helped restore Austrian rule in Lombardy, but at the same time, Palmerston sent the message that both England and France aimed at seeing Italy unified eventually, though for quite different reasons. A subtle but real shift occurred during this final period, and Taylor concluded that when the dust had settled, the old system (the Concert) had virtually ended, and the new (*realpolitik*) had commenced.

Taylor described the unrest in Lombardy and Venetia in 1847 as the result of changes induced when Napoleon Bonaparte marched into northern Italy in the 1790s at the head of a revolutionary army. He brought French revolutionary ideas with him, and they were received eagerly. 'At the present day Italy is prevented from being French only by being Italian', Taylor wrote, a fine example of both his famous epigrammatic style and his perceptive judgement.[24] After 1815, Italians wanted good government and administration, 'careers open to the talents', and a consistent system of law and justice. For a time, these 'French' advantages were obtained in the Francophile Kingdom of Sardinia and in Lombardy, where Austrian rule was both benevolent and efficient. Demand for these advantages continued and intensified when Austrian administration broke down in the 1840s. Italians began agitating for reform, independence, and, finally, national unity.

In the circumstances, Metternich pursued a reactionary course, calling upon the Concert to intervene in the name of legitimacy, stability, and, an added inducement, the curtailing of French influence. His position, as Taylor explained it, was that Europe owed Austria, because Austria occupied northeastern Italy as the 'trustee of European peace', keeping Italy free of French influence and therefore closing off any avenues leading to a European war. It mattered little if the Italians were satisfied as a result.[25]

But Europe did not agree, Taylor went on, and did not respond according to the Concert to Metternich's appeal for intervention against the rebels in 1847. The chancellor was simply out of date. He confused Louis Philippe, the so-called bourgeois King of France since the revolution of 1830, with the Louis Philippe of 1792, who had marched into the Rhineland with the French revolutionary army and drove the Metternich family into exile.

He also imagined that English liberalism was only a tolerant fiction maintained in order to avoid class conflict, and that Palmerston actually shared Castlereagh's commitment to the Concert system and would willingly lead England to intervene in Italy. Therefore, Metternich, in 1847, called upon Palmerston to fulfil England's 1815 treaty obligations, to intervene against revolution and to stand firm against France, which, Metternich assumed, would seek to exploit revolution for its own ends.

However, Palmerston failed Metternich, and as a last resort he turned to France, and reminded Louis Philippe's government that France, too, had committed itself to the Concert, repudiating revolutionary *raison d'état* in the process. His next step was to attempt to persuade France to intervene where England would not, but in the name of legitimacy – restoration of Habsburg authority in Lombardy, in this case – and not on behalf of Italian revolutionaries.

But, as Taylor pointed out, Metternich had missed the point in all of this. The Europe outside of the Empire that Taylor described was no longer responsive to reaction and legitimist internationalism, but increasingly to nationalism and liberty (not to be confused with liberality). Such was the case with France after 1830, England after 1832, and Italy by 1847. Austria would have to deal with Italy on its own.

The remainder of Taylor's study concerned the diplomatic events surrounding the Austrian war with Sardinia and Lombardy, threats by Republican France to intervene, Franco-Austrian negotiations at the height of the Italian crisis, renewed outbreaks of revolutionary violence in Vienna – or 'merely street demonstrations' as Taylor termed them – and the dictatorial Austrian policy for the provinces which followed military victory in Lombardy. When the dust settled, a new reality formed. As Taylor explained it, while the old order appeared restored in Italy, and without the events of 1848–9 having left any indelible impression, the reality was that Prince Schwarzenberg was now running Austrian policy. Schwarzenberg saw Austria as a power state, not merely as a symbol of international mediation. He encouraged Radetzky, who ignored diplomatic efforts to invoke the Concert in favour of unilateral Austrian military action. The result was that Austrian, not European, arms restored Lombardy to the Empire, thus maintaining the balance of power without action of the Concert.[26]

Taylor took great pains to make the transformation clear. As he explained it, the Austrian Empire as a symbol of a European international system devoted to peace and equilibrium gave way to a state which took on the trappings of rude and selfish national power. The clique of Radetzky, Windischgraetz, and Schwarzenberg controlled external policy and, boasting of imperial military strength, attempted to bully Europe just as the internal imperial system bullied the Croats, Slovaks, Ruthenians, and other 'lesser', inhabitants of the monarchy. Meanwhile, in France, Louis Napoleon was elected president of the Second Republic. He entered at once into mediation with England over northern Italy, hoping to gain advantage for France. His intention was to make France a bold power state once more. In England, Palmerston operated within a context of diplomatic pragmatism as he pursued, without compromise, England's policy of maintaining the European balance of power. Taylor thought England had never been comfortable with either the Concert or its ultra-conservative legitimist foundations. On this point he was perfectly in accord with the leading historians of the day, who lauded George Canning, Castlereagh's successor, for leading England to support the American Monroe Doctrine in 1825. This would, as Canning himself rather overstated it in the House of Commons, 'call the New World into existence to redress the balance of the Old'. England breathed more easily with a pragmatic foreign policy, Taylor concluded. It permitted policy-makers to sustain national interest, which included European stability and peace – in that, at least, Palmerston and Metternich saw eye to eye – without continental involvement.

Pragmatism, Taylor wrote, made Palmerston a more astute manager of the balance of power than any of his predecessors were, including Canning. Palmerston was convinced by developments in 1848 – and he brought other knowledgeable English statesmen with him – that the 1815 Vienna settlement no longer achieved its purpose, and that peace was threatened rather than preserved by Austrian rule in Italy.[27] The reason was that when Metternich gave way to Schwarzenberg, legitimacy and the Concert gave way to *realpolitik* and the raw exercise of national power. The door was opened in 1848 for other would-be aggrandising states to fish in Italy's troubled waters.

Palmerston acted accordingly. Taylor credited him with understanding that national unity was in the air in the mid-nineteenth century, and that Italy must unify sooner or later. The foreign secretary also knew that the rising tide of sentiment for national self-determination was accompanied by a desire on the part of nations to act out of selfish interest, that is, to adhere on a broader scale to the principles of *realpolitik*. This challenged the balance of power rather than maintained it. The unification of Italy was a way to redress the balance, which was endangered when Austria abandoned legitimacy in favour of *realpolitik*. Palmerston looked forward to Italian unification, not as a nationalist but as a diplomatic pragmatist. Taylor took obvious pleasure in explaining Palmerston's diplomacy concerning the Italian crisis. Nation-building, revolution, war: the Italian crisis had it all. It underscored Taylor's conviction that diplomacy deals with the 'greatest of themes', with the 'contradictions and misunderstandings' which could lead to the 'destruction of nations and civilizations', and with the unique role played by the diplomats themselves.

The Italian Problem in European Diplomacy concluded with Taylor maintaining that the 1815 balance of power was restored after 1848, more or less in its pre-Napoleonic configuration. It was a system which through pragmatic adjustments, including the unification of both Italy and Germany, prevented a general European war for nearly seventy years, and laid to rest once and for all the myth of legitimacy. He maintained further that the European balance of power rested more comfortably after 1848 upon a foundation of independent actors adhering to a flexible system of change and movement, than upon the Concert system with its commitment to static, and for the most part reactionary, precepts.

But while the story followed the line of explaining the interaction of national principles, it also indicated that a great deal depended upon the individual actors. Even if they were simply following the directions that adherence to national principle took them, they could, and often did, commit independent or collective acts which altered the course of events and policy, if ever so slightly.[28] Choice and necessity and chance and premeditation, interacted constantly in Taylor's vision of history. The interaction centred on what the individual actors actually did in imitating and reacting within the framework of diplomatic relations. Taylor found both process and result endlessly fascinating, and sometimes also disappointing.

The Italian Problem in European Diplomacy identified various elements as crucial to the unfolding of cause and effect in diplomacy, but the character of the individual actors headed the list. Their behaviour could, and often did, affect policy formation and execution. Taylor described the leading characters, miniature biographical sketches in some instances, as he brought their activities into play in the course of telling the diplomatic story. He began with Metternich. The Austrian chancellor was both the grand old man of the Concert system and the victim of the increasingly archaic Habsburg system of empire. He was a conservative aristocrat whose mentality, shaped in the first place by having been driven from his Rhenish home as a young man as the French revolution first expanded beyond its own frontiers, reflected the reactionary perspectives of the regime he served. Fear of revolution, especially revolution connected with France, was fundamental to Metternich's state of mind throughout his career. The presentiments of the Habsburg monarchy also were anti-revolutionary to an almost exaggerated degree, and he shared them instinctively.

But, Taylor wrote, Metternich's time had passed. His conception of Europe was no longer valid, though he did see that the Austrian Empire's days were numbered. And because he saw that, Metternich clung to outdated legitimacy and its handmaid, the Concert, as Austria's best last hope of survival. It was inevitable that the now elderly chancellor would fail in the Italian crisis. However, Taylor argued, the reason was Austria's internal decay, not any inability of Metternich to deal with the European powers.[29]

The Schwarzenberg clique which replaced him was more in tune with the mood of the times, but less astute when it came to grasping how dangerous that mood was for the state it served. When Radetzky brutalised Lombardy and got away with it, the clique was persuaded that Austria could also brutalise Europe. But a bullying statecraft was beyond Austria's strength. The clique managed merely to destabilise central and southern Europe. From then on, only force maintained the balance of power.

The Austrian chancellor's English counterpart was Palmerston, a Whig, a pragmatist, and sufficiently independent-minded to ignore the parliament, the cabinet, and the queen when they interfered with his view of what needed to be done. Palmerston was Taylor's hero in this story, so far as he had one. As Taylor depicted him, Palmerston, being a Whig, believed in peace because he believed in material progress. In 1848 he grasped, as few others did, that the revolution in France would not develop into a replay of 1792, that reform did not have to mean revolution and disorder, and that skilful diplomacy could prevent French armies from exporting revolution into neighbouring countries. Therefore, he succeeded where others failed. In August 1848 he agreed to a general mediation of the war in Italy, 'the only step which could keep a French army out of Italy and so avert a general war. Thus to preserve the peace of Europe was a considerable achievement.'[30]

This pragmatic and practical foreign secretary was a fitting representative of England's foreign policy traditions. He achieved his ends in the Italian crisis, which were to keep the French out of Italy and head off a European war. He did not contrive to liberate the Italians, and so he could not be criticised for not doing so. Had he been master of Europe, Taylor continued, offering here in violation of his prescribed historical detachment a might-have-been observation, Palmerston would have worked to unify Lombardy and Piedmont, rather than restore the status quo, and that would have been preferable. Palmerston was 'the hero of England because he deserved to be'.[31]

Alphonse de Lamartine was foreign minister of revolutionary France during the middle months of 1848. Taylor saw in him the essence of a French statesman, a true practitioner of *realpolitik*. The foreign minister appeared in public to be a classical revolutionary idealist, at once noble and unrealistic. But in private he was a hard-nosed realist capable of the most exquisite dissembling. As Taylor described him, Lamartine delivered fiery orations before the chamber of deputies, calling for a war of liberation in Italy. Then privately he assured Lord Normanby, the English minister in Paris, that the French people would never stand for intervention. This demonstrated to Taylor's satisfaction that French statesmen were the real masters of *realpolitik*, even when, or particularly when, they were also revolutionaries.

Austrian Field Marshal Radetzky was one of several actors in the story whom Taylor saw as a negative contributor. A narrow-minded, arrogant reactionary committed to military action as a solution to all political problems, Radetzky frequently frustrated Metternich's political efforts in Lombardy. He was contemptuous of civilians, and had little regard for the government in Vienna to which he was openly hostile throughout the course of events in northern Italy.[32] At one point the Field Marshal refused permission to Metternich's representative, Count Fiquelmont, to enter military headquarters. Radetzky thought as a military man, and imposed a military solution upon Lombardy.

A military figure of quite different outlook, but equally influential in his way, was French General Oudinot. A genuine revolutionary, at least in appearance, he responded to the Italian situation with overtly radical sentiments. On May 1, 1848 he told the army of the Alps which he commanded: 'The Republic is the friend of all peoples; above all, it has profound sympathy with the peoples of Italy', and then proclaimed that he would lead this army into Italy to liberate the Italian people.[33] These were not the sentiments of the French Government, nor of the Italians, who did not want to be liberated by the French. Oudinot's words raised blood pressures in Paris, Vienna, and Turin, and may have induced the statesmen to hasten their efforts at finding a diplomatic solution.

Palmerston's special envoy to Turin in 1847 was Lord Minto. He, too, played the role of an apparently genuine nationalist and liberal, and created as many problems for his chief as did Oudinot for the French Government. Upon reaching Turin, Minto exceeded his terms of reference by his inclination to encourage 'cheering crowds to disperse by calling for cheers for "*l'independenza Italiana*"', which did not have quite the calming affect Palmerston might have liked.[34] It was indicative of Palmerston's unflappable character that, rather than withdrawing Minto, he discovered ways to use his outbursts to keep Metternich off-balance.

The foreign secretary was less fortunate with Lord Ponsonby, the English minister in Vienna. Taylor recognised in Ponsonby's character and behaviour all of the weakness of the diplomatic system in nineteenth-century Europe. As a general rule, diplomats were aristocrats, by inheritance or purchase, who spoke and wrote French, regarded themselves as in a class by themselves, separate from and perhaps above other people, including the government ministers who gave them their instruction and whom they tended to ignore. Moreover, the cumbersome communications of the period kept these diplomats cut off from contact with home for extended periods. They lived, therefore, in the cultural and political atmosphere of the courts to which they were assigned, their minds attuned to hearing something other than the call of duty, often with unfortunate results.

Ponsonby was a case in point. He was enthusiastic for his host, Metternich, and for the chancellor's conservative view of Europe. At the same time, Ponsonby became Metternich's advocate against Palmerston. Throughout the Italian crisis, Ponsonby altered the foreign secretary's instructions and gave Metternich only those messages that he thought the old man would be glad to hear, and which the ambassador thought would not be offensive to him. For a critical period, neither Metternich nor Palmerston knew entirely what the other was trying to communicate. As Taylor described it, Ponsonby tended to ignore his instructions from London until Metternich, as exasperated as was Palmerston, remarked: 'the attitude of Lord Ponsonby is in every direction most singular and independent in thought and action, quite beyond the usual rules.'[35] Palmerston could not turn the situation to his advantage, nor could he remove Ponsonby, who was so well connected at home as to be beyond Palmerston's reach.[36] Taylor's point was clear: this arrogant and irresponsible diplomat, representing the worst potential of the nineteenth-century aristocracy, had contributed immeasurably to the inability of Metternich and Palmerston to find a common ground regarding Italy. His performance had been positively dangerous to the peace and security of Europe.

Other elements Taylor identified as central to the explanation of diplomatic form and process included national principles, misunderstood national principles, public opinion (defined by his, not Prîbrâm's, usage), the nature of political systems and administrations, military strengths and weaknesses, and general economic and social attitudes, and, finally, the element of chance, or accident. National principles, Taylor began, were those axiomatic assumptions regarding aim and purpose by which statesmen measured the success of their diplomatic relations and procedures. He opened *The Italian Problem in European Diplomacy* by asserting that diplomatic cause and effect in northern Italy began with the national principles upon which Austria, France, and England based their policies. He did not, at the same time, argue that these national principles had to be constant or consistent. Austria and France both changed courses midway, for sound historical reasons, namely that in 1815 Europe had announced in Austria's favour. Austria approached the Italian episode from the internationalist perspective of commitment to the Concert system and legitimacy. Consequently, it was regarded by its representatives as the guarantor of the European treaty system. Wrote Taylor: 'She had all she wanted and therefore was an eager, and sincere, advocate of peace. . . . It is easy', he continued, epigram held high, 'after a good dinner, to condemn the dissatisfaction of the hungry'.[37] Metternich represented Austrian principles with a devotion that suggested they were carved in stone.

However, a gulf separated Metternich from his immediate successors. They tried to adapt Austria to the requirements of *realpolitik* which, as Taylor explained, was the cornerstone of the emerging diplomacy of nationalism. In 1847, the Metternichian policy, diplomatic, timid in a manner of speaking, presenting Austria in rationalist, eighteenth-century terms, restrained the European powers by insisting upon recognition of the 1815 treaty, and the form of international law that accompanied it. But in 1848 Schwarzenberg, aggressive, almost a bully, presented Austria as a modern power state fully capable of competing on equal terms with any other, and ready to overthrow treaties and law in favour of territorial aggrandisement and national self-interest.

Austrian policy actually represented a historic paradox that ran through the modern period of Habsburg history, a fact which Taylor suggested made paradox itself a principle within Habsburg foreign policy. He couched it this way: Metternich's perspective in 1847 had also been Maria Theresa's in the eighteenth century, and would, again, inform Emperor Franz Joseph's after 1871. Similarly, the post-1848 Schwarzenberg view had once been the perspective of Joseph II, Maria Theresa's son, and resurfaced at the end of the nineteenth century when Count Aehrenthal and Count Berchtold advised Franz Joseph on foreign policy. Inner conflict was characteristically Austrian, as Taylor understood the Empire, and during the Italian crisis it worked particular hardships on all concerned. Schwarzenberg thought in terms of Austria having power; Metternich had known better. Therefore, whereas Metternich avoided even discussing power, Schwarzenberg boasted of it. 'Perhaps', Taylor wrote, 'the greatest mistake of this policy was that the boasting

misled not the foreign statesmen alone, for whom it was designed, but very often the Austrians themselves'.[38]

What inner conflict did not do in 1847–9 or in other periods,
was to prevent any statesmen from operating in foreign policy
on the basis of axiomatic assumptions.

France, too, followed historically-rooted national principles
containing an inner contradiction: the perspective of revolutionary Bonapartism on the one hand, and *realpolitik* on the other.
Realpolitik prevailed. Since they had begun 'exporting revolution'
in 1792, the French had styled themselves populist champions
against monarchs, and nationalists opposed to legitimists. Under
Napoleon all of this was put to the test, and, in important
respects, failed to measure up. Consequently, after Napoleon, the
French gave way to a more pragmatic national interest. After
1815, French national principles paid only lip-service to revolution, through a particular rhetoric that was equally idealistic and
practical: 'How glorious to expel the Austrians from Italy and
how noble to give the Italians control of their own destinies! –
is the first thought in 1848', Taylor explained. 'But, how undesirable for France to have a strong, unified kingdom beyond
the Alps! – is the second and decisive one. The phrases are those
of sentimental idealism: the deeds are those of *realpolitik*.'[39]

Briefly, when Louis Napoleon gained power and attempted to
act both as war lord and apostle of peace, idealism blended with
unscrupulousness in French policy. The result was an end to
sensible French *realpolitik* in favour of adventurism, which was
the essence of Bonapartism. Within a decade after 1848, the bold
and aggressive principles of Bonapartism in France and the
realpolitik of Schwarzenberg in Austria, led states to the brink of
ruin. Austria, under Franz Joseph, was sensible enough to pull
back following a short but bloody war with France in 1859.
Napoleon III, on the other hand, launched his Mexican
adventure soon after.

Only England was consistent in both defining and following
its national principles, Taylor wrote, displaying in this earliest
scholarly exercise a hint of the peculiar populist, Little England
patriotism that would inform his later writing. To be sure,
England did not experience revolution in 1848, nor did it have
continental interests in the nineteenth century beyond maintaining the balance of power, the neutrality and security of Belgium,
and access to European markets. England's viewpoint remained

'Peace – the preservation of peace, if Europe is at peace, the restoration of peace if Europe is at war.'[40] England often had both supported and denied national rights, but never went to war on either ground. Caring for peace rather than justice – supposedly the sentiments of a nineteenth-century English authority on international affairs – Taylor believed was an appropriate motto for English policy.[41]

Palmerston was the ideal statesman for this period and this philosophy, Taylor argued. He was not only devoted to peace and the balance of power, but he acted upon these national principles from a pragmatic perspective. Pragmatism, rather than the inflexible legitimist Concert system to which Metternich was committed, was the best hope for maintaining both peace and the balance of power, which, Taylor argued, remained the best hope for Europe in the long run.

Statesmen misperceiving one another's perceptions of national principle, was as important in Taylor's explicatory framework as the principles themselves. It was obvious to him that when rival statesmen misunderstood each other, the result would affect the outcome of diplomacy, both immediately and in the long-term. Taylor saw Austria intervening alone against the Italian rebels as the result of Metternich misreading both England and France on the matter of whether or not sustaining the 1815 system balanced with their overriding national interests. In fact, the chancellor made overtures to both states in 1847, employing in the process his considerable skill at manipulating and manoeuvring, but with little success.

First, Metternich approached England in expectation that he could commit Palmerston to intervention in Italy, and then when Palmerston refused to be drawn in, he offered France an accord. The approach to France had a dual purpose. On the one hand, Metternich thought that the French could hardly remain to profit from a revolution they had entered Italy to suppress.[42] On the other, they were supposed to keep the English, who had shown themselves to be uncooperative, from interfering with Austrian policy in Lombardy. Palmerston not only had refused to intervene in Italy, but had warned Austria to grant administrative reforms in the Austrian provinces. Therefore, Metternich told the French that England actually hoped to establish a northern Italian kingdom, assuming that the French would regard this as a threat to their security, and would behave in response as Metternich wished them to.

But the chancellor missed the point all along, Taylor argued. Approaching France at all, suggested the extent to which he was at a loss concerning Palmerston's disregard for the principles of 1815. Metternich's French policy further suggested that he believed France still had expansionist notions regarding Italy. This was utterly wrong, Taylor claimed, and explained what really happened. In 1847 France had no intention of intervening in Italy, for or against revolution. When French Foreign Minister François Guizot expressed encouragement for reform in the provinces, he spoke not as a spectre from 1792 but as an apostle of the *juste milieu*, who wished to see progress made by 'men of the rich and enlightened classes'. This was not a surprising conclusion for Taylor to draw, his socialist principles notwithstanding. In the first place, it was accurate; in the second, he was himself the heir of North of England progressives, many of whom were also 'men of the rich and enlightened classes'.

In his dealings with Palmerston, meanwhile, Metternich failed to grasp that the political changes which had occurred in England since Castlereagh's time were real. He did not understand, Taylor explained, that while Whiggism might mean 'factious opposition', it might also mean – as it did with Grey and Russell – reform in preference to revolution.[43] Consequently, Metternich did not understand that Palmerston would never go to war in order to uphold a repressive Austrian rule in Lombardy, nor, for that matter, in order to liberate the Italians from it. What he would do was insist upon reforms. And that, Taylor concluded, coming full circle, indicated that Palmerston also missed Metternich's signals, which were that the Austrian chancellor *would* risk European war before he would submit to 'the perils of constitutional concession', and that he would do anything before trying to reach accord with the liberals in Italy.[44] Taylor thought the episode illustrated French *realpolitik* and English pragmatism, and Metternich's inability to understood either one. He was convinced that such misunderstandings were among the elements most common to foreign policy, and often led to the point where solutions to problems could be reached only through 'the arbitrament of war'.

Taylor dealt with public opinion as a reactive rather than implementory factor in diplomacy. Opinion, he argued, was important to policy-makers only as something to be exploited. Policy-making was the prerogative of governments, foreign offices, statesmen and diplomats, and only rarely was a policy altered in any substantive way as the result of public sentiment. And, having said that, he went on to stress that if statesmen could use public opinion for their own ends, they would and frequently did. As one instance, Taylor described a rising tide of public outcry in Italy inspired by the liberal attitudes of Pope Pius IX. First, demands were made for concessions from Austria, and then for the Austrians to withdraw from Lombardy altogether. Metternich ignored these expressions of public opinion until they led to outbreaks of revolution. Only then did he respond, and negatively. Public opinion did not influence him to actually initiate reforms or consider independence for the provinces, but when opinion contributed to revolution, he called upon Austria to react with armed force.

In another example, Taylor described Metternich manipulating opinion in England which favoured the Italian cause, and creating difficulties for Palmerston with the queen, cabinet, and parliament. The notes the chancellor sent to Dietrichstein, the Austrian minister in London, were meant to influence parliament, not the foreign secretary.[45] The effect was futile, of course, because Palmerston did what he thought necessary despite anyone's opinion, including Queen Victoria's. In still another, Taylor described Lamartine using public opinion, which in revolutionary France naturally would favour helping oppressed peoples, to persuade Apponyi, the Austrian *chargé d'affaires* that France might have to intervene in Italy.[46] Then, when Lamartine talked to Lord Normanby, the British ambassador, he employed the same sources of opinion to argue that France would *not* intervene in Italy.

Taylor could only conclude that what passed for public opinion in the nineteenth century might provoke a precipitous response if statesmen were sufficiently indecisive or desperate, or it might indicate a variation on policy. Both eventualities were important and had to be taken into account. But rarely if ever did public opinion lead to policy formation, or describe the ultimate aims a policy would pursue. Of what use to the historian was public opinion in these circumstances, Taylor asked, except as simply another tactic to be exploited by statesmen?

Always in the background of diplomacy, and occasionally

emerging into prominence, were such factors as political systems and administrations, military strengths, weaknesses, ambitions, and general economic and social attitudes. Together these constituted a sort of framework within which diplomatic activity took place. As has been noted, Taylor sprinkled references to military influence on policy-making liberally throughout *The Italian Problem in European Diplomacy*: for example, General Oudinot addressing his troops in the Alps, and Field Marshal Radetzky acting on his own in Lombardy. Less frequently, but with no less conviction of their importance, Taylor referred to the trade considerations which lay behind many English foreign policy assumptions, and which Palmerston took into account when determining his course of action. Taylor claimed that economic attitudes were a factor in England more than in either France or Austria.

In Austria, Radetzky notwithstanding, the political system and imperial administration played the largest role in influencing policy. One of the most critical moments in the Italian crisis, Taylor wrote, was decided by the nature of imperial administration, compounded by a particular weakness inherent within Metternich himself. The chancellor was convinced that some kind of reforms were needed in Lombardy, and he dispatched Fiquelmont to examine the situation and suggest a plan. Fiquelmont obeyed, reporting back that policy should continue to be made in Vienna, but that greater responsibility for its implementation should fall upon local officials. Count Hartig was privy to Fiquelmont's efforts and pointed out that this plan would create needless additional administrative staff. He urged that all Lombardy really needed was greater energy on the part of existing officials. Metternich should cut specific orders, and if they were not followed, confront the guilty parties face-to-face. Less effective officials could even be recalled, if need be.

Therein lay the rub, Taylor explained. Metternich was an ageing veteran of the Ballhausplatz, and could hardly follow Hartig's brusque, though useful advice. Knowing full well that no energy could be expected from the senile Viceroy, Archduke Rainer, or from his equally senile officials, Metternich accepted Fiquelmont's proposal in letters containing 'a tone of great relief'. The chancellor, Taylor explained, always preferred means which avoided the sort of unpleasantness that was inevitable had he acted upon the advice that the archduke was past it, even if they led to vagaries or to abandoning his policy totally.[47]

Finally, Taylor added the element of chance, or accident, to his considerations. For example, chance played a key role in the 'diplomatic revolution' of October 1848. Prince Schwarzenberg was convinced that Austria was a power state the equal of France, and that both were after national aggrandisement in Italy. With this in mind, he set out to complete the Austro-French accord begun months earlier by Metternich, an arrangement by which France and Austria would intervene jointly against Lombardy and Sardinia. A letter containing the proposal was prepared, to be sent to Paris for the perusal of M. Bastide, the French foreign minister. It was ready for Count Wessenberg, the chancellor after Metternich, to sign on October 5. But revolution broke out again in Vienna on October 6, and the letter was left unsigned when the government fled the city. Only Lebzeltern, the under-secretary in the foreign ministry, remained behind. Taylor's description of the scene was a model of the dramatic understatement he brought to his historical narrative over the years:

> There on October 12, Lebzeltern, who had been unable to keep away from the scene of his labour and was wandering disconsolately through the Chancery, found it; realizing its importance he signed and dispatched it. . . . In so accidental and casual a manner was the diplomatic revolution inaugurated.[48]

That was as far as it went, because another set of chance occurrences intervened. When Bastide learned of the letter's contents, he agreed in principle and expressed willingness to join in the accord, but only after the coming presidential election for the newly formed Second Republic. Meanwhile, the revolution in Vienna kept Austrian officials too busy to pay much attention to foreign affairs, and Sardinia made plain its intention to press the conflict in northern Italy to a military conclusion. With both the Austrian and French governments temporarily neutralised, it remained for Radetzky to defeat the Italians alone, which he did, at Novara. That battle turned the tide in Austria's favour, and French aid was no longer required or desired.

What were the issues involved in this situation? First, the letter itself and French agreement with its contents in principle, represented specific policy lines characteristic of what the Austrians and French perceived as their separate national interests. But Lebzeltern discovering and posting the letter constituted a chance occurrence in an unexpected situation. So, too, did Bastide's refusal to act upon the letter's contents prior to the presidential election, though this development was at least predictable, assuming the Austrians understood the meaning of 'presidential election'. When Taylor asked what would have been the result had the first chance occurrence not been neutralised by the second, he answered that as a historian, he was not required to second-guess events, and that such speculation was fruitless. And, having said that, he speculated all the same. By itself the first accident could have produced a general war, had not the second prevented the Franco-Austrian accord and thereby limited the war to the conflict already in progress.

It is an oversimplification to say, as some Taylor critics have done, that his was the 'accidental' view of history. Rather, Taylor always followed the line, beginning with *The Italian Problem in European Diplomacy*, that broad patterns are discernible in what happens, and that these occur because unpredictable events effect what the statesman does, even when the statesman is motivated by historical or other forces extant within his culture, society, and state.

For the most part, Taylor built *The Italian Problem in European Diplomacy* around an interesting, informative, and occasionally provocative story, predicated upon an objective analysis of events, in which he explained what had apparently happened and why. He offered no judgements, except, perhaps, with reference to the stupidity or, conversely, insightfulness of a given diplomatic move. 'I don't deal in moral judgements', he wrote many years later in an effort to make this point clear. 'From whose standpoint can they be made . . .? Or do historians pretend that they speak an eternal truth? . . . I don't praise or blame. I record.'[49] He did offer interpretations, however, and criticism, and in *The Italian Problem in European Diplomacy* they were supported by careful documentation drawn from the *Archives des Affaires Étrangères*, Paris, the *Haus-Hof-und Staatsarchivs* [sic], Vienna, the Public Record Office, London, and a wide collection of published diaries, memoirs, biographies, and letters. In fact, Taylor had so much additional primary material in his footnotes that the reader was confronted with what amounted to a second book.

For a first book, *The Italian Problem in European Diplomacy* indicated surprisingly well, though not perfectly, developed methodological and conceptual lines, and received a mixed response from critics.[50] It was based upon a careful reading of archival evidence and enlivened by the stylistic cheekiness familiar to Taylor readers since. In later years, the cheekiness was often combined with startling conclusions drawn from documents which other historians claimed to have understood differently, and then Taylor was accused of playing games with his evidence, with changing his conclusions and arriving at perverse interpretations solely in order to 'turn history on its head' and create a sensation. To this he replied, 'a conscientious historian can change his mind simply because of new evidence or further thought'.[51] He could also claim, as he did in 1956, that conscientious historians once thought the history of state-craft contained lessons for the future. No longer. 'Nowadays they know better, and read diplomatic history for purposes of entertainment.'[52] It is difficult to argue, convincingly at any rate, that twenty years, and five serious contributions to diplomatic historiography after *The Italian Problem in European Diplomacy*, that Taylor was not talking about himself.

2

Slav Troubles

The Habsburg Monarchy 1815–1918 (1941)

Sitting in England in 1943 with the Second World War raging about him, Taylor observed: 'The German problem is, and has always been, the gravest problem of our European order.'[1] The point might seem dictated by circumstances, but this was simply coincidence. From the moment he began reading about late nineteenth-century diplomacy more than a decade earlier, Taylor was conscious of the danger Germany appeared to represent to other Europeans. Once *The Italian Problem in European Diplomacy* was behind him, he turned his attention to study of the German situation. From 1934 to the end of the 1940s, most of his historical and political writing concentrated on the German in central and eastern Europe.

The problem attracted Taylor because it was so elemental. It concerned the struggle for mastery among the various states and peoples of Europe, and it went on endlessly, changing shape and direction, but never substance. It began with the Germans, who were numerous, rich, and assertive, possessed of the potential to master Europe and of the urge to try, whether as part of the Holy Roman Empire in medieval and early modern times, or as the Germany of Prussian creation, closer to the present. Their actions in pursuit of this aim always threatened the balance of power, and the result was frequently war.

In the 1930s, Taylor looked at Adolf Hitler's revisionist Germany and concluded that its intention was to succeed in eastern Europe where the Germans of the Habsburg monarchy had failed. This suggested certain issues which he thought needed resolution, and urgently, if the future was to be more than simply a repetition of the past. These issues included Prussian militarism, German racial consciousness, ethnic variations within the successor states to the Habsburg monarchy, the bases of internal authority and external security within the nations of the region, and the nature and function of nationalism within the international community. Could Germany, amorphous and unsettled, achieve 'a proper place' in Europe, by which Taylor meant a place of equality, rather than dominance? The question articulated at once the problem posed by these issues, and the objective that any viable solution to it had to achieve.[2]

Taylor was convinced that the Habsburg monarchy and its historic, imperial relationship with the Slavs of eastern Europe was the root of the German problem. He seemed convinced that the events of his own day, Nazi revisionism and, ultimately, the European war of 1939, were simply contemporary manifestations of a long-standing problem. The Habsburg monarchy was not German as such, nor did the Habsburg emperors encourage the nationalist ambitions of their German subjects. Their empire became the focus of an idealistic German nationalism, all the same. He explained it this way. For a long time, the monarchy was the core of a German dream in which the medieval 'Holy Roman Empire of the German Nation' revived under the Habsburgs (who had, in fact, inherited it from other German princes in the fourteenth century) to become a modern German nation holding mastery over all of central and eastern Europe. No European power would be able to stand against this 'Great Germany', which would dominate Europe by its natural economic and political weight. The Great Germany dream was projected as reality at the revolutionary *vorparliament* in 1848 in Frankfurt, only to be rejected by the Habsburgs. Disillusioned, the dreamers turned to the more realistic and limited Little Germany unification scheme advanced by the Prussian delegates, which excluded both Austria and the Slavic peoples of the empire. This truncated version of the German nation was born in 1871 and was the foundation of the Germany which existed at the time of the First World War, and, with some modifications, at the beginning of the Second World War.

However, as Taylor argued in *The Habsburg Monarchy, 1815–1918*, a book he was writing just as the events leading to war in 1939 were reaching their climax, the compromise of Little Germany did not end the dream of a Great Germany, it was only postponed. Adolf Hitler's revisionist foreign policy was the proof. Hitler's Third Reich was the true heir of the Habsburg monarchy, and only by knowing the history of the monarchy could one understand the European dilemma the Germans represented. Taylor saw an unrestrained and irresponsible German nationalism as the essential ingredient in that history.

Taylor described German nationalism within the Habsburg Empire as merely cultural arrogance and racial intolerance enhanced by class consciousness. Not high praise, by anyone's standards. The Habsburgs had opposed German nationalism in 1848 and later, but ineffectually, and Taylor had little sympathy for them. In his version of the story, the Habsburgs were as intolerant, narrow, and irresponsible as were these nationalists, whom they had failed to tame. They did not provide enlightened rule for the Slav subjects of the dynastic empire, which fact simply enhanced German nationalism and increased the difficulties endured by the Slav peoples. Taylor noted in 1935 that there was talk of a Habsburg revival as a way to bring the disparate peoples of the former empire together. The prospect appalled him.

> [T]he Austrian Idea – that German Austria can be the centre for the co-operation of the peoples of the Danube Valley – could only have been achieved by liberalism and tolerance . . . it can never be achieved by clericalism, dictatorship, and a Habsburg restoration.[3]

A year later he added:

> [W]hat good did the Habsburgs do their people except provide picturesque ceremony? . . . At a time when the results of the Great War are being increasingly assailed, one unquestionable good stands out – the destruction of the Habsburg Empire.'[4]

However, breaking up the empire into the successor states of Czechoslovakia, Yugoslavia, Hungary, Austria, and Poland did not resolve the problem endemic to central and eastern Europe: ethnic and national inequality, which again and again produced rivalry, conflict, and even war. In a surprising burst of pragmatism, given the subject, Taylor observed in 1941 that given its history, central Europe could not be settled without some of its inhabitants experiencing injustice. That did not justify indulging in injustice, but to pretend that injustice was not inevitable was to succumb to romance.[5]

On a break from his studies in Vienna in 1929, Taylor travelled within the former monarchy to Carinthia, Trieste and Split, where he discovered that there was more to the former monarchy than German Austrians. It occurred to him then, if it had not before, that the peoples of the successor states constituted a crucial ingredient in the evolution of the German role in Europe. Reading and hearing Adolf Hitler's rhetoric of Great Germany in succeeding years only strengthened this view. It was a simple additional step to understand the history of the Habsburg monarchy as the history of German, and to a lesser extent Magyar, manipulation and exploitation of political incompetence, perverted nationalism, and racial and cultural intolerance, in order to gain mastery over the lesser peoples of the empire.

The Habsburg Monarchy was published in 1941. It contained the results of Taylor's reading and thinking about the Habsburg role in modern Europe over the decade before. The book was a historical explanation of the subject, and included an appendix in which the ethnography of the empire was explained in some detail. At the same time, the bibliography, presented in essay form, contained two memoirs and the Metternich papers, and otherwise the secondary works Taylor had consulted, 'some with profit, most without'.[6] The polemical style and absence of scholarly references, at least compared with *The Italian Problem in European Diplomacy*, leads to the conclusion that *The Habsburg Monarchy* is actually a long essay meant to serve a political purpose rather more than a historical one.

Taylor wasted no time in establishing his context and sympathies. Regarding the former, he declared: 'The history of Austria is the history of the Habsburg Monarchy.'[7] The aim of the monarchy for centuries simply was survival, and, so far as the Habsburgs were concerned, their many subjects, German, Magyar, Slav and others, existed to further this aim. Habsburg policies were simple: oppose nationalism, and make the monarchy an indispensable pillar of the European order, so that if ever the Habsburgs could not control their subjects, the European powers would do it for them.

A crucial point was the European orientation of the monarchy, a point Taylor also elaborated in *The Italian Problem in European Diplomacy*. The Habsburg Empire, he wrote here, was unique among the great powers for being primarily organised for the conduct of foreign policy.[8] For centuries, foreign policy had been the key to Habsburg power, not to mention survival, whether the monarchy was defending Christian Europe against Muslim Turks, Catholic Europe against Protestantism, or the European balance of power against expansionist France. In 1815, the monarchy was concerned mainly with whether its subjects were *kaisertreu*, and proposed itself as Europe's saviour by offering to stand as the principal defender of traditional Europe against the twin evils of revolution and nationalism. By preserving Europe from these horrors, the monarchy could sustain its image as a European necessity while at the same time preserving its own internal order.[9] This was Taylor's interpretation, and it was neither entirely new nor easily refuted, given the evidence.

Taylor projected most of his criticism of the imperial legacy from his view of the relationship between Habsburg domestic and foreign policy. He described the empire as a polyglot of nationalities over which the monarchy ruled in medieval fashion. The Habsburgs regarded their subjects as chattels and their ministers as mere seneschals, and they continued into modern times, categorically opposed to any change in this feudal system. They fell when, in Taylor's phrase, 'their tenants insisted on becoming a free peasantry'.[10] He could not resist letting his readers know that so far as he was concerned, it was not before time.

The futility of the feudal Habsburg system was well represented in the character and performance of both emperor and seneschal in the nineteenth-century empire. Francis Joseph was the best example of the former, Taylor thought. He succeeded to the throne in the midst of the revolution of 1848 and left it in the middle of the First World War. Franz Joseph was the last Habsburg but one, and that by only two years, and had once remarked to US President Theodore Roosevelt that he was 'the last ruler of his kind'. Taylor thought this an apt commentary both on the emperor and the system he ruled, explaining that, in truth, nothing mattered to Franz Joseph save the dynasty, to the existence of which he had been educated and to which he was enslaved. This had nothing to do with improving the lives of imperial subjects, but everything to do with upholding the tradition of preserving dynastic power. The strength of the army and the prestige of the monarchy abroad were this emperor's only policies, and experience had never shown him that these aims were inadequate, or that he ought to have concentrated on making the empire 'something worthwhile belonging to'.[11]

Meanwhile, Prince Metternich, who served Francis Joseph's immediate predecessors, had been the perfect seneschal. A Rhenish *émigré* who had fled from the armies of the French revolution, Metternich had no political base in Austria except the emperor. He had witnessed the behaviour of French revolutionary soldiers in Strasbourg during his student days in 1792–3, and remained thereafter as appalled as any Habsburg ever was at the idea of opposition to duly constituted authority. Hence his insistence upon legitimacy in 1815 as the basis for European restoration following the overthrow of Napoleon. His own legitimacy, meanwhile, was tied to survival of the Habsburg Monarchy, and he rarely argued with the dynastic principle, or advocated reforms he actually believed should have been introduced, if there was even a hint that the throne might disagree with them.

Metternich's successors were much like him, though not so astute. Under their inept government the peoples of the empire learned to expect nothing good, and were alienated from their rulers. In consequence, the peoples became increasingly susceptible to the appeal of nationalism when it invaded the empire after 1848. Taylor observed in passing: 'It is perhaps doubtful whether an alien government can permanently provide any real answer to the appeal of nationalism; that self-government is better than good government is no new discovery.'[12] All the same, there was poor government in abundance, and he treated it as something to be expected. Ironically, Taylor claimed, poor government short-changed the monarchy as fully as it did the peoples. The Habsburgs, he wrote, believing that the Danube without the monarchy was unthinkable, were prevented as a result from taking realistic measures to reform the government that might have ensured their own survival.

Individually and collectively, the last rulers of the Habsburg Empire were inept but also reactionary. Francis I, the last Holy Roman emperor and first Austrian emperor, was, in Taylor's words, 'slow-witted and fearful, he hated ability and initiative in his servants or relatives, and took care to exclude capable men from all positions of responsibility'.[13] His two death-bed political testaments were a study in absurd contradiction. The first ordered his heir to free the Catholic Church from all the controls that had been placed upon it a generation before by Joseph II. The second ordered the heir to alter nothing in the bases of the state, which included Joseph's Church reforms. As Taylor explained it, Joseph's reforms were 'enlightened', and therefore unsettling; but since they existed, they must not be interfered with. Ferdinand, the imperial heir upon whom these improbable directives were laid, was 'epileptic and rickety', and scarcely able to deal with their inherent paradox – or with much else, for that matter. His character, Taylor noted tongue-in-cheek, was indicated in his only recorded saying: 'I am the emperor and I will have dumplings!'[14] Ferdinand was not missed when he abdicated in favour of Francis Joseph in 1848.

Even so, in Taylor's view, Francis Joseph, the last but one Habsburg emperor, was the most futile dynast of all. He described Francis Joseph as an administrator rather than a statesman, who was committed to routine and incapable of formulating general views. Moreover, he distrusted those who were capable of forming ideas. He was a desk-bound bureaucrat who tried to make the Empire work by signing documents throughout each workday, and was mystified when this was found not to be enough.[15] His only goal was to maintain dynastic powers as feudal overlord, and to sustain that power with his conscript peasant army. Taylor thought it no surprise that ministerial morale reached new lows under Francis Joseph, or that, at the same time, imperial ministers were ever more intensely loyal. The state of the Empire worsened and ministers were convinced that to change would invite destruction. Low morale and high loyalty stemmed from the single, negative, assumption that, bad as the empire was, there simply was nothing viable with which to replace it.[16]

The imperial system was a veritable study in inefficiency, which only grew worse with time. Taylor described an over-lapping tangle of councils, boards, chambers and conferences, some created to replace others, but all, including those replaced, continuing to function. The tangle simply expanded and became more inflexible after nationalism penetrated the monarchy and the nationalities problem unfolded.[17] The monarchy then chose ministers because they possessed a power-base in a particular ethnic group (the Magyars, for example), and directed them to operate against the interests of that group. Ministers rarely performed either comfortably or competently in such a context, and yet there was a certain logic to it: that is, furthering – or at least not suppressing – ethnic conflict within the empire was almost the only way to maintain the monarchy over its many contentious parts. Meanwhile, the system had the potential, and indeed the mentality, of a police state. It never quite became one, however, because its institutional absolutism, as Viktor Adler observed, was tempered by inefficiency to the point of being nearly benign. One searched in vain for the real earmarks of oppression, Taylor wrote, the concentration camp, the executioner, and the organised brutality, all justified through propaganda.[18]

Had ministers been made responsible, things might have improved. Taylor argued that the cure for bureaucratic bumbling was to give able men a task and guarantee that while they would be punished for failure, they would also reap rewards by succeeding. This had nothing to do with democracy, he continued, pointing out that all of the great absolutist rulers had great ministers.[19] However, Taylor concluded, as the Habsburgs distrusted change and ministers who suggested it, even as they distrusted their subjects, so ministerial responsibility never entered into the process of imperial government. The crisis in Lombardy and Venetia in 1847–8 was a case in point. The Habsburgs relied on the senile, incompetent viceroy, Archduke Rainer, rather than on Count Hartig, whose suggested administrative reforms might have prevented revolution and war. Administrators who wanted to keep their posts in Lombardy or elsewhere, took their cue from the emperors and worked 'uncomprehendingly', in Taylor's words, 'in a self-sufficient world of paper, divorced from reality'. The object of the imperial system 'is not achievement, but to keep the bureaucrats at their desks from ten till four'.[20] Consequently, imperial officials typically believed that it was a miracle to get through today, without worrying about getting through next year.

Ministerial responsibility might have cured systemic anomalies and even the grosser forms of incompetence, Taylor wrote, but only an appeal to the citizens of the empire, 'calling in the ruled to the assistance of the rulers', could have saved the monarchy itself.[21] But, having argued this, he went on to indicate that if ministerial responsibility was unpopular with the Habsburgs, the idea of popular participation in the political process was more so. The failure of the monarchy to resolve cultural, ethnic, and political divisions among its peoples often based upon some form of injustice, and indeed to encourage such divisions, was the real Habsburg legacy.

Ethnic dissension was epidemic in the later years of the empire, and usually involved either the so-called 'master' peoples in conflict with the monarchy or with each other, or else these groups claiming the right to exploit one of the 'submerged' peoples, who looked in vain to the monarchy for relief. It is wrong to think that ethnocentricity was a recent phenomenon in eastern and central Europe, nor did Taylor suggest that this was the case. He was as aware as any other student of the history of the region that ethnocentricity had been a part of political and cultural life in southeastern Europe for centuries. Taylor did suggest, and rightly, that ethnocentricity fed ethnic conflicts, which in turn contributed greatly to the German problem in modern times, and may even have defined it.

The German problem played, in part, upon historic division between master and submerged peoples within the empire. This division was encouraged by the Habsburg tradition of ruling by playing one ethnic or national group off against the others, a tradition that eventually doomed the empire. The master peoples, by definition, were those conscious through education of their cultural and historic roots. The rest were peoples whose consciousness of such things had been purposely suppressed by the master peoples. These were the Germans, Magyars (Hungary), Italians, and Poles, all having a national past and a ruling class of landed magnates or great capitalists. The submerged peoples included the Czechs, Slovaks, Slovenes, Serbs, Croats, Ruthenians, Little Russians, Roumanians, and others, who comprised an imperial peasantry and, later, a working class for the industrialising cities. The master peoples ruled over these submerged groups, or at least sought to do so.

After 1848, whether they were a master or a subject race, the various ethnic groups demanded some measure of autonomy within, or even independence from, the empire, and local control over cultural and political affairs. For the Germans, Italians, and Poles, this meant union with the 'nation' outside of the empire, while for the Magyars it meant aspirations toward a Great Hungary comprising vast portions of the empire. The rest simply pressed for the right to preserve their own language and to revive whatever of their cultural traditions still existed.[22] The monarchy turned a deaf ear, however, and the empire moved toward a policy, as Count Schmerling once explained it, of keeping everybody in a state of mild dissatisfaction while pleasing nobody.

Dissatisfaction applied mainly to historic peoples, although the Italians were only occasionally a problem, and the Poles almost not at all. The Poles were so quiescent that in the later century, the monarchy regarded them as the only people upon whom it could rely.[23] The real disturbances percolated from the Magyars and the Germans, and they were rarely mild, even before 1848. The Magyars represented a nationalism 'decked out with all the phraseology of the French revolution' (Taylor referred here to Lujos Kossuth's rhetoric in Budapest in 1848), though with little of the reality. In their arrogance (Taylor's phrase), the Magyar's claimed that theirs was the only language of culture, never understanding that non-Magyars, nor anyone else for that matter, would ever voluntarily learn Magyar in the way people voluntarily learn French, English, or even German. It all had to be done by force, making submission to an artificial Magyar monopoly of public life the only means by which people of other races could have a political existence.[24] Of course, it would not be their own.

Magyar nationalism succeeded briefly in 1848, then fell to Russian intervention in 1849. The Magyars bided their time until the Austro-Prussian war of 1866. The empire was defeated then, in part because the Magyars refused to go to war on its behalf. Prussia rewarded this disloyalty by imposing the *Ausgleich* in 1867, an arrangement by which Magyar Hungary became equal partners with German Austria under the monarchy. The arrangement was called the Austro-Hungarian Empire. The Magyars controlled their internal affairs, maintained the right to dispute with Vienna over imperial foreign policy, and controlled their own military, except in war-time.

In effect, the *Ausgleich* realised the Great Hungary striven for in 1848, and within it, the Magyars had a free hand to 'Magyarise' their national minorities. They did so with alacrity. By 1900, though the Magyars were less than half of the population, they comprised 90 per cent or more of officials, doctors, and judges, and 80 per cent of the newspapers were Magyar.[25] Under such circumstances, many non-Magyars emigrated. Those who remained were Taylor's heros: tough, enthusiastic, the potential revolutionaries, resisting 'each ruthless step' in Magyarisation. These fighters were 'the best of their race'.[26]

The Magyar nationalists found their place in 1867. Not so the German nationalists. Their aspirations were of a much higher order. *The Habsburg Monarchy* appeared in 1941, following a half-decade of rising tension in Europe, much of which Taylor laid at Germany's door, and therefore he treated the German problem in the empire with less sympathy or perhaps less patience, than any other. Historical detachment fell well short of an ideal standard on this issue. Taylor began by noting that Austrian Germans lived their own version of the *zerrisenheit* of Goethe's *Faust*: subjects of the monarchy, they nevertheless dreamed of a Great Germany beyond it, which would include the dynastic lands and be ruled by Germans. First, they tried to Germanise the empire, and when that failed, they tried to make the monarchy disappear into a German national state. Taylor explained it this way: the German tradition in the empire was cultural, not political. It also was provincial – Styria or the Tyrol – not nationalistic. The Germans did believe in a theoretical Germany – a *corpus Germanium*, Taylor called it – which was embodied, again theoretically, in the lands of the 'Holy Roman Empire of the German Nation', to which the Austrian Empire was the successor. German lands were part of this empire, which was dominated by German culture. The universities, music and the arts were heavily Germanic, until the later nineteenth century at any rate, and if there was an Austrian 'language of state' it was German. The empire had never robbed the Germans of their cultural heritage as it had others. What the Germans lacked was a political identity. Were they part of the Austrian Empire, or a national Germany that did not exist? Or, in Taylor's clever language: 'Were they to be loyal to Vienna or to the Kingdom in the skies?'[27]

The Germans complained constantly – and with little justification, Taylor thought – that they were mistreated, charging that as the principal professional and capitalist class they bore the greater share of taxation without receiving a correspondingly greater share of privilege, or, on a different level, that they were the race who had 'made' the Empire centuries before, but now were expected to be satisfied as the mere equals of other nationalities. Taylor thought the Habsburgs contributed to these complaints indirectly because they were Germans themselves.

German middle-class liberalism annoyed them, he wrote, but they were never quite certain that the Germans were not entitled to special treatment.[28]

After 1848, German Austrians thought of little except their national 'liberation', Taylor continued. In the early 1860s they believed they had won the empire when Count Schmerling and Count Taafe administered policies that aimed at linking the monarchy more closely to the German minority. However, the dynasty clung to its ethnic non-alignment and turned against this programme. In 1866, the monarchy lost its war with Prussia, and the Great German dream of 1848, of a Catholic German confederation under the Habsburg monarchy, was gone once and for all. With this, they turned on the empire, became disruptive in their actions and anti-Habsburg in their language, and looked more and more, for realisation of their aspirations, to Hohenzollern Prussia, which was imperial Germany after 1871.[29]

The cloak of secrecy of German nationalism came off completely in 1882 with publication of the Linz Programme, the document which became the foundation of the German Nationalist party. The Linz Programme appealed to a 'mythical time' when the Austrian Empire was a German state. It also introduced a new brand of fanaticism in imperial politics. Taylor argued that German Austrians were inspired by this fanaticism to indulge in both intellectual and physical violence, as, for example, in the Friedjung Case.

Heinrich Friedjung, author of *The Struggle for Supremacy in Germany, 1859–1866*, the book Taylor later claimed was his model for writing history, was, Taylor also later claimed, a 'great historian'. More to the point in the present context, he was a cultural and political propagandist for German nationalism and co-author of the Linz Programme. However, German nationalists had no time for liberals or Jews, both of which Friedjung was. He was ejected from the Nationalist Party soon after it was formed, in spite of being a co-architect of its philosophy. His nationalist ardour was not dimmed, however, and when he was commissioned by the Austrian foreign office to write a series of newspaper articles exposing the Croat Nationalist Party as disloyal and subversive, he responded with such enthusiasm that Foreign Minister Aehrenthal was appalled. Only one article was allowed to appear, but it was sufficiently vitriolic that the Croat Party brought a libel action. It was demonstrated in the course of the trial that Friedjung had used some forged documents. He remained unapologetic. Taylor suggested that in spite of being discriminated against by his own party for being a liberal Jew, Friedjung was so convinced that German nationalism was a 'holy crusade', and therefore Slav nationalism appeared 'merely as a treasonable conspiracy', that even if he suspected the documents were forgeries, the cause in which they were used was sacred and so he suspended the critical faculties he possessed as a historian.[30] At least that was Taylor's explanation. 'Damning with faint praise' seems to catch the essence of it, because however much he thought of Friedjung as a historian, Taylor could hardly forgive him for being a German nationalist intellectual during that dangerous epoch, at once fanatical and extreme.

In the 1890s such extremism as Friedjung's was translated into hooliganism in the Imperial Diet. German Nationalist members hurled inkpots, started fist-fights, and called upon the respectable Germans of Vienna to riot and demonstrate each time the government proposed a course of action they didn't like. Their acknowledged leader was Georg von Schönerer, the only non-Jew among the co-authors of the Linz Programme. Schönerer claimed loyalty to the Habsburgs, but Taylor showed how he worked single-mindedly to bring down the empire by forcing German Nationalism upon the dynasty. He was the instigator behind much of the nationalist activism, as for example when German riots forced the Badeni Government to resign.

Badeni was a Pole thought to be above national bias and thus able to form a government that could side-step Nationalist discontents. However, when Badeni appeared in the Diet trying to institute genuinely imperial, as opposed to pseudo-nationalist, programs, Schönerer's 'mobs of well-dressed burghers' rioted. He was forced to resign. Taylor was disgusted. These irrational, irresponsible, and violent nationalists, he wrote, were 'a fit index of the political culture of the "state people"'. The empire could not long survive them. They could render the government helpless, but they could not provide an alternative. All of their negations culminated in opposition to Badeni. The German Nationalists contributed to the destruction of the monarchy more than any single factor, Taylor argued. They prevented transformation of Austria into a non-national state, but they were too weak to achieve the further goal of transforming it into a German national state. The Germans also could not capture the dynasty, and they dared not overthrow it. All they could, do they did, which was to obstruct any positive step the dynasty took.[31]

The German Nationalists were aided in creating disaster by the German Social Democrats. A socialist himself, Taylor saw in this a fine example of hypocrisy. The Social Democrats proved even more unprincipled than the Nationalists *per se*, he wrote. On the one hand they pandered to authority rather than accept responsibility, and on the other, embraced nationalism, with all of its cant of cultural and moral superiority, as the means for achieving socialism. This was not Taylor's idea of socialism. It was bizarre, however, and as one example, he cited Otto Bauer, a socialist leader in Vienna, proposing that the dynasty impose universal suffrage upon the empire, and use the imperial army to enforce it. Taylor thought the plan was both absurd and a despicable betrayal of socialist principles. The Habsburg army was the army of reaction, not revolution, he noted, and went on to accuse the Social Democrats of trying to impose their doctrines on the dynasty because 'they lacked the courage and conviction to win on their own'.[32] The interpretation is probably accurate enough, but Taylor's language is the believer's, not the historian's. He met Bauer in the 1920s, an old man living in Vienna: 'I found him superficial and I never saw him again.'[33]

Taylor was disillusioned by Austrian socialists well beyond Bauer. He described them generally as being like other German Nationalists: Germans first and socialists only when convenient. Not even Marx and Engels escaped their Germanness, he claimed. Engels had 'never ceased to be a German nationalist'.[34] Marx was a revolutionary, who found in socialism, simply the best means of organising the masses for the task of running both industry and the state. He was a typical authoritarian who, because he was a German, assumed superiority over others, and his theories in 1848 'recognized only the claims of the historic nationalities. . . . For him Slav nationalism was a reactionary fraud.'[35] Eventually, in another place, Taylor expanded upon German socialism to suggest that because of its nationalism, it connected directly with Nazism, which he described as a nationally based revolutionary movement with places equally for the small burgher, the peasant, and the worker.

The Austrians were the only, if also the most formidable, exponent of master race nationalism. The victims of all of the master races were the submerged, or 'non-historic' Slavs of the empire. They were human cattle, the cannon fodder of the imperial army, the 'dumb' peasants on the great Magyar estates, and the cowed workers in German factories, oppressed by the aristocratic and capitalistic master peoples. However, 'in the eyes of God' (an odd place for Taylor to search for vindication, given his views on the Deity), there was no preference over poor Rumanians, say, for rich Germans or Magyars. The indictment was clear: the subject peoples 'began their history once more' only after the dynasty 'surrendered to the most violent courses of the Germans and the Magyars', which 'provoked the greatest war in history'.[36]

Slav aspirations were not unreasonable, Taylor thought. Those of the master peoples were. The latter wanted mastery over the Slavs, and tried to conform the dynasty to their wishes. The former merely wanted control over their lives – their own newspapers, legal advice, medical services, and local administration, and some measure of political life in areas where they were the majority. Their role in the empire would be negative until they attained these ends, Taylor pointed out, because they would back whichever of the contending factions offered them some degree of national autonomy. Some few among the master peoples supported them, such as Francis Deak and Count Michael Karolyi, both Magyars. It is an interesting, though perhaps minor, point that when Taylor was writing the first edition of *The Habsburg Monarchy*, he met at Oxford and became friends with Karolyi, who was a revolutionary, a democrat, the son-in-law of Count Andrassy, who had served as a Habsburg minister of state, and an advocate of 'a Danubian confederation of free and equal peoples'. Karolyi introduced Taylor to other aristocratic Magyars, such as Baron Hatvani, a newspaper publisher who like Karolyi was an exile from the Horthy regime. Such connections in 1940–41 almost certainly worked a positive influence on Taylor's hopes for the submerged peoples of the former monarchy.[37] Ironically, the leading Magyar supremacist of the nineteenth century was not a Magyar. Lujos Kossuth, leader of Hungary in the 1848 revolution, was a Slav convert to Magyar nationalism (just as Fichte was a Saxon convert to Prussian mastery in Germany). Kossuth was no democrat, nor a real revolutionary. While advocating liberty, Taylor wrote, he much resembled Mussolini. He assured the Serbs that they would be as free as the Magyars; what he meant was that the Serbs would be free to be absorbed into Magyar culture.[38]

The problem, Taylor continued, was that the minorities were divided on the basis of class even more than of nationality. The master peoples felt equal with one another and enjoyed one another's respect even when in conflict. But when confronting the non-historic nationalities, 'they experienced . . . the degradation which a nobleman would feel at being called out by a new rich grocer.'[39] The object of the master people, then, was to avoid degradation by keeping these 'new rich grocers' firmly in their place, and to enlist the monarchy for the task.

But the monarchy could not take sides, as Taylor explained, as it could not offer acceptable alternatives to the conflict, and consequently, could not survive. As each nationality manipulated the 'lever of power' in one direction or another by being either exceptionally subservient or exceptionally troublesome, the monarchy vacillated helplessly back and forth.[40] No idea of an Austrian state in which all had a stake ever emerged, and each class and nationality grew ever more demanding in serving its separate interests. Finally, Taylor explained, the privileged classes and peoples concluded that it was useless as well as harmful to concede anything, while the subject peoples, or their leaders, came to see total national independence as the only hope for gaining their aspirations. Imperial ministers lost hope, and Count Czernin on the eve of collapse in 1918 observed quite correctly that: 'We were bound to die. We were at liberty to choose the manner of our death, and we chose the most terrible.'[41]

When that war (1914–18) was past, the empire was dismembered and the Slav peoples were organised into the successor states. The future of central and eastern Europe would depend upon how they handled their new states. Could they free themselves from harassment by the master races? Could they free themselves from their own ethnocentricity, for that matter? If toleration was to be learned in central and eastern Europe, the Slavs would have to teach it, Taylor claimed, for whatever democratic impulse there was in the lands of the former monarchy existed because the Slavic peoples had struggled for liberation from the empire. Such an assertion has a hollow ring, now, but Taylor did not know in 1941 what was to happen after 1945.

Taylor produced a new edition of *The Habsburg Monarchy* in 1948, in which he expanded his treatment of Habsburg diplomacy, or at least he emphasised its significance. He admitted to having a 'national bias' in the 1941 edition, and acknowledged that the fate of the Monarchy hinged upon foreign affairs quite as much as upon the behaviour of the various nationalities.[42] Actually, this disclaimer notwithstanding, little was different between the new edition and the old. Both emphasised the critical role of the nationalities in imperial affairs, the latter merely stressed that Habsburg foreign policy was designed to offset the failures of Habsburg domestic policy. That is, beginning with Metternich, Austria gave itself the mission of preserving Europe from liberal or nationalist revolution and war so that in return, Europe would feel a vested interest in preserving the empire.[43]

To be sure, Taylor was a diplomatic historian, but beyond that, he interpreted Habsburg foreign policy, however European in outlook it might have appeared, as inspired by fear of what the future held for the dynastic system. Metternich had seen greater danger in German and Italian nationalism than in French imperialism, because, in Taylor's words,

German and Italian national states . . . must by their boundless ambition inevitably provoke in Europe a war both general and endless. But his vision was sharpened because these national forces threatened in the first place not the European system but the Austrian Empire.[44]

From this premise, Taylor deduced the essentials of nineteenth-century Austrian foreign policy. Prince Schwarzenberg maintained Metternich's dynastic objectives but rejected his technique, which he had watched collapse in the face of revolution. Then, in Italy, Schwarzenberg saw revolution, a revolution of intellectuals who relied more upon liberal ideas than upon force, fall under Radetzky's guns.[45] Schwarzenberg believed in force as the foundation of government, and sought to preserve the Habsburg system by proving that it was a power state. But he missed the point: in order to use power, a state must have it. Metternich had always understood that Austria did not have power, at least not in comparison to the other great powers. It was one thing to crush Italian and Slav revolutionaries, quite another to push Prussia around. Schwarzenberg's policies came to fruition more than a decade after his death, when they produced the monarchy's humiliation at Prussian hands in 1866. This signalled the beginning of the end for Habsburg prestige both at home and abroad, and perhaps most significantly, marked the moment when the allegiance of German nationalists shifted from the Habsburgs to the Hohenzollern kings of Prussia.

After 1866, Taylor wrote, Austrian foreign policy passed into the hands of relative non-entities who practised a blend of Metternichian compromise and Schwarzenberg's empty posturing. For example: attempts to subvert Magyar nationalism through dualism, a Metternichian move; threats of intervention in the Balkans as a sop to Germans and Magyars protesting against Russian support of Slav nationalism – also a Metternichian manoeuvre, but expressed in Schwarzenberg's language; and annexing Bosnia in 1908 and the 'punitive' attack on Serbia in 1914, which were strictly from Schwarzenberg's book. Taylor was certain that such moves failed to impress Austria's neighbours, and asserted that what influence the policies did have only reflected the importance of the Austro-German alliance of 1882. Austrian threats meant little without German backing, and Austria would not have dared threaten war or, as in 1914, actually engage in it without Germany's support. He concluded that attempts at 'solutions by violence' simply forced the cracks in the Habsburg structure into open breaks, and contributed along with so much else to the fall of the monarchy.

The Serbian War which began in July 1914 signalled the end of the monarchy, but did not actually cause it, Taylor argued. Unable to defeat Serbia quickly, the Habsburgs involved Germany and opened the door to the European war that Metternich had always feared. Taylor saw two events proceeding from this disaster. On the one hand, the nationalities lost what little faith they still had in the imperial system and broke into open rebellion. On the other, the Habsburgs defeated Serbia only by becoming Germany's military clients. German success saved Austro-Hungary in Serbia and even held out the prospect of winning the larger war – under German supervision. German generals planned Austrian campaigns, and German soldiers kept the Austrian army from falling apart. Only Germany sustained

Austria-Hungarian engagement in this larger war, for it was a struggle well beyond Habsburg capability. The monarchy could not, in the traditional manner, either negotiate or compromise its way out. It was the ultimate negative for the Habsburgs, Taylor concluded. 'Germany, and so Austria-Hungary with her, was now committed to a bid for the mastery of Europe, and the Habsburgs were no more than German auxiliary troops.'[46] The monarchy, in his view, simply committed suicide.

The fall of the Habsburg monarchy did not end its presence in central and eastern Europe, however. Coming back to his original theme, Taylor argued that the real Habsburg legacy was the long-term impact felt by imperial treatment of the submerged peoples. In 1918, the minorities sought liberation from the empire, the Slavs to win freedom, the master peoples to hang on to their dominant position. In the last days of the war, the latter abandoned the dynasty and tried to declare themselves oppressed peoples who had been conscripted into war, just as had the Czecho-Slovaks and South Slavs.[47] They succeeded to a degree, and Poland, Hungary, and even a left-wing German Austria emerged after the war. However, Taylor continued, their real aim was to continue as master peoples. He explained it this way: the future of central and eastern Europe depended upon the degree to which the submerged nationalities could find happiness amalgamated into the Slav successor states, Czechoslovakia and Yugoslavia. If they could not, instability and insecurity would follow, upon which the other peoples could feed their appetite for mastery.

The prospects were not reassuring. Warned Taylor: 'I have not pretended that the victory of the new nationalities was more than a reversal of the previous order.'[48] Giving independence to the submerged peoples did not satisfy the master peoples, and those others who still found themselves without independence – Croats and Slovaks, for example – were equally, if not more, dissatisfied. The state of mind of all peoples of the former Monarchy was critical. Any of them, if dissatisfied, could open central and eastern Europe to revisionism, which meant restoration of imperial Germany: 'States had to find a new moral basis for obedience at home; they had, more urgently, to find a means of protection against the weight of Germany, the only Great Power on the European continent.'[49]

In analysing the successor states, Taylor revealed clearly a two-tiered paradox inherent within the post-war situation. No master people would accept equality with a submerged nationality; and no submerged people, once awakened to their national identity, would accept rule by the master peoles. Taylor had put his finger on the most important obstacle to stability among the ethnic groupings in eastern Europe, and elaboration of this obstacle was a constant theme as he sought to both explain and reveal the past and future of eastern Europe.

It is important to recognise that Taylor accepted the role of nationalities as a given, his criticism of militant nationalists within the Habsburg Empire notwithstanding. In his view, individual and independent nation states were the only viable components of the European order. However, at the same time he recognised the difficulty of building such nations in eastern Europe. The problem of amalgamation was the first point of consideration. In practice, Czechoslovakia and Yugoslavia simply reproduced the ethnic complications of the monarchy. Seven nationalities comprised constitutional Austria; now Yugoslavia incorporated nine.[50] The essential ingredient was any kind of national identity, which was missing in the new, amalgamated states. By definition (Taylor's):

A national state is one in which the great majority of the inhabitants are of a single nationality and in which the great majority of the inhabitants who are not of the prevailing nationality are not partners but 'minorities', whether protected by special legislation or not.[51]

Neither Czechoslovakia nor Yugoslavia could hope for homogeneity, for too many ethnic groups had to be included. The founders tried to create nations by an act of will, or better, of faith, out of peoples who were alike mainly only in their dislike of the former empire.

The founder of Czechoslovakia was Thomas Garrigue Masaryk, a middle-class intellectual and anti-clerical reformer in the Hussite tradition, who believed political and religious obstacles could be overcome with logic. Taylor described him somewhat hyperbolically as 'the first philosopher-king since Marcus Aurelius'.[52] Masaryk created Czechoslovakia out of Catholics and Protestants, Slavs and non-Slavs, and thus provided the blueprint for the South Slav amalgam of Yugoslavia, where the actual work was done by Bishop Josip Strosmajer of Djakova, a peasant who had risen high in the Roman Catholic Church. Religion was a major stumbling block in Yugoslavia, where many Croats were Catholic and traditionally looked to Vienna, and most Serbs, the majority people and the closest to having a conscious political tradition, were Orthodox Christians who looked to Moscow. Having a large Muslim minority, from the days when the Ottoman Empire ruled the Balkans, only added to the tension. Such differences created enormous barriers in 1918, leading Taylor to state what in the 1990s has become so obvious as to not need statement, that the nobility of the national cause notwithstanding, 'Strosmajer and Masaryk created states; they failed to create nations.'[53]

Masaryk was the master planner of amalgamation, but like Strosmajer, he could not make it work in practice. A Moravian Slovak converted to Czech nationalism, Masaryk lost patience with the pre-war abstractions of the Young Czechs, and offered in their place a commonsense program to be embraced by all Czechs who were prepared to rise above 'a pseudo-historical tradition'.[54] He was prepared to accept both authority and responsibility, because, Taylor explained, Masaryk was one of the few men growing up in the empire who recognised that power without responsibility was an act of denial, but that power with responsibility was the path of progress. He once argued that while democracy is rule by the people, there can be no democratic government without discipline.[55] On this basis, he worked to establish democracy, which he characterised as amalgamation, as the 'new moral basis for authority' in the successor states; no longer Czechs and Slovaks, but Czechoslovakians, all with the same rights and, once the Slovaks caught up with the Czechs culturally and economically, equal responsibilities for governing.

Taylor recognised that even Masaryk could not overcome commitments that were passionate rather than logical. His amalgamation ultimately foundered on traditional sources of ethnic animosity. The reality in Czechoslovakia was continuous disruption from both Sudeten Germans and Slovaks. Both had been incorporated into a state where the Czechs were the 'people of state', and they resented it. To the Germans, the Czechs were inferiors; to the Slovaks, they were simply another master people to be opposed in the name of Slovak nationalism, just as once the Slovaks had opposed the Germans of the empire.

The Pittsburgh Protocol, the document by which the western democracies agreed to recognise the successor states, called for the Czechs to be the people of state, and the rest to have a degree of autonomy regarding education, literature and culture. All would compete equally for jobs in the bureaucracy and the professions. But with statehood, the Czechs took control in all areas and gave every indication of remaining in that condition. The more the minorities agitated, the firmer Czech control became, and amalgamation receded further and further into the background. Taylor drew a comparison between the English and the Scots and the Czechs and Slovaks, in order to emphasise the failure of Masaryk's hopes over time. The English and Scots worked together, he noted, but for Masaryk, 'the Slovaks turned out to be the Irish'.[56] The Germans, on the other hand, turned out to be, well, German.

Yugoslavia, where the Serbs were dominant through numbers and their brief experience at political independence, was similar. They emerged as the people of state, and the Croats (the largest and most important of many minorities) resented them. Neither people possessed a native aristocracy – the ruling Karageorgovitch dynasty descended from peasant partisans against the Turks at the time of the Napoleonic Wars – but the Croats possessed a rudimentary bourgeois tradition which separated them culturally and economically from the wholly peasant Serbs. The fact added fuel to Croat resentment. When the Serbs talked about creating a Great Serbia, Croat intellectuals and Croat patriots, usually enemies, combined to resist. Centuries of Croat resistance to Budapest now turned against Belgrade, and Bishop Strosmajer could not prevent it.[57]

To complicate differences, each Slav state developed what Taylor termed 'peasant democracy', which was a form of fascism. It rested upon various theoretical bases: loyalty to the Habsburgs, populism, or agrarian expansionism. It was singular in its violent methods, however. 'Peasant democracy' had no respect for either democracy or law, Taylor noted, and it used nationalism to fan hatreds that concealed its true aim of territorial aggrandisement.

Meanwhile, German nationalism hovered in the wings as the successor states laboured over amalgamation. In 1935 Taylor offered both a warning and a suggestion for the future. 'Before the war', he began, 'the German Austrians had the opportunity of leading the way to a system of freedom and equality among the nationalities; that opportunity they refused to take.' The Habsburgs disappeared, but 'the opportunity is still there, once the German Austrians make it clear that they have abandoned all belief in their cultural superiority over the races of other states'. An Austria associated with other Balkan states in terms of similar economic, political and strategic interests, could contribute to the stability of the entire region. On the other hand, should the clericalism, dynasticism, and upper-class consciousness that cemented the old empire together be revived, 'then the new system will fail as the old system failed, and a revived Habsburg Empire will produce what the old Habsburg Empire produced – a great European war'.[58]

Which did Taylor believe in the most, the suggestion or the warning? Was he convinced that a contented German Austria living in peace with its Slav neighbours was possible? During 1934–5, when his earliest observations on the past, present and future of the Habsburg lands were written, Austrian fascists murdered Chancellor Dollfuss, disrupted and obstructed normal political life, were outspoken in matters of racial and ethnic prejudice, and revived the old sort of nationalism. Clearly, Taylor had little faith in the German Austrian, and this came through again and again in *The Habsburg Monarchy*. After 1918, they had failed to 'grow up' and accept responsibility for themselves. They played the old games, such as trying to keep German areas of Bohemia out of Czech hands. The Austrian Germans embraced a one-sided version of self-determination. They opposed the socialists when it was proposed that socialism should mean 'the surrender of their domination over others', but they embraced it when the socialists called for a Great Austria. Clericals, old imperialists, and Christian Socialists then marched united behind socialist leaders. Self determination was the rallying cry of all the peoples of southeastern Europe in 1918, and like the Germans they mostly wanted enhancement of their situation: hence, calls for Great Hungary and Great Serbia, for example.

But it was futile for German Austrian to want a Great Austria, Taylor argued. As he explained it, Great Austria was an unworkable collection of such territorial fragments as the Czech

Sudetenland. Austria could become part of a 'great' anything only if it joined with a Great Germany, which was precisely the result of events which occurred between March 1938 and March 1939, and that fact was firmly in Taylor's mind when he was writing *The Habsburg Monarchy*.[59] It is probable that he had recognised the high potential of such an eventuality long before, because in his introduction to an English language edition of Heinrich Friedjung's *The Struggle for Supremacy in Germany* published in 1935, he suggested that only a catalyst was needed to overturn the separation of Austria and Germany. The Slavs had to be completely free of the Germans, he wrote then. Germans had to stop dreaming dreams of a Great Germany. '[W]ere certain extraneous elements removed – the interference of certain powers and the present uncivilized system of rule in Germany – the Germans of Austria would be as content within a national German state as are the Germans of Bavaria and Saxony.' However, millions of Germans were ruled by former submerged peoples, and that 'inclines some German Austrians against the unification of Germany, for they hope still to revive the international organisation once secured by the Austrian Empire'.[60]

Taylor's 'catalyst' came in the form of Adolf Hitler, a charismatic Austrian rabble-rouser who was chancellor of national Germany – which he then called the Third Reich – after January 1933. In 1938 he offered German Austrians union with the Reich, union with other Germans outside of it, and the opportunity thereby to impose themselves once more upon the Slavs of the former monarchy. The Austrians' protest was faint.

Hitler was a natural solution to Austrian German aspirations, Taylor concluded, because he was Austrian in every particular: he learnt his nationalism from Schönerer, his anti-Semitic populism from Lueger, and his demagogy was 'peculiarly Viennese'.[61] Moreover, the Austrian socialists had paved his way. 'Separation from Germany was always a grievance with them, never a principle', Taylor explained.[62] They felt cut off from Germany by circumstance, not by choice, and their only real commitment was to not be reduced to mere equality with the Slavs, not even with Slav socialists. Hitler guaranteed all of this and more. 'Hitler's occupation of Vienna in March, 1938, was an act of national liberation. It freed them from the last relics of the Habsburgs and united them with their national state.'[63] Meanwhile, the German leader borrowed from the Austrian socialists, just as he did from other German Austrians, not least of all his plan for dismembering Czechoslovakia.

Meanwhile, internecine feuds weakened the internal structure of the amalgamated Slav states until they were easy prey to German revisionism. Taylor concluded that the

> separatism of Slovaks and Croats played into the hands of the Germans and was an auxiliary weapon, though the German army was the main one, in destroying both Czechoslovakia and Yugoslavia.[64]

Further, Habsburg nationality policies had left all of the former submerged peoples fearful of the Monarchy even as a ghost, to the extent that they regarded its possible revival as the greatest threat to their security. When the Little Entente of Czechoslovakia, Romania, and Yugoslavia was formed, it was to prevent a Habsburg restoration, and never came to terms with the far larger issue of Germany as a restored great power.[65]

The lesson to be learned was profound. Taylor put it in this language:

> [T]hat Lord and servant, master and slave, the privileged historic nationalities who have won their way to freedom, can never work together. Magyar and Pole, German and Italian can co-operate; but German and Czech, Italian and Serb, Magyar and Roumanian, Pole and Little Russian cannot.[66]

Masaryk understood the lesson as early as 1915, but he had been seduced by the apparent democratic outlook of the Austrian Republic in 1917.[67] Masaryk's proposal sounded very much like Taylor's idea of classic balance of power: as the German Austrians enjoyed the favour and protection of a German nation outside of the former Monarchy, then so must the Slavs enjoy the favour and protection of a Slav nation, specifically one that, like them, had 'won its way to freedom' from a decaying, autocratic imperial dynasty. Specifically, to be free, the Slavs needed 'the protection of a free Russia'.[68]

Taylor never wavered from his conviction that the Soviet Union was the only European power that could counter German weight in eastern Europe, or had genuine incentive to do so. He

explained that the western powers played midwife to the
successor states in 1918, but caved in to German demands in the
1930s, and in any case, their anti-Communist prejudice made
them reluctant to aid the Slavs if to do so might profit the Soviet
Union. This was the lesson of the 1938 Munich Conference,
which dismembered Czechoslovakia to Germany's advantage,
and to which the Soviet Union was not invited. Taylor spoke out
in Britain against Munich, but to indifferent or even hostile
audiences. Throughout the war years, he maintained that in spite
of the Anglo-American-Soviet, the Big Three alliance against
Nazi Germany, the western powers would always sacrifice Slav
interests to German power, in order to prevent the intrusion of
Communist Russia into European affairs.[69]

It must be said that despite these views, Taylor was of two
minds on the role of the Soviet Union in eastern Europe.
Russian involvement was necessary for the security of the
successor states, true; but what might be the impact of Soviet
political influence in the region? The Habsburg experience again
provided insight into the situation. Like the monarchy, the
post-1945 states of eastern Europe had to find a way to achieve
internal authority – running their own affairs – as well as
external security.

Between 1945 and 1950, with the Cold War spreading about
him, Taylor laid aside the historian's mantle and became a
straight political and diplomatic commentator – journalist, as he
might have described it – speaking out as an advocate for the
rights and aspirations of the Slav peoples of eastern Europe. He
wrote as one who believed in what he was doing, for example
attributing his own values and principles to those who voted in
the first eastern European elections in 1945. He was acutely
aware that these elections were being held under the shadow of
the Soviet Union, then characterised by Stalinist totalitarianism.
Therefore, as he explained it in a BBC talk in November 1945, the
eastern European voters were repudiating the 'dictatorships or
semi-dictatorship, kept going by political policy' of their pre-war
governments,[70] and at the same time, they were expunging the
'capitalist illusion' inherent within liberalism, and preparing to
nationalise industry and foreign trade. This was socialism which
in Taylor's view was essential to economic reconstruction so that
the successor states could remain – as the language of the
elections clearly indicated – 'independent and not to be the

satellites of anyone', by which he meant the Soviet Union. In short, the Slavs were voting for political freedom *and* economic security: for strong government direction in economic life, and for the right 'to grumble against it;' for the state to work for individual human beings, not for individuals to work for the interests of the state. 'In other words, they want socialism but they also want the Rights of Man.'[71] The trick was how to manage it, because nothing involving eastern Europe after 1945 was possible without taking the Soviet Union into account.

The centrality of the Soviet Union in eastern European security was also central to Taylor's thinking on the subject during this period. Who was to say that Germany would not one day rise from the ashes to threaten the Slav peoples? But he talked and wrote also about a 'free Russia'. Under Stalin, Russia was not free, nor did it embrace those principles of liberty and democracy to which Taylor was committed. The question in 1945 was this: as the Soviet Union had liberated eastern Europe, would it become not only the external protector of the Slav states but their internal decision-maker as well?

The Soviet Union was not Nazi Germany, Taylor assured his readers, and he rejected any suggestion that being critical of Stalin made him pro-Western in the Cold War. However, he did admit that Soviet military power, and even more, the centrism of Soviet Communist ideology, was as great an obstacle to Slav freedom as German imperialism ever had been. This was particularly true in 1945, because the eastern European elections were being equated with revolutions. The result was a nice dilemma.

This is what all the phrases about 'free' elections run up against: they are elections conducted in the midst of political upheaval not in stable settled societies, and though democracy may be the outcome of revolution, a revolution cannot be conducted by democratic methods.[72]

As the supporter of Communist parties and movements, the Soviet Union naturally was involved on both levels. And, if Communist parties gained power, whether through election or revolution, they would be tied directly to Moscow. That was the nature of Stalinism. Like many other commentators in 1945 and after, regardless of their position on the political spectrum, Taylor accepted the principle that European Communism was Soviet Communism, and assumed that under it, Slav independence and freedom would disappear.

Election returns showed mixed results. In Czechoslovakia, pre-war social democrats Jan Masaryk (Thomas Masaryk's son) and Eduard Bênês returned to office. Elsewhere, elections affirmed Communist partisan leaders in the power they had garnered in war time: Hoxha in Albania, Tito in Yugoslavia, and Dimitrov in Bulgaria, among others. In the Soviet zone of occupied Germany, a Communist regime was established by formal decree. Taylor saw democracy hanging in the balance, and he was certain of nothing for the future except that the Slavs had been shoved around all they wanted.[73]

In 1946 and 1947, Taylor visited the Slav successor states to see for himself. What followed was a sort of political travelogue. In Czechoslovakia, under a coalition government in which Communists shared power with the best pre-war democratic leaders, social democracy seemed to be winning out. 'In Czechoslovakia alone is it possible to be a Socialist without being a Marxist', he wrote in triumphant tone, 'a liberal without believing in capitalism; and religious without being a Roman Catholic.'[74] It was as if the Czechs had embraced Taylor's personal values and beliefs, which, in a sense, they had. There were unresolved questions, of course, and they sounded familiar. 'Can we have nationalization without totalitarian rule?' the Czechs asked. That, Taylor answered, depended upon whether the Communists would accept economic gains without insisting that everyone embrace Marxism, non-Communists would defend liberalism without also espousing capitalism, and above all, on factors the Czechs could not control: a stable European order, revival of foreign trade, and satisfactory relations with the Slovaks.[75]

The Slovak issue connected post-war conditions directly to the Habsburg legacy. The Czechs, industrialised and cultured, still dominated the agrarian Slovaks, who had enjoyed a 'romantic quasi-independence' as wartime collaborators with the Germans. Taylor wondered if they now sought a similar arrangement with the Russians. He noted that mostly Communist Slovak partisans had showed extremely well in the elections, even in areas where the voters had been mostly collaborators, or at least Slovaks who had not resisted the Germans.[76] A new Slovak autonomy, under

Russian protection, was distinctly possible. Taylor considered it to be also dangerous.

In 1947, he was in Yugoslavia, where the Communists won outright in 1945, travelling through the country 'in third-class railway carriage, motorcar, jeep, steamer and peasant's cart', and drawing conclusions both optimistic and cautious. He was confident that his assessments were accurate, because 'one cannot travel thus intimately with a people for three weeks without forming some clear impressions'.[77] Taylor was impressed by the 'energy, gaiety, and enthusiasm which is shown all over the country. . . . There is a Boy Scout spirit of friendship and of confidence; there is also a Boy Scout intolerance of those who stand aside.' The totalitarian impulses of Soviet Communism seemed muted. The Yugoslav Communist Party was concerned mainly with economic and social issues, and seemed to have put ideological purity well down the list of priorities. The leading men in government were professors and intellectuals of various political views. 'The affect is as if the Left Book Club suddenly took over both the central and local government of the country.'[78] In a later decade, Taylor might have written such a line with a chuckle. In 1947 he was deadly serious.

The Serbs and Croats remained ethnically self-conscious, but not so divisively as did the Czechs and Slovaks, he continued. The official position was to dismiss petty conflicts over nationality as inconsistent with the goals of Communism. Therefore, forced integration was unnecessary, or words to that effect. This applied to all ethnic groups. Through the vehicle of Communism, the Croats, Montenegrins, and other minorities were winning equality with the Serbs, though the process was not yet complete, and feelings remained mixed on the nationalities issue. Taylor sensed an exaggerated desire among the Serbs to dismiss the nationalities issue, which he thought simply indicated that they were nervous about their place in Yugoslavia. They ran the state, or appeared to: absence of systematic efforts at reorganisation, decentralisation (every village had its own Peoples' Committee, apparently independent of the centre), and lack of critical argument when plans were formulated, were all elements of government characteristic of old Serbia. However, the Serbs, not behaving as the mainstay of the country as once they had, were uncomfortably unclear on where they belonged in Tito's Yugoslavia. Taylor was sympathetic, for he 'dimly felt' what they knew, that 'Serbs are the only fully adult people in Yugoslavia, without whom Yugoslav independence will be difficult to maintain.'[79] But how to convince Croats, Montenegrins, Bosnians, Slovenes, and Herzegovinians, to name only a few?

Taylor worried about what the Soviet Union would bequeath to post-war eastern Europe: security and freedom for the individual (socialism without Marxism), or control of the individual in the interests of the state (socialism with Marxism/Leninism)? In 1948 he had his answer. All pretence at Communist-Democratic co-operation ended, and the Slav nations slipped under the control of totalitarian regimes, the rulers of which claimed a popular mandate. Outraged, Taylor again took to the airwaves, arguing that power in these now Communist states did not come from the people, but from the police, the centralist Communist Party, and other apparatus of totalitarianism, including outright political murder. In March 1948, Jan Masaryk was found dead in the courtyard of the Czech foreign ministry, a supposed suicide; in May, the Czech parliament was dissolved and a new, Communist, constitution proclaimed. At the same time in Yugoslavia, the Popular Front, an adjunct of the Moscow-centred Cominform, purged 'deviationist' members of Tito's inner circle. Taylor knew that Masaryk was murdered, and that Tito's followers were eliminated in order to impose ideological conformity. Sadly, he concluded, the struggle goes on between those who want freedom and those who want to deny it:

> Ever since the time of Rousseau, the great problem of so-called democrats is how to achieve power, despite the fact that the majority of the people do not intend to vote for those who call themselves democrats of the party of the people.[80]

Taylor's argument with Soviet-style Communism concentrated on the gap between party interest and individual rights. In 1948, he found the same indifference to individual freedom being repeated in the actions of the new governments of eastern Europe that he had seen in 1926 when British Communists remained aloof from the General Strike for party reasons, and in 1929 when Trotsky was expelled from the Soviet party for 'deviationism'. It would not last, he contended, noting that while it was a constant of European history that the ordinary individual was pushed around, exploited by those assuming the right to govern in his name, there was another 'constant', namely that 'the ordinary man has always grumbled and complained as I am doing now, has always put up a sullen resistance to the office holders, politicians, and commissars of the people'.[81] However, lest he be identified with those who waged the Cold War as the answer to Soviet dictatorship, Taylor added: 'Communism is a tyranny within men's souls, not a tyranny from without as German imperialism was; and it can be defeated only by the recovery of courage and self-respect.'[82]

Ironically, it was Yugoslavia, 'less free' in Taylor's phrase than Czechoslovakia had been, which broke away from Moscow at the end of 1948, while Czechoslovakia, for which he had entertained high hopes, became even more hardline. Taylor was jubilant when Tito defied Stalin, and immediately came to the Yugoslav leader's defence against the sceptics. 'This theory of the "put-up" job is the work of those who believe that when a man becomes a Communist he ceases to be a human being. I should have agreed with them until the Tito affair', he proclaimed, adding that the Tito affair 'is the decisive proof that they are wrong'.[83] Taylor's position was that Tito did not stop being a Communist by breaking with Moscow, but rather became a reformer of both Communism and of Yugoslavia's long-standing internal rivalries.

Taylor compared Tito with Henry VIII breaking with Rome in the sixteenth century, drawing analogies that must have taken aback more than one listener. Henry was Tito, Rome was Moscow, and the Pope was Stalin. Henry remained Catholic after the break, just as Tito remained Communist; but when Henry quit Rome, he opened the door to reform of the old religion. When Tito revolted against Moscow, he opened the door to revision of the old ideology. In short, Tito placed human values (never mind what Henry VIII thought *he* was doing) above party or ideological loyalty. 'The other day', Taylor reminded his audience, 'he said again that truth [meaning himself] is above authority [meaning Stalin] and denounced the doctrine that the end justified the means.' If anyone thought Taylor was merely being clever, the notion was dispelled by the next, irrefutable, line. 'The doctrine [the end justifies the means] is essential to Communism, as it was to militant Catholicism; otherwise, you must admit that moral values like truth, justice, tolerance, are more important than the Church or the Cominform.'[84]

As to Yugoslavia's internal divisions, Taylor found in Tito's revolt a solution to historic questions raised by the Habsburg legacy. Tito's revolt proved that 'Yugoslavia is a country which believes in itself', by which Taylor meant that it was, at last, a country, and not merely a geographical expression, a continuation of Serbia, Croatia, and the other, lesser, minorities. Tito had laid the foundation for a new moral basis for its political order that would be 'neither German nor Russian, but something in between. Tito, in fact, is the heir of the Habsburgs.'[85] A startling notion, perhaps, but feasible as an argument. That is, Tito, who was a Croatian, arranged for the two most divisive ethnic elements within Yugoslavia, the Serbs and Croats, to divorce themselves from the external dependencies that had fed their internal rivalry, both in the nineteenth and the twentieth centuries: Russia on the Serb side, and German Austria and later the Reich of Adolf Hitler on the Croat side. Taylor believed that by defying Stalin, Tito had asserted the identity of a nation.

Tito's action added a new wrinkle to the Cold War. Almost immediately he broke with Moscow, the West began to court him, thinking in terms of Yugoslavia as the thin end of a wedge into eastern Europe. Taylor expressed the view, rather grumpily, that these Balkan developments should inspire Britain to become 'America's Tito', rather than the rubber stamp for America's anti-Soviet policies, which closed the door to a genuine solution to post-war problems in Europe.[86] An Anglo-American-Soviet alliance had defeated Germany in war. Why could it not continue as a way to address post-war reconstruction? The answer was obvious, even if deplorable. East–West political and ideological suspicion was mutual and self-fulfilling.

East–West suspicion began well before the end of the Second World War. One of the issues was Trieste, to the role of which Taylor addressed himself in 1944. Trieste, an Adriatic port city at the point where Italy meets Yugoslavia, was built by the Habsburgs, operated by the Italians, who demanded possession of the city in 1919 and again in 1945, and inhabited by a largely Slovene population. The League of Nations supervised it as a free city after 1918, though in Taylor's view it should have belonged to Yugoslavia even then. All logic pointed in that direction, he argued, and gave Trieste its Slavic name, Trst, to stress his point. In Yugoslav hands, he wrote, Trst would free the Czechs from economic dependence on Hamburg. At the same

time, 'Austria and Hungary would be compelled by their dependence on Trieste to co-operate with their two Slav neighbours,
instead of being hostile to them.' The port would become 'the
cornerstone of central European economic unity, as it was originally intended to be: a unity based no longer on German
supremacy but on equal democratic communities'. A Yugoslavian
Trieste would redress 'the worst national wrongs of the peace
settlement of 1919'.[87]

These observations reflected pre-war realities rather than
post-war projections. After the war, Trieste was a Cold War issue.
None of the hopeful possibilities Taylor envisioned in 1944 were
viable without Big Three co-operation, and that did not happen.
Rather, Trieste become a trial of strength between the Soviet
Union and the Anglo-American alliance. Taylor claimed that the
Russians backed Yugoslav claims to the port only in order to
show that they could protect their satellites. The West backed
Italian claims as a way of keeping the Soviet Union out of the
Mediterranean. The Triestian population were not consulted by
either side.

Taylor was tougher on the West than on the Soviet Union on
this issue, claiming that with their democratic traditions, the
British and Americans ought to know better and should show
greater responsibility to fair treatment and justice than could be
expected from the Russians, who had slipped from Tsarism into
Communism with scarcely a glance at democracy. Or, he went
on, perhaps the Western powers were simply inept at the game
of power politics. This view, Taylor, a student of British
diplomacy, could hardly have held seriously. In any event, he
asserted that 'the policy of the Western powers was calculated to
force Yugoslavia even more firmly into the arms of Russia; only
the fantastic pride of the Yugoslavs defeated this outcome'. Then,
as if bewildered by the treachery of which policy-makers were
capable, he added: 'Though I thought poorly of Western policy, I
confess that it never occurred to me that within two years of
signing the treaty of peace, the Western Powers would propose
to hand over the Free City to Italy.' Strange, he observed. Trieste
without its hinterland was unworkable, yet now it was to be cut
off still more completely, and at the demand of 'neo-fascists' in
Italy, in the bargain. 'In my naive view', Taylor concluded, 'the
wisest course for a Great Power, even in its own interests, is to
follow the path of right and justice; this view does not seem to

be held by others.'[88] Perhaps Taylor's analysis was more passionate than precise, but the 'lesson of history' he drew for the region was fundamental. '[T]he political problems of central Europe cannot be solved by intervention from the outside.'[89] Therefore, let the Cold War powers stop fishing in the troubled waters of the former monarchy, or they would have the German problem all over again.

Having said that, Taylor went on to note that it was difficult to see how central and eastern Europe could avoid outside interference, or at least involvement, given the location, the nature of post-war international politics, and the character of the successor states. This was a reality of the Habsburg legacy, he explained. The successor states affected the security of their larger neighbours, notably Germany and Russia, and equally, these neighbours affected the security of the small Slav nations. As Eduard Bênês pointed out in 1946: 'We are not between the East and West, but between Russia and Germany.'[90]

The question was, which outsiders would be the least trouble? Taylor thought Germany would always be Czechoslovakia's nemesis, and rephrased the question as, 'Can we rely on the Western Powers to *act* next time against Germany?' He also thought the Czechs wise when, after 1945, they entered into a defensive alliance with the Soviet Union. This agitated the Western powers considerably, but it was not for the Czechs to choose otherwise. Eduard Gottwald, the Communist premier, made the Czech position clear when he said: 'The Russian alliance is for us not merely a question of safety but even of existence.'[91] Taylor sympathised, observing: 'Anyone who has seen the marks of German terror would find it difficult to condemn this decision.'[92]

These were post-war realities complicated by the Cold War in which the West was two-fisted in its anti-communist prejudice, and the Soviet Union was bull-headed in its knee-jerk antipathy to the West. The latter fact was brought home to Taylor in 1948 at Wroclaw, Poland, where he attended an international Congress of Intellectuals arranged by the Polish Culture Committee. The purpose was to consider the causes of the Second World War and the means for eradicating Fascism from Europe. The Congress was heavily Sovietised, and Russian intellectuals, led by Ilya Ehrenberg, categorically denied that Britain and America had made any contribution to the defeat of Germany compared to

that of the Soviet Union, attacked intellectual criticism as undemocratic, and claimed that western (that is, British and
American) policy-makers now curried favour with neo-Fascists,
just as their predecessors had with Hitler and Mussolini.[93] Taylor
had argued from at least 1945 that America was imperialist; he
came away from the congress viewing the Soviet Union as being
no less so. What chance would the Slavs have in these circumstances, he wondered?

> In 1945 I was fool enough to think the powers could co-operate
> over Trieste. Instead it has become an outpost of American
> imperialism in Europe, and the Yugoslavs, already dealing
> with one imperialist power cannot take on the Americans
> alone.'[94]

Taylor's nightmare was that Cold War power struggles after
1945 simply encouraged the German problem for the Slav
successor states. To some extent, these struggles actually incorporated elements of the Habsburg method of dealing with the
minorities, and thus became part of the legacy of the monarchy.
Just as the Habsburgs did once, as the new imperialists, so too
did the United States and the Soviet Union manipulate the
minorities of the old empire for their own ends. After 1945, the
superpowers quarrelled with rising intensity and frequency until
opinion was hardened into reaction on both sides, and it was
guaranteed that Soviet Communism would dominate eastern
Europe while the western powers would rearm Germany. '[A]ll
Eastern Europe, except for Yugoslavia, has escaped from German
tyranny only to fall under Russian control', Taylor wrote in 1950.
'[O]nly co-operation between Russia and the Anglo-Saxon
powers can give Europe peace and security.' That was not
presently possible, of course, because each side only tried to
arrange defeats for the other. Europe was divided between them,
subordinate on the one side to the Anglo-Saxon powers and on
the other to the Soviet Union, and the nations of Europe were the
poorer for it. 'If there ever is a federation of Europe or of the
world', Taylor alleged fervently, 'it can be based only on free
national states, not on the domination of a single great power.'[95]
    If Anglo-American policy succeeded and Russia was compel-
led to leave eastern Europe to them, what would be the result? A
reprise of the German problem: eastern Europe would not be

liberated if Russia withdrew, Taylor warned, rather, German hegemony would be restored, 'at first economic and then military. Or rather it would be national liberation of a sort, for the unchecked working of the national principle was itself an instrument of German hegemony. Slovakia and Croatia could be "independent nations" only in a German system.'[96]

Perhaps a federated Europe, a concept much discussed in the later 1940s by such western Europeans as Robert Schumann and René Pleven, though in more regional terms than Taylor envisioned, was the solution. In 1946, Taylor suggested 'a coalition of national states, led by France, being resolutely anti-German', which would 'rest on Russian support and yet allow the Russians to withdraw (as they wish to do) from immediate responsibility for European politics'.[97] It is not clear what made him imagine the Russians wanted to be out of Europe, and to be sure after watching events in Czechoslovakia in 1948 and attending the Wroclaw Congress in the same year, he did not raise the point again.

There were observable differences in Taylor's writings in the later 1930s and the 1940s on the Habsburg monarchy and its peoples, as compared to *The Italian Problem in European Diplomacy*. The former were more polemical than scholarly, and historical interpretation was employed as a basis for commentary on contemporary affairs, rather than as an end in itself. *The Habsburg Monarchy* in particular, as history, was far more deterministic than *The Italian Problem in European Diplomacy*. Certainly, much of this had to do with the events Taylor witnessed in the years after 1934, including the diplomatic failures associated with appeasement, the Second World War with its attendant horrors, and the disillusionment which came with the onset of the Cold War.

At the same time there were similarities. Taylor was again critical of system-making, favourable, at least to the extent that it was the lesser evil, to balance of power as a system for maintaining the security of nations, conscious of the role played by individual actors in historical developments, and, above all, individualistic in his northern radical manner to an almost exaggerated degree. It was the northern radical who admired Thomas Masaryk for flaunting historical tradition in the interest of creating a new order for the northern Slavs, who viewed free nations as a corollary of free individuals, and who demanded that historical actors must accept responsibility for their actions.

After a decade of considering the past and present of the peoples of the former monarchy, Taylor advanced two conclusions. First, that the Slavs might solve their internal conflicts by finding in social revolution and economic improvement provided under Marxism, the common loyalty they had not achieved under the Habsburgs.[98] Second, that they might find protection from the Germans in alliance with the Soviet Union, because the Anglo-Saxon powers were intent upon rearming Germany as part of the reconstruction political of Europe. In retrospect, these conclusions resonate with disillusionment, which is hardly surprising in light of the disappointments that characterised the 1940s. Such disappointments hardly improved his state of mind when he took up the history of Bismarck's Germany and made projections regarding its future.

3

Europe and the Germans

The Course of German History (1946)
Bismarck: The Man and the Statesman
(1955)

The German problem, in Taylor's view, was as old as the Germans themselves. However, it took the particular twist that led to the Second World War only after Bismarck unified Germany in 1871. The Bismarckian German Empire, achieved by what Taylor termed the Prussian will to power, furnished pan-German nationalism with the power-base denied to it by the Habsburg monarchy. Unification produced a formidable military and industrial state in the centre of Europe, and consequently the German problem broadened and deepened. The new German Empire pointed directly and unerringly toward the Reich created by Adolf Hitler, under which the pan-German dream was fulfilled to the extent it ever would be. Twentieth-century Europe was shaped to a considerable extent by a Germany wearing the face of an 'intolerant exterminator and overlord', in Taylor's words, that had been imposed by Prussian militarism and barbarism upon the civilised and cultured Germany of the west.[1]

Taylor formed his viewpoint over a quarter of a century of reading, observing, and thinking about the German problem in both its Habsburg and Bismarckian manifestations. During this time he watched the growth of National Socialism, the demagoguery of Adolf Hitler, the diplomatic destruction of Czechoslovakia in Germany's interest, the Second World War, the Cold War, and the reconstruction of West Germany as a western ally against the Soviet Union. He seemed to take Germany and the Germans personally, and perhaps what he had witnessed in this quarter of a century was justification. In any case, his writing on Germany was scarcely objective, though taken in context his conclusions were sometimes compelling. He wrote in one place, referring to the war in 1870 that led to unification, that 'Germany stood for nothing, except German power'.[2] In another, written in the midst of the Second World War, he declared that 'there are too many Germans, and Germany is too strong, too well organized, too well equipped with industrial resources'.[3] Consequently, they were frequently at war with Europe, wars of survival against aggression.

Taylor never believed in war, but neither was he an ardent pacifist. In 1933, Adolf Hitler took office as chancellor of Germany. Espousing a militant nationalism, he began dismantling the Versailles Treaty. German rearmament was underway in 1935, the Rhineland was remilitarised the following year, and in 1938 Austria was annexed by the Reich and the western European powers agreed to the truncation of Czechoslovakia, all in the name of German self-determination. Such events disturbed Taylor to his very bones.

In 1935, Taylor was a leading member of the essentially pacifist Manchester Peace Council. However, as he watched Germany re-emerge as a great power, he advanced the view that democracy would have to go armed in order to survive, and in 1936 urged the Council to shift its moral advocacy away from disarmament and towards resistance to the forces which threatened peace. Armaments are not the cause of war, he wrote in 1937, only 'the symptoms of international conflict; and war can be prevented only by removing the causes of conflict, not by denouncing the symptoms'.[4] The point was well taken, but not by the MPC, which expelled Taylor soon after he penned those lines. Like most Britons at the time, MPC members preferred appeasement to resistance, even if appeasement meant tolerating German militarism and bully-boy diplomacy. Prime Minister Neville Chamberlain seemed to agree, though as an anti-Communist rather than as a pacifist, and organised the Munich Agreement of September 1938 by which Czechoslovakia was dismembered, in order to placate the German chancellor. Taylor was among the first in the North of England to argue publicly against appeasement, and with anti-Communists preferring a strong Germany as defence against the Soviet Union, and pacifists clamouring for peace at any price, he found it an uphill struggle. After Munich he addressed meetings in Manchester on the theme of 'Stand Up to Hitler', in which he plumped for 'national honour, anti-Fascism, Hitler's weakness and the certainty he would climb down'. The response was always the same. 'What you are asking means war. We want peace.'[5]

Taylor was convinced after the Munich Agreement that war with Germany was only a matter of time, and that the policy objectives of the democracies should be to prepare to win it. Their future depended upon it. In October, he left Manchester to become a Fellow of Magdalen College, Oxford. There he joined 'a left-wing luncheon group called the Pink Club', formed in opposition to Chamberlain's foreign policy.[6] It did not accomplish much, but at least in the Club, Taylor found a sympathy and support that had been lacking in Manchester.

Germany occupied Prague in March 1939. Appeasement had failed. Public opinion shifted, if ever so slightly, towards support for a diplomacy of resistance. There were dissenters when Chamberlain announced the unilateral British guarantee of Poland two weeks later, but mostly to urge that it was too little, too late. Taylor shared this view. Nevertheless, the Polish guarantee did draw the line. Taylor saw danger now mainly in the reluctance of the democracies to do more than talk about resistance. He was appalled by the lame-footed fashion in which Anglo-Soviet military talks proceeded in the summer of 1939, talks designed to strike an agreement to oppose German territorial ambitions regarding Poland.

After the talks failed, Taylor was more determined than ever. He argued that Britain must resist even if Russia could not be brought in. In this mood, he welcomed the Nazi–Soviet Non-aggression pact of August, knowing that it meant Britain would be the first to fight against Germany, and the moral argument for democracy resisting Fascism would be made manifest.[7] Germany attacked Poland on September 1, and two days later, joined by its reluctant ally France, Britain declared war against Germany. Democracy was vindicated. Of course, Taylor did not then know that it required a Cabinet revolt on September 2nd to bring these reluctant allies into war on the 3rd.

From that moment, Taylor threw himself into the war effort, convinced that the issues were clear and the cause just. By 1940, he was giving talks for the BBC, and lecturing for the Ministry of Information in Oxford. He claimed that he received no instructions as to what to say. It might be expected that the MOI

expected him to plump for the government's war policies. No
doubt he did, when they coincided with his own views on what
ought be happening. Therefore, on one memorable occasion he
criticised the government for fighting in the Mediterranean on
the grounds that this was solely in order to sustain British
imperialism. He and the ministry soon parted company, and ever
after he doubted that propaganda had much actual affect on
the war, or on domestic public opinion, for that matter. He
did admit, however, but with typical cheek, that overseas
propaganda in the Second World War probably did no harm, and
'provided a useful distraction for politically minded Englishmen
and planners who might otherwise have been a great nuisance'.
Meanwhile, in a BBC talk he called for suppressing the *Daily
Worker*, the newspaper of the Communist Party of Great Britain
which followed the Moscow line, because it advocated a
compromise peace. Needless to say, MOI and BBC lecturing
brought Taylor a certain notoriety. Militant leftists demanded
that he be shut up, and Quintin Hogg, MP, directed the attention
of the House of Commons to 'the irresponsible and ridiculous
statement made by a person in a public position' about the
Mediterranean war, which had upset a very great many people.
MOI parliamentary secretary Harold Nicolson hastily assured
Hogg that Taylor did not represent the views of the ministry on
this question.[8]

Such criticism rolled off of Taylor's back. Nothing mattered
but the defeat of Germany, and to that end he lectured and
wrote, and served his time in the Oxford Home Guard. His unit
was probably not untypical, at least in some respects. He recalled
that they had rifles, but no ammunition, until a single clip was
issued to be shared by the entire unit. It was entrusted for
safekeeping to a veteran of the First World War, who loaded it
into his rifle. One day the rifle accidentally discharged, nearly
blowing Commandant Frank Pakenham's foot off. The clip was
immediately placed in the care of someone else. (Taylor did not
say that it was himself.) The unit's job, Taylor recalled, was to
guard the gas works whenever the air raid alert sounded, 'on the
assumption that the entire German paratroop force would
descend on Oxford. Failing any Germans, our only function was
to demand identity cards from passers-by.' This doughty band
was mostly Oxford academics in the care of a serving sergeant,
who found them strange at best. They offered little danger to any

invader, but reflected a spirit of resistance all the same. In any case, as Taylor remarked many years later, it was all 'great fun'.[9]

Taylor's writing on Germany both before and during the war included essays, book reviews, and books, all full of historical questions having present significance. The effect of German history was all around him; he wanted to know its cause. In these writings, he asked, why had Germany become the principal European menace of the twentieth century? Why had the Germans not acquired a taste for freedom, for themselves and for others? Why had National Socialism, a mindless cause, thrust its tentacles so deep and with such apparent ease into the vitals of the political life of a nation that has been described as the most philosophical of modern times? The answers to these questions and others were presented in summary form in *The Course of German History*, first published in 1946. But Taylor knew the answers to his own satisfaction well before that, beginning with a description written in 1936 of the central importance of the state in German historical development.

The German state in modern times was Baron vom Stein's 'corporate State, in which the nation is everything, and the individual nothing'.[10] Taylor explained it this way. The German state functioned on the basic premise that leaders rule, subjects obey, and the organism of the state assumes responsibility for politics, economics, culture, religion, and social organisation. Through the eighteenth and early nineteenth centuries, this state was identified mainly with Prussia, where its purpose was the exercise of raw power as understood by the Prussian military monarchy. It was an organism for military conquest and the imposition of the ruler's will over his subjects, or over neighbouring states. In the later nineteenth and the twentieth centuries, unification, radical nationalism, and socialism joined together to create totalitarian democracy, which became the principle expression of the state. Totalitarian democracy was National Socialism, in which pan-German idealism connected with Prussian militarism. Thereafter, the German state was an organisation through which the German people asserted their will to power over the other peoples of Europe in the name of national unity.

After 1936, Taylor's consideration of Germany rapidly expanded, but without losing sight of the state as the central organism for manifesting power. Power was the German God, he argued, and in 1848 the Germans surrendered to it and made their peace with the idea of the state. German liberals exchanged freedom for national unity, and even rulers and intellectuals of the petty territorial states who once had opposed central authority as represented by the Habsburg monarchy, developed a national enthusiasm centred in the idea of the German state. Politically conscious Germans endorsed the principle that 'there could be nothing higher than Germany, and that the only task of the State was to be powerful and to use force'. Dazzled by Prussian military success against the French in 1870–1, they became aggressive pan-Germans, recognising 'no higher loyalty than to "the great general staff" and rejecting the common heritage of European civilization'. It was worse at the time of the First World War, Taylor claimed, when the intellectuals acquiesced in the suspension of the rule of law so that the state could organise victory in a war to conquer the peoples on Germany's frontiers.[11] Even Gustav Stresemann, despite his reputation as a great European German who wanted Germany to co-operate with Europe after the war, 'abandoned German imperialism only when it had failed'.[12]

When the German masses became politically conscious, the absolutist state was transformed into the totalitarian democratic state. Taylor thought Germany fulfilled its historic destiny at this point. The moment followed the revolution of 1848, when German nationalism interacted with Marxism to create that peculiar form of German socialism which, in his interpretation, led straight to Hitler's Reich. Taylor described nineteenth-century German socialism as aiming to both liberate the people from the old order and assert German supremacy over non-Germans. The means were economic penetration, claims of German philosophic superiority (the Hegelian core of Marxist determinism, in other words), and control over the Second International. The attempt failed, of course, and achieved neither a successful German revolution nor European supremacy for Germany. It did pave the way for the National Socialist revolution, however, which simply inherited the socialists' mantle and 'expressed, in somewhat violent form, their outlook and wishes'.[13] In Taylor's description, the National Socialists preached class-war and pan-Germanism, claimed to represent the collective will of the nation, decried 'bourgeois' civilisation and decency, and asserted the right of the masses to have mastery over all of their old enemies, foreign and domestic. They produced 'the only German government ever to spring from the initiative of the German masses'.[14]

Subservience to the state and worship of state power was total in Germany, as Taylor read it, and all Germans bore equal responsibility for the German problem and the war which was its most recent manifestation. All were guilty of believing in their 'historic' interests, and following whatever leader claimed to represent these interests. Therefore, the Germans repudiated liberal European civilisation with its emphasis on law, toleration, and highmindedness, and embraced the barbarism and demagoguery of the Nazi State. In the past, the populace had been excluded from political life, and submitted without resistance to the dictates of the state. Under National Socialism they were included in political life, glorified the state, and found in it their own will to power and the mechanics for achieving pan-German unity. In this way, Taylor shaped the view that the tyranny of the Third Reich was a tyranny of the Germans over themselves. Therefore, the Germans would have to free themselves from the tyranny – with some help from the allies, to be sure.[15]

This wartime writing, and much of *The Course of German History* which followed it, was subjective and polemical to an exaggerated degree. However, Taylor was a diplomatic historian of skill, and as capable as any other scholar of writing objectively, even on the subject of Germany. At least, until the war began. *Germany's First Bid For Colonies, 1884–1885: A Move in Bismarck's European Policy*, a short, carefully researched and documented study of German power diplomacy under Bismarck, was such a work. This did not mean it did not have a contemporary political element, however. The book was published early in 1938, a time when appeasement policy guided Britain's relations with Germany. *Germany's First Bid For Colonies* concentrated upon the abrasive and heavy-handedness of German statecraft, and the almost obsequious timidity of British statesmen in response to it. In the circumstances, Taylor seemed to have written a *pièce d'occasion*, a point his critics did not miss. Llewelyan Woodward wrote: 'There is a contemporary moral in this story of fifty years ago', and Mary Townshend added that connecting the European situation of the 1880s with colonial questions was 'particularly significant in view of the present German demands'.[16]

Germany's First Bid For Colonies told the story of how imperial Chancellor Otto von Bismarck tried to re-order Anglo-French-German relations by engaging in some sleight-of-hand in southwestern Africa. As Taylor explained it, the idea was a Franco-German *rapprochement* which would isolate Britain from the continent. He described Bismarck's reasoning for the manoeuvre as suspicious and one-dimensional, in other words typically German:

> [T]o the German mind friendship with one power necessarily implies hostility against another, and Germany, to make herself presentable to France, had to provoke a quarrel with England so that Franco-German friendship would have the solid foundation of anglophobia.[17]

Bismarck hoped to achieve his end by playing on French mistrust of 'perfidious Albion'. The British had a base at Walfish Bay, but refused to lend the Germans protection for their own trading factory at Angra Pequeña. This could only indicate expansionist aims, Bismarck told the French ambassador in Berlin: see what happens when we demand that Britain cede southwestern Africa to us.

That was not how it worked, of course. When the demand for southwestern Africa was made, Britain gladly withdrew. Bismarck was left with some useless colonial territories, 'the accidental by-product of an abortive Franco-German entente', and even more strained relations with the French.[18] Such was Taylor's thesis.

The themes of the book were more complex than the thesis, and sought to shed light on contemporary events. One theme was the aggressive nature of German politics, as disruptive to European stability in 1884–5 as in the 1930s. Then as now, Germany had no historic place in Europe. Taylor described the German empire as 'an artificial reproduction of French nationalism tinged with echoes from the Holy Roman Empire', required to 'ape' the political heritage of others as it had none of its own.[19] Imperial Germany had only what Prussia gave it, a tradition of rude and even violent behaviour in statecraft, predicated upon an assumption that if a policy was in the interest of the state it was a good policy, no matter what had to be done to implement it. Bismarck's methods were crude and arrogant after the Prussian manner, and as evidence Taylor cited a conversation between Bismarck and Courcel, the French minister in Berlin, in which the chancellor expressed the view that Germany should not be held accountable for territorial aggrandisement at French expense in the war of 1870–1.

> The moral was clear – France was to make it up with Germany as Austria had done, consoling herself with the thought that, while Bismarck would not give back Alsace-Lorraine he was sorry he had taken so much.[20]

The chancellor was a regrettable model for those who came after him, who matched his lack of scruples but not his genius.[21]

Taylor also drew parallels between the inept British statesmen of the 1880s and the appeasers of the later 1930s. Lord Granville, for example, read suspiciously like Neville Chamberlain:

> That a foreign secretary should have a policy hardly occurred to him. . . . His sole endeavour was to be polite and considerate, in the hope that no foreign government would be so cruel as to oppose the wishes of a benevolent old gentleman.[22]

Also, while he believed that peace was preferable to war, Taylor made *Germany's First Bid For Colonies* suggest very specific limits to what statesmen should tolerate. British muddling was preferable to German belligerence and intimidation, at least to the extent that the former attitude indicated a preference for peace, while the latter indicated a willingness if not a preference for the use of force. But Germany's drive towards a 'place in the sun' under Wilhelm II was characterised by a belligerence which, like that expressed by Adolf Hitler's Germany, pushed those powers interested in peace, to the wall. British politicians, in the last pre-1914 years, learned that only agreeing to what Germany called security but what everyone else saw as European hegemony for the Germans, could resolve Anglo-German quarrels and win German friendship. Taylor was pleased to conclude that even Little England gentlemen such as Gladstone and Granville would not have paid that price for German friendship.[23] It is not clear that he expected the 1930s appeasers to find their backbone in like manner.

The second German war of the twentieth century, as Taylor

termed it, ended in May 1945, and *The Course of German History* appeared a year later. It began in 1944 as a chapter on Weimar for a Political Warfare Executive handbook on Germany. However, PWE found Taylor's piece too depressing and did not use it.[24] The object of *The Course of German History* was to explain exactly what had led to the war, beginning with Martin Luther's worship of authority in the sixteenth century and finishing with an indictment of the German people for loving power more than freedom throughout time. The study stressed that German history was a history of extremes, that 'only the normal person, not particularly good, not particularly bad, healthy, sane, normal – he had never set his stamp on German history'.[25]

The Course of German History 'came out of my feelings about the war', Taylor wrote, which was no surprise to anyone who read it.[26] He wanted 'to explain to the conquerors what sort of country they were conquering', and to remind them that people usually get the leadership they deserve and want – a lesson for Germany's future and, incidentally, for the conquerors as well.[27] Structurally, the book resembled a standard narrative history, following the threads of German development chronologically and incorporating a sense, from page to page, of 'what happened next?', always Taylor's favourite way of describing his approach to historical exposition. Interpretively, the book had the character of an essay, which, as noted above, it had started out to be. The information contained in its pages was detailed and authoritative, but no sources were indicated, either in footnotes or bibliography. Taylor knew the history he was relating, of that there was no doubt. Likewise, there was no pretence that the book was a scholarly treatise. It was what it was meant to be, a contentious critique which opened by observing that German history contained everything but moderation, and ended by proclaiming that with the defeat of Hitler, German history had 'run its course'. In between, Taylor argued that Germany had begun divided, and should end that way, for anything else meant disaster for the rest of Europe. No other book in Taylor's bibliography more pointedly departed from the concept of history as accident so often imputed to him, than did *The Course of German History*. This study bore the appearance of determinism from start to finish. That is hardly surprising, since the point of the book was to demonstrate how German history led the Germans to do the horrid things they did in the twentieth century.

Taylor began by describing three sources of tension which, he believed, prepared Germany over a thousand years for the role it played in Europe in the nineteenth and twentieth centuries. First, the Germans had no natural frontiers, which explained their constant expansionism at other peoples' expense. Second, they were the 'barbarians on the edge of a great civilization', suspended between this civilisation and the Slavs pressing them from behind. Hence they imitated western civilisation as an aid to exterminating the Slavs, but did not learn its loftier ideals. Third, being in the middle, they looked east and west simultaneously, which created the dualism central to German political traditions, and made theirs the least clearly articulated historical tradition in Europe.[28]

As Taylor explained it, dualism was the key element. For centuries, Germany was kept in turmoil by conflict between the central authority of the German Reich, the 'Holy Roman Empire of the German Nation' which grew out of Charlemagne's great Frankish Empire of the ninth century, and the local interests and power of territorial princes within the Reich. Though it was more form than substance, the Reich was the ideal of unified Germany, and it provided the Germans with their only continuous political history. By contrast, the territorial princes were particularist in outlook and cared little for the idea of a German nation. They were ranged against the Reich historically, and resisted it with vigour and prevented it ever becoming more than a loose confederation of German kingdoms, principalities, and petty states. This was dualism: the parallel existence of the central Reich and the particularist states, each claiming rights which the other would not, or could not, admit.

Dualism was a political paradox with ethnic complications. Not all Germans lived within the Reich, and not all who were its citizens were Germans. When Taylor recounted efforts to unify Germany in 1848, he noted that the plan for a Great Germany demanded a unified state including Slavs living within the boundaries of the ancient Reich. The Germans did not propose this creation as an equal partnership, however, despite their talk of universal suffrage and socialist programs. Rather, they intended to impose German economic, cultural, and political hegemony over non-Germans. The idea of a Germany carried forward the principle of the ancient Reich, but was opposed by the supporters of Little Germany, who expressed the sentiments of traditional particularism. The Little Germany plan called for a smaller but ethnically homogeneous Germany, at least more homogeneous than Great Germany. Little Germany would be founded upon co-operation between Prussia, the largest and most powerful of the particularist states, and the territorial princes, who were non-radical, anti-nationalist, and opposed in principle both to social change and pan-German expansionism.

Taylor regarded 1848 as the climax in the long tradition of conflict between central Reich and particularist state. The argument between Great Germany and Little Germany in the revolutionary Frankfurt Assembly demonstrated that dualism could never be wholly set aside, and the unification that did occur in 1871 was a negative, compromise solution. Bismarckian Germany was created by force, and exclusive of the Habsburg monarchy, the heir of the ancient Reich. A German nation came into existence which left those in favour of the Great Germany of 1848 dissatisfied and 'vaguely resentful', their aspirations still unfulfilled. Dualism was overcome finally only when Hitler annexed Austria in 1938, and then conquered the Slav lands of eastern Europe in 1939 and 1940.

But this is to get ahead of the story. Taylor noted more political complications along the way for dualism than just Frankfurt in 1848, including the failure of early German capitalism to develop along lines similar to England and France. The Hansa was a great trading league with medieval origins, which spread across northern Europe from Novgorod to Iceland, and included many German cities. Had it continued to flourish, Germany, through economic centralisation, might have followed the French and English example towards political centralisation and the founding of a modern nation state. But the reverse occurred, explained Taylor. Geographic discoveries outside of Europe contributed to trade shifting away from the Hansa and towards the Mediterranean, so that instead of leading a 'national awakening', the Hansa cities turned in upon themselves and became jealous of their political and economic rights. They became the urban counterparts of the territorial princes of the hinterland. This was their nationalism, a sort of vague town-centred provincialism. They used the term German merely to distinguish themselves from non-commercial or non-artisan people in Germany or elsewhere, and to disassociate from any form of authority outside of their city walls. When Martin Luther initiated the Reformation, the Hansa merchants left off quarrelling with the territorial princes and joined them in backing him against Rome and the Empire. Luther preached the independence of German Christians from Rome, and of German citizens from the Reich, and both merchant and prince found the sermons attractive. This was a story with paradox enough even for Taylor.

Both Hansa merchants and territorial princes lacked confidence in themselves, Taylor continued, and therein lay the root cause of the next stage in German development. When, through Luther, they experienced a crisis of conscience in political understanding, economic life, and religious conviction, their worst side surfaced. The issue was the Peasants Revolt of 1525, a turning point from which Taylor believed the Germans never fully recovered. As he explained it, Luther had to decide between defining the German nation as the German people or as the princes (established authority). It was no surprise, to Taylor, at any rate, that Luther decided for the princes and became 'the wild, unrestrained advocate of a policy of absolutism and ruthless repression'. Luther felt the same lack of confidence in the Germans as they felt in themselves. 'The Luther who howled against the peasants spoke for a Germany whose markets had crumbled away.'[29] Ironically, after the madness of that episode, Luther gave the Germans the criteria for overcoming the dualism that prevented the building of a nation. He gave them a national language (through his German bible), a national cause, and a national consciousness which, if he meant what he said about individual conscience, might even have become the basis for a liberal tradition.

But it all went wrong. Taylor blamed Luther's 'antediluvian view of religion' for strangling the growth of free minds and a thinking morality. By individual conscience, Luther only meant a detached spiritualism (in Prussia, this became Pietism) not defined by Church ritual. Otherwise, he stressed princely power. The state was always right: there could be no conflict between what the state ordered and what the pious man could do with a clear conscience. The greater individual devotion, the more eagerly that princely orders were obeyed, however violent and unscrupulous.[30] It was not difficult to see Taylor bridging the distance here between Luther and Hitler, as he explained how Luther confronted with the Peasant's League lent spiritual sanction to policies of absolute repression and mass murder. In the process he turned his back on modernisation, reason, and the elevation of the mind, just as Hitler would do four centuries later. Taylor's tone was bitter when he wrote of Luther:

> He objected to the sale of indulgences in order to raise money for the building of St Peter's; if it had been for the purpose of massacring German peasants, Luther might never have become a Protestant.[31]

In this interpretation, Luther was not a departure for Germany, but simply the embodiment of its oldest dilemma, dualism. 'Luther was the barbarian who looks over the Rhine, at once the most profound expression and the most decisive creator of German dualism', Taylor wrote. Luther taught Germans that liberty meant obeying the state. He used the language which, in a sense, he had created, to attack reason, and after giving the Germans a cause and a basis for achieving unity, led them into 'the nightmare of particularism'.[32] The German princes followed his lead and established, as the will of God, an absolutism unprecedented in Europe. Meanwhile, the Hansa merchants asserted their right to be free from all outside authority, also as God's will. In consequence of both, 'authority, so far as it existed, had no sympathy with national sentiment; national sentiment, so far as it existed, was opposed to authority'.[33] This was the Germany of the *Kleinstaaterei*, the 'buffer zone' of states along the Rhine, created for religious reasons by the princes and merchants and affirmed a century later by the great powers as a matter of European policy. The *Kleinstaaterei* remained intact, a collection of contented, culturally thriving absolutist states and municipalities which served as a balance and buffer between the powers. Taylor thought this was no bad thing. Then Napoleon crossed the Rhine with better effect than his Roman ancestors, and Germany entered its modern history, the period when its political development was effected by outsiders: the French, the Habsburgs, and finally, the Prussians.

The remainder of *The Course of German History* was Taylor's story of how the Germans managed to translate a particularist, absolutist past characterised by dualism, into a nationalistic authoritarian present, without managing to achieve either political maturity or a sense of responsibility along the way. He was especially compelled by the influence wielded by the evolution

Europe and the Germans 89

of the state and all of its attendant institutions. He began by observing that when Luther backed the princes' violent response to the peasants and justified their claims to absolute earthly power as the will of God, he destroyed any initiative the Germans might have had to mature politically. In the three hundred years of particularist experience which followed, the Germans learned well how to avoid accepting responsibility for themselves. The reader could almost hear Taylor's teeth grind as he worked out the permutations of the situation he described.

Particularism ended, Taylor continued, when Napoleon re-organised western Germany into the Confederation of the Rhine, and his French followers introduced the Germans to nationalism imbued with the spirit of liberal reform. Many German intellectuals responded by developing a rudimentary liberalism and a nationalism based upon resentment of French interference to go with it. However, as children of the German version of the Enlightenment, they were used to having reforms handed down from above. Therefore, every enlightened reform simply made them more dependent upon authority.[34] So too with nation building. For liberation from the French, the Germans turned to Prussia, the least liberal and most anti-national of all German states. Paradox piled upon paradox. Taylor appreciated them, every one.

Prussia itself was a sort of paradox, Taylor wrote. When Napoleon came to make war in Germany, Prussia was an organisation for conquest and expropriation run by agrarian capitalists, a landed aristocracy called Junkers who worked their estates without feudal dependents, but kept an army of landless labourers living in a state of abject serfdom. The Junkers were Prussia's peculiarity and its strength, the interlopers in a Slavic land who survived by applying the most rigid military discipline to themselves and their system. They had no national sentiment, and were as contemptuous of German burghers as they were imperious to the suffering Slav labourers on their estates.[35] Their sole function was to overcome odds and be powerful. They were simply oppressors.

The Prussians were capable of extraordinary achievements, Taylor wrote, and cited Prussia's greatest king, Frederick II, who transformed Prussia from an obscure frontier kingdom into a European great power in the space of only forty years. He described Frederick as a typical Junker, in that he worked only for Prussia's advantage, making war with foreign powers against the emperor, and ignoring the idea of a common Germany and the existence of a German people.[36] All the same, in serving Prussia, he laid the foundations of the state that in time would unify Germany. It was no accident, Taylor pointed out, that Berlin and not Vienna became the centre of German power. Curiously, he referred repeatedly to Frederick's authoritarian efficiency as an improving monarch, but never to the king's cultural and intellectual contributions.

The process of making Prussia the centre of German power began with Frederick, but continued after him with the Germans themselves. Unable to save Germany from the French, they called upon Prussia to do it for them, and then convinced themselves that they had saved Germany after all. But in Taylor's eyes, presenting the 1813 battle of Leipzig as a 'Battle of the Nations', that is, of 'Germany' against France, was fraudulent. Leipzig was the victory of a professional Prussian army. Of 300,000 Prussian troops, only 10,000 were 'national' volunteers, and only two battalions were present from all of the rest of Germany. The fraud was expanded afterwards in the writings of the nationalist philosopher, Fichte, who glorified Prussia and proclaimed it the leader of the German cause.

But Fichte was a convert to German nationalism, as Taylor explained it. His glorification of Prussia as the powerful nationalist leader came about only because his native Saxony had failed in its expansionist ambitions. Only then did he become a nationalist. He was a great figure at the new University of Berlin, founded 'in the days of humiliation after 1806', where he lectured on nationalism. Yet another paradox: the most appreciative members of Fichte's audience were French officers, who were connoisseurs of the rhetorical.[37] This was appropriate, Taylor argued, because, devoid of reality, Fichte's lectures were only useful as models of the rhetorician's art. They appealed to nothing but an 'unreasoning assertion of the superiority of everything German'. There was no appeal to history or tradition because there was little to appeal to. Any German preference for King Frederick William III of Prussia over Napoleon rested on nothing more than that the former was German while the latter was French. The logic was absurd, but of course also inescapable. If being German made Frederick William III superior to Napoleon, then why should he not rule over the French – and, indeed, the rest of Europe as well – rather than only over Germany and the Germans?[38] Here was the future structure of pan-German nationalism, the connection between German European aspirations and Prussian power. Taylor had described Luther's rebellion as releasing German authoritarianism and intolerance from all restraints. Now he described Fichte's Prussianism as unleashing German aggressiveness, arrogance, and determination to master the peoples of Europe.

One ingredient was missing, however. Fichte provided no role for the German masses. He wrote of the German people, but he meant a sort of free peasant, living happily and obediently under the cultural and political guidance of the Prussian-German State. No such peasant existed, Taylor countered. The Germans who did exist at that level were the workers and landless rural labourers who would join the German nation only when a demagogue, preaching a blend of nationalism and socialism, emerged from their own ranks. He referred to the apotheosis of Adolf Hitler, of course. Hitler, at the head of the German masses, brought to full flower the barbarism Taylor regarded as inherent in the German and Prussian experience.

Fichte did not address Germany's masses, but the Prussian state did. That, Taylor argued, was the ultimate purpose of government, military, and education reforms instituted after 1806. The initiator was Baron vom Stein, a Rhinelander imposed upon the Hohenzollern monarchy by Napoleon. Actually, Stein hated the French (for reasons similar to Metternich's) and meant to transform Prussia into the spearhead of German resistance. He wanted Prussia to be a model for Germany, to create a free peasantry, a constitutional state with a parliament, and an economic system responsive to bourgeois interests. All of this was too radical for the Hohenzollerns, who soon dismissed him. They did not, at the same time, scrap his work. Rather, they altered it to benefit their absolutist version of Prussia. As Taylor explained it, after Stein was gone, the regime emancipated the serfs in order to create an obedient and exploitable class of army conscripts. They reformed the government in order to upgrade administration and strengthen the central state. Stein's economic reforms were redefined to benefit the landed Junkers of east Prussia. Prussia was stronger as a result, but in its own interest, not Germany's. Even so, Stein made Prussia conscious of Germany, and he made it inescapable that one way or another, the

Prussians would have to deal with the Germans or else be overwhelmed by them.

Subsequent to Stein, Taylor continued, General Gneisenau and General Scharnhorst instituted military reforms. They created the General Staff, an institution for co-ordinating and organising all aspects of military operation and supply. The middle class was allowed into the officer corps for the first time, and in the process was won over to aristocratic dictatorship in government. Finally, through a process of selecting army leaders on the basis of locality rather than family connection as in the past, they tied the army to the grass roots of village and estate, and made it an extension of the Junker agricultural system.

Then followed Humboldt's education reforms. They were the key to everything else as Taylor described it, because the Humboldt system militarised the whole people. Actually, Taylor passed over describing the system itself and concentrated on calculating its purpose and consequence. The purpose, he determined, was the deliberate militarisation of a people. The consequence was that the weapons of civilisation – philosophy, history, science – were adapted to serve uncivilised ends, and were dished up in this way with enthusiasm by the schoolmaster and university professor. With characteristic 'let there be no mistake about that' certainty, Taylor concluded that 'Prussian, and later German, education was a gigantic engine of conquest, the more effective in that it was conducted by volunteers.'[39]

All of these reforms extended downward and outward, Taylor continued, serving first the conventional purpose of all Prussian state activity, the preservation of the military monarchy and ruling caste.[40] However, they served the discredited Stein's purpose also. In the 1860s it was this 'reformed' Prussia that led Germany toward unification. The crucial questions in Taylor's mind were two: why did Prussia do it? And what was the effect upon Germany? His answer to the first was, to protect traditional Prussian social organisation from radical German nationalism. Unification occurred under the protection of Prussian guns, at the bayonet-points of well-disciplined Prussian conscripts, and for the Prussian soldier-king to rule. German soldiers became Prussian soldiers, learning to march farther, live longer on hard rations, and stand heavier casualties than their European counterparts. To the second question, he provided this answer: a formidable Prussian military tradition, modernised by technology and education, was imposed upon Germany so that after 1871 Germany joined Prussia in standing for nothing but power. Freedom came to mean only the freedom to impose the German will on others, and German critical intelligence and scientific curiosity were made to serve the ends of conquest. The tone was bitter as Taylor concluded that under Prussian leadership: 'The highest faculties of the mind, and these the Germans possessed, were put to the service of a mindless cause.'[41]

Taylor frequently reaffirmed his conviction that 1848 was the turning point. The Prussians never had wanted to be Germans, he argued, and had remained 'unGerman' until 1848. However, faced with a revolution having German nationalist overtones, the Hohenzollern state was faced with a choice: become German or else turn the Germans into Prussians. The revolution of 1848 came to Berlin as elsewhere in Germany, in the name of German unity, a liberal constitution, and the rule of law. Prussia sent a delegation to join the professors, doctors, lawyers, and businessmen assembled at Frankfurt, whose object was to write a constitution for a united Germany. But the idea of a Germany including Habsburg lands and ruled by the Habsburg monarchy threatened to overwhelm all other considerations, and at this, the Prussian delegates balked. Not that they minded ruling Slavs, which they did already in any case, but they could not stick being themselves ruled by the Habsburgs, Prussia's rival within Germany for more than a century.

In the event, they did not have to. A paradox raised up to confound both revolutionary idealism and the plan of unification. In Taylor's explanation, the German masses, inspired by the example of middle-class intellectuals, rebelled in their turn in the name of radical social revolution. Meanwhile, Slav nationalists convened a Congress in Prague which demanded that the Germans renounce their claims to Slav lands within the Habsburg Empire. In the face of such developments, Frankfurt highmindedness vanished in a wave of panic combined with resentment over thwarted ambition.

The Course of German History essentially retold a story from *The Habsburg Monarchy* with regard to the Slavs, with only a shift in emphasis toward future national Germany and away from the Habsburg monarchy. Once again, the Slavs were a critical issue because their place in eastern Europe held the key to the aspirations of a Great Germany. Seeing themselves as representatives of a superior civilisation, the German nationalists couched German mastery over the Slavs in the language of a great cultural mission, proclaiming that to withdraw would be to betray 'the values of civilization'. That was veneer, Taylor argued. The real point was that Germany must have Bohemia in order to become an empire, whether on the Carolingian model or as the Greater Germany advocated by radical idealists. The Slav Congress, therefore, opposed German hegemony in eastern Europe, which had little to do with cultural missionary work.[42] Consequently, Frankfurt called upon the Habsburgs to put down the Slav revolutionaries, which they did, and to acknowledge that this was in order to serve the aims of German civilisation, which they did not. The Habsburgs merely were reclaiming a dynastic possession. They had no interest in Great Germany expansionism. After Prague, they repudiated the Frankfurt assembly altogether, and the Prussian delegates breathed easier, even if their south German colleagues felt betrayed.

Meanwhile, the Frankfurt Assembly also called upon the Prussian army to save it from riotous peasants and workers. Prussian arms performed as expected, and in the process of restoring order, demonstrated that the Hohenzollern state had never actually lost its power. This power which had 'saved' Germany from the lower orders, was in a position to impose unity upon Germany in line with Prussian interests. With this in mind, the Prussian delegates introduced the Little Germany plan of unification.

It was typically Prussian, as Taylor described it, in that where Great Germany was an ideal, Little Germany was a practical expedient.[43] Little Germany offered a curious combination of moderation and mass nationalism. The advocates of a Great Germany were a collection of radicals needing a revolution to carry their aims forward, Catholics fearful of Prussian Protestantism, and the friends and dependents of the Habsburg monarchy. Their counterparts for a Little Germany on the other hand, were largely north German Protestants and moderates, who proposed a constitutional monarchy with limited suffrage, and the Prussian king as German emperor. The supporters of Great Germany united against this alternative plan, and the argument raged until finally what Taylor termed an 'astonishing compromise' was worked out. The Frankfurt Assembly embraced the Little Germany program which excluded Austria, and offered the imperial crown to Frederick William IV of Prussia. At the same time, the Assembly proposed a centralised democratic constitution based on universal suffrage for this Little Germany, a concept compatible only with Great Germany ideas. Therefore, by failing to achieve its Great Germany goal, the Assembly 'postulated the ultimate destiny of Germany and Prussia', which was that Prussia could rule Germany only on condition of embracing the cause of German nationalism.[44] Taylor's explanation was a remarkable piece of intellectual symmetry which formed a virtually unanswerable case. Of course, for the moment nothing actually happened, as Frederick William IV contemptuously rejected the Little Germany plan as the offer of a 'crown from the gutter'. However, the die was cast, and Prussia ultimately did serve national Germany, even as national Germany served the cause of Prussian militarism, just as Taylor argued that each inevitably must.

Prussia emerged from 1848 with its collective eyes opened. Any Germany but a Prussian Germany represented a threat to traditional Prussian interests. It was Bismarck, who, with his Junker military friends, began to work for German unification under Prussian guidance, a solution from the top. Bismarck once wrote to War Minister von Unruh that Prussia must make an ally of the German people in order to achieve its agenda. This upset von Unruh until Bismarck explained that the alliance would be solely for the purpose of manipulating the Germans. Taylor did not refer to this exchange directly, but he did describe accurately the cynicism lying behind Bismarck's thoughts on the Prussian role as German leader. In 1866, Bismarck arranged a war between Austria and Prussia which removed Austria from leadership within Germany. In 1871, he did the same to France, and a Germany dominated by Prussia was born. The disparate elements from 1848 remained, of course, and Taylor described Bismarck as a chancellor of the German Empire who operated on the principle of divide and conquer.[45]

But for how long could he maintain it? A Germany unified under Prussian military leadership, but a Germany with all of its nationalist and political extremes alive and well – where would it go from there? On the one hand, in order to sustain his exploitative divide and conquer 'dictatorship', Bismarck had to produce justifications; that is, successes in foreign policy, war scares, puffed-up religious controversies, social programs, tariff reforms, colonialism and even a 'sham constitutionalism'. But on the other hand, each policy that justified the dictatorship also inspired some segment of the body politic to assume that the chancellor was on its side against the others, and still further justifications had to be produced. Above all, Bismarck's policies were meant to preserve Prussian interests, but in advancing them, he conceded Great Germany ambitions: permanent alliance with Austria, isolation of France – or its alternative, isolation of Russia and Britain – and acquisition of a colonial empire.

In explaining Bismarck's German Empire, Taylor brought his interpretation of German history to a critical point. In 1888, a king-emperor was enthroned who, though a Prussian, believed himself a German and everything was changed, at least on the surface. Bismarck was forced from office, the dictatorship ended, and the advocates of the Great Germany, thwarted in 1848 and in 1871, came into their own. Dualism ended, pan-German nationalism informed the philosophy of will to power expounded by Heinrich von Treitschke, among others, and Great Germany aspirations were made the ultimate policy goals of the State. Germany under William II embarked on a course of *Weltpolitik*, and the divergent elements Bismarck had ruled merged behind the cause of national unity and the will to power. As Taylor described it, the 'horse' that Bismarck had 'ridden' was now turned loose. His successors simply 'threw the reins on the horses back'. The horse then took the bit in its teeth and became a 'run-away' in every sphere of activity. After 1890, Germany exploded in economics, politics, foreign policy, and claims of national superiority. The struggle for European mastery that culminated in the war of 1914 was set in motion. The irony, Taylor thought, was that Germany could have had Europe without violence – except that to do so required the patience, tact, and political direction that the Germans lacked.[46] Taylor's Bismarck was not an alternative to, but an aberration in, the course of German history. He slowed the process of Great Germany radical nationalism, but he did not prevent it. Taylor presented this argument unaltered in *Bismarck: The Man and the Statesman*, a decade after *The Course of German History*.

The First World War ended in Germany's defeat, or, better, Germany's willingness to accept a cease-fire. Taylor contended that the experience of the war demonstrated the ideological victory of Great Germany, and pointed directly toward the next war. This view was generally shared by historians in the decade after 1945, though without the populist element that Taylor made central to it. As he explained, in 1916, General Ludendorff, a Prussian but not a Junker, became dictator of the army and of Germany. Ludendorff defined war-aims as territorial aggrandisement, the defeat of England, the creation of an independent Poland, and German supremacy throughout the Habsburg lands. These blended Great and Little Germany aims as Taylor had described them. However, Ludendorff was only moderately successful in implementing these aims because the army, still Prussian and Junker, opposed him. It required a populist demagogue, not a general, to achieve the Greater Germany programme; 'in fact a corporal, not a general', in Taylor's words.[47] The First World War had shaped the mentality upon which this demagogue, when he emerged, would base his appeal. In war, the Germans found the unity which eluded them in peace. Taylor argued that the overall German war-aim – German mastery over Europe – reflected popular desires rather than merely those of the ruling elite. In that mastery, the Germans could feel vindicated for having forfeited freedom at home.[48]

But first military defeat and a democratic revolution, which produced the Weimar Republic, had to be endured. Taylor described the Weimar Republic as resting upon a 'constitution for the professor of political science', which few Germans actually wanted, or at least did not want the responsibility for making it succeed. As he explained it, the Constitution was a device that made it possible to wreck the democratic element in Germany, if the undemocratic element ever attacked it.[49] The democrats wanted a unitary, constitutional nation, while the conservatives wanted strong, independent states which would act as a brake on democracy. The anti-democratic element revived particularism and dualism for the specific purpose of overturning Weimar democracy. Reich governments of the left could not afford constitutional conflicts, and therefore dared not interfere with undemocratic practices of state governments of the right. Reich governments of the right cared nothing for the constitution, and did not hesitate to overthrow state governments of the left. In 1933 when particularism and dualism had done their work, the conservative Germans of the petty states were happy to rejoin a nation the leadership of which was suitably authoritarian and committed to statism and the worship of power. None of this was as those 'Professors of Political Science' had envisioned it.

The German people, regardless of class or condition, did nothing to save the democracy that had been established in their name, Taylor continued. By their action, or better their inaction, they demonstrated a preference for authoritarianism and demagoguery over democracy. At this point Adolf Hitler entered the picture. Playing upon popular grievances real and imagined, against democracy and against the Versailles Treaty powers, he, the 'man from the gutter', grasped the 'crown from the gutter', and Great Germany was at last triumphant.[50] In Taylor's words, Hitler's Reich 'was a tyranny imposed upon the Germans by themselves', and while very few liked National Socialist barbarism or the tensions it engendered internally and externally, they accepted it because only through National Socialism could the Germans attain their ends. National Socialism merged the disparate elements of left and right, expansionism, conservatism, and demagoguery, in the single cause of German military, industrial, cultural, and popular supremacy everywhere.[51]

The Hitler Reich ended in 1945, in war and destruction. Taylor concluded that while it lasted, it demonstrated all of the fundamental conclusions to be drawn from the German historical experience: that Germans never would accept Slavs as equals, nor accept Slav independence, because that contravened their idea of national unity; that Germans were devoted to militarism, and in the presidential election of 1932 had disputed only over whether to have the orderly militarism of an elderly field marshal, or the unrestrained militarism of a 'hysterical corporal'; that Germans worshipped the state, and were prepared to accept totalitarian principles in government and society in its name; and that Germans were determined to have their Great Germany, a point clearly demonstrated in 1938 when they annexed Austria and dismembered Czechoslovakia. Referring to the abortive July 1944 conspiracy, Taylor noted that only 'Germans of high character and weak politics' ever opposed Hitler, and then only when it was clear he could not produce the military victory he had promised. Given all of this, it was beyond Taylor's comprehension how the second German war might have come as a surprise to anyone.

The Course of German History concluded with the victorious powers meeting at war's end, in the summer of 1945, outsiders come once again 'to liberate the Germans from themselves', as Taylor put it. 'German history had run its course', he wrote. Or had it? War ended when the 'armies of western civilization and of the Slav world met on the Elbe'. To Taylor it was simple justice that the Slavs were the instruments of the downfall of their German and Magyar tormentors. With that in mind, he called for the western democrates to recognise that the Germans were hopeless, and to make common cause with the Slav world to keep them under control. The Slavs had been gaining strength throughout eastern Europe for years, he argued, and it had been to push them back that Germany fought the war that began in 1939. German–Slav conflict was the point with which Taylor's book opened, and it remained a major theme throughout. Taylor waxed eloquent in pleading for a pro-Slav policy in the west. The Slavs loved equality, freedom, humanity, he wrote, and held the key to ending 'the artificial lordship of German and Magyar' in eastern Europe.[52] The Slavs that Taylor described here were not altogether recognisable, given the eastern European history he had so recently chronicled in *The Habsburg Monarchy* and other writings. Nevertheless, he was convinced that European security depended upon linking the west, including the United States, with the Slavs, including, naturally, the Soviet Union.

Regrettably, it did not happen, at least not at Potsdam, the conference convened by the Big Three powers in the summer of 1945. Quite the opposite. The Cold War, pitting the Anglo-American alliance against the Soviet Union, broke into the open at Potsdam. Taylor believed that its roots lay in western antipathy to Bolshevism as manifested in allied intervention in Russia against the Bolsheviks in 1919, and in the exclusion of the Soviet Union from the Munich Conference in 1938. To Taylor, the Cold War represented the failure of diplomacy and of commonsense, and, personally, a betrayal of all the passion and energy he had put into writing *The Course of German History*, the object of which was to persuade everyone who read it that the historical continuity of the German menace could be ended only through East–West co-operation. Many of his colleagues did not see things the same way, and complained that his indictment of the Germans was overdone. Their message was no less political than was his: Germany had to be rehabilitated; the exegeses of Cold War politics demanded it.[53]

Germany's role in Cold War politics expanded in the years

after the war, and so did Taylor's criticism, expressed in essays and radio talks between 1945 and 1950 on Germany and the western powers. It was irresponsible to talk about a restored, independent Germany, he claimed, in one instance. 'A Germany free from foreign control will seek to restore the united Greater Germany which Hitler achieved in 1938: nor will democracy provide an automatic safeguard against a new German aggression.' Then, reiterating a theme from *The Course of German History*, he argued that Hitler 'could have achieved nothing if the German people had not been taught to worship power above everything else'. In another instance, he termed the debate over post-war German reconstruction a 'wily German trick', urging that the Nazis deliberately created economic chaos at the war's end so that the Allies would have to restore German heavy industry, and with it a restored militaristic Germany. '[Y]ou can see Nazi policy succeeding already, when people argue that we cannot afford to destroy or to diminish the industries of the Ruhr.'[54] Reconstruction might alleviate misery for the Germans, but it would increase the misery for everyone else. Clearly Taylor was on the side of Henry Morganthau, at least where German re-industrialisation was concerned.

During the post-war decade, Taylor frequently attacked writers whom he labelled German apologists.[55] Have we learnt nothing, he asked, when we call for Europe to show compassion for the 'good Germans' who were duped by Hitler and victimised by his Nazi policies? Who were these dupes, he asked? Why, they were no-one at all. They did not exist. There are no 'good Germans', only Germans. Again and again, Taylor hammered this thesis home: *every* German embraced German unity and the will to power as the ultimate expression of German rights, and *no* German ever accepted that Germany owed responsibility to humanity or the spirit of western civilisation. He cited many examples of 'good Germans', as these apologists defined them, and then explained how 'good Germans' actually behaved. Nineteenth-century historian Leopold von Ranke was an example: 'Ranke and his followers . . . regarded the State, whoever conducted it, as part of the divine order. They never opposed; they rarely protested. Inevitably, therefore, they usually found themselves apologizing for what the State had done.'[56] Ernst von Weizsäcker, a German state secretary who claimed to have opposed Hitler, was another. Weizsäcker wrote down his objections to Hitler's foreign policy, and in so doing, imagined he had resisted. But then what, Taylor asked? He locked them in a desk drawer and went about his duties. 'To tell the truth, Herr von Weizsäcker did nothing to harm Hitler and Ribbentrop; he did nothing to harm the allies; in fact, like most of the other "good Germans," he did nothing at all.' Then there was Friedrich Meinecke. His book, *The German Catastrophe*, was well received by historians as a profound analysis by a distinguished German scholar of German historical failures. Again Taylor objected. Meinecke was just another 'wily German', possessed with that 'crude cunning peculiar to the German mind'. Meinecke wrote that simple chance explained Hitler's success, thereby letting the German people off the hook. They were not responsible for Hitler's rise to power.[57]

No evidence or argument presented by any apologist for Germany could shake Taylor's faith in his indictment of the German people as supporters of Hitler, National Socialism, and the subsequent war of conquest. This would never change.

Being prepared to blame the Germans, Taylor naturally also was opposed to a growing body of opinion that adhered to what came to be known as the Nuremberg thesis. This thesis was the product, in a manner of speaking, of the Nuremburg War Crimes trials following the war. In essence, it placed blame for wickedness upon Hitler and the Nazis and excused everyone else. Few were quite comfortable with German assertions that they knew nothing about what was going on in the concentration and extermination camps, but that was only one issue, albeit an important one. Historical and political literature continued to absolve the Germans of collective guilt for the war itself, in favour of dumping it all on Hitler and the Nazis. Taylor knew, or thought he did, that this all had to do with Cold War politics, and therefore in the preface to a 1961 edition of *The Course of German History*, he reaffirmed his determinist thesis for Germany, and took a shot at those who accepted the Nuremberg thesis in the process. It was 'no more a mistake for the German people to end up with Hitler than it is an accident when a river flows into the sea', he wrote. 'The Germans were enthusiastic for a demagogic dictator and engaged in a war for the domination of Europe.' Then, his words dripping sarcasm, he added: 'But I ought to have shown that this was a bit of bad luck, and that all Germans other than a few wicked men were bubbling over with enthusiasm for democracy or Christianity or for some other noble cause which would turn them into acceptable allies once we had liberated them from their tyrants.'[58] Acceptable allies, indeed. As Taylor explained it, correct post-war policy was to deplore the idea that a new German aggression was possible or that precautions against it were necessary. Now the problem was, how could Germany be resuscitated as a great power and used without risk as an ally against the Soviet Union?[59] Freely interpreted, Taylor's view was this: 'If the Cold War turns hot, we must have Germany on our side, and hang the peevishness we might have felt in our naive outrage in 1945.'

As time went on, more and more historians and commentators took umbrage at Taylor's dire warnings about Germany, until, inevitably, The Course of German History turned into a sort of joke. In 1971, H. Russell Williams, argued in a book edited by Hans Schmitt, son of Bernadotte Schmitt, the famous historian of the origins of the First World War, that Taylor's book was itself the result of peevishness, and misplaced peevishness at that. Williams saw it as a period piece, amusing in its way, but not to be taken as serious history. He even suggested, tongue-in-cheek to be sure, that Taylor wrote The Course of German History 'at the height of the blitz, crouching under a table, bombs raining about him, and with but a typewriter between him and oblivion'.[60]

Williams had a point, though his 'under the table' reference must be accepted as hyperbole. The Course of German History was polemical, argumentative, subjective, and indicated clearly that Taylor condemned the Germans and their history well before he began writing. Williams' argument reflected an important reality. Taylor, a disgruntled critic of the Cold War and campaigner against nuclear arms, was pro-eastern Europe, whereas many critics of his interpretation of the German problem were anti-eastern Europe, or at least anti-Communist, though sometimes the line between was thin. Taylor's language tended towards intemperance, and his judgements were so value-laden, that though his arguments sometimes made sense, especially with regard to Germany's future place in European politics, his less radical colleagues were far more often irritated than convinced by his arguments and evidence.

Obviously, there would be lively discussion of Germany's future during the 1950s and beyond, and it would be in the context of the Cold War. Obviously, too, whether or not to incorporate western Germany into a western defence and security system would be part of the debate. Informed opinion viewed western Germany as essential to European security, and accepted the idea of German contrition for past sins. Policy followed suite. NATO, formed in 1949 with the clear purpose of creating a western European defence system against possible Soviet aggression, soon began to consider how and on what basis western Germany could be worked into it. In 1952, the European Defence Community (EDC) was formed, with the newly created Federal Republic of Germany as a member. The EDC did not replace NATO, as some hoped it might, but it strengthened the idea of Germans participating, more or less as equals, in western European affairs.

Such developments distressed Taylor, who still did not trust the Germans. Western statesmen, he seemed to be saying, had learned nothing. They appeared determined to allow anti-Soviet prejudice to blind them to the lessons of history. The occupation regime ended with the Bonn Conventions, accompanied by a plan for German rearmament, the day before the EDC was introduced. In 1954, to circumvent France voting against the EDC and prevent the United States' threatened withdrawal from Europe, Britain organised the Western European Union. An armed Germany was part of the package. All Taylor could see was a revitalised Germany, imposed upon Europe by the Americans with the aid of the United Kingdom; a Germany, moreover, with which they now had to bargain. In order to gain German co-operation as an armed ally, NATO members pledged to work for German reunification. For their part, the Germans had only to exclude nuclear, biological, and chemical weapons from their military arsenal. Germany entered NATO on these terms in 1955, apparently on its way to great power status once more as a participant in the Cold War. As Wolfram Hanrieder phrased it, 'without the Cold War polarization of tensions and interests, there would have been little reason for the Western powers to press for a reconstruction of Germany's military potential'.[61]

Such naïveté – or cynicism, as the case might be – appalled Taylor. He thought he understood what western statesmen, especially the Americans, were up to. *Bismarck: The Man and the Statesman*, published in 1955, was his attempt to remind them of a few hard realities about Germany. It appeared, by no means coincidentally, in the year when the Federal Republic became part of NATO, and, significantly enough, was published by an American press.

The book was inspired by what Taylor regarded as a contemporary effort to resurrect Bismarck as a viable alternative to Hitler. Bismarckian Germany was the Little Germany of 1848, after all, conservative, realistic, and with no great expansionist ambitions. If reconstructed, (that is, if Germany was reunified) Little Germany would stabilize East–West equilibrium, which is to say it would protect the West from the Soviet Union. In the bargain – being conservative and realistic and without expansionist ambitions – it would safeguard Europe, including the Germans, against the Great Germany of Adolf Hitler. In short, Taylor concluded, Bismarck's ghost was being raised in order to bring back *realpolitik*; practical diplomacy once more, and away with the League of Nations, or, to be accurate, the United Nations. By way of explaining what had happened and putting it at the feet of the United States in the process, Taylor noted that the American historian, W. L. Langer, had written the most profound scholarly analysis of Bismarck's post-1871 diplomacy, and had approved of its *realpolitik* character. Some of America's foreign policy-makers after the Second World War had been Langer's students, and had been taught *realpolitik* by him. Now, Bismarck, once repudiated as 'the type of German power', thanks to Langer was fashionable again as a guide to foreign policy. The doctrines of Little Englanders like Gladstone, or Little Americaners such as Woodrow Wilson, meanwhile, were repudiated.[62]

Bismarck was scholarly in a way *The Course of German History* was not. Taylor consulted not only the principal biographies of the Prussian statesman, but also his political writings and his comments on foreign policy, which occupy the first six volumes of *Die Große Politik der europäischen Kabinette*. It was a full-scale biography, complete with descriptions and interpretation of Bismarck's youth and education, family connections, social, economic and political background, and the manner in which he rose to importance, all necessary to clarify his *Weltanschauung*. Mainly, the book detailed his policies and aims as Prussian minister-president and as German chancellor, and ended with a description of the petulant way in which he left office in 1890. That, too, was an expression of his world view, as Taylor interpreted him. *Bismarck* was a personality study, because Taylor always regarded the human role as the essence of statecraft. After all, human beings made and implemented policy.

Taylor found Bismarck interesting, but hardly sympathetic, and the book tried to make a shambles of any arguments that made him out to be substantially different from his successors. The book was addressed to those who would reconstruct his Germany. They had missed the point of Bismarck's *realpolitik*, Taylor argued. The thesis was simple: Bismarck used power ruthlessly and without regard for the rule of law, and built a power state predicated on self-interest and domination, whether in domestic or international affairs, which had laid the groundwork for William II and Hitler. His policies did not hold the key to the European stability sought by western powers involved in the Cold War, and his Germany certainly was not anyone's bulwark of freedom. Of course, it was hardly surprising that the neo-Bismarckians would think *realpolitik* guaranteed stability, peace, and freedom. They were system-makers, Taylor pointed out, who thought policy could be planned and made to work to plan, and that Bismarck had showed the way. Rubbish, he countered, and laid out the evidence.

It was a popular notion, Taylor began, that Bismarck was the master-planner who created Germany and a European system of balance of power by design, and that he had done this for a general European purpose. In fact, it was quite the opposite. Bismarck planned little and controlled less. Rather, he was a manipulator and opportunist who merely responded to what came up, a traditional statesman who for three decades enjoyed an extraordinary run of luck. When his manipulations caught up with him he was forced from office, and all that he had supposedly constructed came crashing down. Germany consisted of forces he had controlled only to the extent that he played them off against each other.

Bismarck lived each day as it came and acted according to circumstance, Taylor continued, the same as any statesmen. He was, variously, the 'honest broker of peace', the hawk, the Junker conservative, and the supporter of industry and free trade. But he played each role from necessity, not from belief or calculation. In Taylor's words, 'he always lived in the moment and responded to its challenge'. Moreover, he believed in nothing except the Prussian system with which he had grown up, and his own will, which, to make prevail, sometimes forced him to contradict the system. Even so, his only sustained motive was to hold and wield power for Prussia, and this, not a master-plan for Germany and Europe, was the secret of his success. In Taylor's view, Bismarck unified Germany solely because in that way alone could he preserve Prussia. After orchestrating three wars he became 'the great buttress of European peace' in order to protect the Germany he had unified. And, in order to achieve unification, he 'stumbled, without knowing it, through the door which led to victory', when circumstances reopened the Schleswig-Holstein question.[63] There was no master planner in this, and no visionary.

Bismarck also was often thought to have been a constitutional statesman. True, Taylor admitted, he did sometimes appear to favour government which worked for the individual rights and happiness of its subjects, and he did proceed as chancellor in a manner that any competent parliamentary statesman would consider useful. However, that was Bismarck the opportunist once again. His reality was Prussia and the Junker aristocracy Taylor explained, as the history of his youth made clear. He believed the old Prussian dogma 'unless we grow greater we shall become less', and acted accordingly, both as Prussian minister-president and as German chancellor. His foreign policy depended upon 'the aggrandizement of Prussia "according to the principles of Frederick the Great"; and he acknowledged loyalty neither to legitimacy nor to German nationalism'. Simply put, Bismarck's dedication to the supremacy of the state was nearly total. Only the state was efficacious, only the state could determine policy, and only the chancellor, representing the king-emperor, could speak or act for the state.

Taylor described Bismarck's constitutionalism as an illusion created by the necessity of manipulating the contending and contentious elements in the Reichstag, the nationalists, pan-German imperialists, industrialists, Catholics, socialists, and agrarian reactionaries who wanted the state to serve their separate interests. Bismarck had only contempt for the Reichstag, and often referred to its leaders as 'sheepsheads'. He used parliamentary connections and arguments when it suited his purpose, and spurned or conspired against parliament with his Junker friends, and the emperor, when it did not. For Bismarck, political action derived from the state, not from individuals, and he used it and the institutions associated with it, to keep political power out of any hands but his own. When he forced social legislation through the Reichstag, it was not because he sympathised with German workers but because he wanted to make German workers subservient.[64]

It was supposed that Bismarck was the master system-maker of the nineteenth century; not quite that, in Taylor's view. Bismarck created systems, both in imperial German politics and in European diplomacy; but he also created such dissatisfaction with his manipulation and opportunism that his systems were dismantled almost the moment he left office. At home, he constructed the Second Reich in such a way that he would only need the support of the emperor to implement his policies; then he hinted at excitement and adventure in external policy in order to divert attention from his Prussian-oriented domestic policy. Bismarck had no intention of doing more abroad after 1871 than occasionally rattling a sabre in the direction of France. In Europe, he created a conservative balance of power, but raised such distrust of his motives among the great powers that they assumed it was in their interests to work against the system. It *was* in their interest, Taylor agreed: Bismarck's balance allied Austria and Germany and isolated France, Britain, and Russia, and aimed at German mastery in Europe.

Clearly, in Taylor's view, Bismarck as a master system-maker was an illusion. His objectives were conservative and limited in scope. He sought a secure Prussia within a quiet Germany, which in turn would be secure within a quiet Europe, which Germany would dominate economically and diplomatically. Perhaps that was acceptable in and of itself, in an age of international anarchy. But Bismarck's method was to manipulate and dissemble. That alone, Taylor argued, was his system. He was resented and mistrusted for it, at home and abroad, and when William II, who had been raised to think in German terms rather than in Prussian terms, assumed the imperial throne in 1888, Bismarck had to go. His system went with him, for under William, the external excitement and adventure Bismarck had promised but not delivered became basic policy. In Taylor's language, 'the generation of Germans that had grown to maturity in the Reich . . . wanted great new achievements, not a quiet life. William II, not Bismarck, represented German feeling'.[65]

All the same, it was the Germany of Bismarck's creation that

William drove to destruction in 1914–18, and with which Hitler launched his expansionism in 1938. Taylor claimed that present-day admirers of Bismarck did not see the real 'Iron Chancellor', but rather one whose reputation was reconstructed in the 1920s. Bismarck was then rediscovered as the German leader in whom honour, tradition, order, and the rule of law had existed co-equally, the German chancellor 'who sought to preserve Europe's traditional civilization'. Following this lead, Winston Churchill after the Second World War called Konrad Adenauer 'the greatest chancellor since Bismarck', which Taylor thought only indicated how little Churchill understood of the German experience: 'Adenauer was a Roman Catholic from the Rhineland, for whom the unity of western Europe came first.' This was a far cry from the Prussian Junker who had wanted to use Germany to control Europe.[66]

Therein lay the problem. Bismarck himself created the legend of his greatness in his memoirs, written solely in order to convince William II to restore him to power. They were couched in language that made Bismarck appear the master of events and the creator of Germany. Later, the so-called 'good Germans' who did not embrace Hitler's system (but also did not resist it) read Bismarck's explanation and rallied to his memory. These were the old national liberals, conservatives, monarchists, and military traditionalists. However, such Germans were remote from the German people, distrusted democracy, and were prepared to combine militarism with the rule of law, in hopes of finding an authority 'that would be moderate from its own decency'. What they got was Hitler, the leader of a mass revolution. When he arrived, they remained silent though disapproving, inactive and hopeful, waiting for him to become the reincarnation of Bismarck. They turned against him only when he failed in war. Meanwhile, they tolerated him, and even tried to capture him for their own ends. To be fair, Taylor noted, he gave them what they wanted, at first. But one day they awoke to discover that everything they valued was gone. 'The *Rechtstaat*, the rule of law vanished. In its place Nazi barbarians ruled.'[67]

Bismarck, Taylor concluded, offered no solution to the German problem, whether taken at his own valuation or as he really was. The German problem was the will to power focused on the ideal of Great Germany, and far from resolving it, Bismarck's policies and methods actually encouraged it. In order to make his will prevail, he had to compromise with the very energies he was seeking to subvert. 'Bismarck feared nationalism and socialism', Taylor had written in 1948. '[P]artly by resisting them, partly by compromising with them, he both postponed their victory and made it inevitable.'[68] By unifying Germany, the chancellor precipitated a nationalist revolution. By extending social reforms to the masses, he precipitated a socialist revolution. And, by introducing the centralised Prussian power state into particularist Germany and militarising the Germans thereafter, Bismarck gave nationalism and socialism the tools by which they could fulfil German expansionist desires. He had prevented neither Great Germany nor war, but actually made them inevitable. That was Bismarck's great achievement, and Taylor could see no reason why anyone in the present day should wish to see it repeated.

In Taylor's view, the solution to the German problem, assuming there was a solution, lay with the Germans themselves. It was a point he made repeatedly. Germany's pacification would come only when the Germans learned to accept Europe as a community of free peoples, rather than as a hunting ground for German ambitions. Barring that, and Taylor remained convinced that such enlightenment would likely be long in coming, he heartily recommended that particularism had been a wonderful principle when practised in Germany, and a modern version of it, the division of Germany into two parts, should be maintained as the best guarantee of European security.[69]

Taylor's apprehensions regarding Germans and Germany did not change over the years, or at least not very much. The typical German, he wrote in 1962, was former SS officer Herr Pruller, a seller of religious articles in Vienna and a diarist. He was 'a conscious, rejoicing Nazi. . . . His diary is a little demonstration that Hitler, far from misleading the Germans or tyrannizing over them, gave them exactly what they wanted.' In 1965, Taylor warned European statesmen against listening to German grievances. 'The lesson of the inter-war years is clear. Once started on the slippery slope of meeting nationalist grievances, there is no stopping until Germany is the dominant power in Europe. Therefore don't start.' And in 1969, he was adamant on the question of reunification. 'We should tell Germany we don't want them reunited', he wrote. 'This would improve our relations with Russia and in the long run with Germany. There are not many morals to be drawn from history. But one is certain: A divided Germany means peace. A united Germany means war.'[70]

Keeping Germany divided to prevent a European war was Taylor's principle theme in two and a half decades of writing on the German problem. It was always Germany's ambition to achieve mastery over Europe, he reiterated, and since the time of Bonaparte, preventing it had been the primary objective of the European balance of power. However, given the record of European diplomatic history since 1848, Taylor was not convinced that as a system for maintaining international security, the balance of power was all that it was cracked up to be. On the other hand, he seemed convinced that it was well ahead of whatever was in second place, at least among practical approaches to international security.

4

The Precarious Balance

The Struggle for Mastery in Europe, 1848–1918 (1954)

No phenomenon in Taylor's lifetime affected him so profoundly as did the Cold War, which dominated international relations after 1945. In consequence, he was inspired to write at length about European diplomatic relations during a period when the European states were still sovereign. The rationale was obvious. The Cold War engaged the two post-war superpowers, the United States and the Soviet Union, with Britain as poor relation to America and the European continent caught in the middle. The subordination of both Britain and Europe to the superpowers, and in such a hateful context, disturbed Taylor to his bones. The Cold War 'devastated my life', he wrote later, adding that he had 'dreamt of a Europe that would be free from both America and Russia'.[1]

This 'dream' was never far from the surface in a number of Taylor's post-war articles on nineteenth-century European diplomacy, and especially in a volume he began in 1948 as the introduction to the *Oxford History of Modern Europe*. That volume was *The Struggle for Mastery in Europe, 1848–1918*, published in 1954, which was a scholarly study of European balance of power diplomacy over seventy years. It was arguably Taylor's best book on diplomatic history. The period 1848–1918 encompassed a Europe that was the centre of the world; it was a period also when that world was assuming its mid twentieth-century character. The relative independence of Europe – including Britain – in international affairs when compared to post-1945, was compelling from Taylor's perspective. He thought it would be instructive to describe the foreign policies of independent nations in an era between epochs of 'ideological' diplomacy, an era when balance of power had prevailed.

The pre-1914 era seemed a useful contrast to the international relations of the Cold War of Taylor's own times, that global conflict which was waged between the superpowers in the context of a 'system' for conducting foreign policy. This conflict reminded him of the contest after 1815 between the reactionary Holy Alliance and the ongoing revolutionary spirit of post-Napoleonic France. In both instances international relations were reduced to absolute rules which allowed neither flexibility nor independence for the participants. The twentieth-century version, however, found the European states which had dominated the Concert in 1815, caught between extra-European superpowers. While they appeared sovereign and independent, they were, in fact, dependent upon the superpowers for their security and, indeed, for their survival. And that, Taylor believed, was no security at all.

When was Europe most secure, Taylor asked? Whenever balance of power diplomacy prevailed, seemed to be his answer, and he justified it on the grounds that when each sovereign European state had 'acknowledged no superior and recognized no moral code other than that voluntarily accepted by its own conscience', there were long periods of peace only occasionally interrupted by war. The periods of peace were produced by the balance of power, a process of diplomacy through which the sovereign states, or at least the great powers, acting alone or within loosely structured alliances, were able to prevent continental mastery by a single power.[2] But in the era of 'ideological', or 'systematic' foreign policy – the age of Metternich or the Cold War – individual states were expected to give up their independence and freedom of action in the name of some greater purpose or good. In the era of the Cold War, real control lay outside of Europe and with the superpowers. The European states had ceased to be sovereign in a way meaningful for international relations. The existence of nuclear weapons, an element in the Cold War to which Taylor objected most strenuously, deepened both European dependency on the superpowers, and the danger inherent within that dependency. Meanwhile, the superpowers constructed their international systems and compelled the European states to become part of them. Was this, as they claimed, the path to peace and security? Or was it, as Taylor suspected, the road to World War Three?

Balance of power is a concept basic in the modern history of diplomacy. Taylor explained it, criticised it, despaired of it, even on occasion applauded it, and described it as at once chimerical, mythical, real and inescapable. He never ignored it. He was not always consistent in his explanation of its role, however. Sometimes he credited the balance of power with being the only process that kept the peace, or, as in *The Italian Problem in European Diplomacy*, limited an aggrandising power. Other times, in *The Struggle for Mastery in Europe* for example, he maintained that the balance of power preserved the peace in the short term but not in the long, and that it could never achieve permanent European security. Still, he thought balance preferable to system-building, which denied the political progress without which security became a form of slavery. Balance, by contrast, rested upon flexibility and freedom of action, in short, upon the willingness and ability to change and adapt. In fact, Taylor regarded a conservative, or static balance of power as a contradiction in terms.

In the second half of the nineteenth century, the great powers preached balance of power, negotiated on the assumption of its validity, strove to achieve it, and each worked long and hard to upset the Balance in its own national interest, while also working to prevent others from doing the same. In a piece written in 1942 and clearly inspired by war-time, Taylor accounted that it was strange that with all the writing on pre-1914 diplomacy, historians had ignored the story of the 'Struggle for the Mastery of Europe', and instead spent their time on 'such crudities as the international anarchy or the iron ore of Morocco; and the inevitable result is the policy of appeasement'. Having blamed his colleagues for the shortcomings of present-day statesmen, he went on to assert that the story of balance of power in the later nineteenth century had to be told, meaning, perhaps that by telling it, some future round of appeasement might be avoided. Whatever he meant by this reference to appeasement, he clearly was convinced that a major gap existed in the history of diplomacy that needed filling.

But who should fill it? Not an American historian, because Americans 'do not understand what was at stake'. Not a German, because for the Germans 'the struggle (that is the resistance to German domination) seems merely wrong-headed'. Taylor did not offer the task to a French, Austrian or Russian scholar, either, and offered no explanation as to why. Who, then? An English historian, to be sure, who would be ideal for the task 'if one could be found with real standards of scholarship and understanding'.[3] Was Taylor announcing his intention to be the historian of the balance of power? Not if he was to be believed when he maintained that 'I cannot think of a subject for myself' and that 'all my life subjects have been thrust upon me by circumstances or by others'.[4]   Perhaps. In any event, in this instance the subject was 'thrust' upon him by Alan Bullock and F. W. D. Deakin, the editors of the modern European history series for the Oxford University Press. They wanted Taylor to write a book on nineteenth-century diplomacy. Perhaps, too, the dead hand of Heinrich Friedjung was a factor, for it is hard to escape the notion that Taylor, who once claimed Friedjung's *The Struggle for Supremacy in Germany* was the model for his own writing, simply co-opted the sense of Friedjung's title for *The Struggle for Mastery in Europe*.

As to the 'circumstances', it may be argued that Taylor's personal confrontation with forces engaged in the Cold War had something to do with his decision to accept the OUP commission. In 1948, the year he began reading for the book, he ran afoul of both sides in the Cold War. In the West, Herbert Morrison from the House of Commons, described Taylor's radio commentaries as 'anti-American, anti-British and not particularly competent'. Subsequently, Taylor was 'struck off' the BBC's Third Programme. In the East, Taylor attended the Congress of Intellectuals held in Wroclaw, Poland, where the Soviet delegates dominated and turned the Congress into a propaganda session. Those who refused to accept the Soviet version of recent history were overwhelmed with abuse, disaragement and insult. 'Of these idiots and imbeciles (Mr Ehrenburg's phrase) I am glad to be one', Taylor remarked when safely back in London, where he found himself to be something of a hero for having 'stood up' to the Communists. His speech before the Congress had defied Soviet interpretations of events, pointing out that the Soviet Union did not save Europe single-handedly from fascism, and indeed only entered the war when attacked by Germany. 'The British dissenters displayed glorious individualism to the last', he proclaimed when writing about the Congress, and then warned that those who believed that 'the Russians can be won over by soft words and one-sided gestures of good will' were fools.[5]

There was nothing new in Taylor writing about the past with his feet planted firmly in the present, although he often denied it. After 1948, he had a bone to pick with both East and West, and he made this clear in *The Struggle for Mastery in Europe* as well as in other writings, all of which appear, at least, intended to educate the two sides in the Cold War. He had already interpreted European history, or aspects of it, in the context of rivalries for power, in *Germany's First Bid For Colonies* and *The Habsburg Monarchy*. Moreover, the themes of German power, militarism, and the desire to master Europe which informed *The Course of German History* were firmly in his mind even as he told the story of the Habsburgs. One need only read *The Habsburg Monarchy* to see *The Course of German History* taking shape. If diplomatic history was to have any practical purpose – and Taylor was usually the first to deny that it had, characteristically, in a sentence either immediately preceding or following one in which he insisted that diplomatic history must have a practical purpose – it should be to educate statesmen as well as the private reader regarding how and why diplomatic relations are the way they are. He viewed European diplomatic history, at least in modern times, as the story of a struggle for mastery of the continent, a characteristic feature of which was manipulation of the balance of power.

Manipulation was never an end in itself, however, and mastery, as often as not, was motivated by a desire for security. As early as 1936, writing on the diplomacy surrounding Franco-Austrian conflict in northern Italy in 1859, he observed that when Austria appealed to the European powers it was on the bases of 'international rights and treaty obligations', and the danger of a 'Napoleonic dictatorship over the whole of central Europe' should France prevail. He repeated the sense of this in 1963 when he wrote: 'European relations in fact were always a tangle of forces, with high principles and apprehensions usually stronger than the will to conquer.'[6]

The Struggle for Mastery in Europe brought together the two distinct forms that were a regular part of Taylor's writing on European diplomacy: scholarly explanation and political argument. The volume was a thorough job of scholarship, but in telling the story of balance of power diplomacy after 1848, Taylor went beyond mere *wie es eigentlich gewesen* (how it actually happened). In the two decades following *The Italian Problem in European Diplomacy*, he read voraciously in published as well as archival diplomatic sources on the second half of the nineteenth century, and produced scholarly analyses of very specific events for *The English Historical Review* and *Revue Historique*. These were notable for their detachment and attention to detailed minutiae, but nevertheless followed his penchant as established in *The Italian Problem in European Diplomacy*, for trenchant observations on statesmen and policies and paradox and irony. When combined with his scholarly books, such pieces as these provided Taylor with an academic reputation. (One hesitates to include *The Course of German History* on the list of 'scholarly books', albeit it is among the most important sources for comprehending how he connected the historical past with the political present. It was scholarly in its way, and yet . . .) In the early 1950s 'Professorships were thrust upon me', from the universities in Manchester, Leeds, Edinburgh and elsewhere, far away from the archives in London, all of which he declined. Oxford University did not offer him any of its three Chairs of Modern History, but he was given a university lecturership, which he accepted.[7]

Meanwhile, Taylor reviewed books in language both political and scholarly, made current affairs radio broadcasts – the *Forces Programme* in 1941, an American wartime series aired from London called *Freedom*, then *London Forum* after the war, until he ran afoul of Herbert Morrison – and discovered television (*In The News*, beginning in 1951), all in the space of a decade. In these venues he commented on historical and contemporary events, drew general rather than specific conclusions, and saw politics, past and present, in terms that clearly reflected aspects of his Cold War concerns. From these performances, Taylor gained a different kind of reputation, and it is almost certain that his television notoriety, along with official hostility provoked by his public criticism of the government's invasion of Suez in 1956, kept him out of the Regius Chair of Modern History at Oxford.[8]

Taylor's scholarly short pieces developed many interpretations, criticisms, and judgements that would be included in *The Struggle for Mastery in Europe*. For example, the thesis of 'European Mediation and the Agreement of Villafranca, 1859' (1936), was that while no third power intervened in the Franco-

Austrian war of 1859, fear that one might, based upon Franco-
Austrian *perceptions* of what Great Britain, Russia, and Prussia
were up to, produced the preliminary Peace of Villafranca that
ended the war.[9] 'Fashoda' (1948) which concerned the Anglo-
French confrontation in the Sudan in 1898, made the point that
'the abiding importance of the Fashoda affair was in the affairs
of Europe; and the fate of Marchand ultimately turned the scales
in the balance of power'. That is, an Anglo-French accord rather
than a war over the Nile fortress, 'fixed the pattern of the Triple
Entente', the eventual partnership of Britain and France in
opposition to German militarism, 'and so of the war of 1914'. He
carried the argument forward in *'Les premières années de l'alliance
russe'* (1950). Though the Franco-Russian alliance evolved in the
context of Anglo-French tension, that was only a temporary
disruption of the steady progress toward improved relations
between the western democracies, a French alliance with Russia
notwithstanding. Taylor wrote:

> La diplomatie français ne misait pas uniquement sur l'alliance russe:
> même aux moments de grande tension, elle ne perdait jamais de vue
> la nécessité d'une réconciliation avec l'Angleterre. L'alliance russe
> n'était pas, en effet, en contradiction avec l'entente franco-anglaise,
> c'était, au contraire, un moyen de la réaliser dans des conditions plus
> favorable pour la France.[10]

Other, similar, points of interpretation and criticism included
that: 'In the eighteen-nineties Africa dwarfed all other questions
in British diplomacy', and that, regarding the French,

> the Egyptian question was for them a matter of internal poli-
> tics – to find some compromise which would reconcile French
> public opinion to the loss of Egypt, and so enable good rela-
> tions between England and France to be restored.[11]

When Taylor turned to British Moroccan policy, he discerned that
Britain's point was to promote reform and maintain the indepen-
dence of Morocco against France, a policy that worked so long as
Morocco remained stable. There was, in this, 'no foresight, no
calculation, no preparation'. Then, referring to the 1906 Algéciras
Conference which brought the Moroccan situation to a sort of

conclusion, Taylor argued that everything had been, as was normal in diplomacy, touch-and-go.

En plus d'une occasion, une affaire de quelques heures aurait complètement altéré le caractèrê des négociations, et alors le cours inévitable de l'histoire aurait évolué dans une direction tout à fait différente.[12]

Trenchant, sometimes witty, but rarely sympathetic judgements of statesmen characterised *The Struggle for Mastery in Europe*. So, too, these pieces. Buol, Austrian foreign minister in 1859, 'had based his whole policy upon Schwarzenberg's theory that the strength of Austria lay in her army, and he had attempted to bully his way through one problem after another'. Lord Dufferin, British ambassador to France during the diplomacy preceding Fashoda, was 'a *grand seigneur*, who knew nothing of African trivialities; besides, he was annoyed by the fact that his arrival in Paris had not led to an immediate improvement in French feeling towards England, and was hostile to the French as a result'. Kimberly, then just arrived in the foreign office, fared no better because he was 'garrulous, elderly, and had no experience of foreign affairs for twenty-five years;' moreover, he was 'dominated by Rosebery, and followed Rosebery's violent promptings without demur'.[13]

A similar style coloured Taylor's judgements of policies. Referring to the Upper Nile policy, he concluded that the 'supreme German blunder was to suppose that there was for France any "great game" other than the maintenance of French independence and the redress of the national wrong (the loss of Alsace and Lorraine)'. Then, at the Algéciras Conference, the Germans relied on the United States, overlooking the fact that, so far as the Americans were concerned at all with Morocco, clearly, '*ils préféreraient la côté de l'Entente*'. Taylor characterised Anglo-French relations over Morocco as somewhere between foolishness and wisdom. '[W]hen not actually quarrelling, they tended to establish an unacknowledged condominium, much to the annoyance of the other Powers'. Meanwhile, seeking a piece of the action, the Italians 'played at being a Moorish Power' and forced the Moroccans to buy an Italian cruiser to compensate for having also bought arms from France.

[T]his proved a great embarrassment, as the Moors had no sailors with which to man the ship when it was completed, and it had finally to be sold off as a job-lot in part payment to Spain of the indemnity of 1893'.[14]

These articles and essays represented a still young Taylor at his most historiographical; a trained, careful scholar with a taste for the ironic as well as a commitment to objectivity, and a capacity to turn a phrase that was unique for his generation – or perhaps any generation – of diplomatic historians. It was good preparation. These pieces were well crafted, reasonably argued, and thoroughly supported with documentary evidence. It is hardly surprising that he was asked to write the first volume of the *Oxford History of Modern Europe*.

Meanwhile, Taylor's 'occasional' writing, as it has sometimes been described, much of which also concerned diplomatic history, was of a different character though it covered much of the same material. In the pages of the *Manchester Guardian Weekly*, for example, he placed more emphasis on personalities and frequently made references which could only be taken as commentary on contemporary affairs. The commentary made no bones about having a 'point of view', and it is clear that this writing was aimed at a popular audience with an eye towards persuasion. It is clear that its existence in no way lessened the Oxford history editors' regard for Taylor as a diplomatic historian.

In 1944 and 1945, the European war was moving toward the total defeat of Germany. That fact scarcely proved to Taylor that either militarism or an affinity for aggression had been expunged from the German mentality. He frequently addressed such doubts in his writing on pre-1914 diplomacy. A piece on the Entente Cordiale and another on Anglo-French diplomacy over Tangiers in the *Manchester Guardian* were set in the diplomatic arena of the Mediterranean in 1904 and after, and aimed from the start to reaffirm the western democracies against German aggrandisement. With the Entente, Taylor wrote, Britain secured both ends of the Mediterranean from French interference, and gave no thought to the idea of 'co-operation between the Western democracies against German militarism'. But the French understood better. Advocates of entente 'knew that they were staking the future of France for the sake of Western democratic civilization. . . . [A]t the crisis of their destiny they remained faithful to the ideas of the Revolution.' The French grasped what the British failed to understand, that Germany wanted European mastery. The Entente assured them that 'the prospect of a German hegemony over Europe achieved by peaceful means vanished forever'. His contemporaries should be grateful, Taylor concluded, that German mastery had been thwarted forty years before, and British Governments should express their gratitude by trying to get on with the French, even to the extent of 'acting in the spirit, instead of on the letter, of the Entente Cordiale'.[15]

In 1945 the shooting war was over and the Cold War began, and Taylor focused squarely on the diplomatic issues of the times in which he lived. Bismarck had understood something that present-day western statesmen seemed to have missed, he wrote in 1946, namely that Anglo-Russian co-operation was the only protection for Europe against Great Germany. 'German power in Europe was ended when Russia and England were reconciled, first in 1907 and then in 1941.'[16] The following year he repeated the point, concluding that

> the more I reflect on this record of Bismarck's life, the more convinced I am that it – and therefore German history – cannot be comprehended without as full a grasp of Russia's place in Europe as western historians have shown for that of England or France.[17]

His historiographical point was certainly valid in both cases, but the principal point was that the western powers must co-operate with the Soviet Union as security against future German aggression.

Taylor took up Bismarck again in 1951. 'I have recently been fortunate enough to start examining Bismarck's diplomacy all over again', he wrote, and went on to express his disinterest in the subject: 'I am prepared to believe that Europe is finished, and I am only curious to know what happened to Europe in the second half of the nineteenth century without worrying any more about the outcome.'[18] It is likely that the phrasing of this line meant very little except as an expression of stylistic individuality, but the point was clear otherwise: Taylor intended to challenge what he regarded as misunderstanding of Bismarck's foreign policy, current among advocates of the Cold War.

Such was the theme later of his final chapter in *Bismarck: The Man and the Statesman* in 1955. Taylor set the stage for this biography by asserting that Bismarck's principle achievement was in domestic politics rather than in foreign policy, and that in any case, his foreign policy was inspired mainly by domestic requirements. '[T]he Bismarckian compromise or contradiction within Germany – it comes to much the same thing – is what mattered most in European history'.[19]

From this beginning, Taylor went on to 'debunk' other interpretations associated with Bismarckian Germany. For one thing, where was the evidence to support the 'widely held' contention that France or Russia, or both, would have prevented German unification in 1848? For another, it was untrue that Bismarck won Russian gratitude for upholding Russia's position in Poland. Instead, the Russians resented Prussian patronage. Still another was Bismarck's claim that the Schleswig–Holstein affair was a trap for Austria from the start. Wrote Taylor: 'I think rather that, as so often, Bismarck, always impulsive and always exaggeratedly nervous of the aggressive designs of others, rushed himself into a commitment and then had to exercise all his great genius in order to get out of a tangle of his making.' Nor did Bismarck control events. Napoleon III, not Bismarck, 'made the moderate programme possible and enabled Prussia to win hegemony north of the Main without a general European upheaval'. Indeed, Napoleon 'took Bismarck's breath away by insisting on Prussia's annexing the whole of north Germany – a victory for the revolution over moderation'. Moreover, Bismarck did not provoke war with France in 1870. That France had news of the renewed Hohenzollern candidacy for the Spanish throne at all, was 'due to the blunder of a cipher-clerk in the German legation at Madrid'. No-one, Taylor claimed, could have guessed that the French would turn the crisis into a war; in short, the French, not the Germans, provoked the war of 1870. (Taylor gave his reasons for this revision of history in *The Struggle for Mastery in Europe*, where he related it to the effect upon French policy of declining French power.) He also debunked Bismarck's claims of diplomatic mastery over Russia and Austria-Hungary at that moment, arguing that the chancellor's diplomacy did not secure Russian and Austrian neutrality in 1870 because they had no inclination to go to war in any case.[20]

At the end of the piece, Taylor made oblique references to Cold

War misunderstanding of Bismarck's role in Europe. Great man that he was, Taylor claimed, Bismarck made mistake after mistake, not least of which was ignoring his own warnings and tying his 'trim Prussian frigate to the worm-eaten Austrian galleon'. However clever he had been in manoeuvring Prussia into control in Germany, Bismarck was never able to control Europe. Rather, 'the diplomacy of Bismarck's later years was simply an elaborate jugglery to conceal the fact that he had abandoned his earlier visions and had been forced to repeat, or even to outdo, the mistakes of his predecessors'. A curious coincidence: the very week when Bismarck made the Austro-German alliance, Gladstone announced his principles of international co-operation. Both claimed they were taking the path to peace. It was no accident, Taylor wrote in fine, epigrammatic form, 'that in every subsequent world-conflict, Bismarck's heirs, the boasted real-politikers, have always been defeated by the heirs of Gladstone, those who hope to make the world anew'.[21]

Which brought Taylor to *The Struggle for Mastery in Europe*, begun in 1948 and published in 1954. He was delighted for the opportunity to write it, thinking it would be fun to 'fill in the gaps' in his other writings on the period after 1848. When the book appeared, it dazzled some reviewers and irked others. But it also 'established my academic reputation instead of being merely a public entertainer'.[22] The contents, meanwhile, reminded Europeans what had changed after 1918, and what they had lost, perhaps forever, after 1945, and this was the point, of course.

Taylor's introduction included this curious footnote: 'I have written throughout this book as though states and nations were monolithic units, with defined personalities.' However:

'France' or 'the Germans' means no more than "those particular Frenchmen or Germans who happened to shape policy at that particular moment"; and even these few usually differed among themselves.

It is not clear why he felt required to explain a style of reference he shared with most diplomatic historians of the time, and the nature of which readers of diplomatic history most probably understood without explanation. Otherwise, the introduction

laid the foundations upon which Taylor rested his understanding
of both the meaning and purpose of balance of power.

Balance of power, he wrote, simply was the absence of single
power domination among a group of sovereign states. Lacking a
dominant controlling force, balance of power took on the appearance of international anarchy wherein a number of sovereign
states were in competition with one another. International anarchy led to arguments for limiting sovereignty in order to end the
anarchy – hence the struggle for mastery among the sovereign
states. Thomas Hobbes had argued for single power mastery as a
solution to anarchy in the seventeenth century, Taylor pointed
out, and noted that mastery had often been attempted, referring
as examples to Philip II of Spain, and Louis XIV, and Napoleon
Bonaparte in France. Each of these attempts failed because the
balance of power had worked to prevent their success. Having
proved itself, the balance emerged unscathed from each such
conflict. Taylor wrote: 'No one state has ever been strong enough
to eat up all the rest; and the mutual jealousy of the Great
Powers has preserved even the small states, which could not
have preserved themselves.'[23]

Sustaining the 'perpetual quadrille' of the balance of power
was a strain, however. Statesmen 'have often wished that they
could sit out a dance without maintaining the ceaseless watch on
each other', Taylor wrote. With the interests of their countries in
mind, statesmen sent diplomats to conduct secret agreements,
and behaved as honestly as their several moral codes allowed, in
a world much like the business world, wherein respect for
contracts does not prevent 'startling reversals of fortune'. Even
as Europeans practised balance of power as the safeguard of
their sovereign interests, they dreamed of alternatives, usually
based on some form of moral authority: the Roman Catholicism
of the Counter Reformation, the Rights of Man of the French
Revolution, international socialism, or, after 1917, Lenin's appeal
to the proletariat 'over the heads of the established governments'
and Wilson's Fourteen Points.[24] One way or another, Taylor
claimed, balance of power had worked 'untrammelled' for
seventy years to prevent single power or ideological domination
of Europe, and a general European war, until finally it was
dwarfed by the internationalism of both Lenin and Wilson.

It was not easy to sustain the balance, however. Even in the
days of the *ancien régime*, which, Taylor noted, often was credited

with a 'divine stability', there was an ever-changing configuration of the powers: 'In fact Powers ran up and down the scale
with a dizzy rapidity', he wrote. In 1648, Sweden, Holland, Spain
and Poland were great powers. By 1815 three of these had ceased
to be great powers, and Poland had simply ceased to be.[25] The
mark of a great power, he explained, was its ability to wage
war. In the nineteenth century this meant the size of the army (or
navy, in Great Britain's case), sophistication of armaments,
strength of the economy, social stability, and, in lieu of being put
to the test, reputation for military prowess.

To illustrate the point, Taylor provided tables for those ranked
as great powers between 1870 and 1918, indicating comparative
growth and decline of populations, army, navy, and defence
estimates, and various kinds of industrial productivity. These
tables indicated who was greater and who lesser among the six
major powers. The German population grew the most, the
French the least. German army estimates increased the most,
British and French the least. German navy estimates increased
the most, and the French the least. Germany also led in
percentage growth of defence estimates, followed by Austria-
Hungary and Russia. Russia spent the highest percentage of its
national income on armaments, and Great Britain the greatest
per capita amount on arms. In each table, the extremes of growth
were almost invariably found in Germany, Great Britain, or
Russia, with France, Italy, and Austria-Hungary lagging behind.

These tables told Taylor that Austria-Hungary declined, Italy
never actually became a great power, Great Britain opted for
naval power, Germany became the greatest land power, Russia
kept up only with great strain, and France slipped backward,
though less than Austria-Hungary. Tables indicating industrial
growth supported his conclusions. Among the European powers,
Great Britain produced the most coal, with Germany a close
second, while Russia produced the least. Germany led in pig iron
and steel production, with Britain in second and Austria-
Hungary last. Taylor added the United States to his industrial
tables, and for good reason. The Americans nearly doubled the
production growth, even of Germany, in all categories, and
showed the highest rate of manufacturing growth between 1860
and 1913. That pointed to the future; only no one then recognised it.[26]

The Struggle for Mastery in Europe narrated the story of

European diplomatic relations between 1848 and 1918. It was the story of a contest for domination of the continent. Taylor's thesis was that through the process of maintaining the balance of power, Europe managed for seventy years to avoid a major war and to prevent any single power, or combination of powers, from gaining continental ascendancy. Finally, the balance broke down in the general war of 1914, a war no-one wanted and few anticipated, and when it ended in 1918, the struggle for Europe became a struggle for the world. 'Henceforward, what had been the centre of the world became merely "the European question"'.[27] The Balance of Power was the central theme, and Taylor supported it with such secondary themes as the movement of power within Europe, the dividing of Europe into alliances, the developments which led to the First World War, and the gradual dwarfing of Europe by the potential global powers, Russia and the United States. As he went, Taylor described how each great power saw Europe and its place therein, indicated characteristics of leaders and statesmen which influenced or even determined their conduct of foreign policy, and pointed to central elements of 'how the game was played'.

After 1848, Taylor began, the 'game' replaced the Metternichian 'system' which had kept the peace in Europe from 1815 to 1848. Before 1848 this 'system of principle and design', the creation of the Congress of Vienna, was maintained by the semi-mythical 'Holy Alliance' of Russia, Prussia, and Austria. These states were able to maintain the territorial and political settlements of 1815, and to prevent progress and change, or at least the appearance of it. Russia and Austria mutually guaranteed each others' Polish lands and the status quo in Turkey, and, along with Prussia, were committed to intervene against liberalism, if asked, on behalf of any independent sovereign. They all 'looked west against France'. The system broke down after 1848, unable to withstand the territorial and political assault by liberal and nationalist revolutionaries in France, Italy, Germany, and the Slav lands of the Austrian empire. The Germans and Italians wanted unification; the Slavs wanted cultural autonomy within the Habsburg monarchy, or even independence from it; and France wanted to be rid of the 1815 treaties in order to play a dominant role in future European relations, the natural consequence of throwing over the Metternichian system in the name of nationalism. The French, Taylor wrote, assumed that Paris would naturally lead a Europe of nation states, just as Vienna had naturally led the congress system.[28]

Between 1848 and 1850 Metternich's system was swept away and himself with it, both replaced by the 'realists' who moulded European affairs for the next thirty years. The Austrian Schwarzenberg was the first of these. He claimed to judge 'from facts, not from principles'. Louis Napoleon and some of the French revolutionaries of 1848 were also realists. Lamartine, poet and revolutionary historian, was also the first foreign minister of the revolutionary government. He showed his realism in foreign policy by dissembling in order to satisfy radical French opinion and, at the same time, reassure statesmen outside of France. For the former, he repudiated the 1815 treaties; to the latter, he promised that France would continue to recognise the treaties. Revolutionary France was also realist over nationalism. While they supported the 'national principle' across Europe in theory, the French knew they risked creating neighbours, Italy and Germany, who, together, could overcome them.[29] Taylor concluded that revolutionary France could not help but be relieved when both Italy and Germany failed at unification in 1848, owing to the intervention of conservative Prussia and Austria.

The Holy Alliance powers defeated the revolutionaries in 1849, but that did not lead to reconstruction of the Metternichian system. Quite the contrary, as Taylor explained it. Tsar Nicholas I refused to make Russia a third in the Austro-Prussian alliance of 1851 aimed against France, for fear of a western alliance forming in turn against Russia – a foreshadowing, in principle at least, of the two great treaty systems of the end of the century. The Tsar was glad to have Austria and Prussia as a buffer between Russia and France, but he would not go to their assistance. Meanwhile, the Near East heated up, which led to the Crimean War in 1854, and the very western alliance that Nicholas feared. The war grew in part out of Britain's suspicion that Russia planned to dismember Turkey, and in part from Russia's equivalent suspicion that the western powers threatened its security in the Black Sea. It reflected Napoleon's desire to have 'disturbance for its own sake'. Crimea was a war against Russia, but not for Turkey, a war viewed by the principal western powers from opposite perspectives. Taylor explained that Britain assumed that defeat of Russia, whose presence in the Black Sea Britain resented, would make the European balance of power stronger. On the other side,

Napoleon assumed the opposite, that a Russian defeat would overturn the balance.[30] Taylor loved this kind of contradiction, seeing it as proof of his contention that statesmen do not control developments, but are controlled by them. Meanwhile, the Crimea War killed Metternich's system and the Holy Alliance, and introduced a period of anarchy.

British statesmen Palmerston and Lord John Russell brought the war to an end in 1856 through negotiation. They often disagreed, and sometimes were political opponents. The bellicose Russell was an isolationist to whom all foreign governments were suspect. Palmerston was a man of liberal principles, but also a realist. He backed Russian intervention in Hungary in 1849, and then invited Kossuth, the Hungarian revolutionary whom the Russian army overthrew, to lunch. For that the 'pro-Turk lunatic David Urquhart', as Taylor described him, vilified Palmerston while Karl Marx went so far as to claim that Palmerston was in Russian pay. Both Russell and Palmerston disliked any development that disrupted the even flow of British interests, interests that were served far more by peace than by war. The Crimean War, which they ended, had been waged in condominium with France against Russia, and was justified on both sides of the channel as a war of liberation against the 'tyrant of Europe'. Just who was being liberated was not quite clear, Taylor wrote, but certainly it was not Europe, which as an indirect result of this war, fell prey first to the machinations of Napoleon III, and then to those of Bismarck.[31]

Taylor had little respect for the post-1848 'gang of adventurers' in France, Napoleon's advisors and ministers, who were realists of a different sort. In Taylor's view, they did much damage to both France and the practice of diplomacy between 1850 and 1870. They included Walewski, Drouyn de Llys, and Morny, among other of Napoleon's 'swell mob' (British Foreign Secretary Clarendon's phrase). They made lying and cheating the basis of diplomatic method, and were equally free of conscience and policy. Moreover, rather than confronting problems, they worked to escape from them, even if that led to greater problems later on – which it usually did. European statesmen were not equipped to deal with a state run by liars, Taylor argued, claiming that they found negotiating with Drouyn or Walewski to be singularly unproductive and confusing. In any case, the French foreign ministers made no decisions; only Napoleon did – and he was as dishonest as his 'gangster' (Taylor's word) followers.[32]

Taylor argued that the Empress Eugénie was key to the operations of this gang. In the midst of Bonapartist negotiations with Prussia in 1863 over what France would do if, as the French ambassador phrased it, 'things hot up in Germany', she persuaded Napoleon to dismiss Foreign Minister Thouvenal and recall Drouyn de Lluys. It was 'the most disastrous step in the history of the Second Empire'. Then, on the eve of the Austro-Prussian war in 1866, she tried to persuade her husband to make an alliance with Austria. There was much 'drifting to and fro' on the question before Napoleon decided on neutrality, the course which favoured Prussia. Austrian supporters condemned Napoleon for being feeble and lacking will, and indeed the Emperor was thought to be ill at the time. In fact, when negotiating with Goltz, he seemed both competent and resolute. Perhaps, Taylor speculated, 'like many sick men, he was most sick when it suited him'.[33] Curiously, while Taylor clearly had little use for Napoleon's followers, his comments always suggested that he was not altogether dismissive of the Emperor himself.

With the arrival of the Bonapartists, the French believed that power was again flowing in their direction. Taylor thought the opposite was true, and offered the Italian situation in 1858–9 as evidence. Napoleon turned to Italy in 1858 precisely because he already knew, perhaps instinctively, that dominance on the Rhine was beyond French capability, given the mood of the Germans and the rising power of Prussia. As Taylor told the story, it was a typical Bonaparte fiasco. France concluded the Pact of Plombières with Sardinia, the leading state of northern Italy. The agreement laid out a joint military venture directed against Austria. The bases of the pact were that Cavour, the Sardinian prime minister, wanted to unify northern Italy, and that Napoleon was sentimentally attached to Italy. There was also the matter of overthrowing the 1815 treaties once and for all, which Napoleon believed could be achieved in Italy. Once overthrown there, he thought, they would break up elsewhere on their own and a further war would be unnecessary. A vague agreement was made with Russia that the tsar would be benevolently neutral, the price-tag to be attached later – in Taylor's prosaic language: 'the Russians hoped to cheat Napoleon at some time in the future; they therefore gave Napoleon an immediate opportunity to cheat them'. This enabled Napoleon to have war with Austria in northern Italy, despite the objections and apprehensions of the other powers.

The struggle, such as it was, ended in the compromise Treaty of Villafranca, and Napoleon returned to Paris convinced – wrongly Taylor thought – that he had laid the foundation of a new system for Europe in which France could behave not only as an independent power, but as a masterful one. However, within two years, the upheaval in Poland which Napoleon sought to exploit, killed his Russian alliance. Taylor explained that Napoleon's Polish policy could have worked only with British support, which he did not have.[34]

It remained for German unification to complete the destruction of the European order Napoleon thought he had created in Italy, and to demonstrate once and for all that French European hegemony was a thing of the past. Bismarck was the unifier and the most dominating figure in European diplomacy of the later century. However, he was not also the controller of events that he made himself out to be in memoirs. Certainly, Bismarck was 'the most daring of Prussian diplomats' and may have been the most clever. But his policies were not always terribly original. Taylor assured his readers yet again that the German chancellor simply was an opportunist for whom the important thing was to make things move and keep them moving. The future could be dealt with when it arrived. Bismarck was arrogant, impatient, and needed quick foreign policy successes to offset his domestic unpopularity: At the beginning of his career he was rash and impatient. Only later did he mature into a diplomatic genius. It was Taylor's view that he might have hoped to manoeuvre Prussia into dominance in Germany by diplomacy in 1866, which would have been a marvel, but that he was capable of such a stroke only in his later years. By the late 1870s, Bismarck had become a conservative, a maker of alliances, leaving impatience behind. 'He ceased to be Cavour and became Metternich', Taylor wrote. 'Henceforth he, too, was "a rock of order".'[35]

German unification was Bismarck's first great achievement. It happened, Taylor explained, because Austria feared to lose the leadership of Germany to Prussia over Schleswig-Holstein, and in desperation provided the excuse for Prussia to bring its military might to bear against Austria and the German states which supported the Empire. Other factors included Napoleon's policy of inaction, German national sentiment and the other powers supposing that a Franco-Prussian war would not much affect the European balance of power.[36] Unification occurred in the context of such a war in 1870–1. But, unlike the Austro-Prussian war in which supremacy in Germany was its prize, the Franco-Prussian war was simply a trial of strength which Prussia – and with it Germany – won. French resentment thereafter was a given: hostility, whenever there seemed a chance to defeat the Germans, and bitter resignation the rest of the time. The harsh reality, Taylor concluded, was that any hope France had for dominating, even mastering Europe was dashed forever by Prussian guns at Sedan.

However, Bismarck took no chances. Having defeated France, he set about creating a diplomatic system that would prevent France or any other continental power from upsetting the balance of power.[37] After 1871, Bismarck, like Metternich in 1815, was thinking in terms of a 'system' for Europe, maintained and directed by a single power, Germany, and by a single statesman, himself. He became more conservative as time passed, also like Metternich, and wanted his system to be permanent, static, and finite. In the process, Taylor concluded, he lost whatever control he ever had over events.

Having made that point, Taylor went on to describe the system, or perhaps systems, that the 'Iron Chancellor' tried to effect. It began with the League of Three Emperors (Germany, Russia, Austria-Hungary) created informally in 1872 in opposition to a proposal advanced by the Austrian foreign minister, that 'self-confident Magyar aristocrat' Andrassy, to raise an alliance of Austria-Hungary, Germany and Great Britain directed against Russia. Bismarck said no. Great Britain, a 'liberal' power, would be an unreliable ally, he thought, whereas conservative Russia had to be an integral part of his conservative system aimed at security for Germany against France.

Taylor appeared convinced that Bismarck genuinely believed in a French danger. Perhaps he did. Certainly he used French sabre-rattling to manipulate German internal politics. An example Taylor used to illustrate the point: in 1875, Bismarck forbade the export of horses from Germany, 'always a routine signal of alarm'. Then he inspired a press campaign which asked 'Is War in Sight?' Meanwhile, Radowitz, Bismarck's confidential agent in St Petersburg who tended to be 'indiscreet after dinner', defended the doctrine of preventive war in a conversation with the French ambassador, Gontaut. Fair enough for a professor of strategic theory; but coming from Bismarck's henchman, the views expressed could only be taken as an indication of a turn in German foreign policy. Gontaut duly reported the conversation and an account of it made the rounds, even appearing in *The Times*, with unsettling effect upon European policy-makers.[38]

In 1878, Russia, victorious in war over the Turks, imposed the Treaty of San Stefano upon them. The Treaty satisfied Russia's demands for a Great Bulgarian national state and Christian emancipation, but it also alarmed the western powers. The British feared that the Russians would occupy Constantinople, and ordered, countermanded, then ordered again the fleet to pass the Straits, which it did on 13 February. Exhausted from the war, the Russians made no effort to stop them, which caused Bismarck to fear that worse might follow later. He invited the western powers to Berlin to revise the Treaty of San Stefano and avoid war. Bismarck played the 'honest broker' at the ensuing congress, Taylor wrote, because he had been so successful at raising Germany's power while reducing that of France and Austria-Hungary. At the congress, Germany attained 'full stature' as a European power, and with it full responsibilities. Bismarck's 'conservative order' began here, Taylor explained: the preservation of France and Austria-Hungary as great powers, not pressing for German one-power dominance over the continent, and preventing an Anglo-Russian war. After 1878 'a new Balance of Power, centred on Germany, had come into existence'.[39]

In order to maintain a German-centred and conservative balance of power, Bismarck had to manipulate the other powers. He formed a new League of Three Emperors in 1881 as an expression of conservative principles. Actually, in Taylor's view, the only principle involved was that if one of the three powers was involved in war with a fourth, the others would remain neutral. Principle had little to do with it; however, practical benefits had a great deal. Russia achieved security in the Black Sea, Prussia was freed from choosing between Russia and Austria-Hungary in the Balkans, and Austria-Hungary achieved security from Italy. Taylor claimed that this last item was only an invention, because Italy was not genuinely a great power. Bismarck had 'invented' Italy as a great power by claiming that the Italians were capable of threatening Austro-Hungarian security, solely as a ruse to persuade Austria-Hungary to become part of the League of Three Emperors. It appeared to Taylor that Austria-Hungary got nothing real out of the League except disruption of their British connection and worthless Russian promises. Bismarck's invention of Italy had a further negative consequence to Austria-Hungary. In 1881 he formed the Triple Alliance of Germany, Austria-Hungary, and Italy, which made Austria-Hungary's place in the League redundant in any practical sense. Again, the chancellor was forced to go beyond his intentions in order to maintain what was central to his interests. In theory, the Triple Alliance banded central Europe into a sort of re-created Holy Roman Empire, at least for foreign affairs. In reality, the alliance only provided a prop for the Italian monarchy and guaranteed Italian neutrality should Austria-Hungary go to war against Russia, which eventuality was to be prevented by the League.[40] One's mind reeled at the complexities of Bismarck's diplomatic game, yet Taylor managed to make the chancellor's manoeuvres clear. And, as he explained Bismarck's alliances, it was equally clear that they did add complications to the game. They did not make improvements, however, and that was Taylor's point.

Meanwhile, Britain lost interest in the balance of power and turned its back on Europe. Taylor explained it this way:

> Most Englishmen had by now accepted Cobden's doctrine that events on the Continent were not their business; whatever happened, Great Britain and her trade would not be endangered. The few Englishmen who still thought of the Continent at all regarded the Balance of Powers as something that worked itself out without British intervention.[41]

What Britain did do was form a 'liberal alliance' with France, the only other colonial power in Europe in the 1870s. (Spain, Portugal, and Holland possessed colonies, but they were scarcely powers.) This was not an alliance so much as an expressed sentiment of friendship, which was disrupted for a period of time over Egypt, the Nile, and Morocco, but revived in the 1890s when Germany set out on its 'new course' under William II.

In the 1880s, Bismarck tried to create a so-called Continental League directed against Great Britain. The scheme broke down when he failed to drive a wedge between France and Britain over southwestern Africa in 1884–5. He failed, Taylor wrote, because he assumed that Anglo-French conflicts were so profound that France would put itself under German protection. The reverse was true, as time demonstrated. Neither France nor Russia were prepared to accept German hegemony in Europe, Taylor explained, and so they rejected the Continental League. This did not mean that the struggle for mastery in Europe was abandoned; rather it was postponed while the powers 'scrambled' for Africa and Asia. Bismarck, only peripherally interested in colonies, continued to explore ways to range the great powers behind Germany against Britain. He was unsuccessful. Taylor argued that: 'The continent of Europe would unite against Great Britain only after it had been conquered by one of the Great Powers.' (This had happened under Napoleon, and would again only under Hitler.) Therefore, Bismarck was able to form no continental alliance against Britain, and even the Triple Alliance was still a decade and more away from being directed specifically against the western powers. It was just as well for Britain that the continental powers remained immune to Bismarck's manoeuvres, as the next few years demonstrated that 'it was awkward for the British empire when the Powers of Europe were on even reasonably friendly terms with each other'.[42]

Bismarck fell from power in 1890, and William II abandoned his former chancellor's conservative foreign policy in favor of an aggressive world policy. Bülow became its symbol, and because world policy was encouraged in order to reconcile opposing forces within Germany and enhance the Emperor's status, he practised both democratic statesmanship and Byzantine sycophancy. World policy involved Germany in colonialism in Africa and Asia, interference in British affairs in South Africa, and a naval arms race with Britain. It also encouraged the Anglo-French Entente by providing both powers with a bogy greater than each other. But this was unintended. World policy was a fake, Taylor argued. European politics were the real object of a world policy that chased after colonies. '[T]his alone was the meaning of "the Age of Imperalism"', he wrote. 1905 saw a 'revolution in European affairs', occurred in 1905 because at that moment Germany determined to make a bid for mastery of Europe, albeit peacefully through diplomacy, and thus free itself to challenge the British overseas empire. Taylor brought it all together with that determination: after 1905, Britain rediscovered the balance of power in Europe and constructed a foreign policy around maintaining it. Every subsequent German move was seen rightly or wrongly as aiming at European hegemony, and a counter to it was sought in Whitehall.[43]

Meanwhile, Taylor continued, it was difficult for either Britain or France to think in terms of permanent estrangement from any single power, and both were reluctant to acknowledge that Germany was striving for hegemony at their expense, except in specific instances. All the same, Anglo-French military talks took place in 1906 even though the French placed little faith in the British army. The French understood that France would bear the brunt of any German attack, and would have considered an arrangement with Germany, so long as it did not require France to give up its freedom of action as a great power. Such an arrangement was unlikely in the atmosphere of 1906. Britain, meanwhile, clung to the idea that its relations with Germany were improving – which in fact they were – and regarded the 1906 Algéciras conference, at which Britain backed France against Germany and for which the French were grateful, as merely an unfortunate and hopefully short-term breach in Anglo-German rapprochement. Only Eyre Crowe argued that Germany was after mastery of Europe.[44]

From time to time, the powers found respite from tension during this last decade before general war, and on that basis Taylor argued that at no time before 1913 or 1914 did the powers seriously think that they were heading for war. The Anglo-Russian entente of 1907, which led to the Triple Entente of Britain, France, and Russia, was not directed against Germany, but was intended to resolve Anglo-Russian differences in Persia. Germany, having no vital interests in China, was willing to be co-operative in Far Eastern diplomacy. At the same time, the powers remained mutually suspicious, perhaps a natural by-product of 'international anarchy.' The Anglo-Japanese agreement of 1902 was preceded by French Foreign Minister Delcassé's remark that: 'We must prevent England finding in the Far East in Japan the soldiers that she lacks.'[45] Also, by the summer of 1908 the naval race had clearly produced strain between Great Britain and Germany.

Taylor found the roots of the 1914 war in Germany's commitment to Austria-Hungary after 1882, and that the blame for it lay in Vienna. The alliance began, as Taylor phrased it, as 'a tug-of-war between Vienna and Berlin' (probably not intended as a pun, howevermuch one might wish that it had been) that did not stop until the Austrians had dragged Germany into the conflict that quickly expanded into the Great War. World war was foreshadowed in the conflict over Morocco in 1906, only it was then still a shadow. Taylor described war threats being voiced only in 'discreet private conversations', and there was no mobilisation of forces. The local wars in the Balkans in 1912–13 held significance for the great powers, and especially for Austria-Hungary and Russia, since Serbia, a regular participant in these clashes had been an anti-Austrian client of Russia since 1903. An explosion was possible at any time during these Balkan wars, and that one did not occur, in Taylor's view, was due to the powers' refusal to be drawn in. Lord Grey ordered that the Triple Entente should be nothing 'hostile or aggressive' against the Triple Alliance, while on the other side, Germany forced Austria-Hungary to remain calm. Of course, the opposite note was struck by Wilhelm II in February 1914 when he announced: 'Russo-Prussian relations are dead once and for all! We have become enemies!'[46] The Kaiser had a way with words to be sure, and Taylor could only speculate upon the consternation this particular outburst may have caused in the Wilhelmstrasse.

Everyone, including the Germans, worked to avoid war, even in 1914. However, Germany did not abandon its fundamental aim of continental domination. Here Taylor took a shot at Bethmann Hollweg, who had succeeded Bülow as chancellor in 1909, for being a prototype of the ineffective 'good German'. Inexperienced in foreign policy, Taylor wrote, but filled with goodwill, Bethmann 'was the first of a type common later in the century – "the good German", impotent to arrest the march of German power, deploring its consequences, yet going along with it'.[47] The consequences, as Taylor described them, were as follows: on June 28, Franz Ferdinand, the Habsburg heir, was assassinated by Bosnian students, put up to it by the same Serbian terrorists who had assassinated pro-Austrian King Alexander of Serbia in 1903. Then the Austria-Hungary Government did the two things that made a general war probable: it held the Serbian Government accountable, and it insisted that Germany back a war of revenge. When the Germans agreed, the general war was guaranteed.

Austrian Foreign Minister Berchtold dawdled 'in the usual

Viennese fashion', and sent an ultimatum a month after the assassination. The Serbs accepted most of it, but Vienna said it was not enough and declared war. Statesmen who after June 28 had not opposed the Austrian-Serbian war, now grew alarmed. Russia advised the Serbs not to resist; Grey offered to mediate between Serbia and Austria-Hungary; and France affirmed its loyalty to the Triple Entente, but encouraged Russia not to go to war for Serbia.[48] To no avail. Everything that produced the First World War followed from that declaration of war on Serbia.

The powers mobilised as a precaution. The Germans invaded Belgium in order to ensure that the French would not outflank them, or rather to ensure that they could outflank the French. The British declared war on Germany because of commitments to France and Belgium . . . and so on, and on.

Taylor thought war started because Austria-Hungary attacked Serbia, and that it expanded because the balance of power broke down. General peace had obtained so long as there was a 'real European Balance'. But in the decade before the general war, Russia fought Japan and lost, which weakened the balance. Germany interpreted this as a shift of power in its direction, and responded with a diplomacy increasingly harsh and aggressive. That was the irony of it all, in Taylor's view. Taking a conclusion straight from the pages of *The Course of German History*, he wrote: 'peace must have brought Germany the mastery of Europe within a few years. This was prevented by the habit of her diplomacy and, still more, by the mental outlook of her people. They had trained themselves psychologically for aggression'.[49] The process ended in 1918 with Germany's defeat, and Taylor ended his story with the contest for European hegemony shifting onto a global stage to become the Cold War, an evolving struggle between the outsiders of the later nineteenth century who had now become superpowers, the United States and the Soviet Union.[50]

Taylor's history of European diplomacy between 1848 and 1918 featured a wholly self-interested foreign policy (save for Gladstone, of course, who aimed at 'a more virtuous foreign policy', and believed that the Concert of Europe 'would do good') usually conducted cynically and in secret, and with few scruples against cheating and duplicity. The Franco-Russian agreement in 1859 was made in secret, and proposed a straight trade: the French forgetting the Black Sea and Bessarabian clauses of the treaty ending the Crimean War, in exchange for Russian support of French policy on Italy. There was talk in 1870 of Russian and Austro-Hungarian involvement in the Prussian conflict with France. Prussia needed security on its eastern and southeastern flanks, and Russian wished to 'localise' the war. An informal three-way deal was struck. Tsar Alexander II told Chotek, the Austro-Hungarian ambassador, he would stay neutral if Austria-Hungary neither mobilised nor stirred up the Poles. He also guaranteed Austria's frontiers 'in the name of the King of Prussia'. Bismarck had not been consulted about this, but quickly endorsed the offer. Austria-Hungary accepted the deal with relief, which was disappointing to the French, who had rather looked forward to help from Austria.[51]

After 1871, Bismarck believed peace depended upon a balance of power in Europe. However, as Taylor described it, his 'system' of the League of Three Emperors and the Triple Alliance, with Prussia at the core, was only a 'conjuring trick'. Bismarck made promises to everyone so he would not have to honour any of them; so too his competitors. Indeed, every participant in the system pretended one thing and intended another, Taylor explained. The League was based on Austro-Russian co-operation, yet the Alliance was preparation for an Austro-Russian war. Meanwhile, the Italians, historically interested in central Europe but, also historically, even more interested in the Mediterranean, worked on the principle that trouble in the Mediterranean was good because it opened doors for them.[52] Taylor called this the 'Jackal principle' in diplomacy.

Statesmen used whatever weapons were at hand. That, Taylor knew, was the nature of the game. Bismarck exploited French revanchism successfully to get Reichstag backing for his policies, and Anglo-French colonial rivalry, unsuccessfully, in an effort to isolate Great Britain from the continent. Austrian Foreign Minister Aehrenthal annexed Bosnia and Herzegovina to Austria-Hungary in 1908 in order to restore the monarchy's declining prestige among the European powers, and Russian Foreign Minister Izvolski acquiesced. His price was Austro-Hungarian support of Russian plans in the Straits, which involved revision of the 1878 Treaty of Berlin. Izvolsky was rebuked by his own government, however, and got nothing. German Chancellor Caprivi tried unsuccessfully to use Anglo-French differences over Siam to gain British backing for German interests in the Near East, and his successors, also without luck, tried to force Britain out of the balance of power in 1912 with an accelerated naval building program. In 1915, Italian statesmen used British suspicion of Russian intentions in the Straits to get the price they wanted for entering the war against their former allies.[53] And they all used public opinion and sometimes were used by it.

This was an important departure for Taylor. He admitted public opinion as a factor in the conduct of foreign policy in *The Struggle for Mastery in Europe* to a degree that he had denied it in *The Italian Problem in European Diplomacy*. The spread of literacy and democracy, and the decline of press censorship in the nineteenth century forced statesmen to take public attitudes into account. 'We have to consider public opinion much more than in Prince Bismarck's time', Caprivi remarked in 1890.[54] That was true, Taylor agreed, but noted that Bismarck still had to justify the Austro-Hungarian alliance by appealing to a highly nationalistic public opinion. Meanwhile, Grey's conduct of foreign policy followed from his assumption that British public opinion could make or break his Liberal Party.[55] Of course, Taylor's definition of public opinion continued to hold that it was sharply limited by contrast to the public opinion of his own day.

Taylor regarded the conduct of foreign policy as dependent to an important degree upon the individuals who conducted it; on their ideas, principles or lack thereof, character, intelligence, cupidity, or whatever else seemed relevant. Without turning *The Struggle for Mastery in Europe* into biography, he nevertheless provided insight into the personalities of the principle statesmen he encountered as a natural corollary to explanation of events and policies. It provided added understanding, for example, not to mention style, to note that Decazes carried out his ambassadorial duties in Berlin in 1874 'with aristocratic frivolity', and without troubling 'to speculate whether a showy diplomatic success would be worth the price that France might have to pay'. Izvolsky, humiliated over the Bosnian affair, 'dragged himself complainingly over Europe, still hankering for the opening of the Straits'.[56] Wessenburg was 'a diplomat of experience and courage', Buol 'lacked daring', Andrassy displayed 'Hungarian arrogance', and Berchtold was 'irresolute and feeble'. Stratford Canning was 'an outstanding British diplomat', Palmerston was frequently impatient, indignant, and always resolute in carrying out his policies, and Disraeli 'prided himself on his knowledge of the Near East, based on a visit to Palestine forty years before', an observation which damned with faint praise if ever one did. Lord Grey brought 'north-country sturdiness' and 'moral earnestness' to the conduct of British foreign policy in his time.[57]

Taylor also regarded that diplomacy – and diplomatic history with it – was burdened with a certain amount of mythology, and he set out to 'debunk' such myths whenever he encountered them. Russia did not aim at dismembering the Turkish empire, for example. The myth that it did, was established by the British for reasons of their own, out of dealings with Russia before the Crimean War. The reality of Russian policy, Taylor argued, was to regain the influence with Constantinople which had been lost when the French had their way over the sacred shrines in Palestine on the eve of the Crimean War. In another instance, Taylor challenged the 'unanimous approval of posterity' of the 1859 war for northern Italy by denying that liberation had anything to do with it. It was open aggression and nothing more, he wrote, in which Austria had law and treaty rights on its side, and France and Sardinia had only ambition.[58]

Debunking myths was what historical study was for, Taylor seemed to say through his various efforts at 'setting the record straight'. Examples included that Prussia was not planning on war with France in 1870, a myth started by Bismarck himself, that Anglo-French conflict over Egypt had been much exaggerated by historians, since the French had no realistic hope of acquiring Egypt, and that French Foreign Minister Delcassé was supposed to have committed France to Russia's aggressive plans in the Balkans and so involved France in war in 1914, 'an absurd exaggeration' which ignored that the Schlieffen plan alone committed Germany to war with France. However, Taylor was quick to point out that the Germans had not planned the war which began in August 1914. The Wilhelmstrasse could not formulate a consistent policy, he wrote, and the chief-of-staff 'could not conduct a campaign, let alone make a war'.[59]

Taylor's view that nothing is inevitable in history (save, it would seem, German militarism) emerged first in *The Italian Problem in European Diplomacy* and was continued, perhaps emphasised, even, in *The Struggle for Mastery in Europe*. The 1914 war which no one wanted nor expected, was never inevitable. 'No war is inevitable until it breaks out', he wrote. Likewise, European international relations were largely the result of opportunism, not determinism. The moment, not grandiose schemes, occupied the judgement of European statesmen. This was even, or perhaps especially, Taylor's view of Bismarck, who, he claimed, never knew until it had happened what he could – or must – do in order to achieve the rather 'mundane' scheme of making Germany secure, and he often missed the mark. The statesmen's intended result frequently was not the actual result. Witness, Taylor urged, Izvolsky's failure to use Austro-Hungarian annexation of Bosnia to further Russian interests in the Straits in 1908; Bismarck's misreading of both British and French policy at the time of his southwestern Africa manoeuvre in 1885; and Napoleon III's character flaw – he was 'an adventurer' – which ruined his gains from the 1859 Villafranca agreement.[60] European diplomacy functioned in this undetermined way in the nineteenth century, Taylor argued, and he saw little change from that standard in the twentieth century. Statesmen formulated policies in the interests of their state and nation, conducted the diplomacy meant to implement them, and if everyone behaved as the policy-maker hoped that they would, and no unexpected event turned up, then the policy would succeed and the statesmen would appear omniscient and omnipotent, providing they knew what to do with victory. If they did, or appeared to, then, like Bismarck, they could write their memoirs and appear to have been the master of events and of destiny, whose methods deserved emulation by later generations. Taylor found few instances of such control.[61]

It was clear that Taylor believed the story of the balance of power rise, decline and fall between 1848 and 1918 held significance for his own times. When America arrived at the front in January 1918, he wrote in the final pages, Europe passed from the world centre-stage. The causes of European conflict – Alsace-Lorraine, African colonies – were as nothing compared to the coming struggle for world mastery. 'Even the German aim of dominating Europe became out of date.' In its place came ideological statecraft. Both President Wilson and Bolshevik leader Lenin wanted a world without the conflict of nation states, the one offering the Fourteen Points and the other world revolution. Each was a Utopian programme with permanent peace as the goal. The United States and the Soviet Russia were each capable of being a world power on its own; but only by combining under the hegemony of one power state could the

European continent achieve status as a world power able to challenge either of them. The German attempt to be that state between 1914 and 1918 failed; the result was Bolshevic and American intervention in Europe. The European stage now became the global stage. After 1918: 'A new Balance of Power, if achieved, would be world-wide; it would not be a matter of European frontiers. Europe was superseded.' There now began 'a competition between communism and liberal democracy which has lasted to the present day'.[62]

The Struggle for Mastery in Europe was among Taylor's most important works of serious scholarship, despite his perverse insistence upon using only English spellings of Germanic names, such as 'Sleswick' for 'Schleswig', as one example, and 'Francis Joseph' for 'Franz Josef' as another. The book was well received, but not uniformly so, and Taylor's approach to spelling was remarked upon. *The Struggle for Mastery in Europe* was called witty, an admirable survey of its subject, stimulating, even Hegelian in its rationality; but also narrow, too much limited to diplomacy, too little concerned with political ideas, cultural trends, and the social structure of players (nation states) in the game, intellectually inadequate and even repugnant.[63] Nor did its connections with the present go unnoticed. Using the metaphor of a formal ball, Asa Briggs observed that: 'There are features of the quadrille which not even the square dance has rendered obsolete, and, although the music sounds very different now, it still goes on.' For his part, J. M. Thompson noted that as a result of the collapse of the balance of power, Europe had become a 'precarious makeweight' between two non-European states. 'This is the moral of *The Struggle for Mastery in Europe*', he wrote, and added that

to understand it is as necessary for the statesmen and peoples of the present generation as it was for their predecessors to understand the decline and fall of the Roman Empire.[64]

Taylor hoped that they had understood, but he doubted if the understanding went deep or would last long. A year after *The Struggle for Mastery in Europe* was published, he reviewed the published papers of Frederick von Holstein, one of the key figures in German foreign policy between 1890 and 1906, and concluded the review with this observation:

> When Russia and the Western Powers are on bad terms, Germany is the only gainer. Holstein could play his tricks at the beginning of the century; the present rulers of Germany do much the same now. Very nice for the Germans, no doubt, but I have never been able to understand why we or the Russians should get any pleasure from it.[65]

5

'Speak for England!'

The Troublemakers: Dissent Over Foreign Policy, 1792–1939 (1957)

Statesmen and others who never learnt or forgot anything, stirred Taylor to dissent, and to admire those who dissented against them. As a diplomatic historian, he was particularly interested in foreign policy dissenters, and he also had a few things to say about the guardians of diplomatic archives who, he complained, took it upon themselves to keep their treasures from the prying eyes of diplomatic historians. Dissent had always been a part of Taylor's life, at least since he repudiated the Diety as a schoolboy in York. He had campaigned against Baldwin's Austrian policy in 1934, against appeasement in 1938, and argued the cause of the Slavs against the Germans throughout the 1940s. By his own admission, he was further left in those years, more radical than at any time in his life. However, also by his own admission, he was 'far more concerned to be a good technical historian', and was only 'radical in my response when something came up'.[1]

Taylor came into his own as a dissenter in the 1950s. Even *The Struggle for Mastery in Europe* and *Bismarck: The Man and the Statesman* with their concern over the Cold War, contained a Dissenting agenda absent from his earlier writings. The 1950s encompassed developments on several levels that affected his thinking directly as a diplomatic historian, and as a politically conscious individual. These included what he regarded as the censorship of official records, the Suez Canal crisis, the Cold War, and above all, the nuclear arms race which lay at the core of the Cold War. These developments provided the impetus for a much expanded quantity of polemical writing and speaking out on the public platform, and for his Ford Lectures given at Oxford University in 1956, and published in 1957 as *The Troublemakers: Dissent Over Foreign Policy, 1792–1939*, hereafter referred to as *The Troublemakers*.

Taylor viewed the international order in the 1950s as unstable and unresponsive to human concerns. The United States and the Soviet Union, engaged in ideological conflict while armed with nuclear weapons, dominated the period, leaving western Europe, which had moved off centre-stage after 1945, to find a subordinate place within the international order. The prospects were not encouraging. The search led in disagreeable directions, or so Taylor thought, especially for Great Britain: into NATO, which meant into junior partnership in the nuclear weapons defence systems of the United States, and into Suez in 1956, an ill-fated attempt to recapture lost imperial prestige ('old wine in new bottles', some claimed at the time). Critics of Suez, Taylor among them, were convinced that the attempt could have touched off a world war. Meanwhile, the government denied historians access to official foreign policy records, which Taylor claimed signalled a departure from the democratic promise of the 1945 Labour Party electoral victory and toward continued domination by 'the best people'.

Such things were not to be taken lying down. Taylor campaigned against the Suez policy, against nuclear weapons, against official secrecy, against the Establishment and for popular democracy as he understood it. In the midst of all this, he was invited to give the Ford Lectures, and chose as his subject, English foreign policy dissenters in modern history. He delivered the lectures in anything but objective language, and when they were published in book form, he remarked: 'this book deals with the Englishmen whom I most revere'. There was no doubt where he stood on the subject of dissent.[2]

Its implied criticism of Cold War politics notwithstanding, *The Struggle for Mastery in Europe* was a *tour de force* of scholarly respectability. *The Troublemakers: Dissent Over Foreign Policy* was Taylor's release from it. There was too much needing to be said against complacency and against the present state of international affairs for him to become, in his words, 'an Elder Statesman' of historiography. 'A radical spirit, I fear, does not diminish with age', he assured readers of his 'London Diary', a regular feature of the *New Statesman and Nation* in the 1950s.

'Start off with the desire to pull down the mighty from their seats; and it is with you to the end of the chapter. It is all very disappointing. I shall never be knighted; nor even sink into the easy somnolence of a university Chair.' Rather he would go on, 'in revolt as usual against my surroundings', though not expecting revolution. It was enough simply to be in revolt, and hope that people came to their senses in time; apropos of which he once replied, when accused of holding strong political views: 'Not strong, extreme views weakly held.'[3]

The term dissent has specific religious connotations in English history. Taylor chose it deliberately to describe his and others' opposition to present policies, because, as he explained it, 'I can think of no better one. . . . A conforming member of the Church of England may disagree with the Bishops. . . . A Dissenter believes that Bishops should not exist. And so it has been with foreign policy in this country.'[4] From the moment the Church of England was established, all who did not conform were Dissenters: Baptists, Congregationalists, Quakers, and even Catholics, though the term recusant was reserved for them. It was a matter of conscience. Religion was disputed on moral grounds, and Dissenters always assumed that by dissenting, they upheld the right. To conform would have been to acquiesce in the wrong.[5]

This description of dissent fitted Taylor well for several reasons. He was Nonconformist in background, in the sense of having been at a Quaker school and of having parents and grandparents who belonged to Dissenting sects. Moreover, he expressed a similar moral world view. He repudiated the social and political Establishment, identified freedom of conscience with political rights, defied orthodoxy and those who represented it, and regarded independence as nearly the ultimate virtue. He was, in the 1950s, an interesting if not a perfect example of a secular dissenter.

Taylor's dissent was linked mainly with foreign policy, and was expressed through his journalism, radio and television performances, as well as in the Ford Lectures.[6] Foreign policy was dominated by the Cold War, and, Taylor thought, by academic supporters of the Cold War. He much enjoyed taking on these historians and international relations analysts, whose work was characterised by harsh logic tinged with ideological commitment. Much writing on the Cold War seemed the antithesis of Taylor's own warm-blooded, humanitarian approach to diplomacy. He once described cold warriors as behaviourists, which for him was a term of abuse. As behaviourists, he argued, they misread history – probably on purpose – in order to find constant, predictable, and exploitable patterns in politics and foreign policy. They then transformed these patterns into systems through which choice in politics and foreign policy could be more easily limited, if not extinguished. Taylor urged his colleagues, at least the historians among them, to resist behaviourism, and to derive 'only malicious pleasure from the efforts of present-day politicians to enlist their great predecessors in contemporary disputes.'[7]

No one played the systems 'game' better than the American political scientist Hans Morganthau. In 1951 he published *In the National Interest*, a book Taylor criticised for resurrecting the ghost of Metternich, the greatest system-maker of all. Morganthau, he wrote, followed Metternich straight through to a modern version of his Concert system, an ideologically and diplomatically aligned international front against the Soviet Union. The Cold War repeated the confrontations of Metternich's age. Revolutions then had been directed against the overlordship of the Habsburgs in the name of freedom. In order to save the monarchy, which Metternich believed was a European necessity, he constructed the Concert system and co-operated in the Holy Alliance. Then along came the likes of Morganthau to argue that Metternich was right to internationalise defence against the revolutionaries. NATO and the doctrine of containment were the result. Taylor denounced Morganthau and all like him, when he deplored

the fashion of historians to go wandering about the past regretting what has happened. . . . It is hard enough to find out about it without trying to alter it. Least of all can we put it back. So-called restorations simply create new systems and institutions with old names.[8]

In the manner of the Dissenters he admired, Taylor's views were meant to persuade, as much as inform, and he was not always judicious in sticking to provable facts. In one astonishing fit of candour, he admitted that in such writing as his criticism of Morganthau, 'the important thing is to get something out that week, not to follow a consistent line. All that matters is to fill the paper.'[9] As a statement of principle, if such indeed it was, this was hardly encouraging. It became less so when the loose generalisations and startling contradictions that result became apparent. Taylor's implicit comparison of the Metternich system with NATO, and the 1848 revolutions with the Communist regimes of eastern Europe after 1948, demonstrate the contradictions. The loose generalisations yield to this test. After seeing Taylor's review of *In the National Interest*, Morganthau let it be known that he was not impressed. He dismissed being linked with Metternich as sheer nonsense, and told this story of what had actually transpired.

Taylor called me an admirer of Metternich. I wrote to the magazine in which the review appeared that the name of Metternich did not even appear in the book. Taylor replied that the name of Metternich appeared on the flap and that it was well known that American authors write their own flaps. A few months later, Taylor published a review of a biography of Metternich in which he referred again to me, without any obvious reason, as an admirer of Metternich.

Morganthau went on to say that 'Taylor is essentially a popularizer who enjoys shocking people by expressing utterly unorthodox opinions', and that he was 'generally unimpressive'. When Taylor learned of this, he remarked simply: 'I once tore apart a book by Hans Morganthau, so naturally he does not love me.'[10] Clearly, he was no more impressed by Morganthau than Morganthau was with him. Neither appeared much disturbed by the other's criticism.

Taylor did not take sides in the Cold War, at least in a cold warrior sense. Both sides played the system-maker game, and he repudiated it, instead preaching co-operation between the Soviet Union and the West. This was not because he favoured Soviet Communism over western democracy, but because he saw such co-operation as an antidote to nuclear holocaust – and protection from a resurgent Germany: 'Soviet predominance in eastern Europe was the only alternative to Germany's and I preferred the Soviet one', he reflected in later years.[11]

However, when he looked over the military realities that were part of the Cold War, Taylor took the position that the Americans were more trigger-happy than the Russians. Foreign policy systems required rational control of military, as well as political factors, he wrote. Wars occurred when military factors were out of control. Such had been the case in 1914, when one power (it did not matter which one) decided: 'I can win if I fight now; I shall lose if I fight later.' He saw an analogous situation in 1959. War was only checked by a technological balance between the United States and the Soviet Union. What would happen if that balance tilted? His timetable looked like this: Russia would pull ahead in long-range missiles by 1961, but, underestimating American scientists, would fall behind in inter-continental ballistic missiles and anti-missile missiles. That would be the logical moment for World War Three, about 1965, when America had a momentary advantage.

Taylor thought the Americans believed too much in weapons, and were too much prepared to use them, a view probably inspired by the example of Hiroshima and Nagasaki. Their nuclear thinking contained a vital error: having weapons superiority did not automatically preclude the possibility of war. Rather, as the historical record indicated, one state resorted to war only when threatened by the rising power of another. Therefore, as Soviet power continued to challenge the Americans, 'we will have war in six or eight years. Unless one power manages, with or without war, to dominate the world.'[12] This projection of a past structure, the outbreak of war in 1914, to explain a present situation, was advanced by the same historian who urged his colleagues to repudiate efforts by politicians to 'enlist their great predecessors in contemporary disputes'.

Taylor was right to deny that methodology, as his own use of it demonstrated. There was no Soviet–American war in 1965 – unless one has an active imagination regarding Vietnam – nor was one very likely, nor did one power manage to dominate the world. Taylor would have done better to predict war for 1962, when John Kennedy and Nikita Kruschev faced off in the Cuban missile crisis, though he still would have been wrong. Ironically, the argument can be made, and often is, that there was neither single power world domination nor nuclear war, because statesmen tutored first- or second-hand by the likes of Hans Morganthau and Henry Kissinger helped shape a global balance of power that held the line until a saner mentality took root – assuming, of course, that a saner mentality is the point of the events of 1989–90 in central and eastern Europe, including the former Soviet Union.

The Suez Canal crisis in 1956 was the first major Cold War crisis to involve Britain since the Korean War. It shocked Taylor, probably because of the suddenness of it, and certainly because of the imperialist implications. He was among the first to fire his considerable verbal guns in protest, loudly and without compromise. Taylor was then appearing regularly on *Free Speech* for Independent Television, an alternative to the BBC of which he was an outspoken champion. At a panelists' pre-broadcast lunch on the day the news broke of the Anglo-French invasion of the Canal Zone, he and Michael Foot, caught up in emotional revulsion at what was happening, refused to speak to their conservative colleagues. 'For us they were criminals and outcasts', Taylor remembered. In subsequent days, as public protest mounted and differences sharpened, discussion on the programme became heated over Suez, and every other current issue. The intensity of debate reflected divisions Suez created, not only within the panel, for example between the conservative Robert Boothby and the radical Taylor, but within the country. Television critic Maurice Richardson found a silver lining in the tension, all the same. He observed that on one occasion, 'the team seemed to be not only on the verge of, but actually losing their tempers with each other. . . . Boothby boomed, Foot fumed, Taylor trephined, with apparent real malice. . . . Anyway it was first-class television.'[13]

Outside of television, Taylor addressed one of the first anti-Suez rallies in August, well before the invasion, where, as he remembered years later, 'I told my audience that they had often sneered at the Germans for not resisting Hitler. Now was the time for us to resist a British Government that was following the same wicked course.' When the invasion was actually on, he bemoaned, in writing, the 'respectability' of the Labour Party, and argued that to win the young to the cause of ending the invasion 'there must be no hesitation, no moderation, no half-heartedness'. In later years he reflected that much as he advocated politics by argument and not violence, on this occasion, had the government not backed down, he was prepared to 'raise the banner of revolt'.[14]

Suez was a momentary aberration in the steady decline of the European powers relative to the superpowers. Nuclear armaments, on the other hand, were a constant factor which more and more came to dominate the international politics of the 1950s. Instructions for behaviour in a nuclear attack were repeated constantly in poster campaigns reminiscent of the propaganda posters of the Second World War – including this parody of Civil Defence instructions popular in the United States:

> In the event of nuclear attack:
> bend over;
> clasp your hands firmly behind your knees;
> place your head between your legs;
> kiss your ass goodby.

Meanwhile, newsreels and television news treated the general public to visual evidence of the awesome power of nuclear bombs, while in Hollywood thrillers, nuclear spies by the score were brought to justice by grim-faced, fedora-topped government agents. Both scholars and commentators pondered and advised on the nuclear issue, and serious novelists suggested widely varied scenarios on its effects in war. Mordecai Roshwald's *Level Seven* described a handful of pre-selected humans surviving underground, until radiation seeped down to destroy even the elite at the very deepest level. *A Canticle for Leibowitz*, by Walter M. Miller, allowed for survival, but indicated gross deformities and mutations resulting from radiation, and the irony of civilisation recovering, reforming – and then blowing itself up all over again. Nevile Shute's *On the Beach* argued that no one could survive nuclear war, and depicted the last remnants of humanity committing mass suicide on a beach in Australia, leaving behind a desolate world inhabitable, if at all, only by an army of mutant cockroaches.

It is hardly surprising that there would be dissent over nuclear arms. Taylor participated from the first day. On January 16, 1958, he attended a meeting at the home of Canon and Mrs J. L. Collins of St Paul's Cathedral. Others present included Bertrand Russell, Ritchie Calder (during the Second World War, he was an official of the Political Warfare Executive, which conducted clandestine propaganda activities against enemy countries), J. B. Priestley, Kingsley Martin, Michael Foot, the Bishop of Chichester, Miles Malleson, Gerald Gardiner, QC, Doris Lessing, Peggy Duff, and Reginald Sorenson.[15] The Campaign for Nuclear Disarmament (CND) came out of this meeting. It was led by a truly distinguished group of clerics, intellectuals, and activists supported by hundreds of thousands of men and women who marched, demonstrated, picketed, wrote letters to *The Times*, and made a general nuisance of themselves in a life and death cause. The movement, as Taylor happily admitted, was informal, undisciplined, relied upon argument and demonstration, and eschewed violence. It was made to order, for his rhetorical style as well as his philosophical outlook, and he claimed to have spoken in more halls for the CND than John Bright did when opposing the Crimean War.

Taylor's address was characterised by humour, logic, and the rough edge of his tongue. This letter to *The Times* was typical:

> A number of your correspondents announce that they would prefer suicide to life under communism. So would I. Our wish can be met simply and cheaply by issuing a phial of poison to every registered anti-Communist. But why should we insist that the rest of the population accompany us on this death ride; that many millions of Russians may also be obliterated; and that the atmosphere be polluted so that future generations will be born maimed or monsters?

And this, from the initial mass meeting of the CND on February 17, 1958:

> You and I must bear the responsibility for these weapons. No one will save us but ourselves. Is humanity so degraded that a lead for right is bound to fail? We should stop at nothing to bring this thing to an end. In the days of agitation for woman suffrage, the suffragettes used to interrupt the speeches of cabinet members with shouts of 'Votes for women.' Let us follow their example and ensure that no politicians of any party can appear on a platform if he supports this military policy without being similarly branded, 'Murderer.' Stand by humanity. Find your task.[16]

Sometimes he was impatient with his audiences. 'I often detect restlessness in the audience when I develop the practical, even cynical, arguments that we should be more secure from a military point of view without the H-bomb', he wrote in the *New Statesman*. The reason, he thought regretfully, was that in defining morality, the older generation left out practicality while the younger generation wanted action and were bored with argument, whether moral or practical. But to succeed, the campaign had to advance arguments combining morality and practicality, not pie in the sky. The young had to be 'won back to morality', he wrote, while their elders had to dissipate their intellectualism. It was simple, really: 'The H-bomb is morally wrong, and it is idiotic into the bargain.'[17] What more need be said?

At Easter time in 1959, Taylor participated in the latter stages of the CND march from Aldermaston to London. 'It was quite pointless and yet psychologically uplifting', he recalled. When the 16,000 marchers reached Trafalgar Square, Taylor was among those who spoke, and he was quoted in *The Times* as having proclaimed: 'In all its long history, Trafalgar Square had never seen a demonstration of this size. In all of its long history Trafalgar Square had never seen a demonstration of this intensity.'[18]

But, typical of such things, the CND included hardliners and extremists of one sort of another, and Taylor eventually ran afoul of them. They wanted formal membership and an elected central committee, 'direct action', meaning sit-downs in Whitehall, and to run CND parliamentary candidates to challenge Labour. All of this smacked of doctrinairism and an appeal to potential violence that betrayed the essential moral pacifism of the movement. Running candidates for parliament was ridiculous, Taylor argued, because it would cost the movement most of its Labour supporters. He, along with many of its founders, left the CND over such issues.

Taylor was a 1950s dissenter well before and after either Suez or the CND, over an issue that affected both democracy as he understood it, and his work as a historian. From the beginning of the decade, Taylor was at war with official secrecy. This involved, as he explained it, denying diplomatic historians access to government records for no apparent reason except, perhaps, to undercut British democracy. Why should governments limit access to historical documents? he asked. What were they hiding? Why were they hiding it? Was there anything *to* hide? Official secrecy had been around in Britain since the Official

Secrets Act of 1911, but as Taylor's particular assault on the institution came during the Cold War, he appeared to be motivated by the suspicion that ideological purpose lay behind limiting access to certain archival material. Ideological warfare, after all, was as dirty as any other kind, and one need only look across the Atlantic at the anti-Communist hysteria engendered by Senator Joseph McCarthy and the House of Representatives Un-American Activities Committee, to see it in all of its horror.

To Taylor's mind, government secrecy was linked with the self-righteous complacency and sense of superiority associated with the British governing elite, whether Tory or Labour, known as the Establishment. Official secrecy was, therefore, anti-democratic. Some of his most abusive commentary was aimed at the Establishment, The Thing, as nineteenth-century populist William Cobbett had termed it. The Thing was paternalistic, anti-populist, hedged on individual liberty, and defended property, class, and privilege. It denied historians access to the unpublished record in order to justify its continued existence. Consequently, it ran the archives as it ran everything else, as a mockery of democracy and the popular will. Writing in *20th Century*, Taylor argued that true democracy chose its rulers 'by lot for short stretches'. In Britain, the rulers chose themselves for life. Britain's rulers, he explained, were a select group who met certain arcane standards which, when met, guaranteed permanence. The democratic process was merely a periodic endorsement of their position. By his description The Thing was tolerant, exclusive, dominating, requiring of its members a white skin, a uniform of tie, collar, and dark suit, preference for sitting at a desk over any other activity, a reasonable grasp of grammatical English, and the ability to read from typescript. It was becoming easier to get into The Thing nowadays, he noted, because almost anyone could join providing he met these requirement. Only the most wretched had no hope, and he mentioned blacks and the sons of agricultural labourers as examples. Still, entry was easier if one had the right parents or at least attended the right schools: Eton for the upper classes, Winchester for the Labour Party. Running away to sea was preferable to attending a Secondary Modern. The distinguishing mark was religion, of course: Anglicanism was preferred but not mandatory, but at least some code of morality befitting 'liberal' Christianity.[19]

The Establishment dominated, in Taylor's language, because

the very word, so plummy, so ponderous, so respectable, tempts us to acknowledge the moral superiority of 'The Establishment'. It conjures up benign, upholstered virtues, calm, steady, reliable. They would never pass a dud cheque or cheat at cards. Not intellectually dazzling, perhaps, but patient, understanding, and tolerant – above all tolerant.

This image was an illusion, of course, carefully maintained by The Thing itself. 'They look upholstered', Taylor explained, 'because they are well fed. Their air of moral superiority is really an assumption that someone else will always cook their dinner – and a very good dinner at that.'[20] From his point of view, The Thing might appear on the surface, to be a system of public morals, underneath it was a system of public plunder, a supposedly benevolent despotism, but actually a collection of elitists distrustful of the people, indifferent to democracy, convinced that common sense had no value, and susceptible to the attractions of power, wealth, and privilege. Clearly, he concluded, it should be got rid of.[21] However, The Thing was pervasive. After the Second World War, the Labour Party was seduced into joining it. Taylor was correct in this assertion, at least if photographs of Trades Union Congress leaders from the 1950s are an indication. They appear fully as well upholstered as their Tory counterparts.

The Establishment managed the system for which it existed through control and limitation, Taylor wrote, which brought him to his complaints against official secrecy. Limiting access to official documents struck him as wrong on a number of levels. For one thing, government secrets were not in the public interest. Voters could not make intelligent decisions without adequate information. For another, keeping secrets added to public expense. Documents were kept locked up and guarded, requiring the hiring of keepers until the moment when the government – at still more public expense – hired official historians to publish large collections of documents. To what end? Taylor wanted to know. The contents of these collections reflected selection and editing. How could they be trusted to contain the full story without misdirection?

The official archivists who 'protected' these collections from historians were perfect representatives of the Establishment, Taylor continued. He described the 'type' as bureaucratic, unsympathetic, elitist, and vain – this last because they were 'privileged' to handle documents to which others were denied access. The archivist resented readers because, if let into the archives, they would 'disturb the neat arrangements on his shelves' and perhaps mishandle the precious hoard while they were at it. Readers were his class enemies.

Though Taylor often criticised the United States as a Cold War superpower, he claimed to appreciate American archival practice as preferable to its English counterpart. It galled him that English documents had been carried off to North America, where they were used by American scholars who published in England. His complaint was not against the Americans for having the documents, or for letting scholars read them at will, but against the British Government for denying access to documents in England. He wrote: 'American historians who are ransacking the papers of Roosevelt and Truman would have the true nature of British freedom brought home to them if they were sent to prison for quoting the papers of Lloyd George.'[22] Taylor could see no legitimate point to such restrictions, which, he argued, merely stifled curiosity and restricted freedom, and performed no service to anyone. As he explained it, secrecy thwarted the spirit of democracy, 'which is, no doubt, why officials seek to maintain it. It will go in time, if democracy survives at all'. The Americans had their faults, he acknowledged, 'but they certainly take democracy seriously;' Britain should follow their lead and observe 'Beard's Law' (a reference to the great American historian, Charles Beard): 'Official archives must be open to all citizens on equal terms, with special privileges for none.'[23]

Finally, he brought the Russians into it. The Americans have no secrets, while the Russians have little else. 'I am on America's side in this', he wrote, and complained: 'Our rulers follow their usual practice; American in talk, Russian in practice. Meanwhile, the contemporary historian should tell the public that he cannot do his job properly.'[24]

Official secrets in Britain, in a legal sense, were a twentieth-century phenomenon. The Official Secrets Act in 1911 was followed by the creation of the Cabinet Secretariat in 1916. This office imposed government control over all ministerial papers with the result that even cabinet ministers who refused to hand over personal minutes, official correspondence, inter-office memoranda, and so forth, found themselves threatened. Since the practice was undemocratic, as Taylor defined it, and damaged the quality of historical research and writing, historians had no choice but to dissent. His feelings on the subject were clear, and nowhere more so than in *The Troublemakers*, where he complained against being denied even Gladstone's 'cabinet papers, really private jottings, without the permission of the Cabinet Office'. And to no sensible end, Taylor insisted, save 'to bolster up the self-importance of the civil servants who insist on it. I regard every official as my enemy; and it puzzles me that other historians do not feel the same way.'[25]

In 1952, a controversy erupted concerning the Cabinet Secretariat, when Aneurin Bevan, Minister of Health in Attlee's Labour Government in 1945, published cabinet minutes in defence of his resignation in 1948. In response, Attlee charged that Bevan violated the 1916 Cabinet Secretariat Act in order to betray the Labour Party. Taylor was outraged by Attlee's action, and plunged into the fray. Bevan's transgression had little to do with the law but everything to do with political freedom, he wrote. Attlee was technically correct, of course, the rule being what it was. But the rule ought not to exist in the first place. In Taylor's words: 'The unity of a political party can surely be maintained by other means than the manufacture of a precedent designed to keep the people, and even posterity, in ignorance.' If the rule was debilitating for politicians, it was even more so for historians. Scrap the law, he pleaded: 'Publish nothing, but allow scholars unrestricted use of the records. Editorial susceptibility will be upheld; and the historical story will be made known.'[26] A practical example: was Germany deliberately pushing the naval arms race in 1909? Only the archives of the German Navy contained the answer, but they were being 'rigorously guarded at Admiralty House'.[27]

Worse was to come. In 1958, parliament imposed a fifty-year moratorium on opening official papers to readers. This meant, for example, that documents pertaining to the Second World War would not be opened until at least 1989. 'How can generals learn how to lose the next war unless they know what happened "last time"?' Taylor asked sarcastically. All the same, he understood the thinking behind this new rule – and disparaged it. 'No harm would be done to states or individuals if the records were open

without restrictions', he argued, except to 'destroy the prestige of
diplomacy and of the archives themselves. It is more impressive
to appear to be protecting guilty secrets than to confess that
there are few secrets to defend.' Years later he observed: 'The
rule is in fact an unworthy survival from the time when government was a "mysterie", reserved for the Crown and its servants.
Such rigmarole has no place in a community which claims to be
democratic.'[28]

Taylor's writing on historical dissenters in *The Troublemakers*
was itself dissent, albeit different in form from his arguments
against official secrets, Suez, and for the CND. True, the volume of
lectures was insubstantial as historical research when compared
with *The Struggle for Mastery in Europe*, and far from objective. It
was the product of historical research, however, and was sufficiently critical of the evidence upon which it was based, that it
could be read as history, rather than as merely an exercise in
dissenting hagiography. All the same, Taylor made no pretence
that he was not involved with his subject. At the outset, he wrote
of the dissenters: 'I hope that, if I had been their contemporary, I
should have shared their outlook.'[29] The words set the theme, and
the tone indicated clearly whose side he was on.

The Troublemakers began when Taylor was invited to deliver the
Ford Lectures at Oxford University. The offer surprised him, he
recalled, because it meant he was being taken for a serious
historian. The Ford Lectures are among the most prestigious in
the English-speaking world, given over the years by the likes of
A. F. Prîbrâm, Sir Lewis Namier, and Sir Richard Pares. Actually,
when the invitation came in 1954, *The Struggle for Mastery in
Europe* was just out, and Taylor had every reason to suppose that
he was regarded as a serious historian. His 'surprise', like so
many other such responses, should be taken with a grain of salt.

The lectures gave Taylor an opportunity to read on the history
of English foreign policy dissent, a subject much to his liking.
Typically, he refused to take credit for the topic, insisting rather,
that he had no idea what he would lecture about. In his words:

I wandered out into the night, encountered Alan Bullock and
told him of my plight. He said: 'You have always opposed
official British foreign policy. Now tell us about the men who
opposed it in the past – Charles James Fox, Bright, the Union
of Democratic Control, right down to the Left before the

Second World War.' I was intoxicated with delight. Yet I should never have thought of the subject if Alan Bullock had not suggested it to me.[30]

He read – historic dissenting speeches as recorded in Hansard and *The Times*, while sitting in the Athenaeum – and in 1956, he delivered the lectures. He 'made things up as I went along', but it seemed to work, at least to the extent that he kept his audience enthralled, the sixth lecture being as well attended as the first. Later, he thought that part of his appeal was in using no script, only quotes typed on notecards, which apparently delighted audiences used to the dry-as-dust Ford Lectures of the past.[31] The following year, the lectures appeared in print as *The Trouble-makers: Dissent Over Foreign Policy, 1792–1939.*

Taylor set the stage early, noting that the only consistency in British foreign policy over time, was that far from being universally accepted, it had always generated disagreement and controversy. Some part of English opinion – educated opinion – had always repudiated every aspect of national policy. 'A foreign minister who waited until everyone agreed with him would have no foreign policy at all.'[32] The style was cheeky and defiant, characteristic of Taylor on radio and television as well as in the lecture hall. 'These lectures', he said, 'are a gesture of repentance for having written recently a substantial volume of what I may venture to call "respectable" diplomatic history', by which he meant *The Struggle for Mastery in Europe.* He then heaped praise upon troublemakers and dissenters as the authors of all progress. 'I don't intend to discuss why men were Dissenters', he explained. 'To my mind Dissent is too normal and sensible to demand explanation.'[33] He offered an explanation all the same. Dissent may have been normal and sensible, but it was also a historical force, representing as he described it a variation on the historical dialectic. British foreign policy a generation hence, would reflect what the dissenters were claiming presently. The policy then would be their policy, and they too would be beset by a new generation of dissenters. Taylor concluded that: 'To-day's idealism is the realism of the future.'

This did not mean that the historian of dissent had to agree or disagree with the result. The historian's task was to understand and explain this historical dialectic of dissent, not to resent, regret, or remake it. Taylor expressed annoyance at historians who claimed the power to decide whether historical actors had behaved rightly or wrongly, and claimed that he refused to read such books, which simply replaced history with fancy. 'The present enables us to understand the past, not the other way round', he wrote, which was the same idea with which he opened *The Italian Problem in European Diplomacy* two decades before. In that volume Taylor described the historian as a member of a living community whose perspective on the past would always be influenced accordingly.[34]

Whenever he wrote a monograph, Taylor usually included an observation on the historian's job of work. Why, is not entirely clear, but at least one possibility is indicated. On the one hand, Taylor claimed to be a conventional historian who simply described what had happened without offering praise or blame, and who argued that there are no profound lessons to be learned from studying the past. On the other hand, his historiography frequently was full of praise and blame. The lessons which his readers were advised to draw from his treatment of German history, for example, were obvious to the meanest intelligence. So, too, *The Troublemakers*. One is inclined to see in his repetition that it is the historian's duty to rise above regretting the verdict of history, an implicit apology for his own inability to do so consistently. As Taylor admitted early on in the Ford Lectures, he looked at the past from perspectives conditioned by the times in which he lived. He understood dissenters because he was one himself, and how could he apply any standards to them but those he applied to himself? It is a theory, at any rate.

Taylor's starting date was 1792, simply because 'I cannot leave out Charles James Fox.' In 1792, Fox denounced the idea of war as a moral crusade, proclaimed that the House of Commons should determine foreign policy, and became the first to hold the newly created post of Secretary of State for Foreign Affairs. Taylor decided to close with 1939 because he thought English dissent might have come to an end with the outbreak of war with Germany. This hypothesis was predicated on the argument that the dissenters in the parliament 'established the claim that – despite their previous hesitations and equivocations – the war against Hitler was their war'. They had won, so to speak, because they demanded, through Leo Amery, that opposition leader Arthur Greenwood 'Speak for England!'[35] But in demanding this, they also bypassed idealistic phrases and moral repudiations of official policy. Instead, they called for the government to remember 'the honour and interest of England'. Dissent had come full circle. It had, in a sense, ended.

Whether a valid judgement or not, the fact was that Taylor had to begin and end somewhere. He was, by practice and inclination a narrative historian, and given what fell between 1792 and 1939, those years provided as good a time-frame as any. He described, epigrammatically and often subjectively, English foreign policy dissent as it passed through stages dominated in turn by the radical tradition of Fox, the pro-Russian, anti-Russian, pro-Turk, anti-Turk manifestations of dissent at mid-century, radical anti-imperialist pacifism before 1914, and pro-German appeasers in the early and mid-1930s, many of whom became anti-appeasers after 1938. Along the way, Taylor made clear that foreign policy dissent was never dependent upon religious, ideological, or social lines, nor did dissenters conform to any particular model. Fox was a Whig scoundrel and profligate, William Cobbett a Tory populist and rustic, John Bright followed Quakerism and Free Trade, and David Urquhart was a Tory radical and pro-Turk. William Gladstone opposed the Turks and embodied Victorian Liberal and High Church principles, while J. T. Walton Newbold was a Quaker and the first Communist elected to parliament. E. D. Morel was an intellectual socialist and impractical visionary, while Keir Hardie was a miner, Member of Parliament, and socialist, known as 'the man in the cloth cap' because he was the first Member of Parliament to refuse to appear in the House of Commons in a topper. And so it went.

Dissent and dissenters may have been many different things, but they were always radical. They never were 'good party men who merely wanted an alternative government'. Of course, they did want an alternative government, but they wanted it to be based upon completely different principles, standards, and codes of moral conduct. Dissent, Taylor wrote, repudiated Establishment in favour of some ideal world, wherein war would vanish and peace reign forever. This was always a major line in Socialism before the First World War. 'Every Socialist believed at the bottom of his heart that capitalism produced all the evils in the world; therefore Socialism would end them. The Great War strengthened this belief.'[36]

Most dissenters wrote as well as spoke their dissent, whether they were in or out of parliament. Some examples: Henry

Brougham, *An Appeal to the Allies and the English Nation on Behalf of Poland*; William Gladstone, *Bulgarian Horrors*; G. B. Shaw, *Common Sense and the War*; Norman Angell, *The Great Illusion*; J. T. Walton Newbold, *How Europe Armed for War*; E. D. Morel, *How the War Began*; and Lowes Dickenson, *The International Anarchy*. These writings addressed such specific issues as war and rumours of war, the plight of oppressed peoples, the plight of those whose lives would be turned upside down if oppressed peoples were liberated (Taylor never claimed consistency for the dissenters), and imperialism. They also stressed basic patterns of thought and argument that repeated from generation to generation. Taylor explained that these patterns were the criteria for measuring dissent in each situation where it surfaced.

Foreign policy dissent was almost always anti-war, but rarely pacifist, Taylor noted. That is, dissenters opposed war as a general rule, but advocated it when the cause was just, as they believed it was in 1937–9. But more often than not, the dissenting position was in opposition to policies advocating, or leading to, war. He explained that between 1791 and 1914 Dissenters turned determined governments away from war in two or three instances. Anti-war dissent usually incorporated ideas about morality, democracy, or simply opposition to government policies that the dissenters regarded as idiotic. Thomas Paine argued that governments caused wars, and democracy would end them. (Taylor did not specify whether Paine wanted to end wars or government, but the implication was that he meant both.) Of course, in Tom Paine's day there were no genuine democracies, and that included the infant United States. Various radicals opposed war against Napoleon on the grounds that if the principle of interfering in the concerns of foreign governments is once acknowledged, then 'wars would be eternal'. David Urquhart opposed the Crimean War because such a war 'was bound to be a hoax'. Similarly, for the 'Pro-Boers' of 1899, 'the war became not so much wrong as unnecessary'. After the First World War, dissenters opposed armaments because armaments were not linked with a constructive policy. And so on.

Dissenters also were isolationists as often as not, a natural corollary to opposing war. Richard Cobden's favourite toast was 'no foreign politics', and late nineteenth-century radical imperialists dissented from mainstream policy because they were isolationists regarding Europe, preferring to concentrate on outside of Europe.[37] Similarly, other dissenters then and later advocated in happy contradiction both isolation and universal interference, 'wishing to stand aloof from all Continental entanglement and yet to defend liberty against all the world'. In 1936 dissenters backed the Spanish Republic against Franco. Some even went to fight against this manifestation of Fascism, and ever after refused to visit Spain far as long as Franco ruled.[38] Taylor could easily identify with this, at least if it was true that, as he claimed, he himself refused to visit Italy so long as the Fascists were in power there. Meanwhile, dissenters who fought for the Spanish Republic did so as individuals who concentrated on that single issue. They did not link resistance to Spanish Fascism to resistance to German revision of the Versailles Treaty.

By its nature, Taylor explained, dissent connected with public opinion and assumed its power to force government to alter policy. In 1832, dissenters who backed the Polish rebels assumed that the public opinion they stirred at home would become as irresistible internationally as it had been at home. Gladstone appealed with great success to public opinion over Bulgaria. Dissenters always assumed that they would win through, because the public opinion they helped to create would eventually force the government to revise its foreign policy. It might take longer than these impatient men of conviction wanted, Taylor wrote, but they never doubted that it would happen.[39] Actually, as he made clear at the outset, dissenters did not wish to change foreign policy so much as to abolish it, whatever it was. Urquhart preached that all diplomacy was wicked, John Bright that it was a waste of time and money for everyone except 'the territorial aristocracy', and still others characterised foreign policy as 'a conspiracy, conducted behind the backs of "the people"', the result of a compact between professional diplomatists and the governing class to keep democratic interference out of foreign affairs. Even J. A. Hobson, in Taylor's view, one of the most rational dissenters, succumbed to belief in 'the conspiracy' of international relations: 'Hobson . . . regarded all rich or powerful men as incorrigible and relied on the working classes to bring aggressive foreign policy – indeed all foreign policy – to an abrupt conclusion.'[40]

But having argued that the negative element predominated in dissent, that is, that dissent intended simply to be in opposition without having an alternative policy to offer, Taylor also showed a positive side in which dissenters proposed their own foreign policy, or at least foreign policy principles. Richard Cobden toasted the end of foreign policy, but then advocated a foreign policy based upon a free trade foundation: namely, 'as little intercourse as possible between Governments; as much connexion as possible between the nations of the world'. Similarly Gladstone, though as prime minister he had to formulate something more specific in practice, advocated 'right principles in foreign policy'. These included economy, peace, disentanglement, equal rights for all nations, and love of freedom. After 1906, Liberal dissenters advanced what amounted to a foreign policy by urging satisfaction of 'the legitimate aspirations of Germany', and after the First World War, Labour 'married' the Union of Democratic Control and embraced its foreign policy: friendship with Bolshevik Russia, overthrow of the Versailles Treaty system, the liberation of Germany, and the defeat of 'the French Jingoes'. On this basis, Labour contributed as a party of dissent to appeasement, in the 1920s and early 1930s.[41]

Dissenters usually advocated some moral position, and consequently profited from the tradition of moral passion that characterised British reformers through time, even if their particular perspective was rooted elsewhere. Gladstone, for example, created a stir over the Bulgarian massacres that was neither intellectual radical (Cobden), nor 'blustering John Bull Radicalism' (Cobbett and Urquhart), but rather the moral passion of abolitionists against slavery. Anti-slavery, Taylor explained, had been a cause associated with the Church, more than with dissent, over the years. Still, one could never separate one desire to do good from another, and Taylor described an occasion when two thousand people gathered in a tent to watch a magic-lantern show of *Uncle Tom's Cabin*, and when it was over, voted a resolution demanding aid for oppressed Bulgarians. Whether the film was shown in the first place with Bulgarians in mind, Taylor did not say. Meanwhile, he noted that dissenters often interconnected moral passion and reason, John Bright being almost in a class by himself in this regard owing to his Quaker convictions. Others included historians Freeman, Lecky, Kinglake, Bryce, Seely, Stubbs, Carlyle, and J. R. Green. These dissenters were 'secular missionaries' for progress, Taylor explained, which was seen as a moral good.[42]

But the moral line was subject to change, to limitation, or to being abandoned altogether. As Gladstone said on one occasion, probably in all seriousness Taylor suggested, one could always retreat from the moral position if it created difficulties. When the Pro-Boers agonised over southern Africa, their commitment to the moral position was tempered by concern over British interests. During the 1870s, every dissenter worthy of the name cried out for relief for some oppressed national minority, such as the Poles or Bulgarians; but in the course of the First World War, their heirs in the Union of Democratic Control (UDC) opposed national self-determination in the lands of the Habsburg empire. The argument was that the ultimate morality lay in opposing the war which the proposal to dismember Austria-Hungary, in the name of self-determination, might prolong. Creating national states in eastern Europe was wrong in principle in any case because, as one UDC member said: 'I believe there is no such people as Czecho-Slovak.' It would not be possible to reconcile the Germans to such artificial creations, since they would come at German expense. The best solution, the radicals said, was a form of Home Rule like that granted to Ireland. Taylor pointed out that it apparently had escaped their notice that the Irish were not content with Home Rule, and there was no reason why the Slavs of eastern Europe should be either.[43]

E. D. Morel and the UDC were Taylor's beau ideal of dissent, despite their imperfections. The UDC occupied one entire chapter of *The Troublemakers*. The movement was founded in September 1914, and had more impact upon public opinion and wartime foreign policy than any other group in Britain. Taylor claimed that the organisation was sufficiently influential to ensure that the 'verdict of war' would not last. E. D. Morel was the driving force. 'Morel has never had an equal as organizer and leader of a Dissenting movement', Taylor wrote. He saw 'sharply, clearly, dogmatically. Thanks to him, the Dissent of the war years did not wander complainingly in the void; though a minority, it spoke with a resolute voice.' Morel went to prison for his anti-war activities, by way of setting an example. Most UDC were working class – except for the intellectuals, of course, such as Lowes Dickenson, Bertrand Russell, and Norman Angell. UDC dissent was aimed mainly against secret diplomacy, 'or perhaps against any diplomacy at all'. If there had been less foreign policy, the Union argued, there would have been no war. It did not take long for the UDC to come down on the side of Germany as having been tricked into war by the diplomats, while Belgium, the ostensible touch point for Britain's entry into the war, was simply an innocent victim of rival imperialist powers. The UDC was among the first to advocate a League of Nations for the post-war period and to oppose self-determination for eastern European peoples which, they argued, would simply be the product of imperialist aggrandisement in any case. The post-war Labour Party agreed with them and formulated its foreign policy accordingly. In 1920, the Mayor of Stepney announced that the UDC had been right about the war and the governments which engineered it. Capitalist governments were not to be trusted with armaments, he said. The mayor was Clement Attlee, a future Labour prime minister.[44]

Few historians were better equipped by temperament than was Taylor to write the history of foreign policy dissent in Britain in the nineteenth and twentieth centuries. A dissenter himself, he both understood and appreciated the outlook and motivation of dissenters, saw the paradox and irony as well as the idealism inherent in their views and actions, and was as capable as they, of contributing outlandish points of view to the foreign policy debate, whether as a historian or as a commentator on current events. *The Troublemakers* contained numerous examples of dissenting extremes and contradictions, and Taylor's style in recounting them clearly indicated his appreciation for the characters with whom he was dealing. For one thing, First World War dissenters claimed that the diplomats were prisoners of the permanent officials at the foreign office, who were responsible for all the wicked policies that had led to war. A generation later, their successors charged Neville Chamberlain with ignoring his permanent officials, to the detriment of foreign policy. For another, Edward VII removed Keir Hardie's name from a royal garden party guest-list because Hardie, anti-Russian as were all good dissenters then, had protested against a royal visit to meet the tsar. Hardie had never attended a garden party and only knew he had been excluded when someone mentioned it to him. However, he took issue on the grounds that 'if I am fit to represent the working classes of Merthyr, I am fit to attend the garden party at Windsor'. After a time his name was restored to the list. Taylor summed up the event in words of evident satisfaction: 'This was, I think, the first occasion when the Labour

Party claimed its share in the Establishment from royal garden parties upwards.'

A particularly engaging example of dissenting paradox was Taylor's story of how G. B. Shaw treated the First World War. First, he made the argument that Grey's foreign policy enticed Germany into war in August.

[H]aving thus destroyed the moral case for the war, Shaw then defended it on strictly practical grounds as a struggle for survival: England must defeat Germany (or Germany defeat England), and, as Shaw lived in England, he proposed to support the English side of the equation.

Taylor regarded this as Shaw pricking moral pretensions, and an example of his 'teasing his fellow Dissenters'.[45] Both interpretations suggest clearly that Taylor both appreciated and enjoyed this Shavian twist.

Taylor offered some twists of his own in dealing with his subject. When describing Anglo-American relations at the end of the First World War, he noted that the dissenters thought the Americans were on their side, only to find that they were not taking sides at all. So far so good, until Taylor offered this explanation: 'Englishmen never realized that even the most friendly Americans, including Wilson and House, looked on all Europeans as aboriginal savages.' The Americans were like missionaries who would never commit themselves to one African tribe over another. 'One set of savages might be a bit better than another; but all needed saving by the superior enlightenment of the New World. The Dissenters did not grasp this. They even supposed that they were flattering Wilson by their approval.'[46] An interesting interpretation of American views of Europe, and possibly not entirely wrong. Even so, bizarre on the surface of it, but well matched to the extremes of hyperbole to which dissenters, including Taylor, frequently gave vent.

In considering Taylor as dissenter, certain questions come to mind. Though a Northerner, a self-taught – and genuine, so far as there is such a thing – radical and socialist, a populist, and an atheist with a Nonconformist background, he was also an Oxford don and became in the course of the 1950s a university lecturer, and a member of the British Academy and the Athenaeum Club, all recognition of his abilities and an indication of academic respectability. Was his assault on The Thing an atonement for 'selling out', for joining the Establishment as a don at conservative, medieval Oxford? 'Any socialist who goes into university education must face the fact that he will lead a life compounded of intellectual integrity and social treachery', Taylor wrote in 1963, and added: 'I suppose it is worth it.'[47] Did he really care about ending the Cold War and the nuclear arms race, and getting on with building international peace and co-operation? Taylor always had a penchant for being perverse, and that has been the rub. For example, in 1957 he wrote a piece on Manchester which praised northern radicalism and earthiness as qualities which worked a positive influence on his own life, but claimed later that the essay was 'a deliberate joke and in part a parody'. He said the same thing about his *English History, 1914–1945*, published in 1965, and dismissed *The Origins of the Second World War*, probably the most controversial historical monograph of the past half-century, as a book 'I wrote for relaxation when much taken up with College administration.'[48] Over the years, such perversity was difficult for his contemporaries to swallow, and it raised doubts regarding his seriousness of purpose, either as dissenter or historian. However, when the record is examined, there is no substantive reason to doubt the sincerity of Taylor's moral revulsion against nuclear weapons, of his desire for warmer East–West relations, or of his moral outrage over the Suez Canal invasion in 1956.

This conclusion applies also to *The Troublemakers*. Despite its limitations, including a tendency to be 'too clever by half' in tone and style, as various reviewers thought, the volume was an important contribution to Taylor's bibliography. It underscored his devotion to contrary-mindedness both in politics and historical interpretation, and revealed his life-long affection for unorthodoxy. It also revealed the depth of his commitment to dissent and indicated by its very nature his *apparent* (the word needs emphasis) indifference to rewards and honours that are the natural corollary to success in his profession. This is perhaps more significant than might at first seem, because those rewards and honours are often the criteria by which success is measured, and the lack of them is sometimes construed as indicating a failed career. It is possible that the Ford Lectures, or at least the manner of them, when combined with his dissenting activities at mid-decade and his popularity in the press and on television, cost Taylor appointment to the Regius Chair of Modern History at Oxford.

Consider that evidence. The Regius Chair is among the premier professorships at Oxford University. The recipient is appointed by the prime minister. Its holders are scholars and lecturers of first rank (theoretically, at least, though there have been marginal performers, at least in the latter regard, over the years) who devote their time and energies to leading out and encouraging historical studies. In 1957, Professor V. H. Galbraith stepped down and Taylor's name was among those put forward to succeed him; indeed, Taylor was convinced that Galbraith wanted him to succeed, 'or, to speak more accurately, to keep Hugh Trevor-Roper out'. Taylor went on to explain that all of this had come as a great surprise to him at the time. It was all Galbraith's machinations, he claimed, and as for himself, 'I should have refused the Regius chair if it had been offered me. Macmillan was then prime minister, and his hands were still red from the bloodshed of Suez.'[49] Taylor had busied himself protesting publicly against the Suez Canal invasion, and at the same time letting it be known that in his view, the Anglo-French action was far more wicked than Soviet intervention in Hungary the same year.

Galbraith, reflecting back more than a decade after the fact, recalled that he had more in mind than keeping Trevor-Roper out of the chair. While he respected Trevor-Roper as a lecturer, Galbraith was adamant, in his colourful Northern way, that no one beyond Taylor among Oxford's prominent lecturers was worth a 'tu'penny fuck'. In short, he wanted Taylor and only Taylor for the post, because he was a man to whom people would listen.[50] Apparently others felt the same. G. N. Clark, Austin Lane Poole, and Sir Charles Webster supported Taylor, while only J. C. Masterman recommended Hugh Trevor-Roper. The final decision came down to Sir Lewis Namier, Taylor's old friend and for whom he had co-edited a Festschrift, who was then the doyen of historians in Britain, a Tory, and connected with people in the government. After some dithering which included the abortive nomination of Lucy Sutherland, Namier told Taylor that only he was suitable for the chair, and would recommend him if he would give up television and journalism. Taylor refused, and Namier recommended Trevor-Roper instead. After that 'Namier was dead so far as I was concerned', and they never spoke again.[51] If this, Taylor's version of events, is reliable, then it would appear that Namier more than Suez, the CND, or other political activities, cost him the Regius Chair, and that while his anti-Establishment outlook may have put Namier off, Taylor's television and journalism put Namier off even more. Galbraith apparently liked the 'telly don' little better, but wanted Taylor as Regius Professor all the same.

Having been denied the chair and therefore the 'academic somnolence' he had warned against, Taylor became even more a populariser of history. A note of defiance pervaded his writing as the 1950s shaded into the 1960s. In an exchange with Stuart Hampshire in the *New Statesman* on the relative merits of public as opposed to commercial television, Taylor appeared as advocate for commercial television with such charges as: 'Why should viewers be denied programmes which they enjoyed, and be given only programmes which did them good'; and 'Commercial television was a rare success for democracy' until it was shot down by the programmers. They became a BBC-type monopoly, 'thanks to the idiotic safeguards which the high-minded managed to smuggle in'.[52] This sort of epigrammatic, champion of the ordinary man, response had come to be expected from Taylor over the years, but it seemed to expand in the years after *The Troublemakers*.

Was Taylor hurt by the Regius Chair episode? On more than one occasion he claimed not, even arguing that the chair was of so little moment to him that, prior to the events of 1957, he was scarcely aware it existed. However, he also wrote bitterly of Oxford University in the aftermath, and spoke of Namier with contempt. They 'hounded me out of university work', he lamented; then, upper-lip stiff, he dismissed the fact as being of no importance. 'Oxford's disregard was for me the order of release. In the years after 1956 I ceased to count in the academic world but I had more fun.'[53] Somehow, in retrospect this protestation has a hollow ring. Perhaps, after 1956, Taylor was only biding his time until the next explosion occurred over his work and place in the academic community. Until, that is to say, 1961 when he addressed himself in book form to the origins of the Second World War.

6

Storm Over War Origins

The Origins of the Second World War
(1961)

The Origins of the Second World War, published in 1961, was and remains Taylor's most controversial work, and small wonder. It addressed a historical consensus sometimes referred to as the 'Nuremberg thesis', because of its association with evidence presented before the Nuremberg tribunal just after the war. This thesis held that the most destructive war in history was desired, planned well in advance, and instituted by Adolf Hitler and his Nazi followers, and that the German people had been largely innocent victims of this evil regime. Not a bit of it, Taylor countered. In his version, Hitler was a traditional European statesman and no more responsible for the war than his counterparts, because: 'The war of 1939, far from being premeditated, was a mistake, the result on both sides of diplomatic blunders.'[1]

Critics spoke against the book in a blitz of protest that was often harsh and acrimonious. Regius Professor Hugh Trevor Roper led the charge, claiming that this 'casuistical defence of Hitler's foreign policy' did 'irreparable harm, to Mr Taylor's reputation as a serious historian'. Taylor was not prepared to take such abuse lying down, however, and replied that the professor's method of criticism would harm *his* reputation as a serious historian, 'if he had one'.[2] This sort of repartee was unusual, however. Mostly, Taylor let the critics have their say and ignored them. In time, when the hurricane had died down to merely a brisk breeze, he looked back with a measure of satisfaction – and some trepidation and regret, he once admitted – on the fact that because of him, no one could ever again look at the origins of the Second World War in quite the same way.

What inspired Taylor to take on the sacred cow of Nazi war-guilt? Several possibilities are indicated. For one, he was thinking about the subject matter of the book throughout the 1950s, his 'decade of dissent'. For another, he clearly regarded the Nuremberg thesis as inspired politically more than historically, and was supported by mainly subjective evidence. For still another, he was naturally inclined towards unorthodoxy, to being the 'traitor within the gates' come what might, and this inclination may well have been sharpened by his sense of having 'ceased to count' in the academic world after 1956.[3]

There is another possibility. Taylor's sensational conclusions (as some critics regarded them) might simply represent 'further thought and new evidence', which was what he claimed. The possibility does not preclude pique, dissent, or an inclination to unorthodoxy of course, but it does suggest that for all of the flaws that an army of critics identified in the book, Taylor meant *The Origins of the Second World War* as a piece of serious diplomatic history. If in the process of being serious and scholarly it took exception to the war-guilt consensus, that was neither surprising nor unusual, given Taylor's track record and the fact that sooner or later every generation re-examines its historical past.

The war-guilt consensus was established during the 1950s by some of the most impeccable names in historical scholarship. It became virtually an article of faith, a measure for good and evil, a moral responsibility to uphold.[4] By challenging it, Taylor took on scholarly giants of international stature and reputation. Maurice Baumont, the distinguished French historian, published two volumes on war origins for *Peuples et civilisations* in 1951, which concluded that the Second World War stemmed from Hitler's belief that his New Order was engaged in a struggle with traditional European civilisation, that Hitler wanted war with Poland, and pressed ahead, even after having determined that Britain and France would not stand aside, and that he knew therefore what he was risking and did not mind. Two years later, Alan Bullock (one of Taylor's personal friends at Oxford) published *Hitler: A Study in Tyranny*, which so completely indicted the Nazi leadership as evil that it inspired *The Twisted Cross*, a highly emotional film treatment of Nazi propaganda. Bullock presented a demonic Hitler whose personality was the principle factor shaping pre-war European politics, and whose early writings proved that he had aimed to destroy Europe all along. The book ended with reference to the destructiveness of Hitler's war, summed up in an observation from an ancient book on Julius Caesar: 'If you seek his monument, look around you.' In the film, this line was intoned by narrator Alexander Scourby while an airborne camera surveyed the bombed-out shell of Berlin.

In 1957 an American, Raymond J. Sontag, claimed that Hitler was always determined to crush Europe beneath the German boot, and that if he did not actually intend war in September 1939, he was prepared to threaten it to gain his ends, and to fight when the threat alone proved insufficient. Therefore, the war was his responsibility and his alone. German scholars also got in on the act, and early. Friedrich Meinecke beat even Maurice Baumont with his short but pointed volume, *The German Catastrophe*, published in 1950. Meinecke accused Hitler and the National Socialists of planning the war on their own, and therefore the German people could be excused from complicity. He was followed by Hermann Mau and Helmut Krausnick. They arrived at the general conclusion that Hitler was an awful monster, the conscienceless murderer of millions of helpless civilians, and an aggressor who knew full well that invading Poland in September 1939 risked a world war in which millions more would die.

Taylor never intended to 'excuse' Hitler; but he was determined *not* to excuse everyone except Hitler. He was convinced that historians who condemned Hitler and excused the 'good Germans' were politically, as much as historically, motivated. His own writing on modern Germany, such as *Bismarck: The Man and the Statesman*, published in 1955, the year that the Federal Republic of Germany joined NATO, amply demonstrated this conviction. Taylor charged repeatedly that there was a correlation between the expanding volume of war-guilt consensus among historians and political scientists, and western German economic recovery and the association of the western Germans with NATO defence strategies. Meanwhile, there was a strong moral prejudice attached to Hitler and his Nazi followers based upon the atrocities associated with the Holocaust. That was understandable, Taylor admitted. However, he argued, neither moral prejudice nor political expediency were an excuse for setting aside historical objectivity.

To be fair, Soviet historians were little different than their western counterparts. Taylor had seen the Soviet version of war origins appear first at the Wroclaw Congress in 1948 (see Chapter 2) and in Soviet publications associated with it. The year of demarcation was 1948, when the Cold War emerged full-blown to dominate European politics. Lines between East and West, still fuzzy in 1947 despite Winston Churchill's claims regarding the 'Iron Curtain', were suddenly crystallised by events which placed Eastern Europe firmly under Soviet control. In 1948, the Soviet Information Bureau published *Falsificators of History* which concluded that the West had systematically rejected all Soviet efforts to counter German aggression, thus making the West equally responsible with Hitler for the Second World War.

Western historians responded in kind. William L. Langer, Harvard historian and former intelligence officer, and his colleague, S. Everett Gleason, charged that throughout the 1939 crisis period, Soviet policy had been a shameless deception. Charles Callan Tansill suggested that western policy was mistakenly directed against Hitler and should rather have been aimed at encouraging Hitler and Stalin to knock each other off, leaving the West to profit from their demise. This isolationist viewpoint lent credence to certain of Taylor's interpretations regarding American pre-war foreign policy.

After 1948, whether the line was anti-Hitler and pro-German or anti-Hitler and pro-Soviet, the tendency on all sides was to rewrite the history of war origins in order to make the Germans acceptable Cold War partners – West Germany with NATO, and in the late 1950s, East Germany with the Warsaw Pact. That was why Taylor began rethinking the issue. As he did so, he began to see war-origins from the historiographical perspective that had been part of his outlook from the beginning of his career: namely, that among leaders of modern states, those who are human and make mistakes, far outnumber those who are merely barbarous villains intent on malice. This was the point when he noted that putting all the blame on Hitler as a nihilist who loved destruction for its own sake, was the easy way out. The reality was that far more than nihilism, human 'faults and failures', blunders and errors in judgement among statesmen and peoples, usually shaped history, and that was the case here.[5]

The interpretation Taylor advanced in *The Origins of the Second World War* evolved over time. *The Course of German History* (1946) presented Germans who, while not innocent by virtue of their national history, were not as wicked as were the Nazis. It also indicated that a war was more or less inevitable. At the same time, the book hinted at least that German responsibility for the war was less a matter of planning than of a system out of control. No compromise had ever been possible with Nazi Germany, Taylor wrote then, because the economic, political, and spiritual needs of Germany required endless expansion. Without the victories leading to expansion, both the National Socialist dictatorship and the German order would have collapsed. The distinction was that only a rational diplomacy, operating within a rational system, could establish German mastery without war; the Nazi system and its diplomacy were by this definition not rational.[6] This was not quite the Nuremberg thesis, but neither was it quite a rejection of it. He actually embraced the Nuremberg thesis in an article on the Munich Conference, published in 1948. 'We know that Hitler intended all along to destroy Czechoslovakia and that the Sudeten grievances were humbug', he wrote. Moreover, 'reason and negotiation were ineffectual against German power; the only answer was cannon, the *ultima ratio regis*'. In 1951, Taylor expressed much the same opinion when he claimed that Munich virtually ensured the Nazi-Soviet neutrality agreement of 1939, enabling Hitler later to take on Britain and France with hope of success. 'What happened in 1939 was an epilogue, the working out of a tragedy on predetermined lines', he concluded.[7]

However, in this case predetermined meant inevitable, not planned, an indication that Taylor was shifting direction. Clearly, he still held Germany responsible for the war. But it was not also clear that he recognised a specific plan formulated by Adolf Hitler leading to war. In fact, by 1951 Taylor was beginning to find that the foreign policy of the Third Reich frequently evolved out of unexpected developments. For example: '[T]he Spanish civil war took the Germans entirely by surprise, and it was a long time before they decided what use to make of it.'[8] By then Taylor had to be wondering what significance such 'surprises' might have for German foreign policy during the critical pre-war period.

Taylor reviewed several volumes of German foreign policy documents from before and during the Second World War that were published in the 1950s. They seemed to confirm his sus-

picion that German policy in 1938 and 1939 was far from systematic or premeditated. He wrote that the Germans clearly thought
that after Munich they had won mastery of Europe without a
struggle. Why, then, did they take steps which forced England
and France into war? The first volume of documents suggested
an answer:

> [O]n the one hand the disintegration of Central Europe was so
> great that Hitler could not resist the temptation to go farther.
> On the other British and French policy seemed to imply that he
> could advance eastward without serious protest from the
> Western Powers.

The point was sustained in the next volume. In Taylor's words:

> The reader of these documents will acquit the German diploma-
> tists of deliberately planning a large-scale war of aggression.
> Why should they? They were getting what they wanted
> without war; and there seemed no limit to what they could
> gain by this steady pressure. . . . They had the same aims as
> Hitler's, only more cautious.[9]

He also suggested that Hitler picked up the pace with the
occupation of Prague in March 1939, and the diplomats lost
control of foreign policy. Only then did the pace quicken towards
war. However, Taylor did not argue that Hitler picked up the
pace as part of a specific plan for war.

Two more volumes of German foreign policy documents
appeared in 1957. The first produced a wrinkle of sorts in
Taylor's thinking. 'In 1939 Hitler was relentlessly set on war with
Poland and ignored the diplomatic turmoil', he wrote unequivo-
cally. 'It seems inconceivable that this time any peaceful triumph
would have satisfied him.' The dictator would have gone to war
with or without his pact with Russia. 'It is indeed puzzling why
the Germans went through all the diplomatic palaver against
Poland when the date for the outbreak of war had already been
fixed.' This was the Nuremberg thesis, or at least part of it,
except that Taylor went on to argue that until August 25, when
Britain ratified a defensive alliance with Poland, Hitler continued
to believe that war would not be necessary.

Taylor was back on track after seeing the second volume. Those documents showed to his satisfaction that once Hitler got involved in war with Britain and France over Poland, 'he hadn't the slightest idea what he wanted to do', and that he took up the invasion of Russia in 1941 'merely for the sake of having something to do. Anything was better than planning the empire that he had acquired so unexpectedly.'[10]   This is Taylorian epigram, and should be read as such. What he was really getting at was the absence of evidence indicating a timetable for war, or a blueprint for a European empire to be acquired through military conquest. One might add that neither was there anything in Taylor's commentary to suggest the certain conviction he had acquired from reading the diplomacy of the whole period, that Hitler's one fixed objective was the eventual destruction of the Soviet Union.

That point came out in 1958 when Taylor wrote that Hitler's war with Poland 'was a mishap; the war against Soviet Russia was the real thing'. This was also the 'blunder' theme, to which Taylor added the factor of Hitlerian opportunism that was central to *The Origins of the Second World War*. 'It is tempting to suggest that he hoped to win by bluff over Poland as he had done over Czechoslovakia and tumbled into war by mistake', Taylor wrote. Not so: 'Hitler had indeed a vision of world conquest, but not a defined plan. The seizure of Austria earlier in the year had been improvised at the last moment.'[11] By now Taylor was nearly convinced that the historical record did not support the thesis that Germany under Hitler planned, predetermined, masterminded, or otherwise dictated events as they transpired, nor were his Nazi followers the supermen of manipulation, control, and organisation that historians and others had made them out to be.

In 1960, Taylor wrote an essay, 'Who Burnt the Reichstag?', which pointed straight to *The Origins of the Second World War*. The piece completely reversed the story of the Reichstag fire as Taylor had told it in *The Course of German History*, debunking Nazi 'genius' in no uncertain terms in the process. The Nazis had tried to discredit the Communists ever since Hitler was appointed chancellor, he noted. The fire of February 27, 1933, which they neither planned nor started, provided a new and perfect opportunity. It was 'a stroke of good fortune for the Nazis', Taylor wrote. 'Here was the Red scare ready-made'; not a plan nor a clever stratagem, but luck, an unexpected opportunity the Nazis were able to turn to advantage.[12] The evidence was contained in an article in the German magazine *Der Spiegel* by Fritz Tobias, a retired German civil servant.

The conventional story was that the Nazis started the fire themselves and blamed it on the Communists in order to justify outlawing this potent source of anti-Nazi opposition, and Taylor had agreed. The police arrested a Dutchman, Marinus van der Lubbe, who was the only person actually on the spot when the fire was discovered. The Nazi courts tried him and four Communists as his co-conspirators. Van der Lubbe was condemned and executed. The Communists were acquitted for lack of evidence – German judges then still maintained at least the appearance of due process, Taylor observed dryly. Nevertheless, the judges concluded that van der Lubbe must have had accomplices. Later, German Communists in exile, in a document called the Brown Book, presented evidence that the Nazis started the fire themselves, and blamed the Communists in order to discredit the Communist Party. In this scenario, van der Lubbe came off as a 'degenerate half-wit, and a homosexual prostitute, kept by the SA leader, Roehm'.

Tobias showed to Taylor's satisfaction that this story was wrong, that neither Communists nor Nazis were responsible for the Reichstag fire but that both had tried to exploit it to their own political advantage. First, the Nazis could find no evidence condemning the Communists; the Communists ignored everything in van der Lubbe's testimony that did not suit them, and twisted the rest until it did. Some examples: police evidence indicated that far from being a degenerate half-wit, van der Lubbe 'was unbalanced, but more than usually intelligent, with an exceptionally accurate sense of place and direction'; when Goebbels heard about the fire, he thought it was a practical joke being played by Putzi Hanftstaengel, 'an upper-class hanger-on of the Nazis'; then Hitler showed up to see what was happening, and was beside himself with frenzy, charging that it was a Communist plot, the signal for a coup, and that every Communist leader had to be caught and hanged. 'Maybe he already saw advantages', Taylor speculated. Or maybe not. '[T]hose standing by were all taken in. To them Hitler appeared as a man surprised, outraged, even fearful.'

Finally, the perpetrator himself. Taylor wrote:

Van der Lubbe was clear about his motive. He had hoped that the entire German people would protest against the Nazi government. When this did not happen, he determined that one individual at any rate should make his protest. Although the burning of the Reichstag was certainly a signal for revolt – a 'beacon' he called it – he had given the signal alone.[13]

In short, the Reichstag fire was the work of a single individual protesting against a wicked regime. This was vintage Taylor, a dissenting conclusion characterised by the same radical enthusiasm with which he had approached *The Troublemakers*. When van der Lubbe saw that the court was determined to link his action to the Communists he despaired, a condition confirmed by independent (as opposed to court-appointed) psychologists. 'He had meant to shake Nazi rule. Instead, he had consolidated their dictatorship and, as well, involved innocent men. For most of the time he remained broken and detached, his head sunk on his chest.' He came to life, as it were, on only one occasion. 'For six hours he tried to convince the judges that he had started the fires all alone. He spoke clearly, coherently, accurately. A Dutch observer – himself an experienced criminal judge – was persuaded that van der Lubbe was speaking the truth.'[14]

Taylor concluded that the Nazi claim that van der Lubbe worked with the Communists and the Communist claim that he was a Nazi stooge, were equally based on conjecture, hypothesis, and in the Communist case, forged evidence, and throughout on political expediency. 'If the Nazis had, indeed, set fire to the Reichstag, they would have manufactured evidence against the Communists.' However, when the Brown Book authors produced a 'repentant former Nazi Brown Shirt' to testify against the Nazis, he was 'muffled to the eyes. This was a wise precaution: he was in fact a well-known Communist, and unmistakably Jewish.' The only genuine Brown Shirt to back the Communist claim was Karl Ernst from Berlin, whose evidence conveniently turned up when he was already dead. 'Who Burnt the Reichstag?' emphasised that historical evidence must be sifted to find out what really happened, and when it had been sifted, the evidence would most likely show that 'events happen by chance; and men then mould them into a pattern'.[15] From this conclusion, to *The Origins of the Second World War*, was an easy step.

The Origins of the Second World War was written from published primary sources, all listed in the bibliography: *Documents on International Affairs, Documents on German Foreign Policy, 1918–1945, Documents and Materials relating to the Eve of the Second World War, Documents on British Foreign Policy, 1919–1939, i documenti diplomatici italiani, Papers Relating to the Foreign Relations of the United States,* and various private papers and memoirs. There was no question that Taylor was thoroughly prepared, certainly as well as most writers on war origins. However, the use he made of his preparation rubbed many of his contemporaries up the wrong way. It was no wonder, as he turned the whole question upside down.

The issue of war origins had generated little argument over the years, Taylor began, compared to the origins of the First World War. For that reason he termed it the 'forgotten problem'. Perhaps it was that unlike other great events in history, the Second World War 'had a simple and final explanation which was obvious to everyone at the time'. Or, perhaps the incentive to argue was lacking. After all, Germany ceased to be central to world affairs after 1945, replaced by the Soviet Union. Therefore, people wanted to know 'about the mistakes' made with Soviet Russia during the war, rather than those made with Germany before it began. 'Moreover', he added in typical Taylor language, 'as both the Western powers and Russia were proposing to enlist different sections of Germany as their ally, the less said about the war the better.' Of course, as a reason for ignoring the origins of the war of 1939, this was rubbish.

> [I]t seems unlikely that historians a hundred years hence will look at these events exactly as men did in 1939; and the present-day historian should seek to anticipate the judgements of the future rather than repeat those of the past.[16]

All the same, Taylor pointed out, it was very convenient to say that Hitler had planned the war. 'His will alone caused it', was a view which satisfied equally those who had opposed and those who had appeased Hitler. Appeasement would have been a good policy, the argument went, if only Hitler had not been so wicked. It was also convenient for the Germans to blame Hitler. At first they had 'tried to shift the guilt from themselves to the Allies, or

to make out that no one was guilty'. Then they discovered that
with Hitler safely dead, it was easier to make him guilty. The
Nuremberg tribunal had sanctioned all of this, Taylor charged, a
court in which evidence collected for lawyers' briefs had been
made into a historical explanation. Again, rubbish. 'This is not
how historians would proceed', he wrote. Nuremburg was a
political, not a historical judgement. In Taylor's startling – for the
time – explanation:

> The documents were chosen not only to demonstrate the war-
> guilt of the men on trial, but to conceal that of the prosecuting
> Powers. If any of the four Powers who set up the Nuremberg
> tribunal had been running the affair alone, it would have
> thrown the mud more widely.

In the circumstances

> the only possible course was to assume the sole guilt of
> Germany in advance. The verdict preceded the tribunal; and
> the documents were brought in to sustain a conclusion which
> had already been settled.[17]

There is never enough historical evidence for absolute judgement, Taylor continued, but he added that there was enough to
retell the story of the origins of the Second World War with
different, and more accurate, conclusions than those drawn at
Nuremberg. He cast himself in the role of an honest broker of
historical objectivity. In his words:

> I have . . . attempted to tell the story as it may appear to some
> future historian, working from the records. . . . Like my
> imaginary successor, I have often had to confess ignorance. I
> have also found that the record, considered in detachment,
> often pushed me towards interpretations different from those
> which men (including myself) gave at the time. This has not
> weighed with me one way or the other. I am concerned to
> understand what happened, not to vindicate or to condemn.

Having said that, he added: 'In retrospect, though many were
guilty, none was innocent. The purpose of political activity is to
provide peace and prosperity; and in this every statesman failed,

for whatever reason. This is a story without heroes, and perhaps even without villains.'[18] Given such premises as these, it also was a story likely to meet with the disapproval of Taylor's colleagues, or at any rate of a fair number of them.

Taylor went on to argue that the First World War caused the Second World War, 'in so far as one event causes another'. First, the Versailles Treaty of 1919, by which Germany admitted defeat and responsibility for the war, had to be enforced if it was to work. However, it was not enforced, owing to a tide of moral opposition from such westerners as the economist John Maynard Keynes, who resigned from the British delegation to the Paris Peace Conference in protest over reparations. Second, the Russians were excluded from Europe following the Bolshevik revolution, which removed the only continental power that could maintain a balance against a resurgent Germany, as a factor in diplomacy. Third, post-war territorial settlements, some contained within the Versailles Treaty and some merely the working out of the self-determination principle proclaimed by the Allies, reduced Germany and at the same time created new states in eastern Europe which could not be secure without assistance from one or more of the great powers. Fourth, the United States refused to sign the Versailles Treaty though President Woodrow Wilson was most responsible for shaping it, and withdrew into isolationism almost before the Peace Conference was over. Finally, Germany and the Germans resented the outcome of the war – reparations, arms limitations, and territorial arrangements – and were increasingly attracted to extremists opposed to the Treaty, of whom Adolf Hitler merely was the most successful.[19]

Taylor then dealt with the statesmen and others of the pre-war years, and the specifics of their diplomacy. Here his challenge to orthodoxy was most obvious and extreme, beginning with his characterisation of Hitler and his role in German foreign policy. In the first place, Hitler did not become chancellor by seizing power, however much the National Socialists liked to claim that he did. Nazi delegates, popularly elected, were a plurality in the Reichstag; therefore, President Hindenburg appointed Hitler chancellor 'in a strictly constitutional way and for solidly democratic reasons', because in the context of Weimar constitutional law he could no nothing else. In the second place, though Hitler subsequently 'destroyed political freedom and the rule of law', he also transformed the defeated Germany of 1918 into a great power. His foreign policy merely aimed at what virtually every German desired: a Germany free from the restriction of Versailles, a rebuilt military, and 'Germany the greatest power in Europe from her natural weight.' Still, this policy was not followed nor developed systematically, despite what historians later made of *Mein Kampf* and *Table Talk*. Hitler only day-dreamed about world conquest, Taylor wrote. So far as he planned on anything, it was on war against the Soviet Union at some unspecified time. 'Against all expectations, Hitler found himself at war with the Western Powers before he had conquered the East.' Taylor charged that historians created Hitler's systems for him out of the supposed influence of Friedrich Nietzsche on his thinking. But there was no such influence. When Taylor read Hitler's 'ramblings' – which he might have described resembling Wagnerian libretti rather more than Nietzschian philosophy – 'I hear in them only the generalizations of a powerful, but uninstructed, intellect.' Charlie Chaplin had understood Hitler better than any academic, Taylor claimed, referring to Chaplin's film *The Great Dictator*. The real Hitler was the day-dreamer 'transforming the world into a toy balloon and kicking it to the ceiling with the point of his toe'.[20]

No system, no master-plan, no diabolical blueprint of world conquest drawn up well in advance; the war that began on September 3, 1939 must have some explanation other than Hitler's inherent wickedness. It was a war, after all, and 'wars are much like road accidents. They have a general cause and particular causes all at the same time.' If there were no motor cars, there would be no road accidents, Taylor noted, developing the analogy which attracted so much critical attention later. 'But a motorist, charged with dangerous driving, would be ill-advised if he pleaded the existence of motor-cars as his sole defence.' The police look for something more immediate as causes for road accidents, Taylor went on, and so too should historians writing on war origins.

> 'International anarchy' makes war possible, it does not make war certain. . . . The second World war, too, had profound causes; but it also grew out of specific events.[21]

One such event was rearmament. Wars cannot happen without armaments. Taylor perceived that Hitler was reluctant to throw his weight around in international affairs until German rearmament was complete, and that would not be before 1943. He made demands before then only because 'he had strong nerves'. The British and French declined to stand up to him until they were properly rearmed. Hitler's generals argued against war in 1939 on the basis that German arms were not ready for it. 'Hitler did not deny their case; he rejected it as irrelevant. He was intending to succeed without war, or at any rate with a war so nominal as hardly to be distinguished from diplomacy.' Therefore, 'the state of German armaments in 1939 gives the decisive proof that Hitler was not contemplating a general war, and probably not intending war at all'.[22]

Another event was American neutrality legislation. After the First World War, in Taylor's words, 'American diplomacy was ceaselessly active in European questions.' But neutrality legislation in the 1930s forced the United States government to stand aside from these questions, other than to lend moral support. 'American isolationism completed the isolation of Europe', he wrote, meaning that western statesmen were eager for American material backing – an armed America in the Atlantic – but none was forthcoming, which left them on their own in dealing with the dictators. But Taylor got ahead of himself. His next paragraph connected American isolationism, as an influence on European policy, with western European views of the Soviet Union, and he indicated clearly that European isolation was complete only when the Soviet Union also stayed out of affairs. The point was that western Europe wanted America involved, but not also the Soviet Union, and the Americans did not want to be involved in Europe, whereas Soviet statesmen appeared 'eager to play a part. . . . They supported the League of Nations; preached collective security; and championed the cause of democracy in Spain.'

Therefore, when Taylor put it together, it was not American isolationism but American isolationism combined with Soviet exclusion that put western Europe at risk in dealing with Hitler during the critical 1936–9 period. European statesmen had only themselves to blame where both America and the Soviet Union were concerned, Taylor continued. 'For reasons that then seemed convincing, Western statesmen strove to keep them out.'[23] Western statesmen still imagined Europe was the centre of the world, that European destinies were to be resolved in a closed circle.

Still another event, or series of events, was the role every statesman played in contributing to the coming of war. It was too narrow, Taylor thought, and overlooked too many possibilities, to say that Adolf Hitler was *the* specific cause for war. Who gave the final push for war? 'Neville Chamberlain is an obvious candidate for this position. From the moment that he became prime minister in May 1937, he was determined to start something.' That was not to say that Chamberlain intended to have a war. Far from it. He intended to start something that would guarantee peace, a program for the 'pacification of Europe'. The program was appeasement, the purpose to concede German demands for revision of the Versailles Treaty, resulting in a pacified Europe. Chamberlain did not see the situation being that Great Britain and France could not stand up to Germany; rather he thought that Hitler would be grateful for Anglo-French good faith concessions. What is more, the prime minister also thought that these concessions could be taken back if the German chancellor did not respond with equal good faith. Chamberlain initiated the policies which led to anschluss and the dismemberment of Czechoslovakia, in part by sending Foreign Minister Halifax to Hitler in November 1937 to suggest that the Austrian, Sudeten, and Danzig issues might be resolved in Germany's favour.[24]

Austrian Chancellor Schussnigg also helped push Europe towards war. Taylor showed him forcing the Austrian issue with his threat to hold a plebiscite on whether Austria wanted to join Germany. The move took Hitler by surprise and infuriated him. Schussnigg had openly defied Hitler, and the world knew it. Hitler must act or be humiliated. Therefore, 'Schussnigg had lit the time-fuse of a considerable bomb.' But even after the *Wehrmacht* was on the move – unprepared by the suddenness of the decision to invade Austria, more than 70 per cent of its vehicles broke down along the line of march – Hitler did not know what he would do after he got to Vienna. It was on the balcony of Linz Town Hall, near where he was born, that he reached 'a sudden, unexpected decision: instead of setting up a tame government in Vienna, he would incorporate Austria in the *Reich*'. A month later a plebiscite – not the one Schussnigg had threatened, but one that was submitted to all of Great Germany – produced a 99 per cent approval of the Führer's action.[25]

Taylor concluded then that Chamberlain set the stage for conciliation of Hitler while Schussnigg triggered the invasion of

Austria, which lit the fuse of nationalism among Germans living in the Czech Sudetenland and Danzig. The result was to increase German pressure on eastern Europe until the statesmen of the western European powers could bear the strain no longer. The war of September 3, 1939 was the result.

To accuse any single statesman with responsibility for the war was not Taylor's intent. Rather, he suggested that no-one bore single responsibility because all were equally responsible. He treated Chamberlain, Schussnigg, various French leaders, and Hitler himself as individuals who were wrongheaded, opportunistic, lucky or unlucky in their policies, but not wilfully premeditating war. He did concede, however, that Hitler was prepared to have war if that was the only way to achieve mastery of Europe. Still, Austria surprised him in March 1938, and he was inclined to let Czechoslovakia disintegrate rather than use force, which, with Anglo-French help, it did. Over Poland, he simply miscalculated.

Taylor's explanation for the onset of the European war that began in September 1939 wilfully challenged a generation of historians who had placed the blame squarely on Hitler's premeditation. Rather, he charged, the war was the accidental result of last minute miscalculation on the part of all parties concerned. The only timetable for war to which Hitler ever tied himself was drawn up only a week before the war actually started, and even then it was altered before hostilities began. At issue was the final territorial readjustment that Germany demanded from the Versailles Treaty: Danzig and the Polish Corridor. The Poles were resolutely intransigent, and Hitler, believing finally that war was the only solution to the problem, set August 26 as the invasion date. At 3 p.m. on the 25th he gave the order that the attack actually would go forward. Then came news that Britain and Poland had signed a formal alliance, and he rescinded the order. 'I need time for negotiations', he said to Chief-of-Staff General Keitel, and rescheduled war for September 1. This, Taylor argued, was when he expected war in the first place, in so far as he was thinking that war would be necessary at all.

Preliminaries for negotiations involved Germany and Britain primarily, and they 'proceeded furiously' between August 26 and 29. The British hinted at offers, Hitler at demands, and neither was prepared to commit to actual negotiations. The Poles stood firm against concession. Taylor saw dishonesty on all sides in this jockeying for position. Hitler said there would be no war if he got Danzig. Taylor speculated that the chancellor might well have meant to isolate Poland with this offer, rather than to avoid war. Meanwhile, the British offered to arrange negotiations between Germany and Poland over Danzig, if Germany promised to refrain from violence. That, too, was dishonest because it was an offer inspired by the fact that 'there was no chance of extracting concessions from the Poles once the danger of war was removed'. The Origins of the Second World War is confusing here. This conclusion suggests that Taylor understood Britain to not actually want Poland to concede on Danzig and the Corridor. However, on the following page he noted that Hitler's demand for giving Danzig to Germany and holding a plebiscite in the Corridor, were 'the very terms which the British and French governments had themselves long favoured'.

Be that as it may, the issue came down to the Poles' willingness to negotiate – or rather unwillingness. Deadlock continued until August 29. Then Hitler broke it by relenting, if ever so slightly, because he had set September 1 for war, and 'there was not much time left before 1 September for him to pull off diplomatic success'. Clearly, Taylor thought that Hitler still preferred a diplomatic victory to military incursion. On August 29 he offered to negotiate directly with Poland, if Warsaw would send a plenipotentiary to Berlin by midnight on the 30th. The offer was made through Joseph Lipski, the Polish Ambassador in Berlin, who apparently did not bother to inform Warsaw that it had been made. The British finally transmitted the request themselves, but only in the early hours of August 31 after the deadline had passed. Later that day, Lord Halifax urged the Poles to send a plenipotentiary to Berlin. It was too late. Hitler 'was the prisoner of his own time-table. With his generals watching sceptically, he could not again call off the attack of Poland unless he had something solid to show; and this was still denied him by the Poles.' Lipski finally rang the German Foreign Office to indicate that he could negotiate, but not as plenipotentiary. 'This was enough for Hitler', Taylor wrote. 'The Poles, it seemed, were remaining obstinate; he could go forward to the gamble of isolating them in war. At 4 p.m. the orders for war were confirmed.' Hitler got the war which led to general war in Europe simply because he initiated 'on August 29 a diplomatic manoeuvre which he ought to have launched on 28 August'.[26]

That, Taylor concluded, was the immediate and diplomatic situation which touched off the war of 1939, which in time became the Second World War. It was hardly premeditated, it was hardly the result of evil machinations by Adolf Hitler. Taylor was confident in his demonstration that the war of 1939 'was a mistake, the result on both sides of diplomatic blunder'. Again and again during that last three years as various international crises occurred statesmen examined the situation and concluded that while the danger of war was real, war itself was not necessarily immediate. For example, in early 1939 the British 'talked themselves into a condition of extreme anxiety' which included anticipating a German attack on Holland and Switzerland, or even an assault on Britain from the air. Nevile Henderson in Berlin scorned such panic, observing: 'My definite impression is that Herr Hitler does not contemplate any adventures at the moment.'[27] Taylor clearly agreed with Henderson. Hitler's occupation of Prague in March 1939 was the step in foreign policy which pushed Europe to the brink of war, he argued, but it was a step taken 'without design; it brought him slight advantage. He acted only when events had already destroyed the settlement of Munich.'[28] It was only then that opinion changed, appeasement became anathema, that Chamberlain was impelled toward a policy of confrontation, and war became inevitable, if indeed it ever actually was so. In the end, Taylor concluded, the war of 1939 was the fault of everyone and of no one, an accident of history.

Why, then, had a generation of historians decided upon an interpretation of Hitler as master-planner and premeditator? The documents produced at Nuremberg, certainly, for they depicted a regime committed to policies of mind-boggling horror in domestic affairs. Taylor had no argument with describing Hitler's internal policy as diabolical and evil. But foreign policy was something else again, and after dismissing *Mein Kampf* and *Table Talk* as pipedreams, he found the source of foreign policy aspects of the Nuremberg thesis in the misreading of a single document: the Hossbach memorandum. It had been produced at Nuremberg as evidence that the evil Hitler of domestic policy was no less evil in foreign affairs.

As Taylor described it, the document was a record of statements Hitler made on 5 November 1937 while meeting with war minister Blomberg, foreign minister Neurath, army chief Fritsch, navy chief Raeder, and air force chief Goering. It was called the

Hossback memorandum after Colonel Friedrich Hossbach who made it. Hitler's remarks, as Taylor summarised them, came to this: a general comment on *Lebensraum*, though 'he did not specify where this was to be found'; a reference to solving Germany's problems with its two 'hate-inspired antagonists' Britain and France – that is, boundary questions left over from the Versailles Treaty – 'by means of force and this was never without attendant risk'; and discussion of three 'cases' in which force might be used. Case 1 was 1943–5. After that the situation could only worsen, so 1943 would be the decisive moment to act. Case 2 was civil war in France, in which instance 'the time for action against the Czechs had come'. Case 3 was war between France and Italy, which might occur in 1938, in which instance 'our objective must be to overthrow Czechoslovakia and Austria simultaneously'. None of these cases envisioned a general war. Also, none of them actually materialised. Therefore, 'they do not provide the blueprint for German policy. Nor did Hitler dwell on them. He went on to demonstrate that Germany would gain her aims without a great war; "force" apparently meant to him the threat of war, not necessarily war itself.' It was not a call to action, but rather 'a demonstration that a great war would not be necessary'. The only safe conclusion to be drawn from the Hossbach memorandum, Taylor argued, was that Hitler counted on getting lucky, as he had in the past, in both foreign affairs and domestic – in the latter case, van der Lubbe setting fire to the Reichstag, the unexpected 'miracle' that gave Hitler the Chancellery in 1933. 'There was here no concrete plan, no directive for German policy in 1937 and 1938. Or if there were a directive, it was to wait upon events.'[29]

No historian had examined why Hitler held this conference, Taylor pointed out. They were a curious collection that Hitler had summoned. Goering was the only Nazi present, the rest being old-style conservatives 'who had remained in office to keep Hitler under control'. Why would he reveal his innermost thoughts, his plan for conquest, as it was described at Nuremberg, to men whom he distrusted and whom he would soon sack? Taylor's answer was simple: Hitler 'did not reveal his inmost thoughts. There was no crisis in foreign policy to provoke a broad discussion or sweeping decisions. The conference was a manoeuvre in domestic affairs.' And that was? '. . . to get rid of Hjalmar Schacht, the finance minister, who was trying to dissuade Hitler from pressing forward with armaments'. Taylor quoted from the memorandum: 'The second part of the conference was concerned with questions of armament'; and, he added: 'This was why it had been called.'[30]

How had it worked? After Hitler left the meeting, others spoke their minds, demonstrating to Taylor's satisfaction that they, too, saw armaments as the purpose of the conference. Raeder complained 'that the German navy would be in no strength to face war for years ahead'. Blomberg and Goering took the admiral aside and explained that the sole object of the conference was to 'prod Fritsch into demanding a larger arms program'. Neurath made no recorded comment, but was supposed to have suffered several heart attacks during and after the meeting, which at the Nuremberg trials were taken to mean that he took Hitler's comments as proof of the chancellor's wicked intent. Taylor noted that four days after the conference, Fritsch wrote a memorandum for Hitler warning that the German army was not prepared for war with France. Hitler replied with assurances that Fritsch need not be concerned, and an admonition that he should get on with rearmament and leave political questions to others.

The manoeuvre succeeded:

> [H]enceforward Fritsch, Blomberg, and Raeder had no sympathy with Schacht's financial scruples. Otherwise, none of the men who attended the meeting on 5 November gave it another thought until Goering found the record produced against him at Nuremberg as evidence of his war guilt.

In short, Taylor saw the Hossbach memorandum as a kind of fraud which but for the Nuremberg trials would never have been taken to indicate anything substantive about the origins of the war, never have 'haunted the corridors of historical research'. All it told us, Taylor concluded, was what we knew already; that

> Hitler (like every other German statesman) intended Germany to become the dominant Power in Europe. It also tells us that he speculated how this might happen. His speculations were mistaken. They bear hardly any relation to the actual outbreak of war in 1939.[31]

In the months and years to come, Taylor neither apologised

for, nor altered his views on war origins, which he regarded as perfectly correct. From time to time he pointed this out in print, usually in defiant language. In December 1961, for example:

> Of course Hitler was bent, as other German statesmen had been, on making Germany again the dominant Power in Europe; and this undoubtedly made some war probable, if not inevitable, at some time. This is far different from saying that the war which started in September 1939 was inevitable, a war in which Great Britain found herself fighting Germany without any effective ally.[32]

For another, in 1963 on the anniversary of the Munich conference, he argued that existing diplomatic evidence was sufficient to challenge the traditional historical view of that event, but that historians – in this specific case Keith Eubank – continued to 'present the accepted version of Munich', even though that version could not be sustained from the record. Still defiant, he wrote also that 'my doubts of the accepted version cannot be removed by abusing me as an apologist for Hitler, nor even by dogmas about Hitler's wicked nature'.[33]

'Abusing' Taylor began almost at once. Rarely had a historical book, especially a diplomatic history, produced such a response as did *The Origins of the Second World War*, not even those which earlier had debated the origins of the First World War. Actually, until this book came along, there had been no real debate on the pre-1939 period, save for a few 'American revisionists' concerned mainly with the Pacific war, who, in Taylor's words, 'still regard their own government as more wicked than any other', and whose works 'are not impressive from a scholarly point of view'.[34] Now there was a debate, a storm even, at least for a time, and Taylor and his book were at the centre of it. Critics covered broad historiographic and scholarly grounds in their arguments, but the primary objection was moral: Hitler was morally responsible for the origins of the war which began in 1939, and Taylor was wrong to claim otherwise, despite his so-called documentary evidence.

This moral argument was inherent within the critics' response regardless of what they talked about specifically, thus demonstrating that they regarded the Nuremberg thesis as a genuine interpretive framework. The central thesis contained in the findings of the Nuremberg Tribunal, published in 1946, was clearly moral, concluding that the German attack on Poland was straightforward aggression: '[T]he events of the days immediately preceding the 1st September 1939, demonstrate the determination of Hitler and his associates to carry out their declared intention of invading Poland at all costs, despite appeals from every quarter.'[35] Since then, the history of the period had maintained that Adolf Hitler was, purely and simply, a demonstrably wicked man equally in domestic and foreign affairs.

The earliest review, unsigned but reputedly written by E. H. Carr, appeared in *The Times Literary Supplement* (*TLS*) and actually praised the book, albeit cautiously. Carr thought Taylor had raised the war origins issue in a detached and logical manner. The book left unanswered questions, of course, but it was 'the first time that we have been able to read an account of the inter-war period which is the work of a scholar studying history rather than the commentary of a contemporary reliving a part of his own experience'.[36] Within days Carr as well as Taylor were under attack by correspondents in the *TLS*. Said one letter, Taylor's 'methodical and impeccable logic', as Carr termed it, ignored contradictions within the narrative. True, said another, but that was nothing compared to the 'startling statements' which were 'likely to confuse undergraduates and other impressionable readers'.[37] The book was a 'truly Orwellesque' rewrite of history, said a third. A fourth correspondent spurned Taylor's interpretation of the Hossbach memorandum, calling it a document that made it 'perfectly clear that Hitler was talking about war'. And so it went. Of these correspondents, only Georges Bonnin liked the book, and could not understand what the fuss was about.[38]

Taylor sent a letter of his own, one of the rare occasions when he responded to criticism in print. It was nothing if not a gesture of defiance:

Sir, – I have no sympathy with authors who resent criticism or try to answer it. I must however thank your correspondents for the free publicity which they have given to my book.

A. J. P. Taylor
Magdalen College, Oxford

Perhaps the gratitude was earned. It is difficult to know how many additional copies were sold as a result of the controversy, but that the book sold well is clear. Paperback copies of the book were to be found more than a decade later, among other places, on book racks at supermarkets in provincial American cities.[39]

The TLS exchange was in June. In July, Regius Professor Hugh Trevor-Roper wrote a criticism of The Origins of the Second World War for Encounter, followed in September by Taylor's cheeky reply, which purported to instruct the Professor on how to quote and questioned his reputation as a serious historian. This reply was followed on the same page by Trevor-Roper's reply to the reply, which said that if this was the best Taylor could do, 'I am not moved.' No doubt it was all very profitable for Encounter, and perhaps for the two historians as well. Not long after the war had ended, Trevor-Roper, who served in British wartime intelligence and had access to inside information, published an excellent little book on the end of Hitler's career called The Last Days of Hitler which was made into a film of the same title, with Sir Alec Guiness as a rather Shakespearian Führer. Trevor-Roper then supported the Nuremberg thesis, and he had not changed by 1961.

The Regius Professor's assault on Taylor's repudiation of moral judgements began with an examination of his 'general philosophy', the 'accident theory' of historical causation. Trevor-Roper noted that 'the real determinants of history, according to Mr Taylor, are objective situations and human blunders'. Really, he asked? 'Do statesmen really never make history? Are they, all of them, always "too absorbed by events to follow a preconceived plan"?' Trevor-Roper presented Richelieu, Bismarck, and Lenin as obvious exceptions, and added that Hitler must be an exception as well. The German chancellor was more than a 'Mr Micawber sitting in Berlin or Berchtesgaden and waiting for something to turn up.' Rather he was, and considered himself to be, 'a thinker, a practical philosopher, the demiurge of a new age of history', and Mein Kampf was an obvious blueprint for his ultimate intentions. Even if it was written in the 1920s, this blueprint was based on ideological commitments that were bound to lead Germany into war sooner or later. Trevor-Roper also refused to dismiss the Hossbach memorandum and Table Talk, as Taylor insisted, as guidelines to Hitler's plans. These documents proved, he argued, that war origins sprang from actions specifically conceived with war in mind.[40]

It is not clear why Trevor-Roper should have emerged as the principal opponent to Taylor in this debate, unless it was his conservative opinions in contrast to Taylor's radical reputation. 'Whenever I see a radical, my first thought is to knock him down', Trevor-Roper is supposed to have remarked. Actually, it more likely was because Trevor-Roper was Regius Professor and Taylor was not, and there had been some question about that at the time of the election. In any event, they soon were on Independent Television carrying on where the *Encounter* debate had ended, or so ITV hoped. The performance was disappointing, especially on Taylor's part. According to one disgruntled witness, he 'fought a curiously listless battle. . . . Had he actually been a boxer, I should have suspected doping.' Hugh Thomas gave Taylor more credit, at least to the extent of concluding that the encounter 'solved nothing'. Years later Taylor claimed that he debated with the Regius Professor 'solely because I was paid to do so', and that there was no 'personal hostility' between himself and Trevor-Roper.[41] Perhaps he took the money under false pretences.

The debate indeed 'solved nothing', nor, for that matter, did the flood of critical reviews of the book which came after. They did, however, underscore the extent to which the underlying issue was moral, even when critics were arguing historiographical philosophy. F. H. Hinsley offered the most cogent challenge to Taylor's history as accident theory by drawing morality and historical process together. First, he noted that Taylor had admitted the existence of underlying historical factors, the stuff of historical determinism, but 'we never learn what they were'.[42] Then he argued that Taylor's insistence on interpreting war origins from a solely diplomatic perspective did not wash as presented. On the one hand, Taylor implied that the war was caused by a combination of 'acute international anarchy', meaning the normal condition of independent states exacerbated by uncertainties and tensions characteristic to the 1930s, and by an imbalance of power created in 1918 when Germany had been defeated in war by the other European powers. However, Hinsley argued, these essentially objective features of international relations between independent nation states did not cause the war, but only invited it, or at least contributed to the invitation.

Meanwhile, Taylor contradicted the supposed objectivity of this analysis by stressing as vital factors in war origins, Hitler's appetite for diplomatic success and the weak attempts of western statesmen to restrain him. These, Hinsley argued, were highly subjective factors.

On the other hand, Taylor had misunderstood, or at least misrepresented, 'general policy and precise planning' and 'cause and occasion'. Hinsley charged that a long-range policy is rarely planned minute-by-minute, and the apparent opportunism of Hitler's daily actions had little to do with whether or not his long-term ends were premeditated. From the evidence Taylor presented, nothing more could be proved than that German planning did not actually occasion the crises of the period, and so what? This did not alter the fundamental reality of Hitler's impact upon pre-war events, which Hinsley explained this way:

> Mr Taylor's version of the pre-war crises is devoid of all regard for the policy of a man who almost wholly caused them on one level because of his confusion of plan with policy and of occasion with cause. But it also takes this course because the antithesis he has drawn between the profound causes of war and the specific events that lead to war is a false antithesis. It cannot be too much emphasized that, while the profound causes lie in the given conditions that invite war, the causes on the other level are not simply events. They are the ways in which men handle events, react to the challenge which the given conditions put to them.[43]

Hinsley concluded that the relationship between given conditions and the statesman's policies, and those between profound causes for war and decisions that lead to war, are not constant and mechanical, as the accident theory implied. Rather, as he phrased it, 'a war is always an alternative to some other course and is always known to be so'.[44] In other words, individuals have *some* control over the way events develop, at least in the larger if not in the specific sense. Taylor's explanation of the causes of the Second World War simply had provided no viable alternative to Hitler having planned on war, and thereby bearing moral responsibility for it.

P. A. Reynolds looked for less philosophical and more practical evidence of Taylor's incorrectness. He identified Taylor's purpose – which he called the basic flaw in the book – as being to demonstrate 'that wars are caused more by the frailties than by the wickedness of men'. No plans, only crises along the path to war, each evolving in ways which neither Hitler or others could control, and finally a war was unleashed in 1939, the explanation for which 'is to be found in the state of his armaments'.[45] Rubbish, Reynolds retorted, going on to argue that in reaching his error-laden interpretation Taylor had misused, misstated, or omitted important documentary evidence on no less than fifty occasions. He then pointed out several 'facts' which these errors led Taylor to overlook. Firstly, Hitler's armaments proved adequate for two successive years of victories starting in 1939. Secondly, even if each pre-war crisis did not develop according to a specific plan, that did not negate the fact that such crises represented stages in a long-term policy that was realisable only through war. Thirdly, if Slav extermination and *Lebensraum* in the east were Hitler's only military objectives, then France and Britain still had to be neutralised in order to accomplish them, and that probably involved war. 'Whether Hitler was a reasonable man or not, the actions that he said he would perform, and that he did perform, were such as any sane man would expect inevitably to lead to war, protest as Taylor may (and as Hitler sometimes did) that this was not his intention.'[46] Reynolds concluded that Hitler was not pulled around willy-nilly by events, but rather was the initiator of crises that led to war, crises which he had contemplated at least, far in advance of their development.

The moral argument rested upon acceptance that Hitler planned, or at least caused, the world war. A. L. Rowse argued that Hitler's drive for world power was the primary cause of the war, and that Britain and France were to be censured for not opposing him with sufficient firmness – an unsurprising contention of a one-time anti-appeaser. G. F. Hudson asked rhetorically 'whether the picture of Hitler which he presents is one that should be accepted as historically true', and concluded that it was not, as any one would have to agree had they read *Mein Kampf*.[47] One could hardly ignore the parallels between *Mein Kampf* and Hitler's conference with his service chiefs in 1937, the subject matter of the Hossbach memorandum. Then, on May 23,

1939, Hitler had said, 'There will be war.' What, Hudson wished to know, could be clearer than that, 'especially as these were not words spoken in casual conversation, but as an address to the heads of the armed forces charged with the military preparations for the attack which, as a matter of history, actually took place on the date assigned for it?'[48]

History as accident simply would not do, because history as accident was amoral. It did not take into account the conscious will of historical actors, who, the critics argued, had the capacity to choose between right and wrong, and so far as Hitler was concerned, wilfully chose the latter. Taylor was in error when he ignored all source material except diplomatic documents (which included the papers, diaries, and memoirs of diplomats, be it noted), because what statesmen said to one another, or how diplomats behaved around the conference table, scarcely exhausted the list of factors contributing to war origins. Robert Spencer, for example, agreed that *The Origins of the Second World War* helped readers to recognise that some of Hitler's aims followed traditional policy lines. However, Taylor left out the significance of the Nazi totalitarian power structure, of the consolidation of that power with ideological aims, and of the co-ordination between economic mobilisation and external expansion. 'One does not, in short, get the impression that Taylor is dealing with foreign policy of a totalitarian dictatorship of the twentieth century.'[49]

T. W. Mason raised similar objections, pointing to the totalitarian state's 'demonic urge' as a factor that could not be overlooked, and using precisely the language which, in Taylor's view, clouded the issue. Mason objected to Taylor laying aside, as causal factors, German economic patterns under National Socialism, the Reich's concentration on rearmament as the prime object of the economy, and the drive towards autarky. War was uppermost in Nazi minds, he insisted: '[A] war for the plunder of manpower and material lay square in the dreadful logic of German economic development under National Socialist rule.'[50] To maintain the Nazi totalitarian hold, it was necessary to expand economic, political and, ultimately, military horizons; therefore, the interdependence of domestic and foreign affairs was logical and unmistakable, and it was unforgivable that Taylor should have ignored it.

Hugh Trevor-Roper also criticised Taylor for leaving out the emotional aspects of totalitarianism in the Third Reich. Emotion controlled by mass propaganda as only a totalitarian state could deploy it prepared the German nation for Hitler's war, he argued. By ignoring the Nuremberg rallies, the parades, and other examples of Nazi militancy, Taylor did a disservice to future generations even while he was misinterpreting his subject. On the one hand, his diplomatic history with its so-called detachment lessened the moral revulsion future generations ought to feel against the Nazi period on the one hand. On the other, employing what was best described as a distorted dichotomy the emotions generated by Nazi propaganda were 'an element of history no less important than the facts'.[51] Presumably to Taylor, Trevor-Roper concluded, a fact was a fact only when it was a diplomatic detail. Actually, this aspect of Trevor-Roper's critique of *The Origins of the Second World War* was unimpressive either for its logic or its clarity, and it is small wonder that Taylor subtitled his reply, 'Exercise for Beginners'.

Meanwhile, James Joll (who had read Taylor's book in manuscript apparently without comment) wrote that while some of Taylor's conclusions were borne out by documentary evidence, it remained that 'Hitler was in fact more wicked and unscrupulous than any other contemporary statesman. . . . It is misleading to write about Hitler as if he were just another ordinary German politician. If Hitler was a rational statesman, then Eichmann was a conscientious civil servant.' F. H. Hinsley agreed. Taylor was right to see that a Germany following the 'old free way' would 'overshadow Europe even if she did not plan to do so', he admitted. However, this did not mean that Hitler's long-term policy, however imprecisely it was planned, was anything less than an unpardonable craving for success. War did not come because of the Polish crisis or the blunders of western statesmen, but because Hitler would not modify his policy of exploiting Europe's imbalance for his own ends.[52]

Louis Morton also took a moral line, and added a strong presentist political component to it. 'What is the significance of this concern with responsibility for war', he asked. 'Is it purely an historical question, or does it reflect deeper forces and contemporary issues?'[53] His answer showed that the question was rhetorical; the point was 'deeper forces and contemporary issues', of course. Morton thought that because Taylor's thesis did not condemn Hitler's aggression in 1939, and in fact denied that it was an aggression, it actually defended war as an instrument of national interest. This was a case made for the use of force in support of national policy, and in making it, Taylor had merely reflected present realities.

Morton's charge was clear. Taylor had written a Cold War book, a charge which must have startled Taylor if he read the review, because Morton put him on the side of the West in the Cold War. So, too, Isaac Deutscher. He noted that where *The Course of German History* justified popular plans in 1944 and 1945 to dismember and de-industrialise Germany, *The Origins of the Second World War* in its turn seemed in 'striking harmony' with the view of those who presently favoured the western alliance with Germany.[54] Morton's perspective was this: survival in the hostile Cold War world was forcing historians – in this case Taylor – to re-examine the criteria by which they read their materials. The absolutes of right and wrong were giving way to moral relativism. Morton explained Taylor in this language:

> Germany is no longer the major power of Europe seeking to assert its natural weight in affairs. The Soviet Union has taken its place, and the Germans are now British allies. . . . If World War II was a diplomatic blunder for which the Western powers must bear a fair share of the blame as Taylor says, then perhaps Germany deserves the support of its former enemies. Certainly no one wishes to repeat the blunder of 1939 if, indeed, the war was the result of a blunder.[55]

Neither Morton nor Deutscher seemed aware that criticism of the very Cold War mentality with which they saddled him had been among Taylor's most consistent dissenting themes since 1945. Whenever critics linked their moral criticism of *The Origins of the Second World War* with current issues, it was inevitably prompted by one of these apprehensions: firstly, Taylor's interpretation appeared to accept outrageous behaviour on the grounds that no fundamental moral stance can be assumed in politics, which in the final analysis is relative to time and place; secondly, his presentation of Hitler as no more guilty than other statesmen surely would encourage neo-Nazi elements, particularly in West Germany; and thirdly, obscuring the aggressive designs of Nazi Germany during the period before 1939 served also to obscure similar designs presently attributed to the Soviet Union. The first apprehension led critics to argue that by not passing moral judgement on evil ideologies, historians simply encouraged them. By down-playing the enormity of Nazi crimes in favour of explaining war origins solely from the diplomatic records, Taylor played into the hands of peddlers of totalitarian ideas and Machiavellian political manipulation. Louis Morton was adamant that international action involving force is immoral when defended either in terms of national expedience or an ideology which denies human rights. S. William Halperin agreed, but in more blunt language. By ignoring the enormity of Nazi crimes, he wrote, Taylor had given 'comfort to neo-Nazis in Germany and to the forces of evil everywhere'.[56]

The second apprehension derived from the first. To critics who had lived through the experience of the war either as soldiers or civilians, there was no eradicating the memory of Nazi savagery. Likewise, there was no ignoring evidence of resurgent Nazism in the Germany of the later 1950s, even if it was on a small scale. Ernest Pisko quoted a reviewer in the *Frankfurter Allgemeine Zeitung* to the effect that Taylor's volume stood to become a primer for unrepentant Nazis. These were 'those all too numerous who have neither learned nor forgotten anything'. Trevor-Roper concurred, insisting that Taylor's defence of Nazi foreign policy would 'do harm by supporting neo-Nazi mythology'. It was no surprise, he added darkly, to find that the book was well received in radical right-wing circles. Meanwhile, Elizabeth Wiskemann pointed to the jubilant reception *The Origins of the Second World War* received in such neo-Nazi publications as *Reichsruf, Deutsche Soldatenzeitung,* and *Nation-Europa,* and observed that Sir Oswald Mosley's *Action* had 'expressed similar appreciation of Mr Taylor'.[57] The Germany of 1961, fully recovered from the ravages of war, was among the most prosperous nations in the world; but critics of Taylor's war origins, from James Joll to Wiskemann, seemed doubtful that the Germans had outgrown their traditional *Weltanschauung* or were fundamentally changed in any other respect, despite the reminders of their nightmare past.[58]

The third apprehension was quite specifically a product of the Cold War. Indeed, a commentator in *The Economist* observed that the Cold War more than any other single factor shaped the mind of Taylor's critics. Many critics drew analogies between Nazi Germany and the Soviet Union, some urging that *The Origins of the Second World War* was an argument for repeating the mistakes of appeasement in 1938 in a wrong-headed attempt to prevent war with the Soviet Union in the nuclear age. Hugh Trevor-Roper for one, parodied Taylor's Hitler in describing the then Soviet Premier Khrushchev as 'a traditional Russian statesman of limited aims, and "the moral line" consists of letting him have his way more completely than we let Hitler have his.' Louis Morton agreed, extending his view that *The Origins of the Second World War* justified a German war in the national interest by wondering if that logic did not also apply to the foreign policy of the Soviet Union:

> If Hitler had no blue print for conquest . . . how much weight should we attach to Khrushchev's claim that he will bury capitalism? If Hitler was only acting under the pressure of events to secure for Germany only what was right and just, may not Khrushchev be taken as merely a Russian version of the German model?

Not quite the way Taylor would have put it, though he might have admitted that the judgement was not completely off. Years later he wrote: 'If my book had a moral for later it was to preach co-operation between Russia and the West.'[59]

The critics of *The Origins of the Second World War* covered the gamut of censure: Taylor had misused the evidence, refused to make moral judgement, encouraged neo-Nazis, played in with the Cold War – on both sides, apparently – and advanced a historical philosophy which was narrow, shallow, and unresponsive to the requirements for explicating equally, past, present, and future. What was the fuss about, as Georges Bonnin had wondered? Simply the subject matter. A small army of historians and others were not prepared in 1961 to see the Nuremberg thesis challenged, however much many of them might deny that there was such a thing. They were unwilling to accept that Hitler did not plan as well as start the war of 1939, nor that the democracies shared responsibility with Germany for the war, nor again that history merely is a series of road accidents, nor, above all, that 'in principle and doctrine, Hitler was no more wicked and unscrupulous than any other contemporary statesman'. That Taylor had added: 'In wicked acts he outdid them all', seemed to them irrelevant.[60]

Taylor was bothered that historians and other commentators who might have questioned moral judgements on, say, the Anglo-German naval race before 1914, did not hesitate to condemn Hitler in moral terms. It was difficult not to make such judgements, however. Hitler was associated with the Holocaust, and that was a crime impossible for civilised human beings to forgive. Taylor did not suggest that they should. His book was about the diplomacy of the inter-war period, not the Holocaust, and because it was about pre-war diplomacy he rejected the moral premise that his critics urged upon him. Almost a decade after the event, he explained it this way:

> Most of what the critics said seemed irrelevant to me. I don't deal in moral judgements. From whose standpoint can they be made – English, American, Soviet, Nazi? Or do historians pretend that they speak an eternal truth? Hitler was out to make Germany a dominant Power. This was wicked from the point of view of others, but hardly wicked for the Germans. I am still not convinced that he would have marched on to European conquest until he been in part provoked into it. If you say of someone: 'he is mad' and treat him as such, he becomes mad in time. Of course maybe he was mad all along. But his later behaviour does not prove the correctness of the earlier analysis. For instance the gas chambers do not prove that Hitler would have instituted these if there had been no war.[61]

All the same, they were instituted, whether by Hitler directly or by his subordinates acting in his name. The fact was unforgivable to Trevor-Roper, Rowse, Hudson, Spencer, Mason, Joll, Hinsley, Morton and many others. Whether they were objecting to the emphasis on diplomacy, the 'road accident' philosophy of history, or something else, they took a perspective on war origins that was fundamentally moral. Each presented specific reasons for concluding that Hitler was responsible for the Second World War, and each made an implicit argument for viewing war origins in moral as well as practical terms. Rowse ended with the observation that in Taylor's strictly diplomatic interpretation of war origins, 'the heart, soul and matter are left out'.[62] Mason agreed, saying that the 'moral detachment' of Taylor's diplomatic history – a history which by denying the impact of ideology on

foreign policy created a nineteenth-century context for a twentieth-century problem – 'destroys much of the point of studying
history at all'.[63] So, too, Alfred Cobban, who wrote: 'Not for
nothing is Mr Taylor the pupil of the late Sir Lewis Namier, in
whom brilliance of style, mastery of detail (in his case perhaps
more exact detail), and contempt for ideas reached their acme.'[64]

The idea that he was anti-intellectual as well as amoral must
have surprised Taylor, and even annoyed him – he admitted
reacting to Cobban, though only privately and on the matter of
Namier being his mentor. 'I made him withdraw', Taylor recalled
later.[65] Otherwise, he once said as a criticism of Namier's history:
'Thinking myself, I assume others think as well.' But in writing
history, at least diplomatic history, the point was to describe how
statesmen behaved in formulating and implementing policy, not
to insist that in performing their tasks they need to have reflected some ideological or philosophical system. For this reason,
he had looked only at the diplomatic record of the 1930s in order
to discover how Hitler and other European statesman had interacted, and how events had unfolded on the way to the war
which began in 1939. That search led him to characterise Hitler
as having been no more immoral regarding the diplomatic
origins of the war than were his counterparts. Had Taylor chosen
to answer his critics in depth, he might have offered the following arguments, their essentials drawn from the pages of *The
Origins of the Second World War*.

Firstly, the motivations behind international relations in the
1930s were similar on all sides. Secondly, Hitler's actions were
inspired largely by Germany's actual political weight and geographical position, neither of which he had created nor
controlled. Thirdly, these actions were taken in response to the
actions of other European statesmen, and were meant to answer
the aspirations of an independent people. What is moral and
what immoral on this point, Taylor asked? 'If Western morality
seemed superior, this was largely because it was the morality of
the status quo; Hitler's was the immorality of revision.'[66] A fine
line, certainly, and in any case, Taylor had long been convinced
that morality was determined as much by the prevailing climate
of opinion as by any consistent or eternal principles of right and
wrong. (This was a curiously existential perspective for a man
who resembled an existentialist in few other particulars.)
Fourthly, the war in 1939 resulted from general misunderstand-

ings over Poland and Danzig, areas to which Germany had claims recognised even in the west. Fifthly, some responsibility for the war lay with Polish Foreign Minister Joseph Beck for resisting those claims, and with England and France for supporting him – weakly, and not always honestly, in Taylor's judgement. He wrote dramatically at one point of flicks of cigarette ash punctuating the doom of nations, as Beck and the western emissaries discussed the eventuality of war. If there was guilt to consider, it was shared.[67]

But perhaps it did not matter what the critics thought then, because over time Taylor's approach to assessing war origins was reflected – though not merely parroted – in writings by such as Alan Bullock and Sidney Aster, among others. Taylor's counter to the Nuremberg thesis came to be, in his words, 'received and old-fashioned orthodoxy'. *The Origins of the Second World War*, he wrote in his memoirs, 'despite its defects, has now become the new orthodoxy, much to my alarm. Every historian cashes in on my views perhaps without knowing that he is doing so.' Alan Bullock, for example: in 1953 his *Hitler: A Study in Tyranny* argued from the first page that Hitler was responsible for planning and executing the Second World War. Fourteen years later in the Raleigh Lecture to the British Academy, Bullock at least partially aligned himself with Taylor. 'Hitler and the nation which followed him still bear, not the sole, but the primary responsibility for the war which began in 1939', Bullock said, and went on to acknowledge that Taylor had rightly demolished the extreme elements of the Nuremberg thesis, agreeing that Hitler knew where he wanted to go but not how he intended to get there. 'Consistency of aim on Hitler's part has been confused with a time-table, blueprint, or plan of action fixed in advance, as if it were pinned up on the wall of the General Staff offices and ticked off as one item succeeded another. Nothing of the sort.'[68]

This was as close to an affirmation of his views as Taylor could have asked for, and perhaps it verified his theory that even if he had 'ceased to count' in the academic world, he was having more fun.

7

'Land of Hope and Glory'

English History, 1914–1945 (1965)

In 1965, Taylor published his first and only comprehensive study of a major period of English history. With *English History, 1914–1945* he embraced the history of his own time and place – came home, so to speak. *The Origins of the Second World War* would be his last offering in the field that made his scholarly reputation, and to which he had contributed as much as any modern historian. Some thought it had been a remarkable contribution. Douglas Cameron Watt, writing in 1977, described Taylor's work as diplomatic history written with extraordinary skill, and focused on the key elements of the subject, 'the role of individuals in history, the influence of personality, the role of deceit and misrepresentation, the "accidental", and the "unpredictable"'.[1] After 1961, Taylor turned his attention primarily to English political and, so far as he could master it, social and even cultural history – written, of course, in narrative form and style.

Watt regretted that Taylor 'abandoned' what he did best. That he would, Watt thought, was inevitable. In the first place, narrative diplomatic history lost some of its appeal in academic circles in the 1960s, at least in those which Watt described unsympathetically as the 'ambitious, the parochial, the monoglottal, and the trendy'. These were historians who repudiated diplomatic history with its emphasis on elites and governments in favour of social, intellectual, women's, and ethnic histories, including 'even Cliometrics'.[2] Taylor often declared that he did not know how to write history flavoured with 'behavioural sauce', and that in any case he did not want to. For him, history that did not tell a story was not history, but political or social science.

In the second place, Watt continued, Taylor had written the

204

history of European foreign policy from 1848 to 1945, at which point Europe was superseded by the United States and the Soviet Union. What was once European mastery of the world had become, in Taylor's own words, merely the 'European question'. There was simply nothing further to say about European diplomatic history. On the other hand, there was a great deal to say about the course of English history, particularly in the twentieth century when, as Taylor saw it, the common people began to have a history separate from that of the ruling classes. He was, after all, an English radical and by tradition and conviction an advocate of putting the people first: of opposing imperialism, of favouring national independence for England and others, of practising live and let live in foreign affairs, and of the people having a say in affairs, be they foreign or domestic. A national history of his own place and time characterised by populist and Little England perspectives, was a natural next step.[3]

Watt's explanation made perfect sense as far as it went, but it did not go far enough. After *The Troublemakers* in 1957, Taylor wrote more and more on English subjects as both historian and journalist, and emerged as a 'television star', to use his own phrase. This image did harm to his reputation as a historical scholar, in particular as a diplomatic historian. Certain events in those years in connection with his place at Oxford University made this clear. He was passed over for several university chairs, including Regius Professor of Modern History, and in 1963 even lost the University Lecturership in International History he had held for a decade. By definition, the appointment was limited to ten years; but Taylor claimed that exceptions had been made for others, and he assumed that in light of his contribution to written history, exception would be made for him as well. 'I was after all the most distinguished historian of contemporary times in the university', he pointed out in language which though immodest contained an element of truth.[4]

Exception was not made, however, and the lecturership was no longer Taylor's. Soon after he wrote a scathing denunciation of Oxbridge elitism in which he argued that no true socialist, no enemy of Britain's class system that is to say, ever could (perhaps *should* is a better word) be comfortable in the prevailing climate at either Oxford or Cambridge, and that dons who were comfortable had sold out, himself among them, sorry to say.[5] The timing was hardly coincidental. Clearly, Taylor saw himself forced out of Oxford diplomatic history without justification. In his piquish language:

> As the ten-year term drew to an end I assumed that the [History] Board . . . would do something for me. . . . I had given the Ford lectures; I would have been Regius professor if politics had not intervened; I had an unrivalled run of historical works which were acclaimed all over the world; I was the only practising historian widely known on television, though perhaps this was not a recommendation in the eyes of the History Board. . . . As it was the Board did nothing, nothing at all, and was evidently delighted to push me back into the pool of ordinary College tutors.

He claimed that a 'revolt' followed in which the other Magdalen Fellows insisted he be made a Fellow of Special Election. That alone prevented him from leaving the university altogether.[6]

Taylor regarded *English History, 1914–1945* as a form of salvation. It fell to him by chance when G. N. Clark, editor of the multi-volume *Oxford History of England*, unexpectedly invited him to contribute a volume on the twentieth century. As Taylor described it, he and Clark were walking one afternoon when Clark remarked that a historian had not been found to write the twentieth-century volume for the series. 'What about me?' Taylor asked. 'Would you?' was the reply. 'That would be marvellous'. There was 'my future determined', Taylor wrote, 'yet it would never have happened if G. N. Clark and I had not gone for a walk in Wytham Woods that autumn afternoon'. In the preface to *English History*, he thanked Clark for having 'sustained me when I was slighted in my profession', an obvious shot at the Oxford History Board.[7]

However, when all is said and done, Max Aitken, Lord Beaverbrook may have been more responsible for Taylor 'coming home' than any other single factor. Beaverbrook, confidant of political giants from Lloyd George to Churchill, was proprietor of the *Daily Express*, which he made 'the most classless of British Newspapers'.[8] His other papers included the *Sunday Express* and the *Evening Standard*. Beaverbrook was a Tory, but also an independent-minded populist patriot and Little England isolationist. He was critical of the United States in foreign policy, and thought the solution to European security lay in accepting the Soviet Union as a part of Europe. These were Taylor's views also, and the only substantial disagreement they had was over the empire and socialism, a disagreement which proved no barrier to their friendship. Beaverbrook occupied a central place in Taylor's life for nearly a decade, and he wrote of Beaverbrook in nearly reverent tones, describing him variously as an irrepressible character who viewed the world with a twinkle in his eye, a great historian, and a great man. 'I loved him more than any human being I have ever met', Taylor claimed.[9]

As Taylor recalled it, he met Beaverbrook in November 1956. Beaverbrook had read his review of *Men and Power*, the press lord's semi-autobiographical study of politics in the era of the Great War, and was sufficiently impressed to invite him to lunch. The same year Taylor became a columnist in the *Sunday Express*, writing radical pieces, though not socialist ones or pieces against the empire. He was quick to deny that his contract was in any way Beaverbrook's patronage: 'That was a myth like the one that I was Namier's pupil.' This is probably correct, for the contract, drawn up by John Junor, was surely inspired by the fact that Taylor already was widely known as a historian, book reviewer, and broadcaster. In any case, it was signed before he met Beaverbrook.[10] All the same, Taylor has left the impression that the press lord became his mentor, the only man to whom he ever deferred, but one who never directed nor ordered his writing in the *Sunday Express*. Apparently Beaverbrook was not above complaining if he did not like what Taylor had written, however. Taylor acknowledged that Beaverbrook made writing English history sound like fun, encouraged his growing inclination to focus on twentieth-century English political subjects, and provided an untiring sounding-board for his historical as well as political ideas. Who better than Beaverbrook to encourage the populist and Little England proclivities towards which Taylor seemed more and more inclined even as a historian, than Beaverbrook? He had been a populist and isolationist advocate in English politics for more than three decades, and was a competent historian – Taylor's judgement – in his own right.

After 1956, Taylor entered what might be termed his 'Beaverbrook period', when he wrote regularly on English subjects in the *Sunday Express* and other journals, in language that was feisty, humorous, cutting, plaintive, thunderous, argumentative, opinionated, and never dull. The principal theme in this writing was populism with a Little England corollary in which Taylor argued that the interests of the people were best served by England maintaining its independence while not interfering in the affairs of other peoples.

The populist Taylor was for the people and against 'our rulers' on virtually every issue. The examples were endless, and what follows is a mere sprinkling of the whole, written in a style aggressively polemical and meant to stir the emotions. In short, perfect for a populist press – or for equally populist broadcast talks, from which some of the following are drawn. Taylor championed pay-as-you-view television because with 'our spiritual and cultural guides' in charge – which is to say BBC programme controllers – 'the consumer and the producer count for nothing. . . . Ordinary people do not get a look in – or a look out so far as television is concerned.' Similarly, he railed against subsidies for the Covent Garden opera house, which were paid by 'you and me, the taxpayers of the country', for the benefit of a relative handful of 'culture snobs'. Culture simply had become 'a system of out-relief for those who think themselves superior to other people'.[11] Meanwhile, he attacked political polling because it helped shape, rather than merely assess, political opinion. 'An elementary rule of social behaviour is that most people do what other people are doing', Taylor wrote.

> A Government which is told by the polls that it is unpopular loses confidence unnecessarily. Even worse, an Opposition which is told that it is going to win becomes self-confident instead of trying to have a policy.

In each case, the people were the losers. Should polls be banned, he asked on the eve of the general election of 1964? 'YES, YES, YES', was his answer.[12]

Taylor was inspired to language both populist and patriotic in 1964, when an aged and infirm Winston Churchill stepped down from his seat in the House of Commons. He urged parliament to create a special and permanent place in the House for the man who 'was the saviour of his country from the greatest peril which it has ever known'. How could parliament do otherwise? 'In 1940 we stood alone. Sir Winston Churchill raised us up. . . . He saved us all. He embodied the British people. They loved him in 1940. They love him now.' Then again: 'We bless his name on his 90th birthday and on every day when we draw breath as free men.' After Churchill's death in 1968: 'In the Second World War, Beaverbrook and the British people were stuck with Churchill. There could be many worse fates'.[13]

When dealing with the General Strike and the Great Depression, Taylor praised the courage and generosity of those ordinary people who in 1914 had fought to free Belgium and then had gone on strike in 1926 to aid the coal miners. 'I cannot think of any other acts of generosity in history so great as these two acts of the millions of volunteers for Belgium in 1914, and the millions of men who went on strike not to gain anything for themselves but for the sake of the miners in 1926', he wrote. Many of the same volunteers were then victimised by the 'incompetence of governments and of Employers generally' after 1929, which only showed how little workers mattered when placed against the interests of those in positions of power.[14] Similar language and purpose characterised his anti-establishment and anti-traditionalist defence of Princess Anne's right to be in the line of succession and attacks on the House of Lords. Taylor argued for Princess Anne by claiming that women are better equipped to occupy the throne than men, and that 'any man who thinks women an inferior race should try taking on Joan Littlewood or Dame Rebecca West'. As for the Lords, the institution should be scrapped '[F]or anyone who believes in democracy the old rule is unanswerable. "If the Lords agree with the Commons, they are superfluous. If they disagree they are undesirable".'[15] Meanwhile, new universities aroused his ire as they copied the worst of Oxford and Cambridge elitism, while claiming to help England build a progressive democratic society. Taylor charged that they were actually building a new, stagnant aristocracy.[16]

Public figures of all kinds were regular subjects – and targets – for populist commentary. Of the Burgess, MacLean, and Philby scandal, for example, Taylor wrote: 'All our statesmen have this guiding rule: "Not before the children". We are the children. We are not allowed to know when statesmen blunder.' But they would not get away with it. The 'clamour of democracy' would go on causing troubles and scandals until ministers 'realize that their first obligation is to the people of Britain, not to a few selected members of a few public schools'. Taylor gave similar short shrift to barristers, rock and film stars who received tax perks, and political leaders who defied the preference of local constituencies when selecting candidates to stand for election. The former case was easy; the latter put Taylor in the position of defending a group of racist skinheads in Surbiton who objected to their MP 'taking an open line on immigration'. Taylor thought the issue was not race, and assured his readers that he opposed 'all forms of racialism'. Rather, freedom of choice and speech were at issue, and he felt compelled to credit that 'the skinheads of Surbiton have struck a fine blow for freedom in asserting their own freedom of choice'. He concluded with a historical flourish reminiscent of the protestant martyrs in the reign of Mary Tudor: 'I hope that the fire which they have lit will not soon be put out.'[17] One might wish he could have found a less unsettling modern part for this analogy.

Then there was Ernest Bevin, Labour foreign minister in 1945, whom Taylor did not much like. 'There was something lacking in a Labour leader who knew a little of industry and nothing of the North of England.' He liked David Lloyd George, on the other hand, or at least admired him, certainly more than he did those who came before and after the irrepressible Welshman. Always the man of the people, 'he did not belong to the charmed circle of the governing class, and never entered it. The rulers of Britain exploited him, and threw him aside when he had served their turn. His heart never ceased to beat for the suffering and the oppressed.' Moreover, Lloyd George achieved much as compared to Herbert Henry Asquith from whom he took over in 1915. Asquith, Taylor wrote, distinguished himself on the eve of the First World War and after mainly by his dithering.[18]

Above all, there was Lord Beaverbrook. In Taylor's eyes, he was 'one of the Creators', a radical, a man 'always on the side of life', and a nonconformist. 'It is his doing more than anyone else's that there is still some individuality and character in this country of ours', Taylor wrote in 1962. 'This was no slight achievement. I suppose we have to have the great and respectable, though I can't think why. I am sure we need also those who give the game away with a wink or a devastating aside.' On Beaverbrook's 85th birthday, Taylor called him a great man, the populist who created great newspapers appealing to all classes of people, the enemy of the Establishment. For Taylor, that was reason enough to endow his greatest friend with immortality.[19]

Taylor even emerged as an advocate for the release of Rudolf Hess, then the last war criminal from the Second World War remaining in Spandau prison – which perhaps merely confirmed the suspicions of some of those who had attacked *The Origins of the Second World War*. Hess was not the issue; British independence was. That is, as Taylor explained, Hess was locked up only because he had flown to Scotland in 1942 seeking peace between England and Germany. A foolish gesture certainly, but hardly criminal. He was kept locked up as a guarantee that Britain and America would never co-operate with Germany against the Soviet Union. 'We have turned a human being into the plaything of political calculation', Taylor charged, adding that 'there is a black stain on our honour until Hess is released'. In 1967 he signed a petition for the prisoner's release, and was attacked by former Campaign for Nuclear Disarmament associates who criticised him for associating his name with a Fascist. Taylor rounded sharply: 'The champions of liberty have done well out of freedom. They have won public distinctions. Some of them have been made life peers'. However, 'I'll believe that the professed champions of freedom really believe in it when I see them holding a demonstration in Trafalgar Square for the release of Hess.'[20]

Taylor had much to say about newspapers, of which he strongly approved, and about those who complained against them, of whom he strongly disapproved. '[N]ewspapers are the voice of democracy', he wrote on one occasion, and on another that a free press 'is the guarantee for all other freedoms'. He railed against D-notices, government injunctions against publishing certain information on the grounds that to do so would harm national security, 'by which a semi-voluntary censorship is exercised over the press'. He preferred a system where D-notices were not issued to muzzle the press, but to compel government departments to make information available – shades of Taylor's campaign in the 1950s against the Official Secrets Act. But that was a fantasy, and the reality was a prime minister ordering D-notices for newspapers in the name of national security. 'National security is indeed endangered at this very moment, and the man who endangers it is at No. 10 Downing Street', Taylor wrote, and added this sarcasm. 'Only a D-notice prevents my revealing his name.'[21]

Then there was government bureaucracy, which was puritanical, elitist, over-staffed, and wasteful of time and money. Among Taylor's complaints: the government regularly violated tax laws and contracts; it was idiotic for the government to impose a £50 limit on taking currency out of the country for holidays; British Summer Time was a travesty; a ban on gift certificates from cigarette packs was the bureaucrats interfering with the smoking habits of ordinary people; bank holidays were stupid; dawdling drivers were allowed to get away with endangering people's lives on the motorways; and on and on and on. The theme was a populist denunciation of 'frivolous, perverted interference' by 'these self-confident authorities, who take it upon themselves to manage our lives'. The government habitually assumed their right to 'tell us what we ought to do and what we ought not'.[22]

Meanwhile, Taylor as a Little Englander concentrated on the international system that emerged after the Second World War, which to him resembled that following the Congress of Vienna in 1815, and on Britain's declining independence. The issues were numerous, including the United Nations, which Taylor wished to see abolished. The UN resembled the Metternich system too much in practice, he argued, while it espoused a fraudulent international idealism in theory. He called it a 'propaganda box' which prevented world leaders talking sense to one another. He cited as example the Korean War, which was fought in the name of the United Nations, but ended only when the combatants turned their backs on the UN and settled things among themselves. If the UN was scrapped, he argued, 'we would see the relations of the Great Powers improving almost at once'. Taylor accused the UN of slaughtering innocent people in the Congo solely in order

to prove some monstrous rigmarole or other about the merits of international action. . . . Shall we soon have UNO troops in Glasgow, putting down riots after a football match? Or perhaps taking over from the United States forces in Mississippi? Why not? What is good for the Congo should be good for all of us.[23]

It particularly annoyed Taylor that the United Nations discussed Commonwealth affairs. Why do we allow it, he wanted to know? 'We should run our own affairs and uphold the unity of the Commonwealth', he proclaimed, adding that 'no other country has such a noble record'. This claim conveniently overlooked Cyprus and the Suez invasion, both of which brought Taylor into the streets against British policy. But that was beside the point. Here it was sufficient to say that the issue was to rescue national independence from international do-gooders. 'The true idealism in foreign policy is to mind your own business', he wrote. 'All the troubles in the world are made worse by this craze for interfering in other people's affairs'.[24]

Britain's relations with the United States within the Anglo-American alliance always brought out the worst – or best – in Taylor. He noted that the alliance originally meant a co-operative partnership, but had become America leading and Britain following as a junior partner dependent on the United States for its policy decisions on a variety of matters. Who was speaking to America for England, he asked? When urged to display 'even a tiny splutter of independence', Britain's leaders would 'bleat fiercely' against it, warning of all manner of dread consequences if they disagreed with the Americans. But grovelling accomplished nothing, Taylor argued. The United States would maintain the alliance 'as long as they need us and not a moment longer'. Taylor thought this danger was realised in 1961 when Britain seemed about to enter the Common Market: 'The Americans are pushing us into the Common Market so as to be rid of us'. In 1959 when French president Charles de Gaulle defied NATO, Taylor had written: 'What about a little Gaullism on this side of the Channel?'[25] He thought the General's stance was appropriate for Britain to take in all of its dealings with America, all of the time.

Taylor was especially critical of American defence experts, the 'faceless men in the Pentagon', who decided NATO nuclear policy and also British defence strategies. In March 1960, when Prime Minister Harold Macmillan went to Washington to discuss a nuclear test ban treaty, Taylor called upon him to 'speak for Britain'. The time had come for 'our rulers' to look after Britain's interests before those of some other country, meaning the United States – meaning, in fact, Cold War military stratagems. Wrote Taylor: 'If the Americans cannot shake themselves free of the Pentagon, all the more reason for us to do so. This would be a service not only for ourselves, but for the real spirit of the Anglo-American Alliance.' A policy which said '[l]eave it to the Americans' was no good, for Britain or the United States. After all: 'It is a poor sort of ally who behaves like a poor relation waiting for the rich cousin to dish out free meals. Yet that is the guiding principle of all our political leaders, right or left.'[26]

Then there was the Common Market, over which Britain was sharply divided between 1960 and 1969 concerning whether it should join. Taylor preferred that Britain stick with the Commonwealth. His words evoked images of high drama when he warned that entering the Common Market would mean the end of the British Empire and Commonwealth (perhaps the only time Taylor appeared as defender of empire, even if by default), and with that, the end of national independence and even of national history. 'Our lives, our jobs, our security will depend on decisions taken by others. . . . We shall be back where we started, when Britain was a province of the Roman Empire.' Britain's politicians did not tell the truth about the Common Market, he charged. Why would they not admit that membership meant loss of national sovereignty, higher tariffs, devaluation of the pound, and the lowering of real wages? Because British politicians did not trust the people – or, just as appalling, they were being mastered by events and were afraid to admit it. Entry into the Common Market was not a policy, Taylor concluded, but a substitute for policy as well as being a vote of no confidence in the Commonwealth.[27]

Taylor condemned Common Market advocates as 'men of little faith'. They had forgotten that Britain was great because of 'our free institution and our independence of spirit', not because of the mundane factors of population and industrial resources. Moreover, 'these forces are still there, as powerful as ever if we dare to use them'. The Commonwealth prime ministers could stop the slide, he wrote, but they would have to speak for the Commonwealth as once Greenwood spoke for England, 'or we disappear'. Britain shared much with Europe culturally and historically, but not so much as with the Commonwealth which shared Britain's institutions and traditions. 'We have never belonged politically to Europe, and I see no reason why we should begin now. . . . We set an example to the world, not to Europe. . . . I don't want to join with a few rich white nations against the world of colour and poverty'.[28]

Economics, politics, culture, and race: all were reasons against and none of them arguments for the Common Market. Taylor charged that for Britain to join Europe would be to finish off the economy of the North of England, claiming that even to negotiate with the Europeans for entry caused economic uncertainty throughout the country. The solution was simply to break off negotiations and forget about 'going into Europe, once and for all'. He applauded 82-year-old Lord Shinwell, who had told the prime minister in strong words that 'the Common Market was wrong for the British people both morally and economically'. What did Market enthusiasts want, Taylor asked? Did they want Britain to merge with Europe? He could scarcely imagine a more preposterous idea. Again Charles de Gaulle entered the picture. De Gaulle wanted France – meaning himself – at the head of Europe, and to keep Britain out. Never mind that de Gaulle's policy snubbed Britain, Taylor pleaded. Rather, let Britain's leaders seize the opportunity De Gaulle gave them. '[T]he chance for British independence has been thrust upon them', Taylor wrote, and they must take it, because 'independence is our only chance. We should indeed stand upon our own feet and turn back to our kin in the Commonwealth.'[29]

This profusion of highly subjective and always entertaining political commentary over which Taylor spread the light of his populist and Little England torch, was written over the later 1950s and through the 1960s. One wonders how much of it he took seriously, or, rather, one may accept that he took most of it seriously, but may ask to what degree he was serious about the sometimes extreme positions he took. Then, in the middle of this political and social potboiling, English History, 1914–1945 appeared. By comparison, the book was mild in language and character, and its arguments reasonable. It was no less populist and Little England, however, and perhaps more effectively so precisely because its format was scholarly detachment.

Taylor credited Beaverbrook with giving him 'inspiration and guidance' for English History, 1914–1945, and it may be understood that he meant much more than simply in preparing the manuscript. Preparing the manuscript was an important part of it, all the same. Taylor told the story this way. One 'gloomy night' after dinner at Cherkley, Beaverbrook's estate in Surrey, Taylor sat with the old man over whisky. Beaverbrook was depressed and in pain from his gout, and asked listlessly what Taylor was working on. Taylor told him about the book he was writing, and complained that he was stuck on economic affairs after 1931, for which he could generate no enthusiasm. At that, Beaverbrook was transformed.

When he realized I needed help, his face lit up. He kicked off his gout shoe and walked up and down without the aid of his stick. He declaimed about the exciting episodes of the nineteen-thirties. . . . For the rest of the evening he was boyishly gay. . . . I was gay too. Beaverbrook had not given me any new ideas. . . . But he inspired me. I thought: 'If this frail old man can be so excited about history, shame on me if I cannot be excited too'. That night Beaverbrook saved my intellectual life.

Beaverbrook died before the book was published, and in words of great poignancy, Taylor wrote: 'I had hoped to place this book in his hands. Now I set down in bereavement the name of Max Aitken, Lord Beaverbrook, my beloved friend.'[30]

English History, 1914–1945 told the story of 'thirty years in the history of the English people'. It was almost pretentiously scholarly, to the degree that Taylor himself later called it 'something of a joke book, from its title onwards with its implications that its history was sterner than that of any of the previous volumes' in the series. It included economic graphs, maps, extensive bibliography, a detailed index, and footnotes with biographical details of important persons, and others which provided details of a particularly arcane nature, such as a reference to King George V's trousers being 'creased at the sides, not in front and back'. Taylor explained that 'my predecessors delivered the judgement of History in the highest Olympian spirit. I followed their example except that in my judgement the poor were always right and the rich always wrong – a judgement that happens to be correct historically'. Perhaps: in any event, with this judgment in mind, he ignored the history of the upper classes, 'which is what English history usually amounts to', in favour of ordinary people whose history only began in the twentieth century. 'I was glad when Max Beloff described it as Populist history', he wrote.[31]

English History, 1914–1945 was indeed populist in all of its essentials. Taylor's story, in outline, was simple. The peoples' generosity sent England to war in defence of Belgium in 1914, and their patience and strength enabled England to survive the worst and most disastrous mistakes of military men and politicians thereafter. In 1916 their patriotism put Lloyd George in power, accepted his moratorium on labour disputes, and supported his war dictatorship. 'English people were almost unanimous in wanting to win the war, and they wanted it run better', was the reason, and the result was that 'the history of the English state and the English people merged for the first time'. The social revolution of the twentieth century that reached fruition in the welfare state following the Second World War, began in the midst of the First World War.[32] Between the wars, demand grew for a better material life for the people and for their democratic involvement in the social and political decisions that affected their lives, demands often expressed through the expanding popular press such as Beaverbrook's *Daily Express*. English culture was also popularised by the wireless, the cinema, and the inexpensive motor car, all of which opened heretofore unimagined horizons for ordinary people. Meanwhile, owing to outmoded industries and an economy exhausted by the war, Britain slipped backward relative to the rest of the industrialised world. Unemployment rose, wages fell, and exports declined. Labour troubles resulted, including the high drama of the General Strike in 1926 and the hunger marches of the 1930s. The Labour Party grew also, as it was the party of the trades unions and increasingly the parliamentary party of ordinary people. Twice, in 1923 and 1929, Labour formed governments, though with limited success.

The second Labour Government was followed in 1931 by the National Government of Tories – with a few Liberals thrown in for good measure – under former Labour Prime Minister Ramsay MacDonald. Its function was to solve economic problems through cut-backs and belt-tightening. But the people took their own way out of economic crisis, spending instead of economising, improving their standard of living rather than sacrificing 'for the national cause', and seeing as a result, stable wages and falling prices rather than the reverse, insisted upon by the economists. 'Increased consumption by individuals pulled England out of the slump'.[33]

In foreign policy, the people wanted peace and embraced disarmament, collective security, and appeasement policy. They also wanted justice for the peoples of the world, or at least for the working classes of Europe, and so in 1920, London dockers refused to load munitions to support Poland's war against the infant Soviet Union. In 1936 ordinary people accompanied the intellectuals who went to Spain to fight Fascism. In 1939, having seen Nazi Germany tear up the Munich agreement, they were behind Arthur Greenwood, acting parliamentary Labour leader, when he rose to 'speak for England'. They were even more resolute in support of Leo Amery nine months after war began when, quoting Cromwell, he demanded of Chamberlain: 'Will you sit forever? For the love of God, go!'[34] Chamberlain did, and until the war ended in 1945, the peoples' hero was Winston Churchill.

After a quarter of a century of peace, the next world war started in 1939. The people believed it to be a popular undertaking against Fascism and for England, but not for an England of wealth and privilege. In June 1945, the people cheered for Churchill but voted for Labour. This was partly folk memory, part commonsense. The Conservatives offered a manifesto similar to Labour; but Labour seemed more likely to carry it through, which they did. The King's speech of August 16, 1945 described 'nationalization of the coal industry and of the Bank of England; social security; a national health service'. Hugh Dalton wrote: 'After the long storm of war . . . we saw the sunrise.'[35] At war's end the people 'turned in on themselves and thought mainly of social security, housing, and full employment, not of foreign affairs'.[36] This wedding of the popular social revolution and Little England came at the end of the story, and that was that, at least so far as the central theme was concerned.

This was English history in the twentieth century as Taylor perceived it. The writing style was typical of him but only more so. That is, it was more epigrammatic than when he wrote diplomatic history, though not so much as his writing in the popular press, for television, or even in his Ford Lectures at Oxford in 1956. For example, 'In 1934 Chamberlain announced that the country had finished the story of Bleak House and could now sit down to enjoy the first chapter of Great Expectations. The public, their houses stocked with free copies of Dickens after the newspaper war, no doubt took the allusion.' For another, in 1935 'the trenches of class war ran along the floor of the House of Commons'.[37] This was similar to but more good humoured than *The Course of German History* had been, probably because then Taylor was deadly serious. He was serious with *English History*, but he was having fun, too.

The emphasis upon individuals – only partially tempered by the frequent references to the people – was typical Taylor. Also typical was the tendency toward trenchant observations about individuals reminiscent of the style and content of his writing in the popular press. It was on this level only that the epigrammatic judgements characteristic of Taylor's occasional journalism found their way into this serious study of national history. No figure of importance escaped being described, analysed, and judged. These are only a handful of examples. Asquith 'was a strong character, unshakable as a rock and, like a rock, incapable of movement'. Lloyd George 'was the most inspired and creative British statesman of the twentieth century', but also 'devious and unscrupulous in his methods. He aroused every feeling except trust. In all his greatest acts, there was an element of self-seeking'. Ramsay MacDonald 'was the greatest leader Labour has had, and his name would stand high if he had not outlived his abilities'. Stanley Baldwin 'seemed, though he was not, an ordinary man. He presented himself as a simple country gentleman, interested only in pigs. He was in fact a wealthy ironmaster, with distinguished literary connexions.' George Lansbury 'was loved as no Labour leader had been since Keir Hardie'. Beaverbrook 'was already a millionaire when he took to newspapers. He was in this world for political influence and for fun as much as for profit.' And though Churchill 'had some faithful followers, in the last resort he succeeded by calling in the people against the men at the top'; and after the loss of Crete, 'the British people did not doubt that Churchill was the best war prime minister they had or could possibly have. But henceforth they accepted him despite his faults. They expected him to make mistakes, and he made many.'[38]

However, while Taylor described the actions of individual leaders, the main emphasis remained the people. The interaction between events, developments, personalities, and the English people underscored every part of this enormously detailed study. This was particularly true of the popular impact of war. The world wars, both if which were total wars and therefore peoples' wars, occupied about a third of the book. The first indicated that 'the English people could not be ignored so easily'; the second proved that they could not be ignored at all.[39]

Total war in 1914–18, as Taylor described it, meant mass armies, conscription, rationing, war socialism (centralised organisation for war production), censorship of news, propaganda, and even air bombardment of civilian targets. Total war generated a popular view of cause, effect, and process. 'The British people were clear why they had gone to war', he wrote. 'It was for the sake of Belgium. Liberation of Belgium, and full reparation, remained always their primary aim.' They were equally clear that there should be some assurance that suchlike would never happen again. The people went to war in their millions, and in the trenches, 'the humble Englishman found his voice' with crude, often obscene songs. Taylor no doubt enjoyed inserting a footnote at this point which read in part: 'During the first World war use of the four-letter word, as it is now called, became universal, or more probably its universal use was first observed by the literate classes.' Meanwhile, the ineptitude of early war leaders led the people to demand change, and that brought Lloyd George to power as the peoples' prime minister. In Taylor's words: 'In wartime the people mattered; and Lloyd George was home once Labour backed him.' Of course, the people paid a high price for 'mattering' in this context. On the one hand, thousands became conscientious objectors, including Taylor's own uncle, Harry Thompson. On the other, three-quarters of a million were killed, and after the war the survivors re-entered an economy that had been stretched to the breaking point.[40]

The war inspired a flood of writing beyond any war in history. An army of historians worked on the origins of the First World War, and beyond that there was an outpouring of novels and memoirs, and even a play about the war, especially after 1928. Taylor took note of this writing and described its common theme as determination that such a war should never happen again. This theme evoked popular sympathy, and when promoters of disarmament appealed to public opinion the response was favourable. The Oxford Union resolution in 1933 not to fight again for king and country was 'a gesture of loyalty towards world peace rather than an act of disloyalty in the ordinary sense'. It probably reflected what most people felt. Similarly, the majority of the 11 million people who responded to the Peace Ballot in 1934 indicated they preferred economic sanctions to war in order to stop aggression, but that did not mean they were not prepared when the time came to meet Hitler and Fascism with force when there seemed no alternative. Even so, when the time came to fight again, and though the cause was just and the people embraced it with determination, Taylor, writing with a hint of irony in his historical voice, was reasonably certain that 'the British people were surprised at the noble part which events had thrust on them'.[41]

The time was 1939. There was little popular objection when war was declared. The people were ready. The government was not. It 'made nothing of the national mood', and having plumped so long for appeasement, had no clear idea what to do in war. When the people demanded to know what was being done, they were 'more or less told that they should not ask such questions. It was hardly surprising that in return the bulk of people came to feel that the war was little concern of theirs'. Taylor pointed to the worst propaganda poster of the war as characteristic of official attitudes within the Chamberlain government: 'YOUR money will bring US victory', he misquoted. The poster actually read: 'Your courage, Your cheerfulness, Your resolution WILL BRING US VICTORY'. Perhaps Taylor thought his version better captured the essence of the message.[42]

In 1940, the Germans overran Norway, the Low Countries and France, and the people came to life. 'Their wrath turned against Chamberlain, their enthusiasm towards Churchill'. After Dunkirk, which Churchill termed 'a disaster of the first magnitude', he told the English people that 'this was their finest hour', and he sustained them thereafter with radio speeches that mixed together 'Macaulay and contemporary slang'. Meanwhile, other authorities 'showed a misplaced lack of confidence in the British people' by prosecuting grumblers for undermining public morale, and sending around Ministry of Information investigators – 'Cooper's snoopers' they got to be called – to probe public opinion. Churchill made them stop when public response threatened to turn the whole thing into a bad joke. Taylor noted popular enthusiasm for 'doing something dramatic' under Churchill's leadership, and, as well, the ease with which Channel Islanders adapted to German occupation. 'It was perhaps fortunate that British patriotism was not put to the supreme test', he observed dryly.[43]

In 1939–45 the real war for the people was at home, just as it had been in 1914–18. Only this time, the intensity was much greater, thanks to the policy accepted on both sides of bombing civilian targets. The 'Blitz' went on for most of the war and was a failure in England even as it was in Germany. Popular spirit remained unshaken. Indeed, Taylor wrote, the more they were bombed the more certain the people were that the war was just and that by showing they 'could take it', they were well along toward winning. Bombardment strengthened popular morale rather than destroyed it – which was equally true in Germany. After a time 'a British statesmen who had pursued anything less than total victory would have been swept away by a storm of public indignation . . . in which factory workers and housewives would have been as resolute as journalists or politicians'. This view was shared by those in the field. 'The war was a people's war in the most literal sense', Taylor explained. 'The Englishmen who fought the second World war believed that the war was worth fighting. They also believed by and large that they would win it.' In July 1944, by which time the D-Day landings appeared to have succeeded, English people flocked to the beaches for the first time in five years. They knew, or thought they knew, that they had won the war. The people needed that inspiration, Taylor noted, because thousands more would be killed in coming months by flying bombs.[44]

Taylor rarely credited war with doing good for anyone, but made an exception where English women were concerned. Before 1914, the suffragette movement was frustrated by a generation of intransigent males inside and outside of parliament, and then gained momentum during the Great War. In 1915, 30,000 women marched down Whitehall demanding the right to serve in the war. Soon 200,000 women were in government service, half a million in clerical work, and many others were working as conductors on trams and buses. A quarter of a million women worked in agriculture and 800,000 in war industries. When the war was over no one could pretend that women had not merited something by their contributions. The immediate result was the Representation of the People Act in 1918 giving women limited suffrage. In 1919 the Sex Disqualification Removal Act opened most professions and higher education to women, although, in Taylor's dry language: 'The Church and the stock exchange provided two quaint exceptions.' Moreover, he added, though the first woman, Lady Astor, entered parliament in 1919, there were never more than twenty women MPs between the wars, and no women judges, company directors, and very few university professors. All the same, women won full voting rights in 1928, and it was women Labour MPs who forced the hand of their male leaders to join in the call for Chamberlain to step down in 1940. Also,

England conscripted women into the armed services in the Second World War, the only nation at war to do so.[45]

Propaganda was a phenomenon of total war. Taylor was not impressed by it, however, probably owing to his brief association with the Ministry of Information, to whom he offered his services as a speaker about the war, in 1940. As he described it:

> I was given a free hand. I went to the principal towns in the southern region, contacted the local information committees, which were run by the agents of the three political parties, and offered my services. The party agents, though not very keen, usually acquiesced. I went to the main shops and offices, secured a ten minutes break and addressed the staff on the war and what it means. Of course the whole thing was nonsense.[46]

On the other hand, Taylor recognised the importance of the instruments of mass communications through which wartime propaganda was disseminated. As radio was still in the future, he wrote, the press 'reached perhaps its highest point of influence during the first World war'. This was not to say that the press also determined what people thought. Editors succeeded when they voiced or stimulated opinions, and failed when they tried to dictate them. Referring to Lord Northcliffe, Taylor wrote: 'Men did not wear the *Daily Mail* hat; they did not eat the *Daily Mail* loaf'. Many drank the *Daily Herald* pint, however, the socialist daily edited by the 'revered leader of the emotional Left' George Lansbury, and written by such middle-class intellectuals as William Mellor and G. D. H. Cole. They contributed 'a gay, self-confident contempt for the doings of the governing class'. The *Daily Herald* bore witness 'that the people of England were not all thinking as their rulers thought they should'.[47]

It was a constantly recurring theme in Taylor's writing that the class system was England's curse. *English History* was no exception. 'The English were the only European people who sorted themselves out by class at mealtimes', he wrote, 'the masses took their principal meal at midday, their betters in the evening. Even the drinkers of beer divided automatically between the saloon and the public bars.' Most newspapers were linked to the class system, appealing, that is, to a particular social class, and that was true even of the *Daily Herald*. On the other hand, the

Beaverbrook press did not appeal to class, at least not in Taylor's estimation, and he gave the credit to Beaverbrook who had 'the New World view that there was no difference between the rich and poor except that the rich had more money'. Consequently, the *Daily Express* had readers from every class, and was 'what England would have been without her class system'. The *Daily Express* climbed to the top of the circulation heap in the mid-1930s, so perhaps Taylor was correct, if circulation figures in any way indicated a readership which crossed class lines.[48] Otherwise, one suspects some hyperbole in memory of his great friend.

If the press did not make opinion, Taylor thought, it surely reflected opinion. For example, only *Reynolds News*, a left-wing socialist Sunday paper, and the *Daily Worker* (for which Taylor had mainly contempt) opposed the Munich Agreement in 1938, while the rest of the press welcomed it. This seemed to Taylor to be a clear indication of his point, since in his own experience few English people had been prepared to go to war over Czecho-slovakia. If there was a paper which both reflected and made mass opinion it was the *Daily Mirror*, which came into being during and because of the Second World War. Taylor described it as being the only truly 'popular' newspaper in England, and this did not contradict his observations regarding the *Daily Express*. By 'popular' he meant that the *Daily Mail* had no proprietor and was the creation of 'the ordinary people on its staff and especially by Harry Guy Bartholomew, a man who worked his way up from office boy to editorial director'. Consequently it became the newspaper of the masses. 'The *Mirror* was . . . brash, but it was also a serious organ of democratic opinion. . . . The English people at last found their voice.'[49]

Meanwhile, broadcasting arrived. Once the First World War ended, broadcasting challenged the press as a mass medium, though it did not replace newspapers. It became the responsi-bility of the British Broadcasting Company, an organisation Taylor frequently criticised, or at least he did not like its manage-ment and especially not its monopolistic character. John Reith ran the BBC in its formative years. Taylor described Reith as a

Scottish dictator. Calvinist by upbringing, harsh and ruthless in character, Reith turned broadcasting into a mission. It was to bring into every home 'all that was best in every department of human knowledge, endeavour and achievement'. He used what he called 'the brute force of monopoly' to stamp Christian morality on the British people.

Of course he failed in the end. 'Like all cultural dictatorships, the BBC was more important for what it silenced than for what it achieved.'[50]

Taylor always seemed to prefer newspapers to broadcasting, even though he frequently worked on both radio and television. For one thing, he thought broadcasting depersonalised politics. Once politicians began using the new medium, people stopped attending political meetings, preferring to listen to their leaders at home over the wireless. Public political opinion could no longer be determined by gauging the temper of public demonstrations at such meetings. The result was the introduction of what Taylor contemptuously regarded as the pseudo-science of poll-taking. Broadcasting also ruined political figures who looked good in print, but were ineffective on the air. On the other hand, it promoted the careers of those who were good infront of a microphone – sometimes to the detriment of the people. Both Lloyd George and Ramsay MacDonald lost out because they were ineffective on radio, while Stanley Baldwin, leaning back and lighting his pipe at the start of a broadcast, was made by it. His relaxed, plain style 'carried a conviction which his acts did not always sustain'.[51] Taylor claimed that once Baldwin began speaking over the wireless, he was never again seriously challenged, politically. Meanwhile, the English people who stayed home to listen to politicians were 'shut up in a box listening to a tinier box'. Broadcasting promoted isolation rather than engagement, passive acceptance rather than calling leaders to account. Perhaps that was what the people really wanted, Taylor concluded. But his tone was impatient. 'Perhaps they did not care what they heard so long as some noise from the little box gave them a substitute for human society'.[52]

The cinema was also mass communications, but of a different kind. Its impact was mainly cultural, beginning with popular indifference to interwar literature. The masses could make nothing of literature after the First World War, Taylor wrote, implying in the process that neither could he. The great prose writers 'disintegrated the traditions of English literature'. Prose 'cried out for meaning' but got instead James Joyce, in whose

Finnegans Wake 'even the words were gibberish'. Taylor thought serious writers posed a dilemma for the historian, because if literature was supposed to reflect the spirit of contemporary life, then little was to be made of what they had to say between the wars. The leading writers seemed to see the end of civilisation, the decline and fall of practically everything. This was beyond Taylor, who argued that by any reasonable standard, this was the best time the English people had ever known:

> more considerate, with more welfare for the mass of the people packed into a few years than into the whole of previous history. It is hardly surprising that ordinary people found the great contemporary works of literature beyond them.[53]

They turned to the cinema instead, with dramatic consequences. The cinema changed the pattern of English life. It 'took people from their homes; eclipsed both church and public house; spread romantic, but by no means trivial, values', and in consequence became 'the greatest educative force of the early twentieth century'. Not that this was altogether a good thing, Taylor cautioned, for cinema had some of the same effects as broadcasting. That is, 'it provided a substitute for real life and helped people become watchers instead of doers'. This judgement applied to newsreels as well as to feature films. Newsreels made war seem more authentic (gave, he noted, the only real meaning to Stalingrad and El Alamein), stimulated greater passion in politics, and led to wider discussion of international events. However, 'with it all was a feeling that these great happenings had no more connexion with real life than those seen every night in the cinema palace'.[54]

As Taylor described it, the life of the English people changed forever between the world wars. The birthrate fell, population shifted away from the North and towards the South, differences between regional dialects softened – a function of the BBC, it is usually thought – church-going declined, the motor car became less of a luxury and more of a necessity, and the people lost interest in the empire, making it clear that they preferred social amelioration to world power. The Labour Party emerged as a force in English political life, and through the trial and error of holding power in 1923 and 1929 learned how to govern in the interests of the masses. Above all, after five years of struggle with Germany between 1939 and 1945, the 'very spirit of the nation had changed. No one in 1945 wanted to go back to 1939.'[55]

Foreign policy occupied much less space than domestic affairs in *English History*. When Taylor did concern himself with foreign policy it was again from a populist perspective. For example, he credited the people, sick of war and uninterested in foreign adventures, with forcing Lloyd George to back away from the Chanak affair in 1922, just as they had forced him to stop aiding Poland's war against the Soviet Union in 1920. For another, he suggested that far from uniting England behind collective security, the foreign policy of the National Government created bitter divisions. 'Great Britain never knew less national unity than in the days of the National government', he wrote. Still again, he claimed that it was popular protest which killed the Hoare–Laval proposal to accept Italian aggression in Abyssinia in 1935, and that public opinion prevented Britain from opposing Germany's remilitarisation of the Rhineland with force in 1936. A desire not go to war 'because of a quarrel in a far-away country between people of whom we know nothing' dominated popular thinking at the time of the Munich conference in 1938. Chamberlain at Munich simply 'reflected the muddle in most English minds. Munich sprang from a mixture of fear and good intentions'. Churchill also reflected the public mind when he came to power in the middle of a war crisis, only it was an opinion that had come to embrace the will to victory in a just cause – even if that meant Soviet domination of Europe, and pawning the empire to the United States.[56]

Taylor was never more populist and Little England than on the subject of Anglo-American relations, and his views in *English History* were little different, though less strenuous in tone, from those expressed in his occasional writings. He did not want America to lead Britain into the Cold War, or once in, to see an American resolution. He wanted Britain to be free of all such entanglements as the 'special relationship', or membership in the Common Market. Little England was an isolationist perspective. Taylor embraced it as such. Lord Beaverbrook held isolationist views, and Taylor praised him for them. In *Beaverbrook*, Taylor wrote: 'Beaverbrook preached Isolation: great armaments and no European alliances. . . . [T]his was not only the wisest course to follow in a world full of dangers but also more honourable than to distribute guarantees which we could not fulfil.'[57] Taylor was clear that Britain must be free to follow its own lead in order to address the interests of the English people. Part of the burden of *English History* was that this freedom was lost to the United States, or at least it was compromised, during the Second World War. Consequently, there was an edge to his judgements and interpretations whenever he described Anglo-American wartime relations.

Britain's problem with the Americans began, as Taylor explained it, in the dark days when Britain stood alone against the Fascist powers and was forced to use its precious dollar reserves to buy American arms. The result was the building up of American factories at the expense of British ones. It was ironic, Taylor wrote, that 'the expenditure of British treasure served to rearm the United States rather than to strengthen Great Britain'. Then the Americans made it a requirement of the Lend-Lease agreement that no Lend-Lease goods could go into exports, and Britain fell even further behind. 'Thanks to lend-lease Great Britain virtually ceased to be an exporting country. She sacrificed her postwar future for the sake of the war.' As Taylor described America taking advantage of beleaguered Britain, it was easy to read 'immoral' between the lines of his narrative. This certainly is true when reading his description of the United States short-changing Britain over atomic weapons: 'The British handed over to the Americans a mass of scientific secrets for war, including that for a controlled nuclear explosion. . . . The British received no acknowledgment or reward.' And again, when he described the Americans taking direct control of the war after 1941, leaving England to go along, so that when English church bells rang to celebrate victory in North Africa, they also rang to toll 'the end of British independence'. It was a question of money. The Americans had it in abundance, while Britain was impoverished. Britain could continue as a great power only with American assistance. The Americans knew this, and therefore in 1945 at Yalta, Roosevelt co-operated with Stalin, representing the only other superpower, against Churchill. Churchill resisted, but 'he was arguing from weakness: British power was declining, and Roosevelt gave little support'. By the end of the war 'the Anglo-American relationship had become that of patron and client', and when victory over Japan was celebrated on 2

September it marked 'the end of the war and the beginning of Britain's post-war troubles'.[58]

All the same, the last pages of English History, provided a picture of the English people triumphant. They were triumphant in this picture precisely because Britain had been eclipsed. The people abandoned empire and world power and entered into an era that brought them greater contentment and prosperity than they had ever known. Taylor's commitment to the people was genuine and of long standing, and this was not the first time he had extolled popular virtues in hyperbolic language. There was, for example, his essay written in 1950 on how the English people had survived their world wars. At that time he argued that out of these wars the people learned 'to take the world as it is and improve it; to have faith without a creed, hope without illusion, love without God'.[59] Optimism tempered with fatalism, idealism with pragmatism, and belief with scepticism; to this litany English History added patriotism linked to a mild form of xenophobia. It was all Taylor's own creation.

In the final paragraph of English History the people whose history he had written merged with Taylor himself. That is, the values he credited to the people were his own values evolved from historical sources and contemporary experience, and proclaimed in writings over three decades, about past and present. It was a lyrical passage to which no paraphrase could ever do justice, when Taylor wrote:

> The British were the only people who went through both wars from beginning to end. Yet they remained peaceful and civilized people, tolerant, patient, and generous. Traditional values lost much of their force. Other values took their place. Imperial greatness was on the way out; the welfare state was on the way in. The British Empire declined; the condition of the people improved. Few now sang 'Land of Hope and Glory'. Few even sang 'England Arise'. England had risen all the same.[60]

So, too, had Taylor risen, it might be said – with some help from his friends.

8

'What Was It All About, Alan?'

Beaverbrook (1972)

'What was it all about?' is the first and last question every historian asks of his or her subject. That the subject might be A. J. P. Taylor makes no difference. Critics read his work and posed the question, usually in terms of 'Will it stand?' or 'Will he last?' The answers have varied. The critics have been either enthusiastic or dubious, torn between approving or condemning writing, the content of which, seemed to bounce between being substantial, trivial, correct, error-laden, serious, and frivolous. Taylor knew the criticism as well as the approval that his work generated among colleagues and critics, and he made a point of denying that he cared what they thought. Or, perhaps, the fact that he made a point of denying indicated that he cared very much. With Taylor, one could never be sure, and that was part of the problem in trying to answer the question, 'Will he last?'

Over his career, Taylor was a serious scholar, a journalist, and a 'television star', as he liked to put it. But which was he, really? Could he be all three without sacrificing his credibility as a historian? Were his unorthodox historical interpretations to be taken seriously, or were they engendered by his dissenting political views, and thereby made suspect, if not simply wrong? Was his epigrammatic and polemical style, acceptable perhaps in a political commentator, also acceptable in a serious historian? Did the 'journalistic excess' of which he was frequently accused, by which was meant stylistic extremes, indicate that he used evidence too 'creatively?' Could one really trust a historian who also wrote for that 'awful newspaper', the *Sunday Express*?

Taylor's career after *English History, 1914–1945* simply added to critical confusion. *English History* was his last piece of substantial, original historiography, written in a style that was at least nominally detached. However, he did not stop writing when it was completed. The year 1964 was 'very much a period of endings for me', he once wrote. That year he resigned his tutorship at Magdalen, withdrew his support for the Labour Party over Harold Wilson's Commonwealth emigration policies, finished the *English History* typescript, and experienced the death of Lord Beaverbrook, 'the master who never betrayed me'.[1] But Taylor still had to make a living, and thereafter, he lectured at University College, London (and occasionally at the Polytechnic College of North London, now the University of North London), conducted seminars at the Institute of Historical Research, appeared on television, and continued to write for the popular press. He also wrote 'potted' histories such as *From Sarajevo to Potsdam*, (1966), *War By Time-Table* (1969), and *The War Lords* (1976). He also produced a biography of Lord Beaverbrook; however, it is difficult to see this book as a work of scholarship, so much as a eulogy to his hero.

The old man's life ended in 1964, but not his hold or influence on Taylor. In 1967 the Beaverbrook Library opened with Taylor as its director. 'One day', as Taylor described it, 'Sir Max Aitken, old Max's son, said to me in his abrupt way, "we are moving my father's papers to London, and you're to look after them".'[2] The papers were moved, and Taylor did look after them, occupying a simple but tasteful office in St Bride's Street. A Sickert portrait of Beaverbrook hung on the wall near his desk. There Taylor directed – largely by leaving them alone – a steady stream of historians, mainly young, from as far away as Australia and as near as London, who mined the library's contents: papers pertaining to Beaverbrook, Lloyd George, Asquith, and others from Beaverbrook's time.[3] For himself, Taylor edited and published papers relating to Lloyd George and W. P. Crozier, and worked on his biography of Beaverbrook, which was published in 1972.

Taylor insisted that *Beaverbrook* was 'not an authorized or a commissioned biography'. Rather, '[i]t is the work of an independent scholar who obeys no dictates except his own'.[4] The latter point was true in principle, whether or not the rest was also true in fact. The work is anecdotal and fraught with hero-worship, a reflection of Taylor's feeling for its subject. His stylistic skills made *Beaverbrook* highly readable, but they did not also make it great history. The appearance of *Beaverbrook* did little to ease critical doubts regarding what Taylor's post-Oxford career might be doing to his reputation as a historian.

Beaverbrook was quite simply the translation of devotion into words. Tom Driberg, who, like Taylor, had written for the Beaverbrook press and a book of his own about the press lord, used 'hagiography' to describe Taylor's work. He 'does not pretend to be objective', Driberg wrote, noting that it was clear from the start that Beaverbrook was the object of uncritical admiration.[5] Driberg concluded that it was not a book Taylor should have written.

Beaverbrook was Taylor's hero. About this there was not the slightest question. Taylor began by noting that the press lord was 'without doubt a most extraordinary man', and spent the next 670 pages trying to demonstrate it.[6] He excused Beaverbrook's foibles and praised his intelligence, generosity, sense of humour, and capacity to do things better than anyone around him. Taylor's criticism of Empire Free Trade, of which Beaverbrook was the champion, was only a gesture in the direction of detachment. The real message lay in such comments as: 'For me Max could do no wrong', or, of a letter from Beaverbrook to Anthony Eden concerning the Warsaw uprising in 1944: 'The grasp of reality shown in this letter was unfortunately not shared by other western statesmen', or again, referring to the Ministry of Production in 1942: 'later events were to confirm Beaverbrook's arguments for a unified control'.[7]

The work was anecdotal to a fault, including stories that involved Taylor's relationship with Beaverbrook and which indicated admiration, respect, and enjoyment of the man on a very personal level. Beaverbrook indicated a serious side of this relationship when guiding Taylor on *English History*, described in the previous chapter; a lighter side is seen when Taylor gave a talk upon receiving an honorary degree from the University of New Brunswick in Fredericton, as Taylor told the story, Beaverbrook introduced him saying: 'Alan Taylor has come a long way to lecture to you, so listen very attentively.' Afterward, he told Taylor that it was 'the finest lecture he had ever heard', to which Taylor replied by asking if he had heard many others. 'Ah, you're a very clever fellow', Beaverbrook replied, and that was that. Missing from this version was Taylor's later assertion that

Beaverbrook actually slept through the lecture, which if true, made the story even better. Either way, Taylor's affection for the man was obvious.[8]

Throughout the book, the reader was given an enormous amount of detail on Lord Beaverbrook's life, even to his bedtime eating habits, and an emotional ending which said that: 'Max Aitken Lord Beaverbrook was quite a Somebody. Those who loved him have one dream in life: that the telephone will ring again and the familiar voice ask, "What's the news?"' What the reader did not get was analytical or critical depth. Critics were quick to note the fact. 'I think the real trouble is the author's too facile response to his subject', wrote Roy Fuller, while Peter Silcox objected that: 'Taylor does not persuade me that Beaverbrook influenced events to any great extent'. Critics joined Driberg in noting Taylor's subjectivity. As Ronald Blythe observed: 'Biographies are full of autobiography, for who can push his way into another's existence without revealing what he likes and what he simply has to accept?'[9]

Taylor's lighter and perhaps disappointing writing after 1965 – at least in the case of *Beaverbrook* – was part of the corpus of work that critics had to consider in their attempts to determine whether or not he had made an important contribution to historiography. Most critics seemed convinced that they had Taylor pegged, but the differences between their views were enormous, a fact which in and of itself was an important clue regarding his place among the historical and political writers of his generation. The attempt to figure him out became almost an international sport, and with as much subjectivity as sport usually produces. Some critics expressed admiration for Taylor – indicating thereby their belief that he would last – while others thought him trivial, thereby concluding that he would not.

David Marquand ranked among the former. As an undergraduate he sat 'sometimes mutinous and sometimes enthralled' at Taylor's tutorials in Magdalen College. Later, after reading *English History*, he was convinced that:

The England of the 1990s will be to some extent Taylor's creation, just as the England of today is to some extent G. M. Trevelyan's. The men who run it will have been brought up on Taylor or on vulgarizations of Taylor; even in academic circles he will doubtless be regarded as the Grand Old Man of the trade.[10]

That was Asa Briggs's view as well, when he had read *The Struggle for Mastery in Europe*: 'Whatever we do will be influenced by what he had done, for he reopened the nineteenth century rather than closed it down'. Two decades later, Alan Sked and Chris Cook were even more effusive, claiming that

> his works have been so widely read, his views so widely debated that his name is now synonymous with the writing of history in this country. He has interpreted the modern history of Great Britain and Europe with such incisiveness of mind and facility of style that his contribution to his field has been unique.[11]

On the other side were those who regarded Taylor's work as sufficiently questionable, if not downright treasonous, to assure that his impact would be minimal. As Marquand observed, Taylor 'unsettles his academic colleagues because they suspect, quite rightly, that his conception of history is not merely irreverent but seditious'.[12] One such colleague – speaking generically – was William H. McNeill, who saw in *The Struggle for Mastery in Europe* 'a falsification and propagandistic distortion of truth', resulting from Taylor's 'Cartesian' view that diplomacy is 'an intellectual, almost a mathematical, exercise in power politics'. Most reviews of *The Origins of the Second World War* accused Taylor of distorting, misusing, and omitting important evidence in order to advance eye-catching but unsubstantiated hypotheses, resulting in a historically suspect picture of Hitlerian foreign policy. As Robert Spencer put it: 'One does not . . . get the impression that Taylor is dealing with foreign policy of a totalitarian dictatorship of the twentieth century.'[13]

There was also a sense that Taylor's penchant for 'journalistic excess', as it was frequently termed, obscured his real contribution to scholarship. Taylor, it was said, was

> two people: the historian of nineteenth-century Austria and Germany, distinguished from most of his fellow specialists by his gift for lively writing, and the coiner of paradoxes, the

spokesman for the unusual, and sometimes unpopular, point of view whom television has made familiar to a wide audience.[14]

Could not, as this judgement implies, a popular historian – that is, one widely known by people not specialists in history – also be a good historian? Denis Judd, a Taylor pupil at Magdalen College, thought he could, so long as one separated the two sides of his personality. 'I do not think one should confuse Taylor's journalistic excesses . . . with his academic work. He is something of a Jekyll and Hyde in this respect.'[15] Others were not so charitable. It was suggested that the 'journalistic excesses' did indeed trivialise Taylor's work and negate his contribution to history. A critic of *The Course of German History* wrote: '[T]he brightness which sounds so bright in the Oxford Union and keeps its brightness and lightness for 1500 words in a Sunday paper . . . when kept up for 264 pages . . . leads Mr Taylor to make false, superficial generalizations'. Years later, Hans J. Morganthau, seeing little to distinguish Taylor the journalist from Taylor the historian, dismissed him as an 'intellectual entertainer . . . a judgment borne out by the great variety of Taylor's writings, dealing with a great number of disparate topics, all of which Taylor could not possibly have mastered'.[16] For Taylor himself, the explanation was simple. 'There is no reason why history shouldn't be written so that someone wants to read it.'[17]

Taylor made a point of being difficult on various levels throughout his career. However, if he irked and annoyed his colleagues, he also challenged them as he challenged his general readers, and this counted with some critics. Fritz Stern described him as 'Shavian. . . . He is brilliant, erudite, witty, dogmatic, heretical, irritating, insufferable, and withal inescapable.'[18] In similar vein, Edward B. Segel called him 'the gad-fly, the constant critic of the respectable and the powerful, the individualist outside of conventional groupings who pricks the pretensions of the orthodox'. Taylor was 'a dedicated individualist, a scholar devoted to fostering the angularities and oddities in his own personality and in society at large, and to resisting the dulling effect of any kind of orthodoxy or respectability on his cherished orneriness'.[19]

One can follow the rise, so to speak, of Taylor's reputation by looking briefly at critical response to his work over time. The earliest criticism concerned *The Italian Problem in European Diplomacy*, and was remarkably unremarkable. It was merely the standard response to a competent young historian. 'Mr Taylor's judgment of the situation with which he deals and with the techniques of policy and diplomacy is always careful and interesting', yawned W. K. Hancock in 1935. Similarly J. L. Hammond on *Germany's First Bid for Colonies*: 'This is a careful and valuable study in diplomatic history with an obvious bearing on present politics.' *The Habsburg Monarchy* began to alter the situation. R. W. Seton-Watson, one of Britain's great experts on Balkan history and politics, liked the 1941 edition despite Taylor revealing 'very definite sympathies'. However, when the 1948 edition appeared, C. A. Macartney complained about Taylor's 'cock-sureness and a complete intolerance of those of whom he disapproves, whether living or dead'. Comments also began to appear regarding Taylor's style: 'I think that he is over fond of the technique of provocativeness, which, when used too often, becomes a bore to the reader and blinkers to the writer.' Politics gave *The Course of German History*, with its subjective and determinist character, a good reception generally, except that, as R. H. S. Crossman pointed out, while Taylor's 'wisecracks' might contain an element of truth, 'they have no place in a book which, in Mr Taylor's words, is "meant to be history". When he keeps to his central theme and controls his temper, he is not only a brilliant but a profound historian.'[20]

As Taylor began to appear more frequently in his role of journalist, responses to his writing were more and more conscious of style. *From Napoleon to Stalin* and *Rumours of War*, collections of his essays gleaned from various journals, academic and otherwise, produced such comments as 'the dullness of facts, the stupidity of the human race, the tragedy of European history brightened up by the epigram, the *bon mot*, the scintillating quip', and 'his glance is scornful, his wit aseptic, his judgements on the human comedy clinical and chilling'. Concern also began to appear, on the one hand over whether Taylor the historian and Taylor the journalist were compatible, and on the other that the latter encouraged the style which made the former sparkle. History and journalism, it was said, made up his 'historiographical personality. This is the reason why he is so readable and worth reading'.[21]

The Struggle for Mastery in Europe evoked a mixed response which had nothing to do – at least overtly – with Taylor the journalist. Fritz Stern thought it was a healthy correction to diplomatic histories coloured by determinist theories or by the shock of world war, while Henry Fairlie disliked diplomatic history written 'in a kind of Blue book and White Paper vacuum'. He wanted more social context. *Bismarck: the Man and the Statesman* which appeared the following year, was simply high class journalism written in a 'fashionable, light handed, and cocksure method', according to one critic. To another, it was 'better than any earlier biographer', because 'Mr Taylor conveys Bismarck's personality'. Michael Howard (once Taylor's student) accepted as a given the blending of journalism and history in this, as in other Taylor books. 'The pattern is too sharply etched; the epigrams are too neat; the judgements are too final: but how refreshing it is to read a historian who is not afraid of pattern, epigram, and judgement!'[22]

The Troublemakers: Dissent Over Foreign Policy was difficult for many critics to justify when they compared it with Taylor's other work. The book was frivolous, even absurd, the work of an 'intellectual teddy-boy' wrote one reviewer, who then reminded Taylor that his reputation as an *enfant terrible* 'can become an obsession, and the obsession can become involuntary and irreversible'. Another critic suggested that Taylor might have gone too far in tilting the scales away from the Establishment, and that in any case 'it may well be that the business of the historian is not the tilting of scales'. Meanwhile, Kingsley Martin liked the idea of a book that exposed the silliness of both the Establishment and its critics. *The Origins of the Second World* also inspired a wide range of views regarding Taylor's competence, from Sebastian Heffner describing it as 'an almost faultless masterpiece, perfectly proportioned, perfectly controlled', by a historian who is 'a rescuer of forgotten truth, a knight of paradox, a prince of story telling, and a great, maybe the greatest, master of his craft', to G. F. Hudson, who thought Taylor ignored evidence and raised serious questions regarding his understanding of men and events, his accuracy and honesty in reading documents, and his grasp of diplomatic relations.[23]

English History redeemed Taylor with the critics, or at least some of them. Here was 'a history of a generation, comprehensive and comprehensible, well proportioned, seldom rushed, and never flagging in interest', wrote one. Another noted that Taylor might sometimes be 'superficial and slick', but more often he was 'disconcertingly profound and provocative'. Still another vowed that it would be difficult to think of anyone who could have done a better job with the subject.[24]

Critical judgements over many years, their contradictions, agreements, and variety of perceptions, simply underscored Taylor's complexity. They make clear that he was a serious historical scholar and an entertainer – 'intellectually frivolous', as he once phrased it; a scintillating stylist and a writer of tedious description; imaginative but also on occasion simplistic; an infuriating revisionist on the origins of the Second World War, but disappointingly conventional on the origins of the First World War, and on Britain's relations with Europe; a historian impatient with methodological and interpretive models, just as he was with diplomatic systems, but who also wrote as a determinist and was the most orthodox narrative historian since Sir John Marriott with whom he compared himself – in terms of only being a narrative writer.[25] The paradoxes were always evident in Taylor's work. A radical populist, he expended most of his effort over the years in describing the activities of the elite, including *English History*, where his theme was self-consciously populist. All the same the book devoted more space to the peoples' rulers than to the people themselves. A life-long socialist, early on he repudiated Marx and Marxists whether in politics or in history. Taylor was a good, technical historian whose interpretations were often unorthodox and sometimes shocking. In short, the critics' picture of Taylor is of a historian as conventional, unconventional, populist, individualist, radical and orthodox, all at the same time.

Naturally, Taylor could never accept such a paradoxical picture of himself, however much he loved paradox in others. He wrote:

I am not a philosophic historian. I have no system, no moral interpretation. I write to clear my mind, to discover how things happened and how men behaved. If the result is shocking or provocative, this is not from intent, but solely because I try to judge from the evidence without being influenced by the judgement of others. I have little respect for men in positions of power, though no doubt I should not do better in their place. Englishmen interest me the most, and after them Europeans. They may all be of small account now; but their behaviour in the last century and a half is a subject of some curiosity and even of some importance.[26]

Was this picture of himself a true one? Was this, in the final analysis, though written in 1956 at the mid-point of his career, what Taylor was all about?

In an odd way, it was. Taylor appeared to swing to and fro on the issue of profound forces and immediate causes, determinism and choice, and plan and accident within history, arguing with equal conviction for each at one time or another, and rendering the question of responsibility, moral or otherwise, difficult to assess. No war is inevitable until it happens, he argued in one place, but described the 'inevitable' failure of the Habsburg system in another. He claimed that 'it was no more a mistake for the German people to end up with Hitler than it is an accident when a river flows into the sea', but argued that German colonies were acquired by accident. He claimed that both world wars were blunders – the one because the Schlieffen Plan took control of events and the other because the diplomats mistimed their diplomatic initiatives. But, having denied moral judgement in history, he wrote these lines which seemed to assert the undeniability of moral judgements:

> It is all very well to say that we must find out what Cromwell or Napoleon was trying to do instead of having a preconceived notion of what they ought to have done. But where is this process to stop? . . . Is it enough to say: 'the Inquisition tortured and burnt thousands of heretics; Hitler sent millions of Jews to the gas-chamber. They did a find job according to their lights?'[27]

The essential point was Taylor's apparently profound commitment to taking every historical case on its merits, and judging it according to the evidence. For him, nothing was absolute except conforming to that which was required in order to find out what happened next, and adhering to those standards of human progress which involved striving after the liberty and happiness of common people. But this was not meant in any Marxist sense. Rather, it was the individualism of his father, who seemed to believe that socialism meant leaving the workers alone to get on with their lives. Taylor wrote political commentary from the perspective that 'no one is better than me – intellectually, morally, socially . . . I'm not better than anybody else', and history with the view in mind that

> [t]he historian does well to lead a dedicated life; yet however dedicated, he remains primarily a citizen. To turn from political responsibility to dedication is to open the door to tyranny and measureless barbarism.[28]

This was what Taylor was about: a mind steeped in radical English political traditions, reflective of the instincts of a Northern English populist and Little Englander, and comfortable with the idea that there was nothing wrong with writing straight narrative history that told an interesting story that someone might want to read. Along the way, he asserted that he was under no obligation to conform to any view of the world or of his craft but his own. The wide variations to be found within the critical response to his work suggests strongly that he rarely did conform. Taylor's place in the historical community was never assured, and he seemed bent on making it as precarious as possible. All the same, the question 'Will he last?' has, most probably, an affirmative answer. His work was imperfect, but what historian's is not? His views provoked debate and re-examination, which is continuing, of interpretations and conclusions about great events, while his style showed a generation of younger historians that lively writing and good scholarship are not incompatible. Not every historian, or even very many, can claim as much. In any case, his subject matter seems to keep coming around, reminding those who have read him that he always had something useful to say about ethnic politics in the Balkans, the role of Germany in Europe, the role of Europe in the world, and about the role of ordinary people in a political community.

Taylor's description of his profession and by implication of himself, set down as long ago as 1952, seems to go to the heart of the matter. 'The English historian calls no man master', he wrote. 'He works alone, following his own bent, thinking occasionally of his reader (though not often enough), but rarely of his colleagues and never of his critics.'[29]

When all is said and done, A. J. P. Taylor could have no more appropriate epitaph.

Notes

Preface

1. 'A. J. P. Taylor', *The Times*, September 8, 1990, p. 16; J. Y. Smith, 'British Historian A. J. P. Taylor Dies at 84', *Washington Post*, September 8, 1990, p. B6; Richard Gott, 'Great history, little England', *Guardian*, September 8, 1990.
2. Keith Robbins to Robert Cole, January 31, 1969; Denis Judd to Cole, February 2, 1969.
3. See C. Robert Cole, 'A Bibliography of the Works of A. J. P. Taylor, parts I and II', *The Bulletin of Bibliography and Magazine Notes*, 33 (July–September and October–December 1976) pp. 170–7, 181, 212–25, cited below as 'A Bibliography of A. J. P. Taylor'; and Chris Wrigley, *A. J. P. Taylor: A Complete Annotated Bibliography* (Sussex, 1980), cited below as *A. J. P. Taylor Bibliography*. Wrigley's volume runs to more than 600 pages.

Introduction

1. A. J. P. Taylor, 'Received With Thanks', *Observer*, November 20, 1966, p. 26.
2. Taylor, *The Origins of the Second World War* (New York, 1963) p. 15. Cited below as *Origins of the Second World War*.
3. Taylor, 'Accident Prone, or What Happened Next', *JMH*, 49 (March 1977) p. 2. Referred to below as 'Accident Prone'.
4. Taylor, 'Dreyfus', *MG* (May 7, 1939) p. 7.
5. Taylor, 'Diplomatic History', *MG* (May 26, 1939) p. 415.
6. A. J. P. Taylor, quoted in Ved Mehta, *The Fly and the Fly Bottle* (London, 1963) p. 151. Cited below as *Fly and the Fly Bottle*. Nonconformists historically regarded the Anglican Church as their enemy, and Taylor inherited this tradition sufficiently to once claim that his hero, socialist idealist George Lansbury, suffered from the defect of being Anglican. His political views were tainted, in Taylor's estimation, by an innate sense of superiority that was the principal by-product of religious establishment. For himself, Taylor claimed to be closer in spirit and viewpoint to the Quakers than any other religious body because, like him, they were a community resolutely out of step with the larger community.
7. Information on Taylor's early life for this study derives from the author's personal knowledge, much of it given him by Taylor directly over the years, and from *A. J. P. Taylor: A Personal History* (London, 1983). Cited below as *Personal History*.

8. Eric Glasgow, 'The Amalgamation of Birkdale and Southport', p. 6. This unpublished manuscript was supplied by Glasgow, who is a local historian of Lancashire. He described Percy Taylor's involvement in the Park–Common controversy as being populism against privilege.

9. Taylor to Cole, July 2, 1973

10. Ibid.; Henry Pelling, *The British Communist Party: A Historical Profile* (New York, 1958) p. 405. Cited below as *British Communist Party*. Newbold proved to be unreliable as the 'English Lenin'. A Quaker of humble origin, he rose in the world via a Manchester University education and the politics of the Fabian Society. He was a moderately successful journalist and was persecuted for writing *How Europe Armed for War*, an indictment of private arms manufacturers. He was elected to parliament as a Communist for Motherwell in 1922. There it ended. Newbold soon left the Communist Party over differences with the leadership. In 1925 he supported Winston Churchill's return to the gold standard, and in 1929 took a seat on the Macmillan Commission on Industry and Finance. From then until his death, Newold was regarded as a traitor to the Communist cause.

11. *Personal History*, p. 37

12. Taylor to Cole, July 2, 1973; Lord Beaverbrook, 'The Man Who Likes to Stir Things Up', *A Century of Conflict*, ed. Martin Gilbert (New York, 1967) p. 3.

13. See Francis E. Pollard (ed.), *Bootham School, 1823–1923* (London, 1926).

14. John H. Gray to Cole, February 12, 1973. Mr Gray was headmaster at Bootham, and his letter included Taylor's *bene decessit* and the results of a conversation with Leslie Gilbert, who had been Taylor's history master. Gilbert remembered Taylor as 'precocious and likable'. Taylor recalled Gilbert as wanting 'to save my soul from Marxism'. The John Bright oration was in honour of the nineteenth-century MP from Manchester, opponent of the Corn Laws, critic of the Crimean War and Quaker hero. He was also Taylor's hero over the years, precisely because he was a dissenter and critic of war and the wielders of power.

15. *British Communist Party*, p. 36; Taylor to Cole, July 2, 1973.

16. Terence Greenidge, *Degenerate Oxford?* (London, 1930) p. 171. Greenidge tells a depressing – and subjective – story of the treatment of intellectual students by the Oxford 'hearty' types, based upon observations made at the time that Taylor was an undergraduate.

17. Taylor to Cole, February 28, 1967. A look at the *Oxford University Gazette* for Taylor's years indicates that 'modern history' ended with 1815. After that came political science.

18. Taylor to Cole, February 19, 1966.

19. Taylor to Cole, May 11, 1973; Taylor, quoted in *Fly and the Fly Bottle*, p. 151.

20. Ibid., p. 144.

21. Ibid., p. 151.
22. Taylor, *The Italian Problem In European Diplomacy, 1847–1849* (Manchester, 1934) p. viii. Cited below as *The Italian Problem*. Taylor, *The Habsburg Monarchy, 1815–1918*, 1st edn (London, 1941) p. vi. Cited below as *Habsburg Monarchy*, 1st edn. Both Namier and Sir Samuel Alexander had reputations for eccentric behaviour, and Taylor loved them both. Alexander, for example, is reputed to have sat in the front row at Hallé Orchestra concerts and read his *Manchester Guardian* during the performance of pieces he did not like. Namier was given to imposing on his friends for hours at a time, to the extent that one exasperated host composed a couplet which read:

There was a Jew named Namier,
Who came here, and came here, and came here!

Or, there was his response to a matron who asked what he thought was the purpose of secondary education. He replied: 'Elementary education keeps children off the streets; university education provides a place for people like me. As for secondary education, I can think of no reason for it at all.' Taylor recalled both anecdotes in *Personal History*.
23. A. F. Pribrâm, it should be noted, was a major contributor to *Die große Politik* from the Habsburg side. The German side consisted of 54 volumes, which Taylor described in later years as 'the only collection of diplomatic documents which can be recommended as bedside reading to the layman' (Taylor, *The Struggle for Mastery in Europe, 1848–1918*, Oxford, 1954, p. 572; cited below as *Struggle for Mastery*). He also noted that publication of *Die große Politik* 'shamed' the British and French into producing similar collections of their diplomatic documents, all to the advantage of historians such as himself.
24. 'Preserving Civil Liberties. Austria Sympathy Meeting Discusses Democracy in Britain', *MG*, June 25, 1934, p. 11; 'Dearly Won Liberties. Danger of Losing them through Apathy: the Sedition Bill Threat', *MG*, June 25, 1934, p. 11.
25. Taylor to the author, June 6, 1966.
26. John W. Boyer, 'A. J. P. Taylor and the Art of Modern History', *JMH*, 49 (March 1977) p. 72.

Chapter 1 Historian of Foreign Policy

1. Taylor to Cole, January 12, 1966.
2. 'Accident Prone', p. 1.
3. Ibid., p. 6.
4. *The Italian Problem*, pp. vii–viii; Taylor to Cole, January 12, 1966. The editors of *The Italian Problem* did not use diacritical markings in

244 A. J. P. Taylor: The Traitor within the Gates

their spelling of Pribrâm's name, nor did Taylor. Therefore, neither has this author when quoting.

5. Alfred Francis Pribrâm, *England and the International Policy of the European Great Powers, 1871–1914* (London, 1931) p. viii. Cited below as *England and the Great Powers; Personal History*, p. 90.
6. *Personal History*, pp. 90–1. Friedjung was Pribrâm's predecessor at the University of Vienna, and part of the great school of Viennese historians in the late nineteenth and early twentieth centuries.
7. *England and the Great Powers*, p. xi.
8. Ibid., pp. 147–9.
9. Ibid., pp. 1, xi.
10. Ibid., p. 149.
11. *The Italian Problem*, p. 2.
12. Ibid., pp. 1–4.
13. *England and the Great Powers*, p. 103.
14. *The Italian Problem*, pp. 7–8.
15. Ibid., pp. 8, 1.
16. Ibid., pp. vii–8.
17. Ibid., bibliographical note, p. 244.
18. Ibid., pp. 6–7.
19. Taylor, 'Metternich and His 'System' for Europe', *Listener*, 62 (July 1959) pp. 167–8. Cited below as 'Metternich and his "System" for Europe'. Of course, it is not entirely wrong to argue that Taylor employed a similar system, in that he simply reversed this 'political science' process, using contemporary theses to explain history.
20. *The Italian Problem*, p. 17. Taylor described in *The Italian Problem* almost exactly the 'classic' balance of power system as laid out for the Napoleonic war years by Edward Vose Gulick in *Europe's Classical Balance of Power* (New York, 1955).
21. *The Italian Problem*, p. 9.
22. Ibid.
23. A traditional story from the Napoleonic Wars concerns a Tyrolean peasant, Andreas Hofer, who organised and led a successful partisan action against the French in the Brenner Pass. When Hofer was described to Emperor Francis II as a patriot, the monarch replied: 'But is he a patriot for me?'
24. *The Italian Problem*, p. 10.
25. Ibid., pp. 11–12.
26. Ibid., p. 236.
27. Ibid., p. 239.
28. Ibid., p. 8.
29. Ibid., p. 80.
30. Ibid., p. 144.
31. Ibid., pp. 218, 242, 31.
32. Ibid., p. 113.
33. General Oudinot, quoted in ibid., p. 96.
34. Ibid., p. 47.
35. Metternich to Dietrichstein, September 27, 1847, quoted in ibid., p. 43.

36. Ibid.
37. Ibid., p. 3.
38. Ibid.
39. Ibid., p. 6.
40. Ibid., p. 4.
41. Ibid., p. 5.
42. Ibid., p. 25.
43. Ibid., p. 31.
44. Ibid., p. 78.
45. Ibid., p. 42.
46. Apponyi reporting to Metternich, March 8, 1849, ibid., p. 82.
47. Ibid., pp. 21–2.
48. Ibid., p. 177.
49. Taylor to Cole, January 29, 1969, and December 18, 1975.
50. See Howard McGaw Smith, 'Review of *The Italian Problem in European Diplomacy, 1847–1849*, by A. J. P. Taylor, *JMH*, 7 (September 1935) p. 346. Few of Taylor's critics on this study were concerned with his methodology, but rather with its results.
51. Taylor to Cole, May 15, 1967.
52. Taylor, 'Ranke', *Englishmen and Others* (London, 1956) p. 1.

Chapter 2 Slav Troubles

1. Taylor, '25 Years of Czechoslovakia', *MGW*, November 5, 1943, p. 260.
2. Ibid.
3. Taylor, 'Dollfus and Austria', *MGW*, July 12, 1935, p. 35.
4. Taylor, 'The Last Habsburg', *MGW*, May 29, 1936, p. 35.
5. *Habsburg Monarchy,* lst edn. p. vii.
6. Ibid, p. 310.
7. Ibid., pp. 1, 6.
8. Taylor, *The Habsburg Monarchy, 1809–1918*, 2nd edn (London, 1948) p. 7. Cited below as *Habsburg Monarchy*, 2nd edn.
9. Taylor, 'Metternich', *MG*, November 6, 1935, p. 7.
10. *Habsburg Monarchy*, 1st edn, p. 2.
11. Ibid., pp. 81–2.
12. Taylor, 'Introduction', *The Struggle for Supremacy in Germany, 1859–1866*, by Heinrich Friedjung (London, 1935) p. xxiii. Cited below as *Struggle for Supremacy*.
13. *Habsburg Monarchy*, 1st edn, p. 29.
14. Ibid., pp. 46–7. Taylor referred later to one other 'recorded' saying by Ferdinand. Observing the shambles of Habsburg policy in the year after his abdication, the former Emperor supposedly remarked: 'Even I could have done this well.'
15. Ibid, pp. 81–2.
16. Ibid., p. 34.
17. Ibid., p. 30.
18. Ibid., p. 32.

19. Ibid., pp. 35–6.
20. Ibid., p. 31.
21. Ibid., p. 50
22. The revival of 'Irish', the ancient Gaelic language of Ireland, after centuries of being suppressed by the English, is an exact parallel to what Taylor described here.
23. *Habsburg Monarchy*, 1st edn, p. 26.
24. Ibid., p. 55.
25. Ibid., p. 157.
26. Ibid., pp. 160–1.
27. Ibid., p. 25.
28. Ibid., p. 24.
29. Ibid., p. 140.
30. *Struggle for Supremacy*, p. xxviii.
31. *Habsburg Monarchy*, 1st edn, pp. 228, 230.
32. Ibid., p. 253.
33. Taylor to Cole, July 26, 1976.
34. *Habsburg Monarchy*, 1st edn, p. 221.
35. Ibid., p. 220–221.
36. Ibid., pp. 179, 27.
37. Ibid., pp. 127, 138, ix; *Personal History*, pp. 156–7.
38. Taylor, 'Kossuth', *MGW*, February 26, 1937, p. 174.
39. *Habsburg Monarchy*, 1st edn, pp. 21, 24.
40. Ibid., pp. 193–4.
41. Taylor, 'National Independence and the "Austrian Idea"', *PQ*, 16 (July, 1945) p. 236. Cited below as 'National Independence and the Austrian Idea'; *Habsburg Monarchy*, 1st edn, p. 278.
42. *Habsburg Monarchy*, 2nd edn, p. 7.
43. *Habsburg Monarchy*, 1st edn, p. 33.
44. Ibid., pp. 33–4.
45. Ibid., p. 80.
46. Ibid., pp. 279–80.
47. Ibid., p. 297.
48. Ibid., p. viii.
49. *Habsburg Monarchy*, 2nd edn, p. 252.
50. Ibid., p. 254. Taylor specified the following peoples: constitutional Austria included Germans, Czechs, Poles, Little Russians, Slovenes, Serbo-Croats, Italians, Rumanians; Czechoslovakia included Czechs, Slovaks, Germans, Magyars, Little Russians, Poles, Jews; Great Hungary contained Magyars, Germans, Slovaks, Rumanians, Little Russians, Croats, Serbs; and Yugoslavia contained Serbs, Croats, Slovenes, Bosnian Muslims, Magyars, Germans, Albanians, Rumanians, and Macedonians.
51. 'National Independence and the Austrian Idea', p. 235.
52. Taylor, 'Masaryk', *MGW*, May 3, 1940, p. 348.
53. *Habsburg Monarchy*, 2nd edn, p. 253. In the year of Taylor's death, Yugoslavia began to disintegrate, and two years later, Czechoslovakia followed suit.
54. *Habsburg Monarchy*, 1st edn, p. 265.

55. Taylor, 'Thomas Garrigue Masaryk', reprinted in *Europe: Grandeur and Decline* (London, 1967) pp. 182, 179. Cited below as 'Thomas Garrique Masaryk'.
56. *Habsburg Monarchy*, 2nd edn, p. 255.
57. Taylor, 'Black Lamb and Grey Falcon', *TT*, March 7, 1942, p. 195.
58. *Struggle for Supremacy*, pp. xxix–xxx.
59. *Habsburg Monarchy*, 1st edn, pp. 298–9.
60. *Struggle for Supremacy*, p. xxix.
61. *Habsburg Monarchy*, 2nd edn, p. 258.
62. Ibid., p. 257.
63. Taylor, 'The Austrian Illusion', reprinted in *From Napoleon to Stalin* (London, 1950) p. 177; *Habsburg Monarchy*, 2nd edn, p. 240.
64. 'National Independence and the Austrian Idea', p. 240.
65. *Habsburg Monarchy*, 2nd edn, p. 257.
66. *Habsburg Monarchy*, 1st edn, pp. 26–7.
67. Taylor, 'Peace Settlements', *TT*, April 11, 1942, p. 314; 'Masaryk in England', *MGW*, March 12, 1943, p. 48; 'Thomas Garrigue Masaryk', p. 181.
68. *Habsburg Monarchy*, 1st edn, p. 72.
69. Taylor, 'Between Two Wars', *MGW*, January 21, 1944, p. 36. Taylor, 'The European Revolution', *Listener*, November 22, 1945, p. 575.
70. Ibid., p. 575.
71. Ibid., p. 576
72. Ibid.
73. Ibid.
74. Taylor, 'Czechoslovakia Today', *MGW*, August 2, 1946, p. 59.
75. Ibid.
76. Taylor, 'Czechoslovakia Today: The Position of the Slovaks', *MGW*, August 9, 1946, p. 71.
77. Taylor, 'Impressions of Yugoslavia: I – A Regime of Youth', *MGW*, May 15, 1947, p. 9.
78. Ibid.
79. Taylor, 'Impressions of Yugoslavia: II – Economics and Politics', *MGW*, May 22, 1947, p. 13.
80. Taylor, 'Ancestry of the "New Democracies"', *Listener*, July 15, 1948, p. 92.
81. Ibid., p. 93.
82. Taylor, 'The Czech Communist Coup', *MGW*, February 2, 1950, p. 12.
83. Taylor, 'Tito and Stalin: the Revolt from Within', *Listener*, January 20, 1949, p. 86.
84. Ibid.
85. Ibid.
86. Ibid.
87. Taylor, 'Trieste or Trst?', *NSN*, December 9, 1944, pp. 386–7.
88. Taylor, 'Trieste', from a pamphlet written in 1945 for the South Slav Committee and published in New York, reprinted in *From Napoleon to Stalin* (London, 1950), including an epilogue added in 1949, pp. 207–8.

89. 'National Independence and the Austrian Idea', p. 244.
90. Eduard Bênês, quoted in Taylor, 'Czechoslovakia Today: Questions of Foreign Policy and Trade', *MGW*, August 16, 1946, p. 87. Cited below as 'Czechoslovakia Today: Foreign Policy and Trade'.
91. Eduard Gottwald, quoted in ibid.
92. Ibid.
93. Taylor to Cole, February 19, 1966.
94. Taylor, 'Free Territory of Trieste', *NSN*, 38 (October 29, 1949), p. 479.
95. 'Thomas Garrique Masaryk', pp. 181–2.
96. *Habsburg Monarchy*, 2nd edn, pp. 259–60.
97. 'Czechoslovakia Today: Foreign Policy and Trade', p. 87.
98. *Habsburg Monarchy*, 2nd edn, p. 261.

Chapter 3 Europe and the Germans

1. Taylor, *The Course of German History* (Capricorn edn: New York, 1962) p. 115. Cited below as *Course of German History*. This book was first published in London in 1946. It grew out of a chapter on Weimar Germany commissioned by the wartime Political Warfare Executive for a handbook. They decided Taylor's chapter was too depressing and rejected it. Denis Brogan suggested that he turn it into a book, and *Course of German History* was the result.
2. Ibid., p. 115.
3. Taylor, 'German Unity: I – The Background of the Reich', *MGW*, April 6, 1944, p. 189.
4. Taylor, 'Guns, Not Butter', *MG*, March 12, 1937, p. 9.
5. *Personal History*, p. 134.
6. Taylor to Cole, interview, June 15, 1976.
7. Ibid.
8. Taylor, *English History, 1914–1945* (Oxford, 1965) p. 516. Cited hereafter as *English History*. Over a cup of tea at the Institute of Historical Research in London in 1979, Taylor remarked to me that he could see little use in the study of British wartime propaganda, and cited his Oxford experience as evidence. I was then just beginning research into that very subject, and was shaken by this announcement. However, I carried on all the same, defying the implied advice, just as Taylor would have done – or so I have always believed. Happily, the research was successful, resulting in my book *Britain and the War of Words in Neutral Europe, 1939–1945* (London, 1990); Hansard, *Parliamentary Debates*, 365, H. C. Debates, pp. 1143–5.
9. *Personal History*, p. 154; Taylor to Dick Cavett, television interview *ca.*1971. Early in the war, Frank Pakenham had represented the Ministry of Information in Eire, to the extent that it was represented, until he was replaced in 1941 by John Betjeman, who served as press attaché under Sir John Maffey, the UK Representative to Eire.
10. Taylor, 'Popular Biography', *MG*, November 10, 1936, p. 7.
11. Taylor, 'A German Exile', MG, June 18, 1937, p. 7; 'Thomas Mann',

MGW, September 24, 1943, p. 172; 'German History', *MGW*, November 17, 1944, p. 273. Cited below as 'German History'; and 'A German on War's Effects', *MGW*, December 31, 1937, p. 534.
12. Taylor, 'Thiers and Stresemann', *MGW*, April 12, 1941, p. 294.
13. Taylor, 'German Legends', *MGW*, January 5, 1945, p. 8.
14. 'German History', p. 273.
15. Taylor, 'What Can We Do with Germany?' *NSN*, 28 (October 28, 1944), p. 288; 'German Unity: II – The Reich of Bismarck and Hitler', *MGW*, April 21, 1944, p. 217.
16. E. L. Woodward, 'How Germany Obtained Colonies', *Spectator*, March 25, 1938, p. 538; Mary E. Townshend, 'Review of *Germany's First Bid For Colonies, 1884–1885*, by A. J. P. Taylor', *AHR*, 44 (July, 1939) p. 900.
17. Taylor, *Germany's First Bid for Colonies, 1884–1885: A Move in Bismarck's European Policy* (Archon Books edn: London, 1967) p. 6. First published in London, 1938. Cited below as *Germany's First Bid for Colonies*.
18. Ibid., p. 6.
19. Ibid., p. 4.
20. Ibid., p. 31.
21. Ibid., p. 99.
22. Ibid., p. 22.
23. Ibid., p. 15.
24. *Personal History*, p. 172.
25. Taylor, *The Course of German History*, p. 13.
26. Taylor to Cole interview, June 15, 1976.
27. *Course of German History*, p. 7.
28. Ibid., p. 16.
29. Ibid., p. 18.
30. Ibid., pp. 19–20.
31. Ibid., p. 19.
32. Ibid., p. 21.
33. Ibid., p. 25.
34. Ibid., p. 33.
35. Ibid., p. 31.
36. Ibid., p. 30.
37. Ibid., pp. 44–5.
38. Ibid., p. 44.
39. Ibid., p. 43.
40. Ibid., p. 99.
41. Ibid., p. 115.
42. Ibid., p. 78.
43. Ibid., p. 86.
44. Ibid.
45. Ibid., p. 115.
46. Ibid., p. 161.
47. Ibid., p. 173.
48. Ibid., pp. 173–4.
49. Ibid., p. 185.

50. Ibid., p. 211.
51. Ibid., pp. 213, 223.
52. Ibid., pp. 226, 222. In the context of describing what he termed the Magyar and German 'Great Fear' of the 'Slav Tide', Taylor identified these two peoples as being partners in Slav oppression. This had been a major theme in *The Habsburg Monarchy*, where he argued that at one point in the nineteenth century, the Germans and Magyars of the Habsburg Empire worked out a theory whereby the Germans would dominate the Slavs in the western half of the empire, while the Magyars could oppress them, with German blessings, in the east. Ultimately, Taylor concluded that in Europe only Magyars were the equal to Germans in barbaric behaviour.
53. See 'Dream-Play of the German Century', *TLS*, September 29, 1945, pp. 457–8; Leo Gershoy, 'Professional Historians Analyze Germany', *NYHTWR*, July 7, 1946, p. 2; Hans Kohn, 'Germany and the West', *NYT*, August 18, 1946, p. 22; R. H. S. Crossman, 'Can Germany be a Free Nation?', *NSN*, 30 (July 29, 1945) p. 62, cited below as 'Can Germany Be a Free Nation?'; and Elizabeth Wiskemann, 'Light on German History', *Spectator*, 10 (August 10, 1945) pp. 132–3.
54. Taylor, 'The Ruler in Berlin', *From Napoleon to Stalin*, p. 82; 'The Twilight of the God', *Englishmen and Others*, London, 1956, p. 183. Cited below as *Englishmen and Others*; 'German Power-Worship', *MGW*, November 20, 1952, p. 10; 'The Problem of Germany', *Listener*, June 20, 1946, p. 799.
55. Ironically, several German historians, Hans-Adolf Jacobsen and Golo Mann among others, described Taylor as a Hitler apologist for having 'excused' Hitler in *Origins of the Second World War*.
56. Taylor, 'Ranke', *Englishmen and Others*, p. 18.
57. Taylor, 'Another Good German', *MGW*, November 16, 1950, p. 10; 'Germany', *MGW*, July 6, 1950, p. 12. *Course of German History*, pp. 7, 9.
58. *Course of German History*, 1962 edn, p. 7.
59. Ibid., p. 9.
60. H. Russell Williams, 'A. J. P. Taylor', *Historians of Modern Europe*, ed. Hans Schmitt (Baton Rouge, 1971) p. 83.
61. Wolfram Hanrieder, *The Stable Crisis* (New York, 1970) p. 1.
62. Taylor, *Bismarck: The Man and the Statesman* (New York, 1955) p. 270.
63. Ibid., pp. 33, 13, 69.
64. Ibid., pp. 35, 156, 203.
65. Ibid., p. 245.
66. Ibid., p. 273.
67. Ibid., pp. 194, 121, 272.
68. Taylor, 'Bismarck: Fifty Years After', *MGW*, August 5, 1948, p. 6.
69. See Taylor, 'Resistance', *MGW*, July 26, 1956, p. 10; 'Somewhat Passive Resistance', *MGW*, December 14, 1958, p. 11; 'Review of *Geschichte der Weimarer Republik*, by Erich Eyck', *EHR*, 72 (July 1957) pp. 517–18; 'Who Burnt the Reichstag?' *HT*, 10 (August 1960) pp. 512–22, cited below as 'Who Burnt the Reichstag?'; 'Why Must we Soft-Soap the Germans?' *SE*, October 27, 1957, p. 12.

70. Taylor, 'Hitler's Third Book', *NS*, 65 (April 17, 1962), pp. 595–6; 'Let Britain Put an End to This Bad Dream', *SE*, January 10, 1965, p. 16; 'Wilson's Blunder Over Berlin', *SE*, February 16, 1969, p. 16.

Chapter 4 The Precarious Balance

1. *Personal History*, pp. 181, 190–1.
2. Taylor, *Struggle for Mastery*, p. x.
3. Taylor, 'Pre-War', *TT*, 23 (November 28, 1942) p. 956.
4. *Personal History*, p. 190; Taylor to Cole, May 6, 1969.
5. Taylor to Cole, 3 November, 1975; Taylor, 'The Wroclaw Congress', *NSN*, 36 (September 18, 1948) p. 238; *Personal History*, pp. 181, 192–3; 'Are Our Public Men Too Squeamish?', *SE*, October 30, 1960. In this piece, Taylor blamed the Labour Government for his being banned at BBC, claiming that it was 'some man called Morrison.' Taylor knew Morrison very well, at least by reputation; Taylor, 'Congress of Intellectuals at Wroclaw, *MGW*, September 9, 1948, p. 12.
6. Taylor, 'European Mediation and the Agreement of Villafranca, 1859', *EHR*, 51 (January 1936) p. 52. Cited below as 'Agreement of Villafranca'; 'An Unbalanced Pattern', *Observer*, June 9, 1963, p. 26. Cited below as 'Unbalanced Pattern'. Taylor was always inclined, in his historical writing, to use only the last names of his characters.
7. *Personal History*, p. 205. *Wie es eiglentlich gewesen* (how it actually happened) is the famous dictum that the great nineteenth-century German historian Leopold von Ranke (about whose politics Taylor wrote with less than enthusiasm, see Chapter 3) laid before his students as their guide to how history should be presented. Every graduate student in history, at least in North America since that date, has been confronted with it.
8. Ibid., pp. 206–7; Taylor to Cole, May 13, 1967. Taylor remarked in that correspondence that 'I should have refused the Regius Chair if it had been offered me. Macmillan was then Prime Minister, and his hands were still red from the bloodshed of Suez.'
9. 'Agreement of Villafranca', p. 52.
10. Taylor, 'Fashoda', *From Napoleon to Lenin* (New York, 1966) pp. 120, 123. Cited below as *Napoleon to Lenin*. Reproduced from a piece first published on September 18, 1948. Cited below as 'Fashoda'; 'Les premières années de l'alliance russe', *RH*, 204 (July 1950) p. 62. Cited below as 'L'alliance russe'. Trans: 'French diplomacy did not rely solely on the Russian alliance: even at moments of great tension they never lost sight of the necessity of a reconciliation with England. The Russian alliance did not, in effect, contradict the Anglo-French entente, but on the contrary was a means for realising more favourable conditions to France.'
11. Taylor, 'Prelude to Fashoda: The Question of the Upper Nile, 1894–5', *EHR*, 65 (January 1950) pp. 52, 79. Cited below as 'Prelude to Fashoda'.

12. Taylor, 'British Policy in Morocco, 1886–1902', *EHR*, 66 (July 1951) p. 374. Cited below as 'British Policy in Morocco'; 'La Conférence d'Algésiras', *RH*, 208 (October 1952) p. 254. Cited below as 'D'Algésiras'. Trans: On more than one occasion, the chance of a few hours could have altered the entire pattern of negotiations; and then 'the inevitable course of history' would, no doubt, have proceeded in quite a different direction.

13. 'Agreement of Villafranca', p. 55; 'Prelude to Fashoda', p. 60.

14. 'Fashoda', p. 95; 'D'Algésiras', p. 238. Trans: 'they would prefer the side of the [Anglo-French] entente;' 'British Policy in Morocco', pp. 348, 362.

15. Taylor, 'The Entente Cordiale', *Napoleon to Lenin*, pp. 97–100. Reprinted from *MG*, April 8, 1944; 'Tangier in Diplomacy', *Napoleon to Lenin*, p. 108. Reprinted from *MGW*, July 10, 1945.

16. Taylor, 'Review of *Bismarck*, by Erich Eyck, *Zweiter Band*', *EHR*, 61 (January 1946) p. 112.

17. Taylor, 'Review of *Bismarck*, by Erich Eyck, *Dritter Band*', *EHR*, 62 (July 1947) p. 393.

18. Taylor, 'Bismarck and Europe', *Rumours of War* (London, 1951) pp. 87–8.

19. Ibid., p. 88.

20. Ibid., pp. 88, 92, 95, 97, 100, 101.

21. Ibid., p. 102.

22. *Personal History*, pp. 190–1, 198.

23. *Struggle for Mastery*, pp. xxin, xix.

24. Ibid., pp. xx–xxi, xxiii. To the reference to diplomats behaving 'honestly', Taylor appended this footnote: 'It becomes wearisome to add "except for the Italians" to every generalization. Henceforth it may be assumed.'

25. Ibid., p. xxii.

26. Ibid., pp. xxv–xxxi. The actual amounts in Taylor's tables are also revealing, because there, too, Germany almost always led the way. By 1914, Germany was second only to Russia in population; spent 25 per cent more on the army than the nearest competitor, Russia; spent half as much as Great Britain on the navy, but at least 25 per cent more than any other power, and the same with overall defence estimates; produced half as much coal as the United States, but nearly as much as Great Britain, and five times as much as any continental power; and the same with reference to pig iron and steel.

27. Ibid., pp. xix–xxxvi.

28. Ibid., pp. 2–4.

29. Ibid., pp. 22, 5, 19.

30. Ibid., pp. 44, 61.

31. Ibid., pp. 33, 117, 82.

32. Ibid., pp. 75, 81n.

33. Ibid., pp. 132–6, 168.

34. Ibid., pp. 99, 106, 138.

35. Ibid., pp. 62, 86n, 103, 132, 140, 158, 259.

36. Ibid., pp. 145, 169, 200.
37. Ibid., pp. 217–18, 324.
38. Ibid., pp. 218–19, 225–6.
39. Ibid., pp. 247, 250, 253–4.
40. Ibid., pp. 271, 275.
41. Ibid., pp. 283–84.
42. Ibid., pp. 301–3, 370.
43. Ibid., pp. 303, 373, 393, 415, 427, 438.
44. Ibid., pp. 437, 438–40.
45. Delcassé, quoted in ibid., pp. 442, 446, 398, 448.
46. Wilhelm II, quoted in ibid., pp. 263–4, 441, 495, 510.
47. Ibid., p. 460.
48. Ibid., pp. 522–3.
49. Ibid., p. 528.
50. Ibid., p. 568.
51. Ibid., pp. 268, 207–8.
52. Ibid., pp. 277–8, 286n.
53. Ibid., pp. 265, 454–5, 458, 546.
54. Caprivi, quoted in ibid., p. 328.
55. Ibid., pp. 328, 264, 458.
56. Ibid., pp. 223–4, 463.
57. Ibid., pp. 20, 47, 212, 520, 233–4, 439.
58. Ibid., pp. 51, 108–12.
59. Ibid., pp. 202–3, 290, 385.
60. Ibid., pp. 518, 32, 115.
61. This was the final point of *Bismarck: The Man and the Statesman*.
62. *Struggle for Mastery*, p. 568.
63. Henry Fairlie, 'Modern Europe', *Spectator*, November 9, 1954, p. 629, cited below as 'Modern Europe'; Louis Barron, 'Review of *The Struggle for Mastery in Europe, 1848–1918*, by A. J. P. Taylor', *LJ*, 80 (February 15, 1954) p. 459; 'Seventy Years of Diplomacy', *The Times*, October 30, 1954, p. 8g; 'European Diplomatic History', *TLS*, November 26, 1954, pp. 749–50; Fritz Stern, 'Review of *The Struggle for Mastery in Europe, 1848–1918*, by A. J. P. Taylor', *PSQ*, 70 (March 1955) p. 113, cited below as 'Review of *Struggle for Mastery*'; Hans Kohn, 'Review of *The Struggle for Mastery in Europe, 1848–1918*, by A. J. P. Taylor', *AAAPSS*, 298 (March, 1955) p. 230; William H. McNeill, 'A Cartesian Historian', *WP*, 8 (October 1955) p. 133, cited below as 'Cartesian Historian'.
64. Asa Briggs, 'Before the Ball was Over', *NSN*, 48 (November 6, 1954) p. 587, cited below as 'Before the Ball was Over'; J. M. Thompson, 'Epitaph on the Balance of Power', *HT*, 4 (December 1954) pp. 854, 856.
65. Taylor, 'Evil Genius of the Wilhelmstrasse', *Listener*, July 21, 1955, p. 104.

Chapter 5 'Speak for England!'

1. Taylor to Cole, June 6, 1966, and December 18, 1973.
2. Taylor, *The Troublemakers: Dissent Over Foreign Policy, 1792–1939*, London, 1957, p. 9. Cited hereafter as *The Troublemakers*.
3. Taylor, 'London Diary', *NSN*, 50 (December 24, 1955) p. 849; 'John Bright and the Crimean War', *Englishmen and Others*, p. 45. This essay first appeared in the *Bulletin of the John Rylands Library* in 1954; Taylor to Cole, December 18, 1973.
4. *The Troublemakers*, p. 13.
5. C. Robert Cole, '"Hope Without Illusion": A. J. P. Taylor's Dissent, 1955–1961', *The Dissenting Tradition: Essays for Leland H. Carlson*, ed. C. Robert Cole and Michael Moody (Athens, Ohio, 1975) pp. 226–7.
6. It is worth noting that Taylor once defined journalism as 'whatever goes into a newspaper and is paid for', *Personal History*, p. 180.
7. Taylor, 'Books in General', *NSN*, 49 (January 22, 1955) p. 108.
8. 'Metternich and his "System" for Europe', p. 167.
9. Taylor to Cole, 23 March, 1970.
10. Hans J. Morganthau to Cole, May 8, 1973; Taylor to Cole, July 2, 1973.
11. Taylor to Cole, January 29, 1969; *Personal History*, p. 180.
12. Taylor, 'How Near is World War III?', *MGW*, September 3, 1959, p. 5.
13. Taylor to Cole, December 18, 1975; Maurice Richardson, quoted in *A. J. P. Taylor Bibliography*, p. 25.
14. Taylor, 'London Diary', *NS*, 92 (August 20, 1976) p. 238; Taylor, 'Report on the Rising Generation', *RN*, November 4, 1956, p. 3; Taylor, interview with Cole, September 23, 1969.
15. George Thayer, *The British Political Fringe* (London, 1965) p. 160.
16. Taylor, 'Letter to the Editor', *The Times*, March 11, 1958, p. 11; quoted in Charles W. Lomas and Michael Taylor (eds), *The Rhetoric of the British Peace Movement* (New York, 1971) p. 77.
17. Taylor, 'Campaign Report', *NS*, 55 (June 1958) pp. 799–800.
18. Taylor, quoted in *The Times*, March 31, 1959, p. 4.
19. Taylor always used the masculine gender in making general references. This does not mean that he automatically excluded women from the Establishment, and it certainly does not mean that he was opposed to equality for women. Quite the contrary. All that his use of masculine gender indicates is that he remained 'old fashioned' in regard to the use of generalised possessive pronouns.
20. Taylor, 'The Thing', *20th Century*, 162 (October 1957) p. 295. Taylor's preceding description of the Establishment and requirements for membership also was laid out in this waggish, if also cynical, essay.
21. Ibid., p. 297.
22. Taylor, 'Keeping it Dark', *Encounter*, 13 (August 1959) 42. Cited hereafter as 'Keeping it Dark'; 'Review of *i Documenti diplomatici Italiani*, 9th series, vol. I', *EHR*, 70 (October 1955) p. 654. Taylor was being too hard on archivists, who, while certainly they guard their 'hoard' carefully, can have a sense of humour about it. Once when I

was denied permission at the Public Records Office in London to see a document that had been 'retained at the department of origin' (trans: 'This document is being made an exception to the thirty-year release rule') I was told not to worry because no one else got to see it, either.

23. 'Keeping it Dark', p. 44; Taylor, 'A Devil's Advocate', *MGW*, October 30, 1952, p. 11. Taylor repeated the Beard admonition again a decade later in 'Eden in the Thirties', *Observer*, November 18, 1962, p. 24.

24. 'Keeping it Dark', p. 44.

25. *The Troublemakers*, p. 22.

26. Taylor, 'Cabinet Secrecy – Handicap for the Historian', and 'Aid to Historical Perspective', *The Times*, August 6 and 19, 1952, pp. 5e and 7e, respectively.

27. *The Troublemakers*, p. 116.

28. 'Keeping it Dark', p. 42. Since Taylor wrote this essay, the fifty-year rule was amended to thirty years; Taylor, *English History*, pp. 602–3.

29. *The Troublemakers*, p. 9.

30. *Personal History*, p. 209.

31. Ibid., pp. 209–10. Vivian Galbraith, the Regius Professor of Modern History, was shocked when Taylor informed him, in the autumn of 1955, that the lectures had been sold to independent television, even before being delivered. As Taylor never presented them on television, either he was having Galbraith on, or the Professor misunderstood him, or else the conversation never took place.

32. *The Troublemakers*, p. 12.

33. Ibid., pp. 12, 14, 15, 19.

34. Ibid., pp. 17, 23–4.

35. Ibid., pp. 26, 200.

36. Ibid., pp. 20, 170.

37. Ibid., pp. 27, 32, 36, 59, 109, 53–4, 90, 38.

38. Ibid., p. 194.

39. Ibid., pp. 43, 70, 96.

40. Ibid., pp. 47, 63, 97–8, 103.

41. Ibid., pp. 50–2, 85–7, 124, 165–6.

42. Ibid., pp. 76–7.

43. Ibid., pp. 72, 74, 56, 94, 109, 144–6.

44. Ibid., pp. 133–66.

45. Ibid., pp. 97, 113, 138.

46. Ibid., p. 157.

47. Taylor, 'On Satan's Side', *NS*, 65 (May 31, 1961) p. 826.

48. Taylor to Cole, December 18, 1975 and February 19, 1966; *English History*, p. vii. In this correspondence Taylor did not repeat a reference to having written *Origins of the Second World War* in six weeks which he made to me orally in 1969, but did repeat the quoted indication that it was written only for relaxation. The reference to Clark concerned Taylor being denied reappointment as a University Lecturer in 1963, which Clark publicly opposed.

49. *Personal History*, p. 211; Taylor to Cole, May 13, 1967.

50. Vivian Galbraith to Cole, interview December 18, 1969. There is no doubt, from his own words, that Galbraith thought Taylor was the best choice available for the Regius Chair – despite also regarding him as vulgar, shallow, and a historian whose writings were 'a waste of time'. Galbraith also claimed that they were friends. What might he have said of Taylor if they were not?
51. *Personal History*, p. 216.
52. Taylor, 'London Diary', *NSN* 50 (December 24, 1955) p. 849; Galbraith to Cole, interview December 18, 1969; Taylor, 'The Television Wars', *NSN* 62 (July 21, 1961) p. 85.
53. *Personal History*, p. 217.

Chapter 6 Storm Over War Origins

1. Taylor, *The Origins of the Second World War*, American edn, New York, 1963, p. 212. Cited below as *Origins*.
2. Hugh Trevor-Roper, 'A. J. P. Taylor, Hitler, and the War', *Encounter*, 17 (July 1961) p. 95. Cited below as 'Taylor, Hitler, and the War'. Taylor, 'How to Quote: Exercises for Beginners', *Encounter*, 17 (September 1961) p. 73. Taylor's reference to Trevor-Roper's reputation was prophetic. Years later, Trevor-Roper authenticated a set of diaries purporting to have been kept by Adolf Hitler. They were soon proved to be forgeries. That *The Times* paid a fortune for the right to publish the diaries, and then paid Trevor-Roper to authenticate them, suggested to a few cynics that the former Regius Professor might have known the diaries were forged, but authenticated them all the same. This was never proved.
3. This referred to what Taylor regarded as Oxford repudiating him for his protest against the Suez invasion, and Sir Lewis Namier repudiating him with reference to the Regius Chair appointment in 1957. See Chapter 5.
4. The 'war-guilt consensus' was built up by the writings of many historians and others in the years after the Second World War. The principle sources of the consensus, only a few of which are included in my text, include: *Judgement of the International Military Tribunal at Nuremberg*, 1946; J. W. Wheeler-Bennett, *Munich: Prologue to Tragedy*, 1948; Moscow Information Bureau publication, *Falsificators of History*, 1948; Friedrich Meinecke, *The German Catastrophe*, 1950; Maurice Baumont, *La Faillite de la paix, 1918–1939*, 1951; Charles Callan Tansill, *Back Door to War: The Roosevelt Foreign Policy*, 1952; William L. Langer and S. Everett Gleason, *The Challenge to Isolation, 1937–1940*, 1952; Alan Bullock, *Hitler: A Study in Tyranny*, 1953; Raymond J. Sontag, 'The Last Months of Peace: 1939', *Foreign Affairs*, 1957; and Herman Mau and Helmut Krausnick, *German History, 1933–1945*, 1963. My comments here on the war-guilt consensus are distilled from Robert Cole, 'A. J. P. Taylor and the Origins of the Second World War', Harold T. Parker (ed.), *Problems*

in European History (Durham, 1979) cited below as 'Taylor and War Origins'.

5. *Origins*, p. 209.
6. *Course of German History*, pp. 220–1.
7. Taylor, 'Ten Years After', *NSN*, 36 (October 2, 1948) p. 278; 'France, Germany and the Soviet Union', *MGW*, January 11, 1951, p. 11.
8. Taylor, 'Spain and the Axis', *MGW*, May 3, 1951, p. 11.
9. Taylor, 'Heyday of Appeasement', *MGW*, January 17, 1952, p. 11; 'German Diplomacy in the Appeasement Years', *MGW*, August 6, 1953, p. 11.
10. Taylor, 'How Hitler Went to War', *MGW*, February 28, 1957, p. 11; 'When Germany Ruled Europe', *MGW*, August 15, 1957, p. 10.
11. Taylor, 'Out of the Diplomatic Bag', *MGW*, February 27, 1958, p. 11; 'Lights Out Over Europe', *MGW*, March 27, 1958, p. 11; 'Munich Twenty Years After', *MGW*, October 2, 1958, p. 7.
12. 'Who Burnt the Reichstag?' pp. 515–16.
13. Ibid., pp. 519–20, 517, 516, 517.
14. Ibid., p. 518.
15. Ibid., pp. 521, 522.
16. *Origins*, pp. 15, 17.
17. Ibid., pp. 17–19.
18. Ibid., p. 22.
19. Ibid., pp. 23, 28–62.
20. Ibid., pp. 69, 71–2, 70–1. Alluding to Chaplin in this context was perfectly natural for Taylor, who always appreciated satirical comedy in which an apparent buffoon was actually a protest against the pretentious, the power-hungary, or the clever Dick who actually was only silly. Taylor admired Chaplin, but even more so W. C. Fields, whose characters got their own back more often than did Chaplin's 'victim' characters.
21. Ibid., p. 102.
22. Ibid., pp. 107, 210–11.
23. Ibid., pp. 35, 126–8.
24. Ibid., pp. 132–3.
25. Ibid., pp. 143, 145.
26. Ibid., pp. 259, 261, 265, 263, 267.
27. Sir Nevile Henderson, quoted in ibid., pp. 212, 194. The 'panic' of February 1938 was real enough. Cabinet minutes reflected it, as did various minutes and correspondence from within the various committees responsible for planning the Ministry of Information.
28. Ibid., pp. 194, 196, 198.
29. Ibid., pp. 128–30.
20. Ibid., pp. 130–1.
31. Ibid., p. 131.
32. Taylor, 'Unlucky Find', *NS*, 62 (December 1, 1961) p. 834.
33. Taylor, 'Flickering Figures', *NS*, 66 (July 12, 1963) p. 49.
34. Taylor, 'Murder or Suicide?' *The Observer*, March 17, 1963, p. 26; ibid., p. 18.
35. Extract from *Judgement of the International Military Tribunal* at

Nuremberg, 1946. The discussion of Taylor's critics is based upon Robert Cole, 'Critics of the Taylor View of History', *The Wiener Library Bulletin*, 22 (Summer, 1968) pp. 2?–24, cited below as 'Critics of the Taylor View of History'. This was republished later in E. M. Robertson, *The Origins of the Second World War* (London, 1971).

36. E. H. Carr, 'Why did we Fight?', *TLS*, April 21, 1961, p. 244, cited below as 'Why did we Fight?'.

37. David Thomson and W. N. Medlicott, letters in *TLS*, May 5 and June 2, 1961, pp. 339 and 361, respectively.

38. Isaac Deutscher, Margaret Lambert, and Georges Bonnin, letters in *TLS*, all published on June 2, 1961, p. 361.

39. Taylor, 'Letter to the Editor', *TLS*, June 9, 1961, p. 390; I saw a copy of the Fawcett paperback edition of *Origins*, in a supermarket in Logan, Utah, in 1971.

40. Trevor-Roper, 'A Reply', *Encounter*, 17 (July 1961) p. 74; 'Taylor, Hitler, and the War', p. 90.

41. Anonymous, quoted in 'Battle of the Dons', *Newsweek*, 58 (July 31, 1961) p. 72; Hugh Thomas, 'A Controversy Re-Examined: Taylor and Trevor-Roper', *Spectator*, 210 (June 7, 1963) p. 728; Taylor to Cole, May 13, 1967.

42. F. H. Hinsley, 'Review of *Origins of the Second World War* by A. J. P. Taylor', *HR*, 4 (1961) p. 223. Cited below as 'Review of War Origins'.

43. Ibid., p. 223.

44. Ibid., p. 223.

45. P. A. Reynolds, 'Hitler's War', *History*, 97 (October 1961) p. 217.

46. Ibid p. 217. The fifty errors is nothing to the two on every page that one Taylor critic claimed to have found in the pages of *Struggle for Mastery*. Edward Ingram, 'A Patriot for Me', *The Origins of the Second World War Reconsidered*, ed. Gordon Martel (London, 1986) p. 257.

47. A. L. Rowse, 'Beneath the Whitewash the Same Old Hitler', *NYTBR*, January 7, 1962, p. 6. Cited below as 'The Same Old Hitler'; G. F. Hudson, 'An Apologia for Adolf Hitler', *Commentary*, 33 (February 1962) p. 179. Cited below as 'Apologia for Hitler'.

48. 'Apologia for Hitler', pp. 182–3.

49. Robert Spencer, 'War Unpremeditated', *CHR*, 43 (June 1962) pp. 139–40, 142–3.

50. T. W. Mason, 'Some Origins of the Second World War', *PP*, 29 (December 1964) p. 87. Cited below as 'Some Origins'.

51. 'Taylor, Hitler, and the War', p. 89.

52. James Joll, 'The Ride to the Abyss', *Spectator*, 206 (April 21, 1961) p. 561. Cited below as 'Ride to the Abyss'; 'Review of War Origins', p. 224.

53. Louis Morton, 'From Fort Sumpter to Poland', *WP*, 14 (January 1962) p. 387. Cited below as 'Fort Sumpter to Poland'.

54. Deutscher, 'Letter to the Editor', *TLS*, June 2, 1961, p. 361.

55. 'Fort Sumpter to Poland', p. 278

56. *Origins*, p. 288; S. William Halperin, 'Review of *The Origins of the Second World War* by A. J. P. Taylor', *CST*, January 12 1962, p. 8.
57. Ernest Pisko, 'Minority Report on the Origins of War', *CSM*, January 11, 1961, p. 7; 'Taylor, Hitler, and the War', p. 95; Elizabeth Wiskemann, Letter in the *TLS*, June 2, 1962, p. 361. There is no reason to assume that Taylor lunching with Mosley at the Ritz in 1970 was in any way linked to the British Union of Fascists founder's 'appreciation' of Taylor's reinterpretation of war origins. See Craig Brown, 'A Proud Old Man in Love', *TLS*, July 19, 1991, p. 28.
58. 'Ride to the Abyss', p. 561.
59. 'Foresight and Hindsight', *Economist*, 169 (May 13, 1961) p. 655; 'Taylor, Hitler, and the War', p. 96; 'Fort Sumpter to Poland', p. 392; Taylor to Cole, January 29, 1969.
60. *Origins*, p. 72.
61. Taylor to Cole, January 29, 1969.
62. 'The Same Old Hitler', p. 6.
63. Frank Freidel, 'Who Started the War?' *Reporter*, 26 (January 18, 1962) p. 52; 'Some Origins', p. 87.
64. Alfred Cobban, 'Historical Notes', *History*, 47 (October, 1961) p. 227.
65. Taylor to Cole, January 29, 1969.
66. *Origins*, p. 72.
67. Ibid., p. 206.
68. Taylor to Cole, May 13, 1967; *Personal History*, p. 235; Alan Bullock, 'Hitler and the Origins of the Second World War', The Raleigh Lecture on History: British Academy, 1967, pp. 287, 262. According to Taylor, after James Joll heard Bullock's lecture, he remarked: 'Pretty smart to make one reputation by propounding a view and then making a second by knocking it down.' Some younger historians working on war-origins in the 1970s also began to reflect both Taylor's methods and his interpretations from *Origins*. Sidney Aster's *1939: The Making of the Second World War* (New York, 1976) is a case in point.

Chapter 7 'Land of Hope and Glory'

1. Donald Cameron Watt, 'Some Aspects of A. J. P. Taylor's Work as Diplomatic Historian', *JMH*, 49 (March, 1977) p. 20. Cited hereafter as 'Taylor's Work as Diplomatic Historian'.
2. Ibid., p. 19.
3. *Personal History*, p. 336; 'Taylor's Work as Diplomatic Historian', pp. 24–25, 33.
4. *Personal History*, p. 242.
5. Taylor, 'On Satan's Side', *NS*, 65 (May 31, 1963, p. 826.
6. *Personal History*, p. 242.
7. *Personal History*, p. 220; 'Accident Prone', p. 12; *English History*, p. vii.

8. Taylor, *Beaverbrook*, London, 1972, p. 175. Cited below as *Beaverbrook*.

9. *Beaverbrook*, p. 632.

10. *Personal History*, p. 214.

11. Taylor, 'Is This the Way to Get Better TV?', *SE*, July 15, 1958, p. 10; 'The Nerve of these BBC Do-Gooders', *SE*, November 22, 1964, p. 16; 'Why Must You Pay for the Culture Snobs?', *SE*, July 15, 1958, p. 10; November 22, 1964, p. 16 *SE*, May 26, 1963, p. 16.

12. Taylor, 'I Say These Polls are a Farce'; 'Should the Pollsters be Banned? My answer is YES, YES, YES at Election Time', *SE*, May 17, 1964, p. 16 and March 27, 1966, p. 9.

13. Taylor, 'Let Winston Stay!'; 'The Man Who Gave Us Our Finest Hour', *SE*, April 5, 1964, p. 16 and November 29, 1964, p. 9; 'Churchill and His Critics', *Observer*, April 15, 1968, p. 26.

14. Taylor, 'The General Strike'; 'The Great Depression', *Listener*, March 8, 1962, p. 410 and March 22, 1962, p. 506.

15. Taylor, 'Why Should Princess Anne Have to Step Down at All?'; 'I Say Scrap the Lords!'; 'Is it Right to Kick these Men Upstairs?'; 'Why Can a Man Lay Down a Crown – But Not a Peerage?', *SE*, March 15, 1964, p. 16, February 16, 1958, p. 10, November 20, 1960, p. 12 and April 2, 1961, p. 12.

16. Taylor, 'Is This £90 million Being Spent the Right Way?' *SE*, October 7, 1962, p. 16.

17. Taylor, 'Why Should These People Get Tax Perks?'; 'Is it a Crime to Sack an MP?', *SE*, April 25, 1965, p. 8 and November 2, 1969, p. 16. It is not possible to know whether Taylor consciously drew upon Lattimer's famous utterance when he and Ridley were being burned at the stake as heretics in the reign of Bloody Mary: 'We will light such a fire in England, Ridley, as will not be put out.' It would not have been uncharacteristic of him.

18. Taylor, 'Nobody's Uncle', *Encounter*, 15 (October, 1960) p. 77; 'Was He the Greatest Prime Minister of All Time?' *SE*, January 20, 1963, p. 8 – Eva Haraszti-Taylor has suggested that her late husband had much in common with Lloyd George; '1914: Events in Britain', *Listener*, July 16, 1964, p. 82.

19. Taylor, 'Why Do I Write for this "Awful Newspaper"?'; 'The Man Who Deals in Sunshine'; *SE*, May 27, 1962, p. 16 and May 24, 1964, p. 16.

20. Taylor, 'Must This Man Stay in Prison For Ever?'; 'The Strange Silence of the "Freedom Brigade"'; 'Why Can't Wilson Speak Out for This Lonely Man?', *SE*, December 25, 1962, p. 10, September 22, 1967, p. 16 and April 27, 1969, p. 12.

21. Taylor, 'The Faceless Ones Will be Happy – the Day the Newspapers Stop'; 'These Men Imperil Freedom'; 'Are You Wrong to Enjoy Your Newspaper?'; 'Should They Have the Right to Spy on You?', *SE*, July 5, 1959, p. 6, March 2, 1958, p. 12, March 5, 1961, p. 12 and June 18, 1967, p. 12.

22. Taylor, 'Could You Name the Minister of Power?'; 'Is This Churchill Warning Coming True?'; 'The Great Foreign Holiday Fraud'; 'Scrap

This £50 Rule *Now*'; 'What a Way to End a Holiday'; 'Do You Want to Go to Work in the Dark?'; 'Will Christmas Presents be Illegal Next?'; 'Who Says the Tax-Man Has no Favourites?', *SE*, July 6, 1958, p. 10, October 16, 1966, p. 16, September 25, 1966, p. 16, March 26, 1967, p. 16, September 15, 1968, p. 16, October 29, 1967, p. 12, December 24, 1967, p. 14 and October 27, 1968, p. 16.

23. Taylor, 'Let's Scrap This Farce at UNO!'; 'I Say – Let Him Quit!'; 'We Must Not Share the Guilt for UNO's Crimes'; *SE*, August 10, 1958, p. 8, February 19, 1961 and January 6, 1963, p. 16. The reference to United States forces in Mississippi concerned clashes over school desegregation.

24. Taylor, 'Here's One Bill We Could Cut Out', *SE*, August 22, 1965, p. 10.

25. Taylor, 'Why Can't Selwyn Be More Like De Gaulle?'; 'Must We Always Take Orders from America?' *SE*, June 14, 1959, p. 12 and December 31, 1961, p. 12.

26. Taylor, 'Must the Faceless Men in America Rule Us Too?'; 'Kennedy or Nixon? Does It Matter to Us In Britain?', *SE*, March 27, 1960, p. 12 and June 26, 1960, p. 12.

27. Taylor, 'Must We Always Take Orders from America?'; 'Why Don't Our Politicians Tell Us the Truth?'; 'Macmillan Has Not Found the Answer Yet', *SE*, December 31, 1961, p. 12, September 17, 1961, p. 17 and July 15, 1962, p. 12.

28. Taylor, 'Will Menzies Speak for Britain?'; 'Why Don't These 'Top People' Think for Themselves?' *SE*, September 9, 1962, p. 14 and October 23, 1962, p. 16; 'Going Into Europe', *Encounter*, 19 (December 1962) p. 62. The Greenwood reference was to calls for Arthur Greenwood, MP, to 'Speak for England' in a House of Commons debate in March 1939, after Germany occupied Prague. Otherwise, the reference to shared 'institutions and traditions' between Britain and the Commonwealth seems vague. One has the feeling that Taylor was thinking of Canada, Australia, and New Zealand rather more than of Nigeria, Sierra Leone or even India.

29. Taylor, 'The Bitter Truth About Britain's Unemployed'; 'Why Don't We Have an Election Now?'; 'Bravo, Mr Shinwell – Now Do It Again'; 'The Awkward Truth That No One Wants to Face'; 'The Menace of De Gaulle to *Us*;' 'How Much More Must We Take from De Gaulle?', *SE*, December 2, 1962, p. 16, January 27, 1963, p. 16, January 29, 1967, p. 16, May 14, 1967, p. 16, July 30, 1967, p. 16 and November 26, 1967, p. 16.

30. *Beaverbrook*, pp. 658–9; *English History*, p. vii. Taylor first told me this story in his office in the Beaverbrook Library in 1969. He repeated it in *Personal History*, pp. 237–238. Each telling was in nearly identical language, which suggests that the story was not only genuine, but a treasured memory of his association with Beaverbrook.

31. *English History*, pp. vi, 2; *Personal History*, pp. 236–7.

32. *English History*, pp. 66, 2.

33. Ibid., pp. 342–4.

34. Ibid., pp. 181, 439, 452, 472.
35. Hugh Dalton, quoted in ibid., p. 597.
36. Ibid., p. 585.
37. Ibid., pp. 351, 354.
38. Ibid., pp. 14, 192–3, 201, 205, 382, 335, 475, 526.
39. Ibid., p. 18.
40. Ibid., pp. 20, 53, 43–4, 47, 106–7, 50–1, 62, 66, 70, 120.
41. Ibid., pp. 362, 379, 439, 453.
42. Ibid., pp. 457–9. *The Times* responded to the original in this language: 'The insipid and patronizing invocations to which the passer-by is now being treated have a power of exasperation which is all their own.' Ian McLaine, *Ministry of Morale: Home Front Morale and the Ministry of Information in World War II* (London, 1979) p. 86n.
43. *English History*, pp. 471, 488–93.
44. Ibid., pp. 503–4, 548–9, 583–4.
45. Ibid., pp. 38, 115, 128n, 166–7, 472n, 512.
46. *Personal History*, p. 159.
47. Ibid., pp. 26–7, 142.
48. Ibid., pp. 171–2, 310.
49. Ibid., pp. 430, 548–9.
50. Ibid., pp. 232–4.
51. Ibid., p. 246.
52. Ibid., pp. 307–8.
53. Ibid., pp. 179, 180.
54. Ibid., pp. 181, 315–16.
55. Ibid., pp. 165, 167, 168, 303, 300, 542, 569, 585, 600.
56. Ibid., pp. 191, 350, 361, 386, 431, 475.
57. *Beaverbrook*, p. xiii.
58. *English History*, pp. 496, 513, 539, 560, 590, 598–9.
59. Taylor, 'Up From Utopia: How Two Generations Survived Their Wars', *NR*, 123 (October 30, 1950) p. 16.
60. *English History*, p. 600.

Chapter 8 'What Was It All About, Alan?'

1. *Personal History*, pp. 243–4.
2. Ibid., p. 246.
3. It was at the Beaverbrook Library in St Bride's Street in 1969 that I first encountered Taylor. We sat in his office and sipped tea while we talked, with the Sickert portrait, depicting a relaxed, confident Beaverbrook with his hands in his trouser pockets, looming over Taylor's shoulder. It only occurred to me much later that the juxtaposition was symbolic of their relationship of mentor and disciple. Taylor's biography of the press lord made the connection clear. So, too, did the long list of his contentious and polemical writings in the *Sunday Express*. Meanwhile, an army of young historians were beavering away in the reading room. Over that few years when the Library was open, they began the research which

led to, among other things, a set of essays, *Lloyd George: Twelve Essays*, which Taylor edited and which Hamish Hamilton published in 1971. Without exception the authors went on to make important contributions to historical scholarship, some of which reflected Taylor's interpretive influence, Sidney Aster's *1939: The Making of the Second World War* being a case in point. When the Beaverbrook Library closed in the later 1970s – a victim of economic recession – its holdings were transferred to the House of Lord Records Office in Westminster, where reading room facilities are about the same as in St Bride's Street.

4. *Beaverbrook*, p. xv.
5. Tom Driberg, *Ruling Passions*, London, 1977, p. 225; Driberg, 'In the Sight of the Lord', *NS*, 83 (30 June, 1972) p. 908.
6. *Beaverbrook*, p. ix.
7. Ibid., pp. 632, 560, 519.
8. Ibid., p. 646; *Personal History*, p. 238.
9. *Beaverbrook*, p. 671; Roy Fuller, 'Bully of Britain', *Listener*, 87 (June 29, 1972) p. 870; Peter Silcox, 'Beaverbrook', *CF*, 52 (December, 1972) p. 39; Ronald Blythe, 'Eager Beaver', *NYRB*, March 8, 1973, p. 29.
10. David Marquand, 'Opinionated, preposterous and sometimes penetrating', *The Times*, April 11, 1983, p. 9; Marquand, 'Historian of the 1990s', MGW, December 1, 1966, p. 10. Cited below as 'Historian of the 1990s. '
11. Alan Sked and Chris Cook (eds),'Before the Ball was Over', *Crisis and Controversy: Essays in Honour of A. J. P. Taylor* (London, 1976) p. 586, vi. Cited below as *Crisis and Controversy*.
12. 'Historian of the 1990s', p. 10.
13. 'Cartesian Historian', p. 131; 'Why Did We Fight?', p. 244; 'War Unpremeditated?' pp. 142–3. See also 'Critics of the Taylor View of History' and 'Taylor and War Origins'.
14. A. H., 'Twentieth-Century Prelude', *HT*, January 1953, p. 70.
15. Denis Judd to Cole, February 11, 1969.
16. Anonymous, 'Review of *Bismarck: The Man and the Statesman*, by A. J. P. Taylor', *PQ*, 26 (October-December 1955) p. 412; Hans J. Morganthau to Cole, May 8, 1973.
17. Taylor quoted by A. Stanley Trickett to Cole, interview November 3, 1965. Tricket was Taylor's pupil at Manchester University in 1933.
18. 'Review of *Struggle for Mastery*', p. 112.
19. Edward B. Segel, 'Taylor and History', *RP*, 26 (October 1964) p. 533.
20. W. K. Hancock, 'Review of *The Italian Problem in European Diplomacy, 1847–1849* by A. J. P. Taylor', *History*, 22 (June 1935) p. 83; J. L. Hammond, 'Bismarck and Colonies', *MG*, March 18, 1938, p. 7; R. W. Seton-Watson, 'Review of *The Habsburg Monarchy, 1815–1914* by A. J. P. Taylor', *EHR*, 57 (July, 1942) p. 391; C. A. Macartney, 'Review of *The Habsburg Monarchy, 1815–1918* by A. J. P. Taylor', *History*, 35 (October, 1950) p. 274; Leonard Woolf, 'The Habsburgs', *NSN*, 37 (March 5, 1949) p. 235; Louis Wassermann, 'Two New

Surveys of the German People – Studies of Extremists', *SFC*, July 14, 1946, pp. 16, 33; 'Can Germany be a Free Nation?', p. 62.
21. Leonard Woolf, 'The Brighter Side of History', *NSN*, 39 (June 3, 1950) p. 636; G. B., 'History Notes', *SRL*, 34 (March 17, 1951) pp. 17ff; 'Twentieth-Century Prelude', p. 70; Martin Wight, 'Contentious but Creative', *Spectator*, 190 (May 15, 1953) p. 639.
22. 'Review of *Struggle for Mastery*', p. 112; 'Modern Europe', p. 630; 'Review of *Bismarck: The Man and the Statesman* by A. J. P. Taylor', *PQ*, 26 (October–December, 1955) p. 412; Martin Wight, 'Iron Chancellor', *MG*, July 8, 1955, p. 10; Michael Howard, 'The Iron Chancellor', *NSN*, 50 (July 9, 1955) p. 48.
23. 'Public Dissent', *TLS*, June 21, 1957, p. 382; W. L. Burn, 'Review of *The Troublemakers: Dissent Over Foreign Policy, 1792–1939* by A. J. P. Taylor', *History*, 43 (January, 1958) p. 61; Kingsley Martin, 'Dissenters', *NS*, 53 (June 8, 1957) p. 740; Sebastian Heffner, 'Mr Taylor's Masterpiece', *Observer*, April 16, 1961, p. 30; 'Apologia for Hitler', p. 179.
24. C. L. Mowat, 'England in the Twentieth Century', *History*, 51 (June 1966) p. 188; Robert Rhodes James, 'England Arise!', *Spectator*, 215 (October 22, 1965) p. 517; Max Beloff, 'On England in Transition', *Government and Opposition*, no. 21 (April 1966) p. 405.
25. Taylor to Cole, May 13, 1967.
26. *Englishmen and Others*, p. vii.
27. *Struggle for Mastery in Europe*, p. 518; *The Habsburg Monarchy*, 1st edn, p. 4; *Course of German History*, p. xix; *War By Time-Table* (London, 1969), p. 121; *Origins*, p. 102; 'Books in General', *NSN*, 46 (November 24, 1951).
28. Taylor to Cole, May 13, 1967; *Englishmen and Others*, p. 18.
29. Taylor, *Rumours of War* (London, 1952) p. 1.

Select Bibliography

This bibliography is limited to interviews and correspondence involving A. J. P. Taylor, myself, and others willing to talk about him, which I have accumulated over the years; to those reviews and other commentaries on his work or on circumstances in which he found himself, at one time or another, to which specific reference is made in the text or notes; and to Taylor's own writings. As Taylor's writings comprise a bibliography in excess of one thousand entries, I only included those which I have quoted or consulted with an eye towards deepening my grasp of his thinking.

Two lists of Taylor's work have been published over the years. In 1976 I published 'A Bibliography of the Works of A. J. P. Taylor, 1934–1965: Parts One and Two', *Bulletin of Bibliography and Magazine Notes*, vol. 3, nos. 4–5, July–September, and October–December, 1976. This list begins in 1934 and stops at 1965, and therefore is incomplete at both ends. In 1980 Chris Wrigley published an exceptional volume, as complete as it was possible to be at the time: *A. J. P. Taylor: A Complete Annotated Bibliography* (Sussex, 1980). The bibliography listed below does not attempt to recreate either of these collections, and instead consists mainly of those Taylor writings to which I have made reference in the text or in the notes.

Primary Sources

Books by A. J. P. Taylor

A. J. P. Taylor: A Personal History (London, 1983).
An Old Man's Diary (London, 1984).
Beaverbrook (London, 1972).
Bismarck: The Man and the Statesmen (New York 1955).
Course of German History (Capricorn edn: New York, 1962). Originally published in London in 1946.
English History, 1914–1945 (Oxford, 1965).
Englishmen and Others (London, 1956).
Europe: Grandeur and Decline (London, 1967).
From Napoleon to Lenin (New York, 1966).
From Napoleon to Stalin (London, 1950).
From Sarajevo to Potsdam (London, 1966).
Germany's First Bid for Colonies, 1884–1885: A Move in Bismarck's European Policy (Archon Books edn: London, 1967). First published in 1938.
Habsburg Monarchy, 1815–1918, The (London, 1941; 2nd edn, New York, 1948).

Italian Problem in European Diplomacy, 1847–1849, The (Manchester, 1934).
Lloyd George: Twelve Essays, ed. A. J. P. Taylor (London, 1971).
Origins of the Second World War (American edn: New York, 1963). First published in 1961.
Rumours of War (London, 1952).
Struggle for Mastery in Europe, 1848–1918, The (Oxford, 1954).
Troublemakers: Dissent Over Foreign Policy, 1792–1939, The (London, 1957).
War by Time-Table (London, 1969).
War Lords, The (London, 1977).

Periodicals: articles, commentaries, reviews by A. J. P. Taylor

'A Devil's Advocate', *MGW*, October 30, 1952, p. 11.
'A German Exile', *MG*, June 18, 1937, p. 7.
'A German on War's Effects', *MGW*, December 31, 1937, p. 534.
'Accident Prone, or What Happened Next', *JMH*, 49 (March 1977) pp. 1–18.
'Aid to Historical Perspective', *The Times*, August 19, 1952, p. 7e.
'Ancestry of the "New Democracies"', *Listener*, July 15, 1948, pp. 92–3.
'Another Good German', *MGW*, November 16, 1950, p. 10.
'Are Our Public Men Too Squeamish?' *SE*, October 30, 1960, p. 16.
'Are You Wrong to Enjoy Your Newspaper?', *SE*, March 5, 1961, p. 12.
'Awkward Truth That No One Wants to Face, The', *SE*, May 14, 1967, p. 16.
'Bismarck: Fifty Years After', *MGW*, August 5, 1948, p. 6.
'Between Two Wars', *MGW*, January 21, 1944, p. 36.
'Bitter Truth About Britain's Unemployed, The', *SE*, December 2, 1962, p. 16.
'Black Lamb and Grey Falcon', *TT*, March 7, 1942, p. 195.
'Books in General', *NSN*, 49 (January 22, 1955) p. 108.
'Bravo, Mr Shinwell – Now Do It Again', *SE*, January 29, 1967, p. 16.
'British Policy in Morocco, 1886–1902', *EHR*, 66 (July 1951) p. 342–74.
'Cabinet Secrecy – Handicap for the Historian', *The Times*, August 6, 1952, p. 5e.
'Campaign Report', *NS*, 55 (June 1958) pp. 799–800.
'Churchill and His Critics', *Observer*, April 15, 1968, p. 26.
'La Conference d'Algésiras', *RH*, 208 (October 1952) p. 236–54.
'Congress of Intellectuals at Wroclaw', *MGW*, September 9, 1948, p. 12.
'Could You Name the Minister of Power', *SE*, July 6, 1958, p. 10.
'Czech Communist Coup, The', *MGW*, February 2, 1950, p. 12.
'Czechoslovakia Today', *MGW*, August 2, 1946, p. 59.
'Czechoslovakia Today: Questions of Foreign Policy and Trade', *MGW*, August 16, 1946, p. 87.
'Czechoslovakia Today: The Position of the Slovaks', *MGW*, August 9, 1946, p. 71.
'Democracy in Britain', *MG*, June 15, 1934, p. 11.
'Diplomatic History', *MG*, May 26, 1939, p. 415.
'Do You Want to Go to Work in the Dark?' *SE*, October 29, 1967, p. 12.
'Dollfuss and Austria', *MGW*, July 12, 1935, p. 35.

'Dreyfus', *MG*, May 7, 1939, p. 7.

'Eden in the Thirties', *Observer*, November 18, 1962, p. 24.

'European Diplomatic History', *TLS*, November 26, 1954, pp. 749–50.

'European Mediation and the Agreement of Villafranca, 1859' *EHR*, 51 (January 1936) pp. 52–78.

'European Revolution, The', *Listener*, November 22, 1945, pp. 575–6.

'Evil Genius of the Wilhelmstrasse', *Listener*, July 21, 1955, pp. 102–4.

'Faceless Ones Will be Happy – the Day the New spapers Stop, The,' *SE*, July 26, 1959, p. 6.

'Flickering Figures', *NS*, 66 (July 12, 1963) p. 49.

'France, Germany and the Soviet Union', *MGW*, January 11, 1951, p. 11.

'Free Territory of Trieste', *NSN*, 38 (October 29, 1949) p. 479.

'General Strike, The', *Listener*, March 8, 1962, pp. 409–12.

'German Diplomacy in the Appeasement Years', *MGW*, August 6, 1953, p. 11.

'German History', *MGW*, November 17, 1944, p. 273.

'German Legends', *MGW*, January 5, 1945, p. 8.

'German Power-Worship', *MGW*, November 20, 1952, p. 10.

'German Unity: I – The Background of the Reich', *MGW*, April 6, 1944, p. 189.

'German Unity: II – The Reich of Bismarck and Hitler', *MGW*, April 21, 1944, p. 217.

'Germany', *MGW*, July 6, 1950, p. 12.

'Going Into Europe', *Encounter*, 19 (December 1962) p. 62.

'Great Depression, The', *Listener*, March 22, 1962, pp. 505–8.

'Great Foreign Holiday Fraud, The', *SE*, September 25, 1966, p. 16.

'Guns, Not Butter', *MG*, March 12, 1937, p. 9.

'Here's One Bill We Could Cut Out', *SE*, August 22, 1965, p. 10.

'Heyday of Appeasement', *MGW*, January 17, 1952, p. 11.

'Hitler's Third Book', *NS*, 65 (April 17, 1962) pp. 595–6.

'How Hitler Went to War', *MGW*, February 28, 1957, p. 11.

'How Much More Must We Take from De Gaulle?' *SE*, November 26, 1967, p. 16.

'How Near is World War III?' *MGW*, September 3, 1959, p. 5.

'How to Quote: Exercises for Beginners', *Encounter*, 17 (September, 1961) p. 73.

'I Say – Let Him Quit!' *SE*, February 19, 1961, p. 16.

'I Say Scrap the Lords!', *SE*, February 16, 1958, p. 10.

'I Say These Polls are a Farce', *SE*, May 17, 1964, p. 16.

'Impressions of Yugoslavia: I – A Regime of Youth', *MGW*, May 15, 1947, p. 9.

'Impressions of Yugoslavia: II – Economics and Politics', *MGW*, May 22, 1947, p. 13.

'Is it a Crime to Sack an MP?' *SE*, November 2, 1969, p. 16.

'Is it Right to Kick these Men Upstairs?' *SE*, November 20, 1960, p. 12.

'Is This Churchill Warning Coming True?' *SE*, October 16, 1966, p. 16.

'Is This £90 million being spent the Right Way?' *SE*, October 7, 1962, p. 16.

'Is This the Way to Get Better TV?' *SE*, July 15, 1958, p. 10.

'Keeping it Dark', *Encounter*, 13 (August 1959) pp. 40–5.
'Kennedy or Nixon? Does It Matter to Us in Britain?' *SE*, June 26, 1960, p. 12.
'Kossuth', *MGW*, February 26, 1937, p. 174.
'Last Habsburg, The', *MGW*, May 29, 1936, p. 35.
'Let Britain Put an End to This Bad Dream', *SE*, January 10, 1965, p. 16.
'Let's Scrap This Farce at UNO!' *SE*, August 10, 1958, p. 8.
'Letter to the Editor', *The Times*, March 11, 1958, p. 11.
'Letter to the Editor', *TLS*, June 9, 1961, p. 390.
'Let Winston Stay!' *SE*, April 5, 1964, p. 16.
'Lights Out Over Europe', *MGW*, March 27, 1958, p. 11.
'London Diary', *NSN*, 50 (December 24, 1955) p. 849.
'London Diary', *NS*, 92 (August 20, 1976) p. 238.
'Macmillan Has Not Found the Answer Yet', *SE*, July 15, 1962, p. 12.
'Man Who Deals in Sunshine, The', *SE*, May 24, 1964, p. 16.
'Man Who Gave Us Our Finest Hour, The', *SE*, November 29, 1964, p. 9.
'Masaryk', *MGW*, May 3, 1940, p. 348.
'Masaryk in England', *MGW*, March 12, 1943, p. 48.
'Menace of De Gaulle to *Us*', *SE*, July 30, 1967, p. 16.
'Metternich', *MG*, November 6, 1935, p. 7.
'Metternich and His 'System' for Europe', *Listener*, 62 (July, 1959) pp. 167–168.
'Munich Twenty Years After', *MGW*, October 2, 1958, p. 7.
'Murder or Suicide', *Observer*, March 17, 1963, p. 26.
'Must the Faceless Men in America Rule Us Too?' *SE*, March 27, 1960, p. 12.
'Must This Man Stay in Prison For Ever?', *SE*, December 25, 1962, p. 10.
'Must We Always Take Orders from America?' *SE*, December 31, 1961, p. 12.
'National Independence and the "Austrian Idea"', *PQ*, 16 (July 1945) pp. 236–46.
'Nerve of These BBC Do-Gooders, The', *SE*, November 22, 1964, p. 16.
'1914: Events in Britain', *Listener*, July 16, 1964, p. 82.
'Nobody's Uncle', *Encounter*, 15 (October 1960) p. 76–80.
'On Satan's Side', *NS*, 65 (May 31, 1963) p. 826.
'Out of the Diplomatic Bag', *MGW*, February 27, 1958, p. 11.
'Peace Settlements', *TT*, April 11, 1942, p. 314.
'Popular Biography', *MG*, November 10, 1936, p. 7.
'Prelude to Fashoda: The Question of the Upper Nile, 1894–5', *EHR*, 65 (January 1950) 52–80.
'Les premières années de l'alliance russe', *RH*, 204 (July, 1950) p. 62–76.
'Pre-War', *TT*, 23 (November 28, 1942) p. 956.
'Problem of Germany, The', *Listener*, June 20, 1946, pp.799–800.
'Received with Thanks, The', *Observer*, November 20, 1966, p. 26.
'Report on the Rising Generation', *RN*, November 4, 1956, p. 3.
'Resistance', *MGW*, July 26, 1956, p. 10.
'Review of *Bismarck*, by Erich Eyck, *Zweiter Band*', *EHR*, 61 (January 1946) p. 112.

'Review of *Bismarck*, by Erich Eyck, *Dritter Band*', EHR, 62 (July 1947) p. 393.

'Review of *Geschichte der Weimarer Republik*, by Erich Eyck', EHR, 72 (July 1957) pp. 517–518.

'Review of *i Documenti diplomatici Italiani*, 9th series, vol. I, EHR, 70 (October 1955) p. 654.

'Scrap This £50 Rule *Now*', SE, March 26, 1967, p. 16.

'Should the Pollsters be banned? My answer is YES, YES, YES at Election Time', SE, March 27, 1966, p. 9.

'Should They Have the Right to Spy on You?', SE, June 18, 1967, p. 12.

'Somewhat Passive Resistance', MGW, December 14, 1958, p. 11.

'Strange Silence of the Freedom Brigade, The', SE, September 22, 1967, p. 16.

'Spain and the Axis', MGW, May 3, 1951, p. 11.

'Television Wars, The', NSN, 62 (July 21, 1961) p. 85.

'Ten Years After', NSN, 36 (October 2, 1948) p. 278.

'These Men Imperil Freedom', SE, March 2, 1958, p. 12.

'Thiers and Stresemann', MGW, April 12, 1941, p. 294.

'Thing, The', *20th Century*, 162 (October 1957) p. 293–297.

'Thomas Mann', MGW, September 24, 1943, p. 172.

'Tito and Stalin: Revolt from Within', *Listener*, January 20, 1949, p. 86.

'Trieste or Trst?' NSN, December 9, 1944, pp. 386–7.

'25 Years of Czechoslovakia', MGW, November 5, 1943, p. 260.

'Unlucky Find', NS; 62 (December 1, 1961) p. 834.

'Up From Utopia: How Two Generations Survived Their Wars', NP, 123 (October 30, 1950) pp. 15–18.

'Was He the Greatest Prime Minister of All Time?', SE, January 20, 1963, p. 8.

'We Must Not Share the Guilt for UNO's Crimes', SE, January 6, 1963, p. 16.

'What a Way to End a Holiday', SE, September 15, 1968, p. 16.

'What Can We Do With Germany?' NSN, 28 (October 28, 1944) p. 288.

'When Germany Ruled Europe', MGW, August 15, 1957, p. 10.

'Who Burnt the Reichstag?', HT, 10 (August 1960) pp. 512–22.

'Who Says the Tax-Man Has no Favourites?' SE, October 27, 1968, p. 16.

'Why Can a Man Lay Down a Crown – But Not a Peerage?' SE, April 2, 1961, p. 12.

'Why Can't Selwyn Be More Like De Gaulle?' SE, June 14, 1959, p. 12.

'Why Can't Wilson Speak Out for This Lonely Man?', SE, April 27, 1969, p. 12.

'Why Do I Write for this 'Awful New spaper'? SE, May 27, 1962, p. 16.

'Why Don't Our Politicians Tell Us the Truth?' SE, September 17, 1961, p. 17.

'Why Don't These Top People Think for Themselves?' SE, October 23, 1962, p. 16.

'Why Don't We Have an Election Now?' SE, January 27, 1963, p. 16.

'Why Must We Soft-Soap the Germans?' SE, October 27, 1957, p. 12.

'Why Must You Pay for the Culture Snobs?' SE, May 26, 1963, p. 16.

'Why Should Princess Anne Have to Step Down at All?' *SE*, March 15, 1964, p. 16.
'Why Should These People get Tax Perks?' *SE*, April 25, 1965, p. 8.
'Will Christmas Presents be Illegal Next?', *SE*, December 24, 1967, p. 14.
'Will Menzies Speak for Britain?' *SE*, September 9, 1962, p. 14.
'Wilson's Blunder Over Berlin', *SE*, February 16, 1969, p. 16.
'Wroclaw Congress, The', *NSN*, 36 (September 18, 1948) p. 238.

Correspondence

Maurice Fitzsimmons, Martin Gilbert, Michael Gordon, John H. Gray, Della Hilton, Denis Judd, Hans Morganthau, Keith Robbins, Robert Skidelsky, A. J. P. Taylor, A. Stanley Trickett.

Interviews

Vivian Galbraith, Della Hilton, Stanley Hoffman, Michael Gordon, Denis Judd, Hans Morganthau, A. J. P. Taylor, A. Stanley Trickett.

Hansard, *Parliamentary Debates*.

Secondary Sources

Books

Aster, Sidney, *1939: The Making of the Second World War* (New York, 1976).
Cole, C. Robert and Michael Moody, eds., *The Dissenting Tradition: Essays for Leland H. Carlson* (Athens, Ohio, 1975).
Driberg, Tom, *Ruling Passions* (London, 1977).
Friedjung, Heinrich, *The Struggle for Supremacy in Germany, 1859–1866* (London, 1935).
Gilbert, Martin (ed.) *A Century of Conflict* (New York, 1967).
Greenidge, Terence, *Degenerate Oxford?* (London, 1930).
Gulick, Edward Vose, *Europe's Classical Balance of Power* (New York, 1955).
Hanrieder, Wolfram, *The Stable Crisis* (New York, 1970).
Judgement of the International Military Tribunal at Nuremberg (1946).
Lomas, Charles W. and Michael Taylor (eds) *The Rhetoric of the British Peace Movement* (New York, 1971).
Louis, William Roger (ed.) *The Origins of the Second World War: A. J. P. Taylor and His Critics* (New York, 1972).
McLaine, Ian, *Ministry of Morale: Home Front Morale and the Ministry of Information in World War II* (London, 1979).
Martel, Gorden (ed.) *The Origins of the Second World War Reconsidered* (London, 1986.).
Mehta, Ved, *The Fly and the Fly Bottle* (London, 1964).
Parker, Harold T. (ed.) *Problems in European History* (Charlotte, 1977).

Pelling, Henry, *The British Communist Party: A Historical Profile* (New York, 1958).

Pollard, Francis E. (ed.) *Bootham School, 1823–1923* (London, 1926).

Pribrâm, Alfred Francis, *England and the International Policy of the European Great Powers, 1871–1914* (London, 1931).

Robertson, E. M. (ed.) *The Origins of the Second World War* (London, 1971).

Schmitt, Hans (ed.) *Historians of Modern Europe* (Baton Rouge, 1971).

Sked, Alan and Chris Cook (eds) *Crisis and Controversy: Essays in Honour of A. J. P. Taylor* (London, 1976).

Thayer, George, *The British Political Fringe* (London, 1965).

Articles, reviews and other pieces

A. H., 'Twentieth-Century Prelude', *TT*, January 1953, p. 70.

'A. J. P.Taylor', *The Times*, September 8, 1990, p. 16[sic].

Barron, Louis, 'Review of *The Struggle for Mastery in Europe, 1848–1918* by A. J. P. Taylor', *LJ*, 80 (February 15, 1954) p. 459.

'Battle of the Dons', *Newsweek*, 58 (July 31, 1961) p. 72.

Beloff, Max, 'On England in Transition', *GO*, no. 21 (April 1966) pp. 405–13.

Blythe, Ronald, 'Eager Beaver', *NYRB*, March 8, 1973, p. 29.

Boyer, John W., 'A. J. P. Taylor and the Art of Modern History', *JMH*, 49 (March 1977) pp.40–72.

Briggs, Asa, 'Before the Ball was Over', *NSN*, 48 (November 6, 1954) pp. 586–7.

Brown, Craig, 'A Proud Old Man in Love', *TLS*, July 19, 1991, p.28.

Bullock, Alan, 'Hitler and the Origins of the Second World War', The Raleigh Lecture on History: British Academy (1967).

Burn, W. L., 'Review of *The Troublemakers: Dissent Over Foreign Policy, 1792–1939* by A. J. P. Taylor', *History*, 43 (January 1958) p. 61.

Carr, E. H., 'Why did we Fight?' *TLS*, April 21, 1961, p. 244.

Cobban, Alfred, 'Historical Notes', *History*, 47 (October, 1961) p. 227.

Cole, C. Robert, 'A Bibliography of the Works of A. J. P. Taylor, Parts I and II', *BBMN*, 33 (July–September and October–December, 1976).

——, 'A. J. P. Taylor and the Origins of the Second World War', Harold T. Parker (ed.) *Problems in European History* (Durham, 1979).

——, 'Critics of the Taylor View of History', *WLB*, 22 (Summer 1968) pp. 29–44.

Crossman, R. H. S., 'Can Germany be a Free Nation?', *NSN*, 30 (July 29, 1945) p. 62.

'Dearly Won Liberties. Danger of Losing them through Apathy: the Sedition Bill Threat', *MG*, June 25, 1934, p. 11.

Deutscher, Isaac, 'Letter to the Editor', *TLS*, June 2, 1961, p. 361.

'Dream-Play of the German Century', *TLS*, September 29, 1945, pp. 457–458.

Driberg, Tom, 'In the Sight of the Lord', *NS*, 83 (June 30, 1972) p. 908.

Fairlie, Henry, 'Modern Europe', *Spectator*, November 9, 1954, p. 629.

'Foresight and Hindsight', *Economist*, 169 (May 13, 1961) p. 655.

Freidel, Frank, 'Who Started the War?' *Reporter*, 26 (January 18, 1962) p. 52.

Fuller, Roy, 'Bully of Britain', *Listener*, 87 (June 29, 1972) pp. 870–1.

G. B., 'History Notes', *SRL*, 34 (March 17, 1951) pp. 17ff.

Glasgow, Eric, 'The Amalgamation of Birkdale and Southport', unpublished manuscript supplied by the author, ca. 1975.

'German Power-Worship', *MGW*, November 20, 1952, p. 10.

Gershoy, Leo, 'Professional Historians Analyze Germany', *NYHTWR*, July 7, 1946, p. 2.

Gott, Richard, 'Great History, little England', *Guardian*, September 8, 1990, p. 18.

Halperin, S. William, 'Review of *The Origins of the Second World War*, by A. J. P. Taylor', *CST*, January 12, 1962, p. 8.

Hammond, J. L., 'Bismarck and Colonies', *MG*, March 18, 1938, p. 7.

Hancock, W. K., 'Review of *The Italian Problem in European History, 1847–1849* by A. J. P. Taylor', *History*, 22 (June, 1935) p. 83.

Hauser, Oswald, 'A. J. P. Taylor', *JMH*, 49 (March, 1977) pp. 34–39.

Heffner, Sebastian, 'Mr. Taylor's Masterpiece', *Observer*, April 16, 1961, p. 30.

Hinsley, F. H., 'Review of *Origins of the Second World War*, by A. J. P. Taylor', *HR*, 4 (1961) p. 223.

Howard, Michael, 'The Iron Chancellor', *NSN*, 50 (July 9, 1955) p. 48.

Hudson, G. F., 'An Apologia for Adolf Hitler', *Commentary*, 33 (February, 1962) pp. 178–84.

Jacobsen, Hans-Adolf, 'Adolf Hitler, Eine Politiker Ohne Programm?' *Europe-Archiv*, 16 (1961) pp. 457–62.

James, Robert Rhodes, 'England Arise!' *The Spectator*, 215 (October 22, 1965) p. 517.

Joll, James, 'The Ride to the Abyss', *The Spectator*, 206 (April 21, 1961) p. 561.

Kohn, Hans, 'Germany and the West', *NYT*, August 18, 1946, p. 22.

——, 'Review of *The Struggle for Mastery in Europe, 1848–1918*, by A. J. P. Taylor', *AAAPSS*, 298 (March 1955) p. 230.

Macartney, C. A., 'Review of *The Habsburg Monarchy, 1809–1918*, by A. J. P. Taylor', *History*, 35 (October 1950) p. 274.

Mann, Golo, 'Hitler's Britischer Advokat', *Der Monat*, 157 (September 1961) pp. 79–86.

Marquand, David, 'Historian of the 1990s', *MGW*, December 1, 1966, p. 10.

——, 'Opinionated, preposterous and sometimes penetrating', *The Times*, April 11, 1983, p. 9.

Martin, Kingsley, 'Dissenters', *NS*, 53 (June 8, 1957) p.740.

Mason, T. W., 'Some Origins of the Second World War', *PP*, 29 (December, 1964) pp. 67–87.

McNeill, William H., 'A Cartesian Historian', *WP*, 8 (October, 1954) pp. 124–33.

Morton, Louis, 'From Fort Sumpter to Poland', *WP*, 14 (January, 1962) pp. 386–92.

Mowat, C. L., 'England in the Twentieth Century', *History*, 51 (June, 1966) pp. 188–96.

Pisko, Ernest, 'Minority Report on the Origins of War', *CSM*, January 11, 1962, p. 7.

'Preserving Civil Liberties. Austria Sympathy Meeting Discusses Democracy in Britain', *MG*, June 25, 1934, p. 11.

'Problem of Germany, The,' *Listener*, June 20, 1946, p. 799.

'Public Dissent', *TLS*, June 21, 1957, p. 382.

'Review of *Bismarck: The Man and the Statesman*, by A. J. P. Taylor', *PQ*, 26 (October–December 1955) p. 412.

Reynolds, P. A., 'Hitler's War', *History*, 97 (October, 1961) p. 217.

Rowse, A. L., 'Beneath the Whitewash the Same Old Hitler', *NYTBR*, January 7, 1962, p. 6.

Segel, Edward B., 'Taylor and History', *RP*, 26 (October, 1964) pp. 531–46.

Seton-Watson, R. W., 'Review of *The Habsburg Monarchy, 1815–1914*, by A. J. P. Taylor', *EHR*, 57 (July 1942) p. 391.

'Seventy Years of Diplomacy', *The Times* October 30, 1954, p. 8g.

Silcox, Peter, 'Beaverbrook', *CF*, 52 (December 1972). p. 39. Smith, Howard McGaw, 'Review of *The Italian Problem in European Diplomacy, 1847–1849*, by A. J. P. Taylor, *JMH*, 7 (September 1935) p. 346.

Smith, J. Y., 'British Historian A. J. P. Taylor Dies at 84', *Washington Post*, September 8, 1990, p. B6.

Spencer, Robert, 'War Unpremeditated', *CHR*, 43 (June 1962) pp. 136–44.

Stern, Fritz, 'Review of *The Struggle for Mastery in Europe, 1848–1918*, by A. J. P. Taylor', *PSQ*, 70 (March 1955) pp. 112–14.

Thomas, Hugh, 'A Controversy Re-Examined: Taylor and Trevor-Roper', *Spectator*, 210 (June 7, 1963) p. 728.

Thomson, David, W. N. Medlicott, Isaac Deutscher, Margaret Lambert, George Bonnin, and Elizabeth Wiskemann, letters to the Editor, *TLS*, May 5, 1961, p. 339 (Thomson) and June 2, 1961, p. 361 (all the others).

Thompson, J. M., 'Epitaph on the Balance of Power', *HT*, 4 (December 1954) pp. 854–6.

Townshend, Mary E., 'Review of *Germany's First Bid for Colonies, 1884–1885*, by A. J. P. Taylor, *AHR*, 44 (July 1939) p. 900.

Trevor-Roper, Hugh, 'A. J. P. Taylor, Hitler, and the War', *Encounter*, 17 (July 1961) pp. 88–96.

——, 'A Reply', *Encounter*, 17 (July 1961) pp. 73–4.

'Unbalanced Pattern, An', *Observer*, June 9, 1963, p. 26.

Wassermann, Louis, 'Two New Surveys of the German People – Studies of Extremes', *SFC*, July 14, 1946, pp. 16, 33.

Watt, Donald Cameron, 'Some Aspects of A. J. P. Taylor's Work as Diplomatic Historian', *JMH*, 49 (March 1977) pp. 19–33.

Wight, Martin, 'Contentious but Creative', *Spectator*, 190 (May 15, 1953) p. 639.

——, 'Iron Chancellor', *MG*, July 8, 1955, p. 10.

Wiskemann, Elizabeth, 'Light on German History', *Spectator*, 10 (August 10, 1945) pp. 132–3.

Woodward, E. L., 'How Germany Obtained Colonies', *Spectator*, March 25, 1938, p. 538.
Woolf, Leonard, 'The Brighter Side of History', *NSN*, 39 (June 3, 1950) p. 636.
——, 'The Habsburgs', *NSN*, 37 (March 5, 1949) p. 235.

Index

Abyssinia 8, 227
Action 199
Adenauer, Konrad 108
Adler, Viktor 44
Aehrenthal, Count 29, 49, 137
Africa 82, 117, 132–3
Aitken, Max *see* Lord Beaverbrook
Aldermaston 152
Alexander II (Russia) 136
Alexander II (Serbia) 135
Alexander, Sir Samuel 5
Algéciras Conference 117–18, 134
Alsace-Lorraine 83, 118, 140
America *see* the United States
Amery, Leo 218
ancien régime 15, 17, 123
Andrassy, Count 130, 138
Angell, Norman 161, 164
Anglicanism *see* Church of
England
Anglo-American alliance 70, 99,
213, 227–228
Anglo-French entente 133
Anglo-Japanese agreement 134
Anglo-Russian entente 134
Anglo-Soviet military talks 77
Angra Pequeña 82
*Appeal to the Allies and the English
on Behalf of Poland, An* 161
appeasement 76, 113, 143, 179
Apponyi, Count 33
Archives des Affaires Étrangères 37
Asia, 132–33
Asquith, Herbert Henry 210, 219,
231
Aster, Sidney 203
Astor, Lady 222
Athenaeum Club 158, 166
Attlee, Clement 156, 165
Australia 150, 231
Austria, Austrians, *and* Austria-
Hungary 13, 16–17, 19–20,
22–3, 28–30, 32, 34–36, 40, 43,
47–8, 50, 54–6, 60–1, 70, 76, 83,
86, 96, 107, 114, 121, 124–5,
127–9, 131, 134–5, 139–40,
184–5, 234
Austro-German alliance 55, 122
Austro-Prussian alliance 126
Austro-Prussian War 47, 95, 127,
130

Badeni, Count 50
balance of power 2, 9, 12–14,
16–18, 23–4, 31, 41, 73, 105,
107, 111–17, 122–4, 126,
129–33, 136–41
Baldwin, Stanley 143, 219, 225
Balkans 55, 58, 60, 69, 131, 134,
139, 236, 240
Baptists *see* Nonconformists
Bartholomew, Harry Guy 229
Bastide, M. 35–6
Bauer, Otto 51
Baumont, Maurice 171–2
Bavaria 61
British Broadcasting Company
(BBC) *see* broadcasting
Beard, Charles 155
Beaverbrook x, 227, 231–3
Beaverbrook Library 231
Beaverbrook, Lord x, 3, 206–7,
209–10, 215–17, 224, 227, 231–3
Beck, Joseph 203
Belgium *and* Belgians 11, 30, 136,
155, 209, 216, 220
Belgrade 59
Bênês, Eduard 65, 71
Berchtold, Count 29, 135, 138
Berlin 82–3, 90, 93, 131, 134, 138,
172, 178, 186–7
Bethmann-Hollweg, Theodore 134
Bevan, Aneurin 156
Bevin, Ernest 210
Big Three, the 63, 70, 99
Birkdale 2–3
Bismarck, Prince Otto von 15,

Bismarck – *continued*
74–5, 82–3, 95–6, 104–9, 120–2,
127, 129–33, 137–9, 140, 192,
237
*Bismarck: The Man and the
Statesman* x, 7, 96, 103–8, 120,
143, 172, 237
Black Sea, the 126, 136
Blomberg, Werner von 187–9
Blythe, Ronald 233
Bohemia 60, 94
see also Czechoslovakia
bolshevik revolution 181
bolsheviks 99, 141, 163
Bonn Conventions 103
Bonnin, Georges 191, 200
Bootham School 3–5
Boothby, Robert 149
Bosnia *and* Bosnians 55, 67, 135,
137, 140
Bourbons 17–18
Boyar, John W. 8
Briggs, Asa 141, 234
Bright, John 4, 151, 160, 162–3
Britain *and* British *see* United
Kingdom
British Academy, the 166, 203
broadcasting
BBC 77–8, 114, 149, 169, 208,
224–6
ITV 149, 193
radio ix, 1, 100, 116, 158
television ix, 1, 116, 149, 158,
169
Brougham, Henry 161
Brown Book, the 177–8
Bryce, James 163
Bulgaria *and* Bulgarians 130, 163–4
Bulgarian Horrors 161
Bullock, Alan 158, 171–2, 203
Bülow, Prince Bernhard von 133,
135
Buol, Count 118, 138
Burgess, Guy 209

Cabinet Secretariat 155–6
Calder, Ritchie 150
Cambridge University 205, 209

Campaign for Nuclear
Disarmament (CND) ix,
151–2, 157, 169, 211
Campbell-Bannerman, Henry 3
Canning, George 23
Canticle for Leibowitz, A 150
Caprivi, Leo von 137–8
Carinthia 40
Carlyle, Thomas 163
Carr, E. H. 191
Castlereagh, Lord 15, 18, 22–3, 32
Catholicism *and* Catholics 41, 43,
49, 58, 65, 68, 94, 123, 145
Cavour, Count 129
Chamberlain, Sir Neville 76–7, 83,
165, 183–5, 187, 218, 221, 222,
227
Chanak Affair 227
Chaplin, Charlie 182
Charlemagne 85
Cherkley 215
Chichester, Bishop of 150
China 134
Church of England 145, 153
Churchill, Sir Winston 108, 173,
206, 208–9, 218–19, 221, 228
cinema 217, 225–6
Clarendon, Lord 127
Clark, G. N. 4, 168, 206
Cobben, Alfred 202
Cobbett, William ix, 153, 160
Cobden, Richard 132, 161, 163
Cold War, the ix, 6, 63–4, 68–73,
75, 99, 101–3, 105, 111–12,
114–16, 120–1, 136, 143–7, 149,
153, 155, 167, 173, 198–200,
213, 227
Cole, G. D. H. 223
Collins, Canon J. L. 150
Collins, Mrs J. L. 150
colonialism, *see* imperialism and
imperialists
Cominform 67–8
Common Market 214–15, 227
Common Sense and the War 161
Commonwealth 212, 214, 231
communism *and* communists
63–8, 70, 72, 114, 147, 151, 160,
176–8

Communist Party of Great Britain 3–4, 78
Concert of Europe 13, 15–19, 21–3, 25, 29, 112, 136, 146
Confederation of the Rhine 89
Congregationalists *see* Nonconformists
Congress of Vienna 15–17, 124, 212
Conscription Act 3
conservatism *and* conservatives 97–8, 108, 129–131, 133, 149, 153–4, 167, 218
Constantinople 131, 139
Continental League 132
Cook, Chris 234
Courcel, M. 83
Course of German History, The x, 79, 81, 83–102, 115–6, 136, 174, 176, 198, 218, 235–6
Covent Garden 208
Crimean War, the 126–7, 136, 139, 151, 161
Croatia *and* Croatians 23, 49, 56, 57–9, 62, 66–7, 69, 73
see also Slavs
Cromwell, Oliver 218, 239
Crossman, R. H. S. 236
Crowe, Sir Eyre 13, 134
Crozier, W. P. 231
Cuban Missile Crisis 148
Cyprus 213
Czechoslovakia *and* Czechoslovakians 40, 46, 56–60, 62–3, 65–6, 68, 71, 73, 75–6, 98, 164, 174–6, 184–5, 187, 224
Czernin, Count 53

Daily Express 206, 217, 224
Daily Herald 223–4
Daily Mail 223
Daily Mirror 224
Daily Worker 224
Dalton, Hugh 218
Danube River 43
Das Zeitalter des Imperialismus, 1884–1914 5
de Gaulle, Charles 215
Deak, Francis 52

Deakin, F. W. D. 114
Decazes, M. 138
Delcassé, M. 134, 139
democracy *and* democrats 45, 58, 64–5, 67, 77, 80, 98, 108, 144, 152–3, 155, 157, 161, 169, 183
Der Spiegel 177
Deutsche Soldatenzeitung 199
Deutscher, Isaac 198
Dickenson, Lowes 161, 164
Die Große Politik der Europäischen Kabinette 7, 104
Dietrichstein, Count 33
Dimitrov, Georgi 65
Disraeli, Benjamin 138
dissent *and* dissenters ix, 1–2, 77, 114, 143, 145–6, 157–8, 160–1, 163, 165–6
Documents and Materials Relating to the Eve of the Second World War 179
Documents on British Foreign Policy, 1919–1939 179
Documents on German Foreign Policy, 1918–1945 179
Documents on International Affairs 179
Dollfuss, Englebert 60
Driberg, Tom 232–3
Drouyn de Llys 127
dualism 85–8, 96–7
Duff, Peggy 151
Dufferin, Lord 118
Dunkirk 221

EDC (European Defence Community) 103
Eden, Anthony 232
Edinburgh 116
Edward VII 206
Egypt 117, 132, 139
Ehrenburg, Elya 71, 114
Eichmann, Adolf 197
El Alemein 226
Elbe River 99
Empire Free Trade 232
Empress Eugénie 127
Encounter 192–3

Engels, Frederick 51
England *and English see* United
    Kingdom
*England and the International Policy
    of the European Great Powers,
    1871–1914* 11
English Historical Review, The 115
English History, 1914–1945 x, 167,
    204, 206, 215–33, 237–8
entente cordiale 119–20
Ernest, Karl 178
Establishment, the 2, 145, 153–5,
    166–7, 210, 237
    see also The Thing
Eton 153
Eubank, Keith 190
Evening Standard 206

Fairlie, Henry 237
Falsificators of History 173
Far East 134
fascism *and* fascists 7, 59–60, 70–2,
    77, 114, 217, 228
    see also national socialism *and*
        nazis
Fashoda 117–18
Fellow of Special Election 206
Ferdinand I 43
Fichte, Johan 90–1
Fiquelmont, Count 27, 34–5
Finnegans Wake 226
Foot, Michael 149–50
Forces Programme 116
Ford Lectures, the 5, 10, 144–5,
    157–8, 167, 206, 218
Fox, Charles James 157, 159–60
France *and* French 13, 17, 20–1, 23,
    28–32, 34, 73, 80, 82, 86, 88–90,
    96, 103, 107, 114, 117–18,
    120–3, 124, 126–7, 129–32, 134,
    136–7, 139–40, 163, 171, 174–6,
    182, 184, 186, 199–9
Francis I 43
Francis Joseph 29–30, 42, 44
Franco, Francisco 162
Franco-Austrian War 115, 117
Franco-Prussian War 80, 83, 95,
    121, 130

Frankfurt 39, 86, 93–4
Frankfurter Allgemeine Zeitung 199
Franz-Ferdinand 135
Frederick II 89–90, 106
Frederick William III 90
Frederick William IV 94–5
Free Speech 149
Freedom 116
Freeman, E. A. 163
Friedjung, Heinrich 10, 49–50, 61,
    114
Fritsch, Werner von 187, 189
From Napoleon to Stalin 236
From Sarajevo to Potsdam 231
Fuller, Roy 233

Galbraith, V. H. 168–9
Gardiner, Gerald 151
General Strike, the 3–4, 67, 209,
    217
George V 216
German Catastrophe, The 101, 172
German general staff, the 92, 203
German unification 76, 92, 95, 129
Germany *and* Germans ix, 13, 20,
    24, 38–9, 41, 46, 48–9, 51–2,
    55–7, 59, 61–5, 69, 71–110, 113,
    118–19, 121–2, 124, 126, 130–1,
    133–4, 136, 139–41, 143, 147,
    159, 163, 170, 172–5, 179–81,
    183–4, 186, 188–9 194, 198,
    203, 221–2, 227, 234, 239–40,
    218
*Germany's First Bid for Colonies,
    1884–1885* x, 7, 81–3, 115, 236
Gilbert, Martin ix
Gladstone, William Ewart 83, 122,
    156, 160–1, 163–4
Glasgow 212
Gleason, S. Everett 173
Gneisenau, General 92
Goering, Hermann 187–9
Goltz, Count 128
Gontaut, M. 130
Gottwald, Eduard 71
Granville, Lord 83
Great Depression, the 209

Great Dictator, The 182
Great Illusion, The 161
Great War, the *see* World War I
Green, J. R. 163
Greenwood, Arthur 159, 214, 218
Grey, Lord 12, 32, 135, 138–9
Guiness, Sir Alec 192
Guizot, François 32

Habsburg Monarchy, 1815–1918,
    The x, 7, 39, 41–62, 73, 93, 99,
    115, 236
Habsburg Monarchy ix, 5, 17, 19,
    25, 39–9, 40–6, 48, 53–4, 56–7,
    59–60, 62–3, 65, 69, 71–2, 74–5,
    80, 86, 88, 93–4, 97, 125, 135,
    146, 164
    see also Austria
Halifax, Lord 184, 186
Halperin, S. William 199
Hamburg 70
Hammond, J. L. 236
Hampshire, Stuart 169
Hancock, W. K. 236
Hanftstaengel, Putzi 177
Hanrieder, Wolfram 103
hansa, the 86–8
Harastzi-Taylor, Eva xi
Hardie, Keir 160, 165
Hartig, Count 34, 45
Hatvani, Baron 51
Haus-Hof-und Staatsarchive [sic] 37
Heffner, Sebastian 237
Henderson, Sir Nevile 187
Henry VIII 68
Herzegovina 67, 137
Hess, Rudolf 211
Hindenberg, Paul von 181
Hinsley, F. H. 193–4, 197, 201
Hiroshima 148
Hitler: A Study in Tyranny 171, 203
Hitler, Adolf 8, 38–9, 41, 61, 72,
    75–7, 80, 83, 86, 88, 91, 98,
    100–1, 104–5, 108, 133, 149,
    159, 170–6, 178, 180–1, 183–5,
    187–95, 197, 200–2, 239
Hoare–Laval plan 7, 227
Hobbs, Thomas 123

Hobson, J. A. 162
Hogg, Quinton 78
Hohenzollerns 55, 91, 93–4, 121
Holland 123, 132, 187
Holocaust 172
Holstein, Baron Friedrich von 12,
    141
Holy Alliance, the 112, 125–6, 146
Holy Roman Empire, the 38–9, 43,
    82, 85, 132
Home Rule 164
Horthy, Admiral 52
Hossbach Memorandum, the
    187–9, 192–3, 195
House, Colonel 166
House of Commons 78, 114, 160, 208
    see also parliament
House of Lords 209
    see also parliament
House of Representatives
    Un-American Activities
    Committee 153
How Europe Armed for War 161
How The War Began 161
Howard, Michael 237
Hoxha, Enver 64
Hudson, G. F. 195–6, 201, 237
Humboldt, Baron von 92
Hungary *and* Magyars 40–1, 44,
    46–8, 51, 55, 61–2, 70, 99, 130

i documenti diplomatici italiani 179
ITV (Independent Television) *see*
    broadcasting
Imperial Diet 50
imperialism *and* imperialists 54,
    68, 78, 133, 140, 149, 161–2,
    165, 239
Incitement to Disaffection bill 7
International Anarchy, The 161
In The National Interest 146–7
In The News 116
Information, Ministry of (MOI)
    77–8, 221, 223
    see also propaganda, *and* public
    opinion
Ireland *and* Irish 59, 164
Iron Curtain 173

Italian Problem in European Diplomacy, 1847–1847, The x, 9–37, 41, 73–113, 116, 138–9, 159, 236
Italy *and* Italians 8, 17, 20, 22, 24, 26–9, 31, 33, 35, 46, 62, 69–70, 118, 124–6, 128, 132, 137, 139, 188
Izvolsky, Prince 137, 140

Japan *and* Japanese 134, 136, 228
Jews 239
Joll, James 197, 199, 201
Joseph II 29, 43–4
Joyce, James 225
Judd, Denis ix, xi, 235
Junkers 89, 92, 95, 97, 105–6
Junor, John 207

Karageorgevitch 59
Karolyi, Count Michael 52
Keital, General 185
Kemp, Betty ix
Kennedy, John F. 148
Keynes, John Maynard 181
Kinglake, A. W. 163
Kissinger, Henry 148
kleinstaaterei 88
Korean War, the 149, 212
Kossuth, Lujos 47, 52, 127
Krausnick, Helmut 172
Kruschev, Nikita 148, 200

Labour *and* Labour Party 144, 149, 152–4, 156, 163, 165–6, 217, 226
Lamartine, Alphonse de 126, 33, 125
Lancashire 2
Langer, W. L. 104, 173
Lansbury, George 219, 223
Last Days of Hitler, The 192
League of Nations 69, 104, 165, 183
League of Three Emperors 130–1, 137
Lebzeltern, Count 35–6
Lecky, W. E. H. 163

Leeds 116
legitimacy 17–19, 23–5, 29, 31, 43
Leipzig, battle of 90
lend-lease 228
Lenin, V. 123, 140, 192
Lessing, Doris 151
Level Seven 150
Liberal Party 138
Linz Programme 49–50
Linz Town Hall 184
Lipski, Joseph 186
Little England 2, 31, 83, 104, 205, 207–8, 212, 215, 240
Little Russians 46, 62
Littlewood, Joan 209
Lloyd George, David 155, 206, 210, 216, 219–20, 225, 227, 231
Lombardy 14, 16–17, 19, 21–2, 25–7, 30, 34–5, 45
London 28, 152, 231
London Forum 116
Louis XIV 123
Louis Napoleon, *see* Napoleon III
Louis Philippe 21–2
Lubbe, Marinus van der 177–8, 188
Ludendorff, General 97
Lueger, Karl 61
Luther, Martin 84, 86–8, 91

Macaulay, T. B. ix, 221
MacDonald, Ramsey 217, 219, 225
MacLean, Donald 209
Macmillan, Harold 168, 213
McCarthy, Sen. Joseph 153
McCartney, C. A. 236
McNeill, William H. 234
Madrid 121
Magdalen College 6, 8, 77, 192, 206, 233, 235
Magyars *see* Hungary
Main River 121
Malleson, Miles 151
Manchester 2, 6, 77, 116, 167
Manchester Guardian ix, xi, 6, 14, 119
Manchester Guardian Weekly 119
Manchester Peace Council 8, 76

Manchester University 5–8, 10
Marcus Aurelius 58
Maria Theresa 29
Marquand, David 233–4
Marriott, Sir John 238
Martin, Kingsley 150, 227
Marx, Karl 51, 65, 67, 74, 80, 127, 238–9
Masaryk, Jan 65, 67
Masaryk, Thomas Garrague 57–8, 62, 65, 73
Mason, T. W. 196, 201
Masterman, J. C. 168
Mau, Hermann 172
Mediterranean 70, 78, 86, 119, 137
Mehta, Ved 6
Mein Kampf 182, 187, 192, 195
Meinecke, Friedrich 101, 172
Mellor, William 223
Men and Power 207
Methodists *see* Nonconformists
Metternich, Prince Klemens von 14–15, 17–23, 25, 26–35, 41–3, 54, 91, 112, 126, 129, 146–7, 212
Miller, Walter M. 150
Minto, Lord 27
Monroe Doctrine, the 23
Montenegro 66-7
Morel, E. D. 160–1, 164
Morganthau, Hans 146–8, 235
Morganthau, Henry 100
Morny, Duke of 127
Morocco 13, 113, 117, 132, 134
Morrison, Herbert 114
Morton, Louis 197–201
Moscow 2, 64, 67–8, 78
Moseley, Sir Oswald 199
Muggeridge, Kitty 5
Muggeridge, Malcolm 5
Munich
  agreement 8, 76–7, 175, 187
  conference 8, 63, 99, 174, 190, 227
Muslims 58
Mussolini, Benito 53, 72

Nagasaki 148
Namier, L. B. (Sir Lewis) 5–7, 157, 168–9, 202, 207

Napoleon I 18, 21, 30, 88–91, 110, 123, 133, 239
Napoleon III 20, 23, 30, 121, 125, 127–9, 140
Nation-Europa 199
National Government, the 7, 217, 227
national interest 11–12
nationalism *and* nationalists 19–20, 43, 47–52, 54, 60, 76, 79, 86–7, 89–92, 95–6
national socialism *and* nazis 39, 51, 63–4, 75, 79–81, 100–1, 108–9, 170–2, 174, 176–8, 181, 196–7, 199, 201
Nazi–Soviet nonaggression pact 77, 174
North Atlantic Treaty Organization (NATO) 103–4, 144, 146–7, 172–3, 213
Neurath, Alfred von 187, 189
Newbold, J. T. Walton 3, 160–1
New Statesman xi, 152, 169
New Statesman and Nation 144
Nicholas I 126
Nietzsche, Friedrich 182
Nile River 117–18, 132
Nixon, Richard M 1
Nonconformists
  Baptists 2, 145
  Calvinists 225
  Congregationalists 2, 145
  Methodists 2
  Quakers 2–3, 145, 160, 163
  see also dissent *and* dissenters
Normanby, Lord 26, 33
Norway 221
Novara 36
Nuremburg
  rallies 197
  thesis 170–1, 174–5, 190, 192, 203
  Tribunal 101, 170, 180, 187–9, 191
Official Secrets Act 152–3, 155, 211
On The Beach 150
Oriel College 4
Origins of the Second World War, The x, 167, 170–1, 174–6, 179–90, 192, 196, 200, 202–4, 211, 234, 237

Orthodox Christians 58
Ottoman Empire 58
Oxford 72
Oxford History Board 206
Oxford History of England 206
Oxford History of Modern Europe
111, 119
Oxford Home Guard 78
Oxford Union 220, 233
Oxford University 4–8, 9, 77, 116,
144–4, 157, 167–9, 205, 209, 232
Oxford University Press 114
Oudinot, General 27, 34

Pact of Plombières 128
Paine, Tom 161
Pakenham, Frank 78
Palestine 139
Palmerston, Lord 19–28, 26–8,
31–4, 127, 138
*Papers Relating to the Foreign
Relations of the United States*
179
Pares, Sir Richard 157
Paris 26–7, 35, 118, 125, 128
Paris Peace Conferences 181
parliament 26, 160, 222
see also House of Commons *and*
House of Lords
particularism 85, 89, 97, 109
Peace Ballot 220
Peace of Utrecht 17
Peace of Villafranca 117
Peasants Revolt, the 87
Pentagon, the 213
Persia 134
Peuples et civilisations 170
Philby, Kim 209
Philip II 123
Piedmont 26
Pisko, Ernest 199
Pittsburg Protocol, the 58
Pleven, René 73
Poland *and* Poles 40, 46–7, 62, 77,
97, 121, 123, 125, 128–9, 162,
164, 171–2, 175–6, 187–8, 191,
197, 203, 217, 227
Polish Corridor 187

Political Warfare Executive (PWE)
84, 150
Polytechnic College of North
London 231
Ponsonby, Lord 27-8
Poole, Austin Lane 168
Pope Pius IX 33
Portugal 132
Potsdam Conference, the 99
Prague 77, 93–4, 175, 187
Priestley, J. B. 150
Příbrám, A. F. 5, 9–13, 15, 28, 157
Princess Anne 209
Production, ministry of 232
propaganda 7, 45, 49, 78, 212,
220–1, 223
see also Information, Ministry of,
and public opinion
Protestant Reformation 86–7
Protestants *and* Protestantism 41,
58, 88, 94
Pruller, Herr 109
Prussia *and* Prussians 17, 49, 55,
75, 79–80, 82–3, 86, 88–93,
95–6, 109, 117, 121, 125, 127,
129, 136–7, 139
public opinion 13, 28, 33, 77, 138,
162, 221, 225
see also propaganda *and*
Information, Ministry of

Quakers see Nonconformists

Radetzsky, Field Marshal 20, 22–
3, 25, 26, 34, 36, 54
radio see broadcasting
Radowitz, Count 130
Raeder, Admiral 187, 189
Rainer, Archduke 34, 45
Raleigh Lecture 203
Ranke, Leopold von 100
realpolitik 15, 20–1, 23–4, 26, 29–30,
32, 104–5
Redgrave, Vanessa 1
Regius Professor of Modern
History (Oxford) 7, 116, 168,
170, 192, 205–6

Reichstag 106–7, 137, 177–8, 181, 188
Reith, Sir John 224–5
Representation of the People Act 222
revolutions
  1789 25–6, 123
  1848 26, 31, 35, 42, 52, 85, 93, 125–6, 147
Revue Historique 115
Reynold's News 224
Reynolds, P. A. 195
Rhine River 88
Rhineland 108, 227
Ribbentrop, Joachim 101
Richardson, Maurice 149
Richelieu, Cardinal 192
Robbins, Keith ix
Roehm, Ernst 177
Rome 68, 87
Roosevelt, Franklin Delano 155, 228
Roosevelt, Theodore 42
Rosebery, Lord 118
Roshwald, Mordecai 150
Rowse, A. L. 195, 201
Rumours of War 234
Russell, Bertrand 150, 164
Russell, Lord 32, 126–7
Russia *and* Russians 17–18, 62–7, 69, 71–3, 96–7, 99, 107, 109, 111, 114–5, 117, 121, 124–5, 127–9, 131–2, 138, 140–1, 148, 151, 155, 176, 181
  see also Soviet Union
Rumania *and* Rumanians 46, 52, 62
Ruthenia *and* Ruthenians 23, 46

St Petersburg 130
San Stefano, Treaty of 131
Sardinia *and* Sardinians 21–2, 35, 128, 139
Saxony *and* Saxons 61, 90
Schacht, Hjalmar 188
Scharnhorst, General, 92
Schleswig-Holstein 106, 121, 129
Schlieffen Plan, the 139
Schmerling, Count 47, 48

Schmitt, Bernadotte 102
Schmitt, Hans 102
Schönerer, Georg von 50, 61
Schumann, Robert 73
Schussnigg, Kurt von 184–5
Scots 59
Schwarzenberg, Prince Felix von 20, 22–3, 25, 29–30, 35, 54–5, 118, 125
Scourby, Alexander 172
Second Empire 127
Second Reich 107
Second World War, the *see* World War II
Sedan 130
Seeley, J. R. 163
Segel, Edward B. 235
Serbia *and* Serbs 53, 95, 58–9, 61, 66–7, 69, 135–6
  see also Yugoslavia
Sex Disqualification Removal Act 222
Shaw, G. B. 161, 166
Shinwell, Lord 215
Shute, Nevil 150
Siam 137
Sked, Alan 234
Slavs 19, 39–40, 50, 52–3, 56, 58, 60–2, 64–5, 67, 71–2, 74, 85, 94, 98–9, 125, 143, 164, 195
Slovakia *and* Slovaks 23, 46, 56, 59, 62, 65, 73
  see also Czechoslovakia
Slovenia *and* Slovenes 67, 69
Spenser, Robert 234
socialism *and* socialists 7, 51, 56, 60, 62–4, 67, 79–80, 85, 91, 109, 123, 160, 166–7, 207, 224, 239
Sontag, Raymond J. 172
Sorenson, Reginald 150
Soviet Information Bureau 173
Soviet Union 62–4, 67–8, 70–2, 74–5, 99, 102–3, 111, 114, 136, 140, 144, 146–8, 149, 176, 179, 183, 198–201, 205, 207, 211, 217, 227
  see also Russia
Spain 123, 132, 162, 183, 217
Spandau Prison 211

Spanish civil war, the 174
Split 40
Stalin, Joseph 64, 68–9, 173
Stalingrad 226
Stein, Baron vom 79, 91
Stern, Fritz 235, 237
straits (Dardanelles) 131, 137–8, 140
Strasbourg 43
Stratford, Canning 138
Stresemann, Gustav 80
Strosmajer, Bishop Josip 57–9
Struggle for Mastery in Europe, 1848–1918, The x, 7, 111, 113–5, 118, 121–141, 143, 157–8, 234, 236
Struggle for Supremacy in Germany, 1866–1871, The 10, 49, 61, 114
Stubbs, William 163
Sudan 117
Sudetenland, the 58, 61, 174, 184
Suez 116, 143–4, 149, 157, 167–9, 213
Sunday Express x, 206–8, 230
Surbiton 210
Sutherland, Lucy 168
Sweden 123
Switzerland 187

Taafe, Count 48
Table Talk 182, 193
Tangiers 119
Tansil, Charles Callan 173
Taylor, Constance 2–3
Taylor, Percy 2–3
Television, *see* broadcasting
Third Reich 39, 61, 69, 75–6, 80, 98, 174, 196–7
Thomas, Hugh 193
Thompson, Harry 220
Thompson, J. M. 141
Times, The ix, 14, 130, 151–2, 158
Times Literary Supplement, The (TLS) xi, 191
Tito 64–6, 68–9
Tobias, Fritz 177
toryism *and* tories 153–4, 160, 206, 217

totalitarianism 63, 65, 80, 196
Townsend, Mary 81
Trades Union Congress (TUC) 154
Trafalgar Square 152
Treitschke, Heinrich von 20, 96
Trevor-Roper, Hugh 168, 170, 192–3, 196–7, 199–201
Trieste 40, 69–70
Triple alliance 132–3, 135, 137
Triple entente, the 117, 134–5
Trotsky, Leon 4, 67
Troublemakers: Dissent Over Foreign Policy, 1792–1939, The 144, 156–167, 169, 178, 205, 237
Truman, Harry S. 155
Tudor, Mary 210
Turin 27
Turkey *and* Turks, *see also* Ottoman Empire 125–6, 139
20th Century 153
Twisted Cross, The 171

Uncle Tom's Cabin 163
Union of Democratic Control (UDC) 157, 163–5
United Kingdom ix–x, 2, 13, 16, 20, 22, , 29–31, 33–4, 38, 59, 63, 69–71, 76, 81–3, 86, 96–7, 107, 111, 114, 117, 119–20, 124, 129–31, 133, 136, 140, 144–5, 149, 153, 155, 158, 160, 165, 171–4, 176, 182, 184–6, 188–92, 201, 205, 208–9, 211, 213–15, 217, 219–21, 223, 226, 228–9, 234, 238, 240
United States 69–72, 99, 103–4, 112–13, 118, 125, 136, 140–1, 144, 147–8, 150–5, 166, 172, 181, 183, 201, 205, 207, 211, 213, 227–8
United Nations (UNO) 104, 212
University College, London 231
University Lectureships in International History 205
University of Berlin 90
University of New Brunswick 232
Unruh, Viktor von 95
Urquhart, David 127, 160–2

Venetia 14, 45
Versailles Treaty, the 76, 98, 162–3, 181, 184–5, 188
Vienna 5, 7, 10, 27, 34–5, 40, 48, 50, 62, 90, 109, 125, 134, 184
Vienna University 9
Vietnam 148
Villafranca, Treaty of 129, 140
vorparliament 39

Walewski, Count 127
Walfish Bay 82
War by Time-Table 231
War Lords, The 231
Warsaw 232
Warsaw Pact, the 173
Washington, DC 213
Washington Post ix
Watt, D. C. 204–5
Webster, Sir Charles 168
Weimar
  Constitution 97
  Germany 83
  Republic 97
Weizsäcker, Ernst von 100–1
Wessenberg, Count 35, 138
West, Dame Rebecca 209
Whigs *and* Whiggism 19, 26, 32, 160
Whitehall 133, 152, 222

Wilhelm II 83, 96, 105, 107–8, 132–3, 135
Wilhelmstrasse 135, 139
Williams, H. Russell 102
Wilson, Harold 231
Wilson, Woodrow 104, 123, 140, 166, 181
Winchester 153
Windischgraetz, Field Marshal 20, 23
Wiskemann, Elizabeth 199
Woodward, Llewelyan 8, 81
World War I 2, 11, 13, 40, 42, 53, 55, 78,80, 96–7, 102, 108, 136, 160–1, 163–5, 179, 183,190, 207, 210, 217, 219, 221, 224–5, 238
World War II 39, 73, 75–6, 78, 83, 98, 104, 108, 150, 154, 156, 158, 169, 171, 173, 175, 179–81, 187, 194, 204, 209, 211–12, 217, 221–3, 228, 238
World War III 113, 148
Wroclaw Congress 71, 73, 114, 173

Yalta 228
York 143
Yugoslavia 40, 56–9, 62, 66–7, 69–70, 72
  see also Serbia